I0878326

Richer *of* Saint-Rémi

Richer *of* Saint-Rémi

THE METHODS AND MENTALITY OF A TENTH-CENTURY HISTORIAN

Justin Lake

The Catholic University of America Press
Washington, D.C.

Copyright © 2013
The Catholic University of America Press
All rights reserved
The paper used in this publication meets the minimum
requirements of American National Standards for Information
Science—Permanence of Paper for Printed Library Materials,
ANSI Z39.48-1984.
∞

Frontispiece: St. Jerome from a Latin and Old English manuscript
of the *Lives of the Hermits Paul and Guthlac.*

Library of Congress Cataloging-in-Publication Data
Lake, Justin.
Richer of Saint-Rémi : the methods and mentality of a
tenth-century historian / Justin Lake.
p. cm.
Includes bibliographical references and index.
ISBN 978-0-8132-2125-0 (cloth : alk. paper)
1. Richer, of Saint-Rémy, 10th cent. 2. Historians—
France—Biography. 3. France—History—To 987—
Historiography. 4. France—History—Capetians,
987–1328—Historiography. I. Title.
DC36.98.R53L35 2013
944'.02107202—dc23
2012043470

To Natasha

Contents

Acknowledgments

I owe a sincere debt of gratitude to Jan Ziolkowski, Richard Tarrant, and Michael McCormick, without whose advice and assistance this project would never have come to fruition. Nino Luraghi and Kathleen Coleman also provided valuable suggestions and support along the way. In addition, I would like to thank the Catholic University of America Press, Philip G. Holthaus, and the anonymous readers who devoted painstaking attention to the manuscript. My parents, Sim and Carol, my brother, Tim, and Jack Massey offered feedback at various stages of the book's composition and provided the valuable perspective of a nonspecialist audience. Jason Glenn has been unfailingly helpful and a model of scholarly comity. Finally, I cannot thank my wife, Natasha, adequately enough. Without her, this book would not have been possible.

Abbreviations

CCCM Corpus Christianorum, Continuatio Mediaevalis. Turnhout, 1966–.

CCSL Corpus Christianorum, Series Latina. Turnhout, 1954–.

CSEL Corpus Scriptorum Ecclesiasticorum Latinorum. Vienna, Leipzig, Prague, 1866–.

CTC *Catalogus translationum et commentariorum.* Editor in chief, Paul Oskar Kristeller. 8 vols. Washington, D.C., 1960–2003.

Halm *Rhetores Latini Minores.* Edited by Carl Halm. Leipzig, 1863.

HRE Flodoard. *Historia Remensis Ecclesiae.* Edited by Martina Stratmann. MGH SS 36. Hanover, 1998.

Lausberg Heinrich Lausberg. *Handbook of Literary Rhetoric.* Edited by David E. Orton and R. Dean Anderson. Translated by Matthew T. Bliss, Annemiek Jansen, and David E. Orton. Leiden, 1998.

Manitius Max Manitius. *Geschichte der lateinischen Literatur des Mittelalters.* 3 vols. Munich, 1911–1931.

MGH Monumenta Germaniae historica. Hanover, etc. 1826–.

MGH Poetae Poetae Latini aevi Carolini. Hanover, 1881–1899.

MGH SRG Scriptores rerum Germanicarum in usum scholarum separatim editi. Hanover, 1871–.

MGH SRG n.s. Scriptores rerum Germanicarum, Nova series. Berlin, Hanover, 1922–.

MGH SRM Scriptores rerum Merovingicarum. Hanover, 1885–1920.

MGH SS Scriptores (in Folio). Hanover, 1824–.

Niermeyer J. F. Niermeyer. *Mediae Latinitatis Lexicon Minus.* 2 vols. Leiden, 2002.

OLD *Oxford Latin Dictionary.* Edited by P. W. G. Glare. Oxford, 1982.

PL *Patrologiae cursus completus, series latina.* Edited by J.-P. Migne. 221 vols. Paris, 1841–1864.

Szövérffy Jospeh Szövérffy. *Secular Latin Lyrics and Minor Poetic Forms of the Middle Ages: A Historical Survey and Literary Repertory from the Tenth to the Late Fifteenth Century.* 3 vols. Concord, N.H., 1992–1995.

Richer *of* Saint-Rémi

Introduction

BETWEEN THE YEARS 991 and 998 an otherwise unknown monk named Richer *(Richerus)* of the monastery of Saint-Rémi at Rheims wrote a four-volume work of history that begins with the election of Odo, count of Paris, as king of West Francia in 888 and peters out on the final folio of the manuscript in a series of annalistic jottings, the latest of which is datable to 998. Only one copy of Richer's *Historia* is extant, and it is agreed to be the product of the author's own hand. This precious autograph manuscript (Bamberg, Staatsbibliothek, MS Hist. 5) exists in an unfinished state. Its fifty-seven folios are filled with erasures, corrections, and other proofreading marks that testify to various stages of composition and revision.

In the prologue to the *Historia* Richer defines his subject matter as "the conflicts of the Gauls" *(congressus Gallorum)*. He goes on to explain that his intention was "to recall to memory in writing the frequent wars waged by the Gauls during the reigns of [their] kings, their various struggles, and the different reasons for their undertakings" *(bella a Gallis sepenumero patrata variosque eorum tumultus ac diversas negotiorum rationes)*.[1] Most of the *Historia* is devoted to the political fortunes of the West Frankish kings during the turbulent tenth century, in particular their dealings with refractory magnates, Viking invaders, and the Ottonian kings of Germany. Richer also devotes significant portions of his history to the reforms undertaken by Archbishop Adalbero of Rheims (969–989) and to the career of Gerbert of Aurillac (ca. 945–1003), who served as *scholasticus* at the cathedral school of Rheims (972–

1. *Historia*, prologue.

981, 984–989) and as archbishop of the same see (991–998), and to whom the *Historia* is dedicated.

Our knowledge of Richer himself is limited to what we can glean from his history. He was probably born between 950 and 960; his father fought on behalf of King Louis IV (936–954) and his queen, Gerberga; and at some point he entered the monastery of Saint-Rémi. His detailed knowledge of Gerbert's teaching at the cathedral school of Rheims has frequently been interpreted as evidence that he studied under Gerbert, but there is no definitive proof of this. After the last datable entry in the *Historia*—the appointment of Gerbert to the archbishopric of Ravenna in 998—we know nothing more about Richer. Apart from this limited biographical framework we can only speculate about his background and his motivations for writing history.

The *Historia* was not widely known in the Middle Ages. Only three other authors are known to have cited it between the time of its composition and its rediscovery in the nineteenth century.[2] Hugh of Flavigny (1064/65—d. after 1114) drew upon the *Historia* for a passage about Gerbert in his *Chronicon*, but Hugh is not known to have traveled to Bamberg, which raises the possibility that another manuscript of Richer's history once existed in northern France, perhaps at Verdun (the location of Hugh's home monastery of Saint-Vanne).[3] The medieval chronicler Frutolf of Michelsberg (d. 1103) and the Renaissance humanist historian Johannes Trithemius (1462–1516) also used Richer's history, but although both authors consulted the text at Bamberg, where it is at-

2. Hartmut Hoffmann, "Die *Historien* Richers von Saint-Remi," *Deutsches Archiv für Erforschung des Mittelalters* 54 (1998): 508–20.

3. G. H. Pertz, ed., *Chronicon Virdunense*, MGH SS 8 (Hanover: Hahn, 1848), 367. We know that there was once a manuscript of Flodoard's *Annals* at Verdun—a manuscript used by Hugh and later brought with him to the monastery of Saint-Bénigne at Dijon—so it is not a stretch to imagine that there might have been a copy of Richer's *Historia* there as well. The conduit between Rheims and Verdun may have been Richard of Saint-Vanne, who studied at the cathedral school of Rheims in the late tenth century. We have no way of knowing if Richer's own monastery preserved a copy of his work because the library of Saint-Rémi was destroyed by fire in 1774.

tested in a twelfth-century library catalogue, the evidence suggests that they used a manuscript other than Bamberg, Staatsbibliothek, MS Hist. 5.[4] Trithemius states explicitly in his *Annales Hirsaugienses* that Richer's history was divided into two books—not four — and both he and Frutolf restrict their borrowings to books 1 and 2.[5] Moreover, in certain places both authors disagree together against the autograph. The version of the *Historia* that these two authors consulted at Bamberg, therefore, was probably not our codex, but a revised version—still dedicated to Gerbert—that included only books 1 and 2.[6]

After the sixteenth century Richer's text was neglected until the head librarian at Bamberg, Joachim Jaeck, chanced upon the manuscript and presented it to Georg Heinrich Pertz, the first editor of the *Monumenta Germaniae Historica,* in 1833.[7] Six years later Pertz published the first edition of Richer's work, which he titled the *Historiae*; this edition was reprinted in the *MGH* in the same year.[8] Georg Waitz revised Pertz's edition in 1877,[9] and Robert

4. Paul Ruf, *Mittelalterliche Bibliothekskataloge Deutschlands und der Schweiz,* 3.3 (Munich: C. H. Beck, 1939), 368n9: *Liber Richheri ad Gerbertum.* For the borrowings of Hugh, Frutolf, and Trithemius from the *Historia,* see Hoffmann, "Die *Historien* Richers von Saint-Remi," 508–20. Hoffmann argues convincingly that Frutolf and Trithemius had access to a now-lost version of Richer's history, also located at Bamberg.

5. *Annales Hirsaugienses,* 136–37: "Claruit hoc tempore in Gallia Richerus Monachus Rhemensis nostri ordinis, homo studiosus et tam in divinis scripturis quam in saecularibus litteris egregie doctus, ingenio promptus et clarus eloquio: qui scripsit ad Gerbertum supradictum Rhemorum Archiepiscopum pulchrum et compendiosum opus de gestis Gallorum, quod in duos libros divisit." It is important to note that Gerbert is still the dedicatee in the revised version of the *Historia*; this works against the hypothesis that subsequent drafts were intended for a different dedicatee.

6. The version of the *Historia* that Frutolf and Trithemius consulted must have been later than Bamberg, Staatsbibliothek, MS Hist. 5 because they incorporate revisions that Richer made to his autograph manuscript.

7. For an account of Jaeck's presentation of the manuscript to G. H. Pertz and his traveling companion, Johannes Böhmer, see Jason Glenn, *Politics and History in the Tenth Century: The Work and World of Richer of Reims* (Cambridge: Cambridge University Press, 2004), 269–73.

8. *Richeri Historiarum libri IIII,* MGH SS 3 (Hanover: Hahn, 1839), 561–657.

9. *Richeri Historiarum libri IIII,* MGH SRG 38 (Hanover: Hahn, 1877).

Latouche published a two-volume edition with a French translation in 1930 and 1937.[10] Since Latouche's edition four studies devoted exclusively to Richer and his history have been published.[11]

The Manuscript and the Date of Composition

Bamberg, Staatsbibliothek, MS Hist. 5 is one of the few surviving autograph manuscripts from the early Middle Ages, and as such it is an invaluable treasure.[12] Not only do the visible signs of Richer's editing offer us a rare insight into the complicated and messy process of historical composition in the Middle Ages, they also hold out the tantalizing prospect that important clues to understanding the *Historia* might be lurking in the manuscript. For if we could reconstruct the order in which Richer wrote the various sections of his history and date them accurately, it might be possible to determine how political events at Rheims during the turbulent decade of the 990s affected his writing.[13] But while the manuscript has provided fertile ground for speculation, no consensus has emerged about the dating of the manuscript or of the timing of the revisions.

Georg Heinrich Pertz, the text's first editor, used a change in ink tone as the criterion by which to distinguish between two different stages of composition.[14] He maintained that the first half of the codex (folios 1^r–28^r, which contain the prologue, all of book 1, and book 2.1–78), was written in a lighter ink than the second half

10. Robert Latouche, *Richer: Histoire de France,* 2 vols., Les classiques de l'histoire de France au moyen âge 12 and 17 (Paris: Librairie Ancienne, 1930 and 1937).

11. Wolfgang Giese, *"Genus" und "Virtus": Studien zum Geschichtswerk des Richer von Saint-Remi,* diss. Munich 1967 (Augsburg: W. Blasaditsch, 1969); Hans-Henning Kortüm, *Richer von Saint-Remi: Studien zu einem Geschichtsschreiber des 10. Jahrhunderts* (Stuttgart: Franz Steiner Verlag, 1985); Hartmut Hoffmann, "Die *Historien* Richers von Saint-Remi"; Glenn, *Politics and History.*

12. See Hartmut Hoffmann, "Autographa des früheren Mittelalters," *Deutsches Archiv für Erforschung des Mittelalters* 57 (2001): 1–62.

13. This is the approach adopted by Glenn, *Politics and History.*

14. *Richeri Historiarum libri IIII,* 562–63.

(28^{v}–55^{v}) and that the same distinction could also be found on the last folio of the manuscript (57^{v}), which contains nineteen lines of annalistic notices that Richer intended as source material for a continuation. The first eight lines of folio 57^{v}, which cover the years 995–996, are written in a lighter ink, while the next eleven, which cover the years 996–998, are written in a darker ink. If the ink tone of the first eight lines of annalistic notices matched the ink tone of folios 1^{r}–28^{r}, Pertz reasoned, then Richer must have composed the first section of the *Historia* between 995 and 996. Likewise, if the dark ink tone from the eleven final lines on folio 57^{v} matched that of the second half of the manuscript, then Richer would have composed folios 28^{v}–55^{v} between 996 and 998. Richer's corrections, which were also written in this darker ink, would then also date to the years 996–998. Pertz concluded that Richer wrote the first part of his history (from the prologue up to 2.78) on folios 1^{r}–28^{r} and the first eight lines of annalistic notices on a separate sheet of parchment (which became folio 57^{v}) between 995 and 996. He then wrote the second half (2.79 to the end) on folios 28^{v}–55^{v} and the final eleven lines of annalistic notices on folio 57^{v}. Finally, with the same darker ink that he had used for the second stage of composition, he went back and corrected the first half of his work.[15]

Pertz's hypothesis was accepted by Ferdinand Lot and Robert Latouche, and remained unchallenged until recently.[16] In a study of Richer's history that coincided with his preparation of a new edition for the *Monumenta Germaniae Historica* in 2000, Hartmut Hoffmann demonstrated the weaknesses of using ink color as a means of dating the manuscript.[17] He noted that the ink tone of the first eight lines of annalistic notices on folio 57^{v} cannot be determined with any degree of certainty because the ink has almost

15. See Pertz, *Richeri Historiarum libri IIII,* 563n8.

16. Latouche, *Richer: Histoire de France,* 1. vi–vii; Lot, "La date de naissance du roi Robert II et le siège de Melun," in *Mélanges Julien Havet: Recueil de travaux d'érudition dédiés à la mémoire de Julien Havet (1853–1893)* (Paris: Ernest Leroux, 1895), 152.

17. "Die *Historien* Richers von Saint-Remi," 447–55.

completely faded away.[18] Moreover, there is not merely one major shift in ink tone from light to dark. On the contrary, changes in ink occur at various other points in the manuscript, most obviously at 11^{r}, 13^{r}, and 43^{v}.[19] In general, changes in ink tone are both more frequent and more difficult to determine than allowed for by Pertz, making it an inadequate criterion by which to date the various sections of the *Historia.* Instead, Hoffmann asserts that whatever we can say with certainty about the composition of the *Historia* must be based on the internal evidence of the text. When the narrative ends on folio 55^{v}, Richer is discussing events of the year 995, the last of which is a synod to be held at Saint-Rémi on July 1 of that year.[20] The last datable event in this part of the *Historia* is the death of Count Odo I of Blois and Chartres in March 996.[21] The annalistic notices on folio 57^{v} all concern the years 995–998. Thus, Hoffmann reasons, it is likely that Richer finished his history in the summer of 996 and began collecting material for a continuation shortly thereafter.[22] The notes on folio 57^{v} were not written in two separate stages; instead, they were all jotted down after Richer had already completed the main body of his text.[23]

Hoffmann's conclusions run counter to the highly nuanced, but admittedly speculative, reconstruction of Richer's compositional process by Jason Glenn.[24] The complexity of Glenn's thesis

18. "Die *Historien* Richers von Saint-Remi," 454.

19. "Die *Historien* Richers von Saint-Remi," 454.

20. At the conclusion of the Synod of Mouzon, which took place on June 2, 995, a decision was made to hold another council at the monastery of Saint-Rémi on July 1 (*Historia* 4.107). In the first of the annalistic notices on folio 57^{v}, however, Richer (perhaps mistakenly) says that the synod met at Senlis. See *Historia* 4.108 and Hoffmann, *Historiae,* 306, chap. 107n1, and chap. 108n1.

21. Hoffmann, "Die *Historien* Richers von Saint-Remi," 455. For Odo's date of death, see Ferdinand Lot, *Études sur le règne de Hugues Capet et la fin du Xe siècle* (Paris: É. Bouillon, 1903), 178n2.

22. Since the first of the annalistic notices mentions the synod to be held on July 1, which is the last item mentioned in the *Historia* proper, it seems probable that Richer began taking down notes almost immediately after finishing the main portion of the text.

23. "Die *Historien* Richers von Saint-Remi," 455.

24. *Politics and History in the Tenth Century,* 128–65, 285–300. See also Glenn,

defies any attempt to reduce it to a summary, but the main points of his argument are as follows: First, the first and fourth quires of Bamberg, Staatsbibliothek, MS Hist. 5 preserve the remnants of an earlier draft or drafts of Richer's history.[25] Second, contra Pertz, the majority of the fifth and sixth quires, that is, folios 33–44 (*Hist.* 3.13–4.23) and 45–57 (4.23–end) were composed before the first three and a half quires (folios 1–28^{r}).[26] Third, the fifth quire contains fragments of two independent works that Richer composed before he embarked on the *Historia,* a *Gesta Adalberonis* and a *Vita Gerberti.*[27] Glenn ultimately posits at least three different stages of revision, during each of which Richer intended his work for a different patron—his decisions about what to include and what to leave out being dependent on the political currents in West Francia.[28] Glenn's thesis is ingenious, and certain aspects—particularly his suggestion that the material about Adalbero and Gerbert's early

"The Composition of Richer's Autograph Manuscript," *Revue d'histoire des textes* 27 (1997): 151–89, and "The Lost Works of Richer: The *Gesta Adalberonis* and the *Vita Gerberti,*" *Filologia Mediolatina* 4 (1997): 153–90.

25. Glenn posits that the eight folios that make up the quaternion of the fourth quire were written around folios 29 and 31, which were parts of an earlier draft. Folios 10 and 11, which appear to have been later additions to the second quire, may also have been part of this early draft. He also draws attention to the occurrence of the letter 'R/r' in the margins of certain folios (including 10, 11, 29, and 31). See *Politics and History,* 140–46. For Hoffmann's arguments to the contrary, see "Die *Historien* Richers von Saint-Remi," 449–51.

26. *Politics and History,* 146–54.

27. See "The Lost Works of Richer," and *Politics and History,* 146–54, 85–293.

28. See *Politics and History,* 158–63. In brief, he suspects that Richer began work on a revision of Flodoard's *Annals* and that he completed this initial draft upon the death of Count Odo of Blois in 996. Richer might have written the work in Chartres and perhaps intended to dedicate it to someone there. A second stage of work on the *Historia* would have begun in the summer and fall of 996 after a political realignment that followed the death of Odo. Robert, the son and anointed heir of Hugh Capet, courted Odo's widow, Bertha, while Hugh and Gerbert opposed their marriage. Gerbert would have been actively engaged in the defense of his see at this time and, more than ever, he needed Hugh's support. Richer, Glenn hypothesizes, aligned himself with Gerbert and Hugh and added material to his *Historia* intended to bolster Gerbert's claims to the archbishopric of Rheims. At this point he would have written the dedication to Gerbert. A final stage of revision would have most likely begun in 997 or 998, after Gerbert had left Rheims and abandoned his claim

career in book 3 may predate the other portions of the *Historia*—are compelling.[29] Other parts fall more in the realm of the possible than the verifiably true, as he readily admits.[30]

Ultimately almost two centuries of careful scrutiny of the manuscript have left us with few firm conclusions about the dates of its composition aside from the *terminus post quem* of 991 and the *terminus ante quem* of 998, which are based on the dates of Gerbert's tenure as archbishop of Rheims. The manuscript is a puzzle that will not yield up its secrets easily. The question that we would most like to answer is precisely when Richer began writing. The legitimacy of Gerbert's election to the see of Rheims was disputed almost immediately, but he faced his most serious challenge in June 995, when the papal legate Leo, abbot of Saint-Boniface-and-Alexis at Rome, convened a synod at the Lotharingian abbey of Mouzon-sur-Meuse to investigate the legality of his accession to the see.[31] Gerbert had been elected archbishop in June 991 after the previous occupant of the see, Arnulf, was deposed at the synod of Saint-Basle-de-Verzy (June 17–18) on charges of perjury and treason.[32] After swearing an oath of fidelity to Hugh Capet, Arnulf had

to the archbishopric. The final draft of the manuscript could have been intended for Arnulf, the embattled former archbishop of Rheims, who preceded Gerbert in possession of the see and took over for him after Gerbert left Rheims. Under this theory Gerbert was one of possibly three different intended dedicatees.

29. Glenn's hypothesis explains the erasure and lacuna at 33[v] and the awkward transition at *Historia* 3.21, where the *huic* that introduces the chapter has no antecedent in the previous chapter. He also rightly points to the questionable implication of Pertz's hypothesis that after writing the first half of the *Historia* (folios 1–28) Richer took notes for a continuation on the last folio of a quire that he intended to use to continue his history. See *Politics and History,* 135–36.

30. See *Politics and History,* 165. For reaction to Glenn, see Hoffmann, "Die *Historien* Richers von Saint-Remi," 451–54.

31. See Ernst-Dieter Hehl, ed., *Acta concilii Mosomensis,* MGH Concilia 6.2 (Hanover: Hahn, 2007), 495–507, and *Historia* 4.99–107.

32. The Synod of Saint-Basle took place on June 17–18, 991. See Ferdinand Lot, *Études sur le règne de Hugues Capet et la fin du Xe siècle* (Paris: É. Bouillon, 1903), 31–81; Pierre Riché, *Gerbert d'Aurillac, le pape de l'an mil* (Paris: Fayard, 1987), 126–40; Claude Carozzi, "Gerbert et le concile de Saint-Basle," in *Gerberto, scienza, storia e mito. Atti del Gerberti Symposium 25–27 luglio 1983,* ed. Michele Tosi (Piacenza: Archivum Bobiense, 1985), 661–66. Gerbert's elevation to the see of Rheims came

colluded with Charles of Lotharingia, the Carolingian claimant to the throne and Hugh's rival, and turned over the city of Rheims to him.[33] In the course of the synod of Saint-Basle Arnulf admitted his guilt and signed a document of abdication, which paved the way for Gerbert to replace him as archbishop.[34] Pope John XV never accepted the validity of the synod's proceedings, however, and the result was a protracted dispute pitting Gerbert against the papacy and Arnulf's defenders.

In response to the threat posed by the synod of Mouzon, and before the synod itself, Gerbert drew up his own *Acta* of the synod of Saint-Basle to justify Arnulf's deposition and defend his own election as archbishop.[35] If Richer began writing in 995 (as Pertz, among others, suggested), it would be difficult to see the *Historia* as anything other than a piece of pro-Gerbert advocacy couched in the form of a history of the West Frankish kings. On the other hand, if he began writing earlier, then conceivably he could have undertaken the project for any number of reasons. Although definitive proof is hard to come by, there are reasons for thinking that he commenced his history before 995. In the first place, the idea that he composed a history of over 50,000 words in the nine months between June 995 and March 996—while still attending to the full round of daily offices required of a monk—is improbable. More significant is the fact that the abbreviated version of Gerbert's *Acta* that he includes at 4.51–73 was not originally part of the sixth quire. Instead, it was written on three separate folios (the bifolium 49/50 and the single scrap of parchment 51) that were

shortly after the synod. See Gerbert, letter 179, in Pierre Riché and J.-P. Callu, eds., *Gerbert d'Aurillac: Correspondance,* Les classiques de l'histoire de France au moyen âge, 2 vols. (Paris: Les Belles Lettres, 1993), 2.446–51.

33. *Historia* 4.25–36.

34. For the series of events beginning with Arnulf's accession and ending with the Synod of Saint-Basle, see Riché, *Gerbert d'Aurillac,* 111–40; Kortüm, *Richer von Saint-Remi,* 68–78; *Historia* 4.25–73.

35. Ernst-Dieter Hehl, ed., *Acta concilii Remensis,* MGH Concilia 6.2 (Hanover: Hahn, 2007), 380–469. Leo had the *Acta* of Saint-Basle by June 9, 995. See Lot, *Études sur le règne de Hugues Capet,* 96; Carozzi, "Gerbert et le concile de St-Basle," 662.

inserted into the manuscript at a later date and keyed to the surrounding text.[36] If Richer started writing in response to the events of 995, after Gerbert had written his *Acta,* it is hard to see why he did not include an account of the synod in the sixth quire while he was writing it, rather than waiting to add it in later. Indeed, if the impetus for writing was to defend Gerbert, his version of the synod of Saint-Basle should have been the centerpiece of the whole history. In the absence of definitive proof to the contrary, therefore, the safest assumption is that Richer began writing sometime between 991 and 995.[37]

Historiographical Background

Because the stated theme of the *Historia* is political history *(congressus Gallorum)*, and because German and French scholars of the nineteenth century were the first to scrutinize the text, questions of national identity and political ideology have always loomed large in the scholarly discussion about Richer.[38] From Pertz's first edition of the *Historia* in 1839 to Jason Glenn's recent study, historians have answered the vexing question of how Richer's own political allegiances may have affected his presentation of events in different ways. Informing most of these attempts is the

36. Folio 48^{V} contains the end of Richer's account of the betrayal of Arnulf and Charles of Lotharingia (*Historia* 4.47), Hugh Capet's entry into Laon (4.48), and his debate about what to do with the prisoners (4.49), followed directly by Count Odo I of Blois and Chartres's speech to his men about the castle of Melun (4.74). Richer has gone back and inserted his account of the Synod of Saint-Basle at the point in the manuscript where it should fall chronologically. For the division of the manuscript into quires and folios, see Hoffmann, "Die *Historien* Richers von Saint-Remi," 448, and Glenn, *Politics and History,* 138–39.

37. There is one potentially serious textual challenge to this conclusion, the similarity between a passage found in the speech of Ingo at *Historia* 1.11 and the speech of Adalger in Gerbert's *Acta* of the Synod of Saint-Basle which could suggest that Richer only began writing after he had the *Acta* in front of him. See chap. 4 below.

38. See Gian Andria Bezzola, *Das Ottonische Kaisertum in der französischen Geschichtsschreibung des 10. und beginnenden 11. Jahrhunderts* (Graz and Cologne: Hermann Böhlau, 1956), 105–45; Glenn, *Politics and History,* 5–6; Giese, *"Genus" und "Virtus,"* 10–16.

assumption that, in choosing to write about recent political history, Richer must have undertaken the task in order to promote a specific political viewpoint, either his own or that of his patron, Gerbert of Aurillac. This assumption has seemed all the more probable because Richer wrote at a time of acute political crisis in the kingdom of West Francia: the years after the accession of Hugh Capet.

Hugh obtained the crown in 987 at the expense of Charles, the duke of Lower Lotharingia, who, as the representative of the Carolingian line, had an equally valid—if not stronger—claim to the throne.[39] When Charles was snubbed as the successor to Louis V (986–987) by the assembly of West Frankish magnates at Senlis in 987, he mounted a campaign to win back the throne by force. After an initial period of success in which he captured Laon and Rheims, Charles was betrayed and captured in 991.[40] His death shortly thereafter cleared the way for Hugh to rule without rival.[41] Richer wrote the *Historia* in the years immediately following these events, when feelings on both sides of the Carolingian-Capetian dynastic dispute were still raw. He wrote in a city, Rheims, that was a long-standing seat of Carolingian power, and in a monastery, Saint-Rémi, that was closely tied to the Carolingian monarchy through royal patronage, coronations, and burials.[42] Thus, it is only reasonable to suppose that in writing a history of the West Frankish kings, he was attempting to impose his own view of the Carolingian-Capetian dynastic conflict on his audience. Yet identifying any

39. Charles was the brother of the deceased king Lothar (954–986) and the uncle of Lothar's successor, Louis V (986–987).

40. *Historia* 4.47. See Ferdinand Lot, *Les derniers Carolingiens: Lothaire, Louis V, Charles de Lorraine (954–991)* (Paris: É. Bouillon, 1891), 272–77.

41. Charles died in captivity at Orléans before 995, the year in which Odo of Blois and Adalbero of Laon sought to deliver the kingdom of West Francia to Otto III, using Charles's young son Louis as a pawn. See Lot, *Les derniers Carolingiens*, 277–82.

42. See Michel Bur, "Reims, ville des sacres," in *Le sacre des rois: Actes du colloque international d'histoire sur les sacres et couronnements royaux, Reims 1975)* (Paris: Belles Lettres, 1985), 39–48, and Philippe Depreux, "Saint Remi et la royauté carolingienne," *Revue historique* 285 (1991): 235–60.

consistent ideological commitment to either dynasty has proven to be extremely difficult.

One of the rare pieces of biographical information that Richer reveals about himself provides a tantalizing bit of support for the idea that he might have been motivated by partisanship for the recently dispossessed Carolingians. He tells us that his father, Rodulf, was a vassal *(miles)* of the Carolingian king Louis IV and his queen, Gerberga, and he describes with relish his father's military service in their behalf (*Historia* 2.87–90, 3.7–9). Richer's family tie to Louis IV and Gerberga was taken as evidence of his pro-Carolingian agenda by a number of nineteenth-century German scholars.[43] The same scholars tended to view him as a nascent French nationalist who supported the claims of the West Frankish kings on Lotharingia, the old Carolingian heartland, and who was not above changing the details of his history to promote his pro-West Frankish and pro-Carolingian agenda.[44]

The thesis that Richer was hopelessly biased in favor of the Carolingian dynasty and his native kingdom of West Francia dissolved under strict scrutiny, however. Particularly important in this reassessment was Ferdinand Lot, who pointed out that on close inspection neither the historical context in which the *Historia* was written nor the evidence of the text itself offered much support for the early German historiographical consensus.[45] In fact, there are convincing reasons for rejecting the view that Richer set out to produce an overtly pro-Carolingian history.[46] In the first place, his assessments of the Carolingian kings are more nuanced than we would expect from the pen of a devoted partisan; nor do they always come out best when compared with their Robertian/

43. See, e.g., Pertz, *Historiarum libri IIII*, 562, and Karl Wittich, "Richer über die Herzoge Giselbert von Lothringen und Heinrich von Sachsen," in *Forschungen zur Deutschen Geschichte* (Göttingen: Verlag der Dieterichschen Buchhandlung, 1863), 3.107. For a summary of opinions, see Bezzola, *Das Ottonische Kaisertum*, 114n32; Giese, *"Genus" und "Virtus,"* 10–16; Glenn, *Politics and History*, 5–6.

44. Giese, *"Genus" und "Virtus,"* 10–12.

45. *Les derniers Carolingiens*, xvii–xix.

46. See esp. Bezzola, *Das Ottonische Kaisertum*, 114–17.

Capetian rivals.[47] Moreover, he dedicated the *Historia* to Gerbert of Aurillac, who owed his election to the archbishopric of Rheims to Hugh Capet,[48] and he lavishes praise on Gerbert's patron and predecessor Adalbero (969–989), who was accused of treason by the Carolingian king Lothar and played a critical role in persuading the West Frankish nobility to crown Hugh Capet instead of Lothar's brother Charles.[49] It is hard to credit the idea that Richer dedicated to Gerbert a work of history implicitly hostile to King Hugh and his Robertian/Capetian predecessors if both Gerbert and Adalbero were supporters of the Capetian dynasty. In fact, if Richer was working at the behest of Gerbert—as he claims in his prologue—he might have been motivated by a pro-Capetian bias, not a pro-Carolingian one.

Such is the argument advanced by Hans-Henning Kortüm, who contrasts Richer's portrayal of weak and ineffective Carolingian kings (Charles the Simple, Louis IV, Lothar, and Louis V) to his depictions of the energetic and capable Robertian-Capetian rulers Odo, Robert I, and Hugh Capet.[50] Kortüm's thesis is convincing in part; Richer is not hesitant to point out the flaws of the Carolingians. But, with the possible exception of Louis V, he also shows sympathy to the dynasty his father served. Nor does he make any attempt to justify or defend the Robertian-Capetian usurpation of Carolingian power.

Wolfgang Giese's 1969 study of the *Historia* resists the temptation to characterize Richer as a partisan of either the Carolingian or the Capetian cause. Giese posits that Richer was an advocate for

47. Bezzola, *Das Ottonische Kaisertum,* 114–16.

48. See Gerbert, letter 179 (Riché and Callu, 2.446–51), and Ferdinand Lot, *Études sur le règne de Hugues Capet,* 79–81. Later sources confirm that Gerbert was appointed by Hugh. See Ademar of Chabannes, *Chronicon*, ed. P. Bourgain, CCCM 129 (Turnhout: Brepols, 1999), 3.31; Helgaud of Fleury, *Epitoma vitae regis Rotberti Pii,* ed. and trans. Robert-Henri Bautier and Gillette Labory (Paris: Éditions du Centre national de la recherche scientifique, 1965), chap. 3; Rodulf Glaber, *Historiae,* ed. and trans. John France, in *Rodulfus Glaber: Opera* (Oxford: Clarendon Press, 1989), 1.13.

49. *Historia* 4.2–11.

50. See Kortüm, *Richer von Saint-Remi,* 38–49.

a strong king (whoever he might be) whose authority could suppress the civil discord *(dissidentia principum)* that was weakening the kingdom. For Giese, Richer's *Historia* was not meant to be an argument for the legitimacy of Capetian or Carolingian rule in West Francia. Rather, Richer was working at a task set for him by Gerbert: the composition of a history that would help to justify and explain Gerbert's actions in the tortuous series of events surrounding his struggle to maintain his position as archbishop of Rheims.[51] According to Giese, Richer lacked the discipline to adhere to an annalistic format or to maintain the *apologia* for Gerbert as the central focus of his work. Instead, he produced a history lacking concision or unity, the central purpose of which—a sympathetic portrayal of Gerbert—was diluted by frequent digressions and rhetorical flights of fancy.

While Jason Glenn has argued that a close reading of the *Historia* reveals Richer's own political leanings, which are neither straightforward nor easy to discern,[52] Hartmut Hoffmann has recently called into question the ability of historians to locate Richer's ideological point of view at all. Hoffmann concludes that whatever partiality Richer might have felt for the Carolingians or Capetians remains concealed beneath the literary superstructure of his text. Explicit authorial commentary is rare in the *Historia*; when it does occur, it seems in virtually every instance to express the point of view of one of the actors in Richer's history, and not Richer himself. Any attempt, therefore, to separate Richer's personal opinions from those of the characters he describes is almost certainly doomed to failure.

In the end, the most compelling argument against seeing Richer as a political partisan of one dynasty or the other is the inability of scholars to reach a consensus on the matter. If he was producing political propaganda, he was either a writer of extreme subtlety or

51. Giese, *"Genus" und "Virtus,"* 39–41, posits that, in commissioning the *Historia* from Richer, Gerbert directed him toward the *Annals of Saint-Bertin,* in which Hincmar of Rheims had justified his struggle with Pope Nicholas I.

52. Glenn, *Politics and History,* 110–11.

one who failed in his task. Insofar as his political ideology can be discerned from the text, it manifests itself in two ways: advocacy for the church of Rheims and its archbishops—particularly Adalbero and Gerbert, who are the two clear heroes of the work—and support for strong, legitimate kings who ruled by consensus and could suppress the political disorder that plagued tenth-century West Francia.[53] Richer's political perspective is not dynastic, but local and personal, shaped by the interests of his monastery and the city of Rheims, his loyalty to Adalbero and Gerbert, and his familial loyalty to Louis IV.

The intensive focus on uncovering the latent political agenda of the *Historia* is part of a broader trend to view medieval historiography primarily as a form of political discourse and to concentrate above all else on the political dynamics that inform historical writing.[54] While it is undeniable that history writing in the Middle Ages was a political act, a narrow focus on the political context of historiography can obscure the other factors that might have motivated a medieval monk to write, such as the desire to honor a patron, to ward off idleness, or to win prestige and esteem within his own community. We should not assume that political motives were foremost in Richer's mind, particularly given the lack of any consistent agenda in his work beyond a rather conventional indictment of civil disorder and weak kingship. Indeed, there is ample evidence to suggest that literary concerns were as important to him as political ones.

53. Bezzola, *Das Ottonische Kaisertum,* 117–23; Giese, "*Genus und Virtus,*" 107: "Einen Gegner bekämpfte Richer: Den Streit, die Gefährdung, und Bedrohung der Sicherheit des Reiches, die Unordnung." Cf. Geoffrey Koziol, *Begging Pardon and Favor: Ritual and Political Order in Early Medieval France* (Ithaca, N.Y.: Cornell University Press, 1992), 145.

54. See, e.g., Gabrielle Spiegel, "Political Utility in Medieval Historiography," in *The Past as Text: The Theory and Practice of Medieval Historiography* (Baltimore: Johns Hopkins University Press, 1997), 83–98; Hans-Werner Goetz, "Die Gegenwart der Vergangenheit im früh- und hochmittelalterliche Geschichtsbewußtsein," *Historische Zeitschrift* 255, no. 1 (1992): 61–97; Matthew Innes and Rosamond McKitterick, "The Writing of History," in *Carolingian Culture: Emulation and Innovation,* ed. R. McKitterick (Cambridge: Cambridge University Press, 1994), 193–220.

Richer and Flodoard

In the prologue Richer characterizes his work as part of a tradition of annalistic history at Rheims. He writes that he is continuing the annals of Archbishop Hincmar (ca. 806–882)[55] and that his work has drawn upon "a certain book of Flodoard" (894–966), a canon of the cathedral at Rheims who wrote *Annals* covering the years 919–966—the book to which Richer here calls attention—and a monumental *History of the Church of Rheims (Historia Remensis Ecclesiae),* which Richer also uses as a source.[56] Richer borrows heavily from Flodoard, sometimes following his *Annals* closely, at other times using them as a point of departure for his own original narratives. It is in Richer's use of his most important source text that we find one of the keys to understanding how he viewed his own historical project.

Richer and Flodoard are in many ways a study in contrasts. Flodoard's methodology inspires trust among modern historians. With the archives of the cathedral of Rheims at his disposal, he excerpts widely from letters, charters, epitaphs, and wills. He uses a wide range of narrative sources: histories, poems, saints' lives, the acts of martyrs, accounts of miracles, and reports of synods. Some of these Flodoard rephrases and condenses; in other cases he cites his source verbatim.[57] When his citations can still be checked, they

55. The annals attributed to Hincmar by Richer were traditionally known as the *Annals of Saint-Bertin.* They covered the years 830–882 and were the work of three successive writers: an anonymous author, Prudentius of Troyes, and Hincmar of Rheims. Hincmar's contribution covered the years 861–882. See Félix Grat, Jeanne Vielliard, and Suzanne Clémencet, eds., *Annales de Saint-Bertin* (Paris: Librairie C. Klincksieck, 1964), and Janet Nelson, *The Annals of St-Bertin* (Manchester: Manchester University Press, 1991).

56. See Martina Stratmann, ed., *Flodoardus Remensis: Historia Remensis Ecclesiae* (hereafter cited as *HRE*) MGH SS 36 (Hanover: Hahn, 1998), and Philippe Lauer, ed., *Les Annales de Flodoard,* Collection de textes pour servir à l'étude et à l'enseignement de l'histoire (Paris: Alphonse Picard, 1905).

57. For a detailed examination of Flodoard's relationship to his sources, see Martina Stratmann, "Die *Historia Remensis Ecclesiae*: Flodoard's Umgang mit seinen Quellen," *Filologia Mediolatina* 1 (1994): 111–27. In general, Flodoard tends to

have proven to be accurate.[58] Flodoard employs an elegant style free from mannerist excess, and he eschews fictional speeches and entertaining digressions. While the *Historia Remensis Ecclesiae* is a work with a clear agenda —the glorification of the church of Rheims and the defense of its material interests—Flodoard largely refrains from making authorial judgments. Likewise, in the *Annals* he steers clear of moralizing commentary.[59] By current standards of historical scholarship he is as reliable a historian as the early Middle Ages can offer.

Richer has been treated more warily by modern scholars, particularly by historians who have turned to his work as one of the few narrative sources for the political and ecclesiastical history of West Francia in the tenth century.[60] And indeed, there are good reasons for approaching his work with skepticism.[61] Although he sometimes contents himself with paraphrasing Flodoard's *Annals* for a particular year, he almost never reproduces his written sources verbatim.[62] He dresses up Flodoard's bare-bones narrative with freely invented speeches, dialogue, character sketches, descriptions of diseases, and accounts of battles. On occasion he seriously distorts Flodoard by rearranging the order of events or adding material of questionable veracity. Sometimes these errors appear to arise out of carelessness, at other times out of the desire to create a dramatic effect. Moreover, he is remarkably loose with figures. When precise numbers for battle casualties or the size of

---

abbreviate narrative sources like saints' lives, while he usually reproduces charters, wills, and accounts of synods in full or with minimal changes.

58. See Stratmann, *HRE,* 27–28, and "Flodoard's Umgang," 118.

59. Stratmann, *HRE,* 29; Lauer, *Les Annales de Flodoard,* xx.

60. See, e.g., Latouche, *Histoire de France,* 1.xi: "Il est donc dangereux de le suivre et son témoinage est toujours suspect," and Jean Dunbabin, *France in the Making, 843–1180* (London: Oxford University Press, 1985), 19.

61. See Latouche, "Un imitateur de Salluste au Xe siècle: L'historien Richer," *Annales de l'Université de Grenoble,* section lettres droit, n. s., 6 (1929): 289–306; Hoffmann, *Historiae,* 3–8; and chap. 2 below.

62. The exception is the text of Arnulf's profession of loyalty at the Synod of Saint-Basle (*Historia* 4.60), which is virtually identical to the text found in Gerbert's *Acta.*

armies are not available, he invents them. When Flodoard provides numbers, he sometimes changes them anyway.[63] He can be maddeningly careless with names and dates, and he sometimes seems confused about even the most basic facts of the history he is purporting to tell.[64] On three occasions he is guilty of passing off evident forgeries: a letter to Hugh the Great from the synod of Ingelheim (*Historia* 2.77); Lothar's letter to Conrad of Burgundy asking him to ambush Hugh Capet (3.86); and Emma's letter to her mother, Adelaide, asking her to arrange for Hugh's capture (3.87).

Richer's less stringent standard of historical accuracy is not the only way in which he differs from Flodoard. Richer uses classical sources liberally, while Flodoard largely avoids them.[65] Richer is self-assured in his prologue, while Flodoard makes elaborate protestations about his own inadequacy as a writer and the external factors that prevented him from finishing his work. Finally, Richer shows a clear appreciation of the value of secular learning for its own sake. His esteem for knowledge, in fact, is intimately bound up not only with the form of the *Historia*—the classicizing language and rhetorical set pieces—but also with its contents.

On the surface the *Historia* is a work of political history. Richer tells the reader as much in his prologue, where he defines his theme as the "wars of the Gauls" *(congressus Gallorum)*. This is the standard subject matter of the medieval chronicle, familiar to Richer from the *Annals of Saint-Bertin* and Flodoard's own *Annals*. But Richer does not limit himself to writing about politics and church history. Instead, he breaks up his narrative with a number of di-

63. See chap. 2 below.

64. E.g., Richer writes that Charles the Simple's father was "Carloman," and his grandfather, Louis the Stammerer (*Historia* 1.4). In truth, Louis the Stammerer was Charles the Simple's father and Charles the Bald was his grandfather.

65. Richer's vocabulary is littered with reminiscences of Cicero, Caesar, Sallust, Livy, and Hegesippus, among others. See the index in Hoffmann, *Historiae*, 315–25. Flodoard's citations of classical authors are limited to his discussion of the early history of Rheims in the *HRE*. He quotes from Caesar, Livy, Lucan, Eutropius, and Orosius. His references to Virgil, Sallust, and Aemilius Macer in this section are taken from Isidore of Seville's *Etymologiae*. See Michel Sot, *Un historien et son église au Xe siècle: Flodoard de Reims* (Paris: Fayard, 1993), 635; Stratmann, *HRE*, 6–8.

gressions. These include an anecdote about the rivalry between Derold, the court doctor to Charles the Simple and future bishop of Amiens (929–946), and an anonymous doctor of Salerno favored by the queen (*Historia* 2.59); a detailed account of Gerbert's celebrated disputation with the Saxon scholar Otric of Magdeburg (3.56–65); and a description of his own arduous journey to Chartres to read medical manuscripts (4.50). Each of these mini-narratives is focused around the importance of secular learning. Indeed, each one of the characteristics that sets Richer's *Historia* apart from Flodoard—classicism, enthusiasm for specialized forms of knowledge such as medicine and siege engineering, love of rhetorical invention, concern for dramatic effect over factual accuracy, and the insertion of the digressions cited above—can be traced back to Richer's self-professed *aviditas discendi* (4.50). It is a theme that is largely absent from the work of Flodoard.

Why two historians who were educated and lived in the same city, who wrote about many of the same events, and whose most important works are separated by a span of only four decades show such pronounced differences with one another is a question of considerable interest.[66] In some ways Richer is simply sui generis; no other contemporary author exhibits quite the same morbid interest in creating fictional diseases for his characters, for example. But a more satisfying explanation can be found in the changes in the intellectual atmosphere at Rheims that began shortly after Flodoard's death (966) with the election of Adalbero as archbishop in 969 and the arrival of Gerbert at Rheims in 972.

Flodoard was one of the most learned men of his day, "*un homme fort cultivé*."[67] He wrote prodigiously—both poetry and prose—and was a friend and correspondent of the intellectual luminary Rather of Verona.[68] As a literary stylist he is superior to

66. Flodoard wrote the *HRE* between 948 and 954; he made the last entry in his *Annals* in the year of his death, 966. Richer wrote between 991 and 998.

67. Pierre Riché, *Écoles et enseignement dans le Haut Moyen Âge* (Paris: Aubier, 1979), 179.

68. Folcuin of Lobbes records that Rather sent a copy of his *Agonisticum* to

Richer, whose own prose style can seem meager in comparison to the elegant Latin of the *Historia Remensis Ecclesiae.* Yet while Flodoard had received an elite education, none of his writing reveals anything close to Richer's obvious delight in learning for its own sake. Flodoard was the product of a static educational system that was still essentially Carolingian in its outlook. The impetus for the establishment of cathedral and monastic schools under Charlemagne and his successors had been the desire to create a literate clergy to pray, perform liturgical functions, and understand sacred Scripture. The schools that developed to instruct these clerics treated secular learning as a tool to be used in reading and commenting on the Bible. Flodoard was the product of such a school, one that reflected the cultural environment that took root at Rheims under Archbishop Hincmar (845–882).[69]

We know virtually nothing about the school at Rheims in Hincmar's day, although one must have existed to train the canons of the cathedral.[70] We are better informed when it comes to what he thought such a school should teach.[71] Hincmar viewed instruction in the liberal arts as utilitarian. Education was intended to equip the student with the tools he needed to understand the divine word. As a secondary function, it provided the secular clergy with literary skills that could prove valuable in an administrative or legal capacity. Hincmar himself was a formidable administrator, politician, and canonist, but not a classicizing scholar or protohumanist.[72]

Flodoard, among others, for his approval. See *Gesta abbatum Lobiensium,* ed. G. H. Pertz, MGH SS 4 (Hanover: Hahn, 1841), 64.

69. For Carolingian educational ideology, see C. Stephen Jaeger, *The Envy of Angels: Cathedral Schools and Social Ideals in Medieval Europe, 950–1200* (Philadelphia: University of Pennsylvania Press, 1994), 21–27. See also Riché, *Écoles et enseignement,* 111–18.

70. For the scanty information about the school at Rheims before 900, see Sot, *Un historien et son église,* 57–58, and Émile Lesne, *Histoire de la propriété ecclésiastique en France,* 6 vols. (Lille: R. Giard, 1910–1943), 4.276–77.

71. See, e.g., Riché's translation of a canon from the Synod of Savonnières in 859 (*Écoles et enseignement,* 355) at which Hincmar probably played an important role.

72. The manuscripts copied at Rheims while Hincmar was archbishop and his

The school, or schools, that existed at Rheims in Hincmar's day suffered badly in the Norman invasions at the end of the ninth century, so much so that Hincmar's successor, Fulk (883–900), brought Hucbald of Saint-Amand and Remigius of Auxerre to Rheims to restore two schools, one for canons and one for "rural clerics."[73] The restored schools continued to teach according to the Carolingian educational tradition. Students studied the liberal arts as a precursor to reading and meditation on the sacred Scriptures *(lectio ac meditatio sapientie).* This was the intellectual climate in which Flodoard was educated and wrote.[74] His weightiest literary productions—the *Historia Remensis Ecclesiae,* a four-book history of the church of Rheims, and *De triumphis Christi,* a monumental Christian epic of nineteen books comprising almost 20,000 lines—reflect both the spiritual focus of the education Flodoard had received at the cathedral school of Rheims and Hincmar's interest in safeguarding and expanding the power of his see. In this environment we would hardly expect to meet with anything like Richer's *Historia,* a work that mixes lurid portrayals of the savagery and treachery of the West Frankish nobility with fictional speeches, digressions, and personal anecdotes, and which contains very little in the way of spiritual edification.

own pattern of literary citation reveal a distinct preference for the Bible and Church Fathers over secular literature. See F. M. Carey, "The Scriptorium of Reims during the Archbishopric of Hincmar (845–882 A.D.)," in *Classical and Mediaeval Studies in Honor of E. K. Rand,* ed. L. W. Jones (New York, 1938), 41–60. For Hincmar's use of citations from the Bible, Church Fathers, and canon law, see appendices 1–3 in vol. 3 of Jean Devisse, *Hincmar, archevêque de Reims,* 3 vols., Travaux d'histoire éthico-politique 29 (Geneva: Librairie Droz, 1975–1976). For Hincmar's libraries, see Devisse, *Hincmar,* 3.1469–1512, and Sot, *Un historien et son église,* 67–77.

73. *HRE* 4.9, pp. 401–2.

74. Flodoard received his educational training first from Gundacer, a canon at the cathedral of Rheims, and later at the cathedral school itself. See *HRE* 2.19, p. 176; Sot, *Un historien et son église,* 45; and Peter Christian Jacobsen, *Flodoard von Reims: Sein Leben und seine Dichtung "De triumphis Christi,"* Mittellateinische Studien und Texte 10 (Leiden: Brill, 1978), 4–10.

Adalbero, Gerbert, and the Educational Revival at Rheims

Three years after Flodoard's death the cultural environment at Rheims underwent a profound change. In 969 Adalbero, a canon of Metz from a noble Lotharingian family, who had been educated at the monastery of Gorze, was chosen to be archbishop.[75] Under his direction an era of cultural revival began at Rheims. Adalbero reformed the monasteries of Mouzon (971) and Saint-Thierry (972), replacing their canons with Benedictine monks.[76] He compelled the canons of the cathedral of Rheims to live together in a community and organized them under the Augustinian rule.[77] He made major renovations to the cathedral itself.[78] He traveled to Rome (971–972) to confirm the privileges of Saint-Rémi, and he endowed the monastery with one of his own holdings, the Abbey of Saint-Timothy.[79] As was often the case, ecclesiastical reform went hand-in-hand with a renewed emphasis on education. The

75. For Adalbero, see Auguste Dumas, "L'église de Reims au temps des luttes entre Carolingiens et Robertiens (888–1027)," *Revue d'histoire de l'église de France* 30 (1944): 21–30; Rosamond McKitterick, "The Carolingian Kings and the See of Rheims (883–987)," in *Ideal and Reality in Frankish and Anglo-Saxon Society. Studies Presented to J. M. Wallace-Hadrill*, ed. P. Wormald, D. Bullough, and R. Collins (Oxford: Blackwell, 1983), 238–44; and Michel Bur, "Adalbéron, archevêque de Reims, reconsidéré," in *Le roi de France et son royaume autour de l'an Mil: Actes du Colloque Hugues Capet 987–1987, La France de l'an Mil, Paris-Senlis, 22–25 juin 1987*, ed. Michel Parisse and Xavier Barral i Altet (Paris: Picard, 1992), 55–63.

76. For a summary of Adalbero's reforms to the monasteries in the diocese of Rheims, see Michel Bur, "Saint-Thierry et le renouveau monastique dans le diocèse de Reims au Xe siècle," in *Saint-Thierry, une abbaye du VIe au XXe siècle. Actes du Colloque international d'Histoire monastique Reims-Saint-Thierry, 11 au 14 octobre 1976*, ed. Michel Bur (Saint-Thierry: Association des Amis de l'Abbaye de Saint-Thierry, 1979), 44–49.

77. *Historia* 3.24

78. *Historia* 3.22. See Michel Bur, "A propos de la *Chronique de Mouzon* II: Architecture et liturgie à Reims au temps d'Adalbéron (vers 976)," *Cahiers de civilisation médiévale* 27 (1984): 297–302, and Hans Reinhardt, *La cathédrale de Reims. Son histoire, son architecture, sa sculpture, ses vitraux* (Paris: Presses universitaires de France, 1963), 41–45.

79. *Historia* 3.26.

cathedral school at Rheims acquired new prominence, and by the 970s Gerannus, the archdeacon at Rheims, had become famous for teaching *logica* (dialectic and rhetoric).[80] During a trip to the Ottonian court in Rome on behalf of King Lothar he so impressed the brilliant Gerbert of Aurillac that the latter obtained permission to leave Rome to travel to Rheims and study with him. In 972 Gerbert himself became *scholasticus* of the cathedral school, a position he held until 982, when he was appointed abbot of Bobbio by Otto II. Gerbert's stay at Bobbio was brief. Harassed by the monks and threatened by powerful landholders, he left the abbey for good in December 983 and returned to Rheims shortly thereafter. At Rheims Gerbert served as *scholasticus* again from 984 to 989, as secretary to Archbishop Arnulf from 989 to 991, and as archbishop himself from 991 to 997.[81] As schoolmaster of the cathedral, and then as archbishop, Gerbert was the key figure in the educational life of Rheims for a period of nearly twenty-five years.[82]

Gerbert's love of learning went far beyond an appreciation of the utility of *sapientia saeculi* for understanding sacred Scripture. His letters reveal that he conceived of himself as a scholar and a philosopher as well as a cleric, and, as much as any other figure in the intellectual history of the tenth century, he represents a rejection of the Pauline condemnation of the folly of worldly wisdom. For Gerbert, learning was a gift from God to man, and knowledge went hand-in-hand with faith.[83] Those endowed with *scientia* had, in fact, a better claim to faith than the ignorant.[84] Gerbert's reli-

80. *Historia* 3.45.

81. For the chronology of Gerbert's life, see Riché, *Gerbert d'Aurillac,* 279–88. Gerbert abandoned Rheims in 997, though Richer would have continued to honor him with the title of archbishop of Rheims until he accepted the see of Ravenna in 998.

82. For Gerbert's pedagogy, see Riché, "L'enseignement de Gerbert à Reims dans le contexte européen," in *Gerberto, scienza, storia e mito. Atti del Gerberti Symposium (25–27 luglio 1983)* (Piacenza: Archivum Bobiense, 1985), 51–69.

83. Gerbert, letter 190 (Riché and Callu, 2.492): "Multum mortalibus divinitas largita est, o mei animi custos, quibus fidem contulit et scientiam non negavit." See also Riché, *Gerbert d'Aurillac,* 239–55, for an assessment of Gerbert's character and beliefs.

84. Gerbert, letter 190 (Riché and Callu, 2.492): "Huic fidei ideo scientiam cop-

gious devotion had a distinctly philosophical aspect. Pierre Riché points out that Gerbert took the Boethian view that God represented "the supreme good, the perfect intelligence, he who made order rule over the universe."[85]

Gerbert established himself as perhaps the preeminent scholar of his day, so much so that Otto III brought him to Germany as a personal tutor.[86] He wrote widely on the *quadrivium* and was probably the first scholar in the Latin West to make use of the abacus, about which he wrote two different treatises.[87] Moreover, he was marked by a deep and unambiguous love for the classical tradition, one that was not tinged with regrets about the vanity of pagan wisdom. Richer tells us that Gerbert trained his students in the "modes of expression" *(modi locutionum)* by expounding Virgil, Statius, Terence, Juvenal, Persius, Horace, and Lucan (*Historia* 3.47). This literary canon, composed exclusively of classical authors, is a departure from the traditional course of reading in Carolingian schools, which relied heavily on the Christian poets of late antiquity.[88] Gerbert's letters testify to his tenacity in seeking out new manuscripts of classical authors.[89] He was a self-styled Ciceronian who drew on Cicero's works for both his Latin prose style and his moral philosophy.[90] He also followed Cicero in his high es-

---

ulamus, quia stulti fidem non habere dicuntur. Hanc vos habere fidem illa generosi animi praeclara scientia indicat."

85. *Gerbert d'Aurillac,* 246.

86. See Gerbert, letter 186 (Riché and Callu, 2.480–83).

87. See Uta Lindgren, *Gerbert von Aurillac und das Quadrivium: Untersuchungen zur Bildung im Zeitalter der Ottonen,* Sudhoffs Archiv 18 (Wiesbaden: Franz Steiner Verlag, 1976), 17. Gerbert's mathematical works are collected in N. Bubnov, *Gerberti Opera Mathematica* (Berlin: R. Friedländer, 1899). The works on the abacus are the *Regulae de numerorum abaci rationibus* (Bubnov, 1–22) and the *Fragmenta de norma rationis abaci* (Bubnov, 23–24).

88. See Günter Glauche, *Schullektüre im Mittelalter,* Münchener Beiträge zur Mediävistik und Renaissance-Forschung 5 (Munich: Arbeo-Gesellschaft, 1970), 62, 65.

89. See Pierre Riché, "La bibliothèque de Gerbert d'Aurillac," in *Mélanges de la Bibliothèque de la Sorbonne* 8 (1988): 94–103, esp. 96–100, and Gustav Becker, *Catalogi bibliothecarum antiqui* (Bonn, 1885; reprint, Hildesheim: Georg Olms, 1973), 77–79.

90. See Gerbert, letter 44 (Riché and Callu, 1.106): "non is sum, qui cum Pan-

timation of the value of rhetoric, particularly for the active, political life. It was fundamental to Cicero's philosophical program that eloquence and personal morality should go hand-in-hand, a view that Gerbert adopted wholeheartedly.[91] In a letter to Evrard, abbot of Saint-Julien of Tours, he makes just such a connection between personal virtue and the ability to speak well:

> And since the practice of moral behavior and that of speaking are not separate from philosophy, I have always joined my pursuit of speaking well with a desire to live properly, although a proper manner of living by itself is better than the ability to speak well, and to one who has been released from the concerns of leadership one is enough without the other.[92]

He goes on in the same letter to stress the usefulness of rhetorical ability: "But to those of us who are engaged in political life both are necessary. For [the ability] to speak suitably in order to persuade and to keep angry tempers in check with soothing speech is supremely useful."[93]

Gerbert's appreciation of the value of eloquence is not, in and of itself, unusual. Six centuries earlier Saint Augustine had appropriated the tools of classical rhetoric for Christians in his *De doctrina christiana.* In doing so, however, he had restricted the scope of oratory to preaching. The bishop, Augustine believed, had a duty to explain the word of God to his flock and to combat false belief. In the service of these ideals he should avail himself of the appropriate means of making his message clear and compelling; eloquence for its own sake, however, was still suspect. Augustine's attitude was recapitulated in the ninth century in the *De institutione clericorum* of Hrabanus Maurus (776–856). Hrabanus's manual

etio interdum ab utili sejungam honestum, sed potius cum Tullio omni utili admisceam"; and letter 158 (2.394): "in otio et negotio praeceptorum M. Tullii diligens fui executor." See Riché, *Gerbert d'Aurillac,* 247–48, for Gerbert's "Stoic morality."

91. Cf. *De inventione* 1.1.1; *De oratore* 3.55.

92. Letter 44 (Riché and Callu, 1.106): "Cumque ratio morum dicendique ratio a philosophia non separentur, cum studio bene vivendi semper coniunxi studium bene dicendi, quamvis solum bene vivere praestantius sit eo, quod est bene dicere, curisque regiminis absoluto, alterum satis sit sine altero."

93. Letter 44 (Riché and Callu, 1.106).

on clerical duties and education is a perfect encapsulation of Carolingian educational ideology. Each of the liberal arts is valued as one part of the intellectual tool kit needed to read and understand the Bible. Education is assigned the ultimate end of moving the student closer to the *scientia sanctarum scripturarum*.[94] Hrabanus draws heavily on *De doctrina christiana* for his brief discussion of rhetoric, and, like Augustine, he locates the value of eloquence in preaching:

> Rhetoric (as teachers of secular learning relate) is the knowledge of speaking well in civil disputes. But although this definition seems to pertain to worldly knowledge, nonetheless it is not irrelevant to ecclesiastical education. For whatever the orator and preacher of the divine word says fluently and gracefully in his teaching and whatever he brings forth appropriately and eloquently in writing relates to the knowledge of this art. Nor on any account should he be judged to sin who studies this art at an appropriate age and follows its guidelines in composing and delivering a sermon; rather, he does good work who learns it fully to this end: that he may be suitable to preach the word of God.[95]

In contrast to Hrabanus, Gerbert viewed rhetoric not as a tool limited to preaching, but as an integral part of the active life, and the trajectory of his own career testifies to the utility that skill in argumentation and persuasion could possess for a late-tenth-century cleric. Gerbert won renown for participating in a day-long disputation with Otric of Magdeburg at the behest of Otto II at Ravenna in 981; he served as secretary to two archbishops of Rheims, to Hugh Capet, and to the German emperor Otto III; and he expended much of his energy in the years between 991 and 997 defending his title to the archbishopric of Rheims in writing and in person. The power to persuade was a crucial factor in his meteoric rise from monk at Aurillac to *scholasticus* at Rheims, abbot of Bobbio, archbishop of Rheims and Ravenna, and finally to the papacy itself. By stressing the political utility of speaking well, and

94. *De institutione clericorum* 3.2.
95. *De institutione clericorum* 3.19.

by adopting Cicero's ideal of the orator as both eloquent and morally good, Gerbert expanded the proper sphere of rhetoric and endowed it with a value that it did not possess for many of his predecessors.

Gerbert's high opinion of the practical value of oratorical training is clearly reflected in the *Historia,* where speeches are both very frequent and very effective. Indeed, virtually every important act is preceded by an oration of some sort.[96] Rhetoric has a clear practical value for the characters that inhabit Richer's textual world; the ability to "speak suitably in order to persuade" is almost a prerequisite for success. Moreover, Richer states explicitly that studying well-written speeches will benefit students of rhetoric and those engaged in the practical affairs of the church. At the end of his account of the Synod of Saint-Basle he directs the reader to look into Gerbert's *Acta* of the council, a work, he writes, that "will be found very useful not only in cases that come up before synods, but also to those familiar with rhetorical issues [*status rhetoricae*]."[97] He includes Gerbert's speech at the Synod of Mouzon in his history "because it is full of arguments, and the reader will derive great profit from it."[98] Richer's own rhetorical training points directly to Gerbert's influence: not only did he study the *Acta* of the synods of Saint-Basle and Mouzon as compositional models, but his use of rhetorical *termini technici* closely mirrors Gerbert's.[99]

This emphasis on the efficacy and practical benefits of eloquence in the *Historia* is only one aspect of Gerbert's influence, however. As part of his effort to assemble a new rhetorical library from which to teach, Gerbert brought to Rheims three texts—Cicero's *De inventione* and *De oratore,* and Marius Victorinus's commentary on the *De inventione*—which together provided a clear

96. See Kortüm, *Richer von Saint-Remi,* 97ff.

97. *Historia* 4.73: "Qui [liber] non solum sinodalibus causis, sed et status rethoricae cognoscentibus utillimus habetur."

98. *Historia* 4.101: "Sed hanc addere hic placuit, quod plena rationibus plurimam lectori utilitatem comparat."

99. See chap. 4 below.

exposition of the Ciceronian view of the rhetorical foundations of historiography. Herein lies an important insight into understanding the *Historia*. For if there is a single hermeneutical key that will bring the most clarity to Richer's approach to history writing, it is Cicero's conception of history as a *narratio* constructed according to the rules of rhetoric. The true historian, in Cicero's understanding, was not simply a mediator of reliable data; he was a literary artist obligated to describe in detail the circumstances of historical deeds (who, what, when, why, where, how), to explain the motives of his characters, and, when necessary, to use plausible fictions to make his narrative credible.[100]

Robert Latouche drew attention to the rhetorical foundations of the *Historia* some eighty years ago, explaining that Richer's methodology, which had been garnering angry accusations of bad faith and partisanship ever since the first appearance of the *Historia* in print in 1839, was actually the product of overlapping rhetorical impulses: to make sense of his source material (i.e., to make it clear and plausible in rhetorical terms, or as Richer says in his prologue, to explain *rationes negotiorum*) and to embellish and amplify it.[101] Latouche was more exasperated than entertained by Richer's historical imagination; he denied his work the status of history and viewed it instead as a collection of rhetorical exercises worked up for his teacher, Gerbert.[102] He was unsparing in his criticism of Richer's methods, and his footnotes bristle with charges of inaccuracy and outright forgery.[103] Where Latouche

100. See above all A. J. Woodman, *Rhetoric in Classical Historiography: Four Studies* (London: Routledge, 1988), 70–116. For a recent discussion of the nexus between rhetoric and historiography in classical antiquity, see Cynthia Damon, "Rhetoric and Historiography," in *A Companion to Roman Rhetoric*, ed. William Dominik and Jon Hall (Malden, Mass.: Blackwell, 2007), 439–50.

101. "Un imitateur de Salluste," 294–95.

102. *Richer: Histoire de France*, 1.xi.

103. Two of his notes on *Historia* 2.4 serve as representative examples. When Louis IV, upon his arrival in France, masters a particularly spirited horse, Latouche protests: "Encore un trait forgé par Richer!" (1.132n1). He is unconvinced when Richer recounts that Hugh the Great immediately served as the new king's squire: "Ce détail est une forgerie de Richer.... Richer n'a pas de scrupules d'historien" (1.133n2).

erred was in drawing a bright line between rhetoric and historiography. Rhetorical *inventio* was a fundamental element of classical historiography, and the ultimate test of a narrative constructed according to the principles of classical rhetoric was plausibility, not truthfulness. He was, moreover, far too eager to attribute Richer's deviations from the standard of truthfulness to a desire to imitate Sallust. While Sallust was, along with Hegesippus, one of Richer's two most important compositional models, it is Cicero's theoretical conception of a rhetorically inflected historiography that had the greater impact on the contents of the *Historia*.

Although in this larger sense Latouche misses the point of Richer's methodology, his analysis of the *Historia* as principally a rhetorical exercise does a better job of actually explaining its contents than interpretations that view the *Historia* primarily as a means of political commentary. In some sense, then, this study is an effort to rehabilitate Latouche's understanding of the text by focusing on the rhetorical foundations of Richer's work. Thus, rather than concentrating primarily on the manuscript or the political agenda of the text, both topics that have received exhaustive treatment, the following chapters will attempt to shed light on Richer's methods, his way of thinking about the past, and the use that history had for him. It will consider the value of his prologue as a programmatic statement, his amplification and distortion of his source material, his construction of speeches and other rhetorical set pieces, and the ways in which he used his history as a means of self-representation and self-promotion. From these investigations it is hoped that a more fully rounded picture of Richer and his work will emerge, one that is grounded in both the political and intellectual context of late tenth-century Rheims.

[ONE]

Richer's Prologue

ANY ATTEMPT TO UNDERSTAND the *Historia* must begin with two basic questions: Why did Richer choose to write history and how did he conceive of his task? The only place where he comments directly on both the contents of his work and his occasion for writing is the prologue, which makes this the logical place to begin looking for answers.[1] The prologue to the *Historia* must be evaluated carefully, however, for it poses a particular kind of interpretative challenge that characterizes the prologues of medieval histories as a genre. The problem is not that medieval historians are silent about their reasons for writing; on the contrary, they frequently cite considerations such as the usefulness of history, the desire to oblige a patron, or the need to preserve the memory of the past. Instead it is the predictable regularity of these claims that invites skepticism on the part of the reader.

Medieval authors typically built their prologues around certain literary-rhetorical formulae, or *topoi,* intended to please the audience and create a positive impression of the author.[2] These formu-

1. For Richer's prologue in general, see Kortüm, *Richer von Saint-Remi,* 93–96.

2. The task of the speaker or writer in the prologue was to secure the goodwill of the audience *(captatio benevolentiae).* See Cicero, *De Inventione,* ed. E. Stroebel (Stuttgart: Teubner, 1965), 1.15.20; *Rhetorica ad Herennium,* ed. F. Marx (Leipzig: Teubner, 1964), 1.4.7; Marius Victorinus, *Explanationes in Ciceronis rhetoricam,* ed. A. Ippolito, CCSL 132 (Turnhout: Brepols, 2006), 1.20. See also E. R. Curtius, *European Literature and the Latin Middle Ages,* trans. Willard R. Trask (Princeton, N.J.: Princeton University Press, 1990), 70. For the topoi of medieval prologues, see Gertrud Simon, "Untersuchungen zur Topik der Widmungsbriefe mittelalterlicher Gesschichtsschreiber bis zum Ende des 12. Jahrhunderts," *Archiv für Diplomatik* 4 (1958): 52–119 (part 1), and 5–6 (1959–1960): 73–153 (part 2); Tore Janson, *Latin Prose*

lae might have rendered contemporary audiences attentive and well disposed, but they tend to frustrate modern readers. The conventional nature of prefatory topoi frequently obscures whatever truth might lie behind an author's statements, making it difficult to distinguish genuine expressions of authorial intention and practice from the rhetorical devices used to secure a sympathetic audience. Faced with a seemingly impenetrable web of clichés, the reader may be tempted to ignore the author's statements about why he wrote and instead to speculate about unseen social, political, and personal factors that could motivate historical writing. This kind of speculation has an important role to play in understanding the work of medieval historians. Yet there is an accompanying danger that, by disregarding what medieval authors actually tell us, we become too free to read into their work whatever motivations we choose.

Between the equally unsatisfactory extremes of credulity, on the one hand, and unfounded speculation, on the other, there is a reasonable middle ground.[3] Each topos must be evaluated separately and weighed against the other elements of the prologue before it can be accepted at face value or dismissed as a rhetorical fiction. Medieval authors were accustomed to constructing their prologues around certain traditional themes, but within the confines of this system there was room for innovation and individual expression. The author had to choose which topoi to use and which to reject, which to amplify and develop and which to pass over quickly. Accordingly, the degree of emphasis given—or denied—to a particular topos can serve as a signal to the reader of its relative importance to the author.

Prefaces: Studies in Literary Conventions, Studia Latina Stockholmiensia 13 (Stockholm: Almquist & Wiksell, 1964); Curtius, "Mittelalterstudien," *Zeitschrift für Romanische Philologie* 63 (1943): 225–74 (esp. 245–51); Bernard Guenée "Histoire, mémoire, écriture. Contribution à une étude des lieux communs," *Comptes rendus des séances de l'Académie des Inscriptions et Belles Lettres* 127 (1983): 441–56.

3. Helmut Beumann demonstrates an exemplary approach to the interpretation of medieval historiographical prologues in "Topos und Gedankengefüge bei Einhard," *Archiv für Kulturgeschichte* 33 (1951): 337–50. See also "Der Schriftsteller und seine Kritiker im frühen Mittelalter," *Studium Generale* 12 (1959): 497–511.

The text itself may also give some indication of the role that particular topoi played in composition. An author who apologizes for his faulty style in the prologue, but who goes on to write artificial and highly ornamented prose, uses the topos of stylistic inadequacy to ingratiate himself with the reader, not because he is truly embarrassed about his literary skill. Thus, by paying attention to the relevance of certain topoi to the text as a whole, we can get a better sense of the reason for which the author uses them.

A broadly comparative approach can also bring the individual elements of a prologue into sharper relief. By comparing Richer's prologue to those of other medieval historians—particularly those of his contemporaries—we can get a better sense for the originality of his deployment of any particular topos. The application of these three criteria—degree of emphasis, internal consistency, and the comparative method—will show that valuable clues to reading the *Historia* lie behind the seemingly formulaic veneer of the prologue.

At this point it will be useful to reproduce the prologue in full:

To my Lord and most blessed father Gerbert, Archbishop of Rheims, the monk Richer: The authority of your command, most holy father Gerbert, has provided the seedbed for the conflicts of the Gauls to be compiled in a book. Because the advantages to be realized are so great, and because the subject matter is so abundant, I have embraced this task as eagerly as I was drawn by the marvelous good will of the one making the request. I have judged it best to begin with recent events because Hincmar of blessed memory, who was eighth in the office of archbishop before you,[4] so comprehensively wove together the deeds of the more distant past in his own annals.[5] The further back the reader goes from the beginning of my work through Hincmar's history, the earlier the material that he shall find. I say this so that the frequent repetition of the name "Charles" and of other names in each of our works

4. Gerbert was actually the ninth archbishop after Hincmar. The order of succession after Hincmar was as follows: Fulk (882–900), Hervey (900–922), Seulf (922–925), Hugh (925–931/941–948), Artald (931–940/946–961), Odelric (962–969), Adalbero (969–989), Arnulf (989–991), and then Gerbert (991–998).

5. The *Annals of Saint-Bertin (Annales Bertiniani)*. Hincmar wrote the final section, covering the years 861–882.

will not cause any confusion about their respective order. For when the sequence of events is not heeded, error will confound the struggling reader by leading him astray from the proper order. Therefore, because the names "Charles" and "Louis" appear often in both of our histories, the careful reader will distinguish between kings who share the same name by referring to the different time periods of the authors. My particular goal is to recall to memory in writing the frequent wars waged by the Gauls during the reigns of these kings, their various struggles, and the different reasons for their undertakings. If the affairs of others are mentioned, let it be assumed that this is due to incidental reasons that could not be avoided. Now if I am accused of being ignorant of the unknown past, I do not deny that I took some things from a certain book of Flodoard, a priest of Rheims, but the content itself shows very clearly that I did not use the same words, but different ones, and that I employed a very different rhetorical style. I think that the reader will be satisfied if I have treated everything plausibly, clearly, and concisely. For by declining to be long-winded, I will reveal many things succinctly. I will begin the prologue to the work as a whole after I have briefly made a division of the world and divided Gaul into its parts, since it is my intention to describe the customs and deeds of its inhabitants.[6]

Dedication and Commission

Richer begins the prologue with a dedication to Gerbert and an acknowledgment that he is writing at his request. He declares that Gerbert "has provided the seedbed" *(seminarium dedit)* for a historical work recounting the "conflicts of the Gauls" *(congressus Gallorum).* In the next sentence he states more explicitly that he is writing at Gerbert's request.

The nature of Richer's relationship to Gerbert and the role that Gerbert played in the composition of the *Historia* are issues of fundamental importance, for it makes a considerable difference to our understanding of the text whether or not Richer was writing in response to a specific request from Gerbert. If we accept Richer's claim that he was "commanded" to write at face value, then we must

6. *Historia,* prologue.

explain why Gerbert commissioned from him a history of the wars of the West Frankish kings. Possibly he might have been interested in a work that would bolster the legitimacy of the Capetian dynasty, since he owed his appointment to the see of Rheims to Hugh Capet. But as we will see the *Historia* does not make for a very effective propaganda piece in favor of Capetian rule. Another possible scenario is that Gerbert assigned Richer to write a history that would defend and legitimate his title to the archbishopric of Rheims.

By the summer of 995 Gerbert was working tirelessly to clear his name and justify his conduct in the events surrounding the deposition of Arnulf and his own election as archbishop. He attended the Synod of Mouzon despite Hugh Capet's prohibition and argued his case there in person.[7] After the stalemate produced at Mouzon he published his own *Acta* of the Synod of Saint-Basle to defend himself, and he subsequently published *Acta* of the Synod of Mouzon as well. He also wrote a number of letters to garner support for his position, the most important of which was a lengthy *apologia* addressed to the bishops Wilderod of Strasbourg and Notker of Liège.[8] In May 996 he traveled to Rome in the company of the German emperor Otto III to argue his case before a new pope, Gregory V (996–999).[9] It is certainly plausible that he also directed Richer to write a history, or to revise an older history, as part of his public relations campaign. This would help to explain why Richer includes a revised and abbreviated version of Gerbert's *Acta* of the Synod of Saint-Basle (*Historia* 4.51–73) and intended to include Gerbert's speech from the Synod of Mouzon. Presumably the audience for

7. See *Historia* 4.99, and *Acta concilii Mosomensis.* Gerbert alludes to the success of his speech at Mouzon (and perhaps also to the publication of his *Acta* of Saint-Basle) in his letter to Raymond, abbot of Saint-Gerald at Aurillac, in the summer of 995. See letter 194 (Riché and Callu, 2.514–17).

8. See letter 192, to Archbishop Siguin of Sens (Riché and Callu, 2.502–9); letter 193, to Bishop Notker of Liège (2.510–13); letter 194, to Abbot Raymond of Aurillac (2.514–17); letter 197, to Pope John XV (2.524–25); and letter 217, to Bishop Wilderod of Strasbourg (2.582–651).

9. *Historia* 4.108; Riché, *Gerbert d'Aurillac,* 64–167. The synod at Rome reached no decision on the dispute between Gerbert and Arnulf because Arnulf was not present. Another synod was scheduled for later that year, but it never took place.

this work would have been the clergy—and perhaps also the laity—at Rheims, whose hostility Gerbert alludes to in a letter he wrote to the empress Adelaide in the spring or summer of 997.[10] Richer's embrace of Gerbert's *auctoritas* in the prologue could even be read as a profession of loyalty to an archbishop whose position had become increasingly precarious.[11] There is at least one serious problem with this theory, however. As mentioned above, Richer's insertion of his redaction of Gerbert's *Acta* of the Synod of Saint-Basle into an already-complete account of the events of 991 argues strongly that he started writing before Gerbert had composed his *Acta,* and hence before 995. Thus he cannot have originally intended his history as a way of defending his dedicatee from challenges to his occupation of the see of Rheims.

However we choose to interpret the "command" from Gerbert, we run into difficulties. On the one hand, there is no obvious political reason why Gerbert should have been interested in a history of the West Frankish kings (or at least the history that Richer ended up producing). On the other hand, it is very unlikely that the *Historia* was conceived of from the beginning as a piece of pro-Gerbert advocacy. In fact, the whole idea that Richer wrote at Gerbert's bidding needs to be carefully reconsidered, particularly given that references to commissions or commands in prologues are not nearly as conclusive as they might seem at first glance. The claim of an author to write at the request of a third party (the *Auftragstopos*) is one of the most widespread of medieval prefatory topoi, and it could serve a number of practical functions, regardless of whether it reflected a real commission.[12] First, the writer

10. Letter 181 (Riché and Callu, 2.460–62): "Memini etiam meos conspirasse non solum milites, sed et clericos, ut nemo mecum comederet, nemo sacris interesset. Taceo de vilitate et contemptu, nichil dico de gravissimis injuriis sepe michi a pluribus illatis."

11. At the same time, references to *auctoritas* are often a part of the topos of commission, whether or not the author was trying to express support for the authority of the *Auftraggeber.* For *auctoritas* more broadly conceived as grounds for dedication, see Simon, "Untersuchungen zur Topik der Widmungsbriefe," 2.114.

12. See Simon, "Untersuchungen zur Topik der Widmungsbriefe," 1.59–64, and Janson, *Latin Prose Prefaces,* 116–24.

paid a compliment to the giver of the commission *(Auftraggeber)* by working at his request. Second, a commission provided the author with a reason for dedicating the work (if the dedicatee and the *Auftraggeber* were one and the same, as they are in this case) beyond mere flattery.[13] Third, by assigning the impetus for writing to someone else, the writer absolved himself of some of the responsibility for the reception of his work. Finally, and of particular importance for the monks and secular clerics who wrote histories and saints' lives in the early Middle Ages, a commission could insulate the author from charges of pride or literary presumption.[14] The topos of commission, which stretched back to the beginnings of Latin prose literature in the Roman Republic, became so common in the Middle Ages that an author's claim to have received an order to write must be treated with considerable skepticism.

We should be wary, then, of accepting Richer's claim at face value, since it is not difficult to see the advantages for him of linking his work to Gerbert. The *Historia* is a secular political history—in contrast to an institutional church history like Flodoard's *HRE* or a more obviously edifying saint's life—and as a monk, he might have felt it prudent to justify the composition of such a work by appealing to a commission from a church superior. Furthermore, the *Historia* deals with potentially controversial topics, foremost among them the Capetian-Carolingian dynastic struggle and the disputes over the archbishopric of Rheims. By invoking the name of a powerful patron like Gerbert, Richer might have warded off potential critics. Indeed, if he had determined to write his history in the absence of a commission, he conceivably could have secured one—or perhaps even invented it—when it came time to make his work public.

Our understanding of the role that Gerbert played in Richer's composition of the *Historia* depends in part on how we understand the expression *seminarium dare*, which is not attested before

13. Janson, *Latin Prose Prefaces*, 28.

14. Simon, "Untersuchungen zur Topik der Widmungsbriefe," 1.61.

Richer and used very seldom after him. He appears to have coined it by analogy with the more common *principium dare,* which he derived from the opening chapter of Hegesippus's *Bellum Iudaicum,* where the author states that outrage at the sacrilege perpetrated against the Jewish faith by Antiochus IV Epiphanes "gave rise to" *(incentivum principium dedit)* the Maccabean revolt.[15] Apart from Richer's frequent citations from Hegesippus elsewhere in the *Historia,* we know that he was familiar with this passage because he uses the redundant phrase *incentivum principium* again in book 3.[16] In Hegesippus *principium dare* designates the immediate cause-and-effect relationship between the abandonment of the Jewish cult mandated by Antiochus and the uprising against him led by Mattathias and his sons. Thus, if Richer treats *seminarium dare* and *principium dare* as synonymous, it would imply the same kind of direct cause-and-effect relationship existed between Gerbert's command and Richer's history.

The fact that Richer chose to use *seminarium* instead of *principium,* however, suggests that we should consider the possibility that he wanted to maintain the literal meaning of *seminarium* as the "seedbed" from which the *Historia* sprang. This might imply something less than a direct commission.[17] Advice, encouragement, or even a dossier of documents could have comprised a *seminarium.* We know, for example, that Richer used Gerbert's *Acta* of the Synods of Saint-Basle and Mouzon, and that he probably had access to at least some of Gerbert's letters.[18] Alternatively, *semina-*

15. *Bellum Iudaicum,* ed. Vincenzo Ussani, *Hegesippi qui dicitur historiae libri v,* CSEL 66 (Vienna: Hoelder-Pichler-Tempsky, 1932), 1.1: "Bello Parthico . . . incentivum principium dedit sacrilegii dolor."

16. *Historia* 3.67: "horum ergo discordiae incentivum principium Belgica fuit."

17. Giese, *"Genus" und "Virtus,"* 42n1, reads *seminarium* as evidence that Gerbert instructed Richer to write. Glenn, *Politics and History,*16n104, finds the dedication "cryptic" and sees no evidence for Gerbert's direct involvement. Outside of the prologue Richer uses *seminarium* at 2.6 and 4.41. In the latter case he retains the literal meaning of *seminarium* as "seedbed" and builds an agricultural metaphor on top of it: "qui fallatiae seminarium utiliter positum considerans, alcioris machinamenti dolos prodire posse advertit."

18. See Hoffmann, *Historiae,* 3, and Kortüm, *Richer von Saint-Remi,* 20–21.

rium could be an oblique reference to Gerbert's teaching or his intellectual influence on Richer.

If the phrase *seminarium dare* remains vague, the words *imperii* and *iubentis* appear to clarify matters: Gerbert commanded Richer to write. The apparent forcefulness of the verb *iubere,* however, is tempered by its frequent appearance in prologues in circumstances where it appears to express little more than respect for or deference to the dedicatee.[19] How, then, are we to decide if Richer was merely paying a compliment to Gerbert, or if Gerbert did, in fact, ask Richer to write? Here the comparative approach can prove useful. We may be able to get a clearer sense of the meaning behind Richer's use of the Auftragstopos by examining other prologues that employ the same commonplace in contexts where we know more about the relationship between author and dedicatee. Flodoard, for example, refers to a command from his dedicatee in the prologue to the *Historia Remensis Ecclesiae:* "I am turning over to the resourcefulness of your ardent devotion the fourfold work of my labor, gathered from everywhere and arranged in chapters, just as you deemed worthy to command me."[20] Flodoard dedicated the *HRE* to a certain "R," usually identified as Archbishop Ruotbert of Trier (931–956). Ruotbert played a crucial role in the series of councils and synods convened between 947 and 948 to settle the ongoing dispute over the archbishopric of Rheims.[21] The controversy pitted Hugh of Vermandois, whose father, Count Heribert II of Vermandois, had arranged his election to the see in 925 when he was only five years old, against Artald, who had been installed as a replacement to Hugh in 931 and then later expelled.[22] Flodoard was

19. Janson, *Latin Prose Prefaces,*117–20.

20. *HRE,* 57.

21. For Ruotbert of Trier's role in the controversy between Artald and Hugh, see Ernst-Dieter Hehl, "Erzbischof Ruotbert von Trier und der Reimser Streit," in *Deus qui mutat tempora: Menschen und Institutionen im Wandel des Mittelalters: Festschrift für Alfons Becker zu seinem fünfundsechzigsten Geburtstag,* ed. Ernst-Dieter Hehl, Hubertus Seibert, and Franz Staab (Sigmaringen: Jan Thorbecke, 1987), 55–68.

22. For a summary of the conflicts over the see of Rheims, see McKitterick, "The Carolingian Kings and the See of Rheims."

a supporter of Artald, and after Hugh's return to Rheims in 940 he was stripped of several of his benefices and put under a kind of house arrest by Heribert.[23] When the dispute over the archbishopric of Rheims was finally settled at the Synod of Ingelheim in the summer of 948, Ruotbert of Trier played a leading role.[24] Flodoard was at Ingelheim with Artald, and after the conclusion of the synod he spent several weeks in the retinue of Ruotbert; shortly thereafter he began to write the *HRE*.[25]

It is difficult to assess what the nature of Ruotbert's "command" to Flodoard could have been, but it is unlikely that the archbishop of Trier sought out Flodoard and asked him to write a history of the church of Rheims. It is possible that Flodoard discussed his literary project with Ruotbert and received some sort of encouragement, but there is no reason to think that Ruotbert commissioned him to write. Instead, Flodoard's invocation of a command is probably a polite fiction. His dedication is intended to express his gratitude and esteem for Ruotbert, particularly in light of the service the archbishop of Trier had done in helping to maintain Artald's control of the archbishopric of Rheims.

It is not difficult to find other contemporary examples in which the Auftragstopos is deployed as a literary convention rather than a true reflection of the relationship between author and dedicatee. In the preface to his *Historiae*, the Burgundian monk Rodulf Glaber (ca. 980–1046) declares that he was moved to write by the frequent complaints of his monastic brethren and his dedicatee, Abbot Odilo of Cluny (994–1049).[26] Yet in his earlier *Life of St. William* Glaber asserts that it was William (962–1031), abbot of Saint-Bénigne of Dijon, who ordered him to begin work on his

23. See Sot, *Un historien et son église*, 47–49.

24. See Hehl, "Erzbischof Ruotbert von Trier und der Reimser Streit," 60 ff.

25. See Stratmann, *HRE*, 4–5; Sot, *Un historien et son église*, 49; Jacobsen, *Flodoard von Reims*, 52–53; and Heinz Löwe, "Dialogus de statu sanctae ecclesiae: Das Werk eines Iren im Laon des 10. Jahrhunderts," *Deutsches Archiv für Erforschung des Mittelalters* 17 (1961):12–90, esp. 55–57. Löwe presents the case that "R" was Rorico, bishop of Laon (948–976).

26. *Historiae* 1.1.

history.[27] Liudprand of Cremona (ca. 920–972) dedicated his *Antapodosis* to Recemund of Elvira and claims in the prologue that Recemund asked him to write a history of the kings and emperors of Europe.[28] Yet later in the same work Liudprand states that he undertook the *Antapodosis* in order to pay back King Berengar II of Italy and his wife, Willa, for what they had done to him and his family.[29] His intention, he says, was to reveal their impiety to present and future generations. It is highly unlikely that in any of these three instances the authors were actually ordered to write by the people to whom they dedicated their work. In each case the topos of commission was deployed to express esteem for the dedicatee, not to explain the real reason why the writer undertook his composition. These examples should alert us to the possibility that Richer is invoking Gerbert's "command" for the same reason.

On the one hand, it is beyond doubt that Richer intended Gerbert as a reader, and that his choice of dedicatee was not merely an afterthought. Large parts of books 3 and 4 were written with Gerbert specifically in mind. Richer devotes twenty-one chapters to his patron's teaching at Rheims (*Historia* 3.45–55), the spread of his scholarly reputation (3.43, 3.55), and his disputation with Otric at Ravenna (3.55–65), and twenty-three chapters to the Synod of Saint-Basle (4.51–73). He intended to devote several more chapters to Gerbert's speech at the Synod of Mouzon, although this part of the *Historia*, if it was ever written, has fallen out of our manuscript. At the same time, there are grounds for questioning the view that Gerbert actively commissioned the *Historia*. First, and most importantly, the majority of the work has nothing to do with Gerbert. Nor does the earlier history of the see of Rheims in the late ninth and tenth centuries, which makes up one of the major themes of the *Historia*, provide any obvious support for Gerbert's position in the 990s. There is the possibility that Richer chose to

27. *Vita domni Willelmi abbatis*, chap.13.
28. *Antapodosis*, prologue.
29. *Antapodosis* 3.1.

embed an *apologia* for Gerbert inside of a broader political history because there was not a tradition of writing *vitae* of still-living bishops. Still, the effectiveness of a four-volume chronicle of the West-Frankish kings as a tool for promoting Gerbert's cause among the clergy and monks of Rheims is open to question. Moreover, if Richer was writing under orders from Gerbert in an effort to burnish his patron's reputation with wavering or neutral parties at Rheims, it seems odd that he should choose to state in his prologue that Gerbert had commanded him to write. A more deft propagandist might have claimed to write out of love for his patron, or from the desire to make the truth generally known.

A more plausible scenario, therefore, is that the initiative to write the *Historia* came from Richer himself. If so, the commission from Gerbert must be understood as a rhetorical fiction that Richer used to shield himself from criticism and pay homage to his dedicatee, allowing him to show deference to a superior and to express the ideal nature of the link between a monk and a powerful prelate. His laudatory portrait of Gerbert, rather than being the result of a command from his patron, would have been the product of several overlapping impulses: a genuine admiration for his intellectual mentor and a wish to create a lasting literary monument to him; the desire to impose a version of recent events sympathetic to Gerbert and Adalbero upon a Rheims community who were not necessarily united in their admiration for these figures;[30] and the belief that flattery of the powerful was an effective means of winning patronage.

The history of Richer's autograph manuscript confirms that, whatever Richer's original intentions were, the *Historia* ultimately ended up in the hands of his dedicatee. Gerbert's position at Rheims became increasingly untenable throughout the second half

30. For opposition to Gerbert at Rheims, see Gerbert, letter 181 (Riché and Callu, 2.456–65). For hostility to Adalbero, see the continuation to Flodoard's *Annals* in Lauer, *Les Annales de Flodoard,* 160: "Anno DCCCCLXXVI destruxit Adalbero, nomine non merito archiepiscopus arcuatum opus quod erat secus valvas aecclesiae sanctae Mariae Remensis."

of 995 and 996, and his fate was sealed when a council convened by Pope Gregory V at Pavia in February 997 suspended all of the bishops responsible for Arnulf's condemnation, robbing Gerbert of much of his remaining support.[31] By June of that year Gerbert had abandoned Rheims for Magdeburg and the court of Otto III, who subsequently appointed him archbishop of Ravenna.[32] Around the same time King Robert II, a former pupil of Gerbert's who had fallen out with him over Gerbert's opposition to his marriage to Bertha of Burgundy, agreed to release Arnulf from confinement and reinstate him as archbishop.[33] Richer stopped writing in early 998, immediately after the news of Gerbert's appointment to the see of Ravenna reached Rheims.[34] Shortly thereafter his manuscript became part of Gerbert's private library, which passed into the control of the cathedral of Bamberg several years after his death.[35]

Gerbert must have had Richer's *Historia* with him at Rome because fragments of two letters written in the name of Pope Sylvester II are appended to the final folios of the manuscript.[36] If Gerbert did indeed commission Richer to write the *Historia,* then he may have sent for it once he had arrived in Italy. But it is hard to see why he would have still been interested in it after 998, when

31. *Leonis abbatis et legati ad Hugonem et Rotbertum reges epistola,* ed. G. H. Pertz, MGH SS 3 (Hanover: Hahn, 1839), 694.

32. Riché, *Gerbert d'Aurillac,* 286; Gerbert, letter 181 (Riché and Callu, 2.456–65).

33. See Abbo of Fleury, letter 1, *PL* 139.419–21; J. F. Böhmer and Harald Zimmermann, *Regesta Imperii 2.5: Papstregesten, 911–1024,* 2nd ed. (Vienna: Böhlau, 1998), p. 243, no. 796. Bertha, the widow of Count Odo I of Blois and Chartres, and Robert were second cousins; hence their marriage was within the prohibited degrees of consanguinity. Equally problematic was the fact that Robert was godfather to one of Bertha's children from her first marriage.

34. The final two entries among the annalistic notices on folio 57^{v} of the manuscript report on Gerbert's appointment to the archbishopric of Ravenna and Pope Gregory V's decision to allow Arnulf to resume his former see. A papal bull of Gregory V dating to April 28, 998, confirmed Gerbert as archbishop. See Gerhard Schwartz, *Die Besetzung der Bistümer Reichsitaliens 951–1122* (Leipzig: Teubner, 1913), 152.

35. See Hartmut Hoffmann, *Bamberger Handschriften des 10. und des 11. Jahrhunderts,* MGH Schriften 39 (Hanover: Hahn, 1995), 22–30; Riché, "La bibliothèque de Gerbert d'Aurillac"; F. Mütherich, "The Library of Otto III," in *The Role of the Book in Medieval Culture,* vol. 2, ed. Peter Ganz (Turnout: Brepols, 1986), 11–26.

36. Hoffmann, *Bamberger Handschriften,* 22.

the possibility that he would return to Rheims and displace Arnulf (who now had the backing of both Pope Gregory V and King Robert II) was remote. A more likely scenario is that Richer himself took the initiative to make sure that his work got into the hands of his dedicatee. Indeed, it is possible that he brought his manuscript to Italy himself.[37] If he had become identified with a pro-Gerbert faction at Saint-Rémi, then he might have found it expedient to leave the city when Arnulf returned to power. There is certainly no shortage of examples in the Middle Ages of monks forced to change locations due to shifting political currents.

In the end, there can be no definitive answer to the question of whether Gerbert commissioned the *Historia* from Richer. What is clear is that the presence of the Auftragstopos in the prologue is not a sufficient basis on which to establish such a claim. Given that we are dealing with probabilities and not certainties, the following scenario is perhaps the most plausible: Between 991 and 995 Richer began work on a history of the West Frankish kings from a local, Rheims-centric perspective, a history that focused on the perils of civil disorder and dynastic warfare. This topic would have found a sympathetic audience at Rheims, which had been brutally sacked in 989, during the civil war between Hugh Capet and Charles of Lotharingia.[38] Richer intended from the beginning to dedicate this work to Gerbert, the newly installed archbishop of Rheims, but not necessarily in response to a commission. After the Synod of Mouzon he began to use his history as a platform to support his increasingly embattled patron, redacting his own abbreviated version of Gerbert's *Acta* of the Synod of Saint-Basle on three separate

37. Such a journey was hardly unusual. Flodoard, in *Annales,* s.a. 920, p. 4, mentions townsmen of Rheims who had gone on pilgrimage to Rome. He himself went to Rome in 936. See *De triumphis Christi apud Italiam, PL* 135.832.

38. Charles captured Rheims—with the complicity of Archbishop Arnulf—in October 989. His army then plundered the city in brutal fashion and pillaged the cathedral. See Lot, *Les derniers Carolingiens,* 255; and Richer, *Historia* 4.34, 4.53. In a letter written to Remi of Trier in the fall of 989, Gerbert calls attention to the hardships that had been inflicted on the city—and specifically on the clergy—by Charles and his army. See letter 162 (Riché and Callu, 2.402–3).

folios, inserting these into the manuscript, and keying them to the events of 991, which he had already written about. Once Gerbert had accepted the archiepiscopal see of Ravenna, and it had become clear that he would not be returning to Rheims, Richer either sent the *Historia* to Gerbert or went to Italy with the manuscript.[39] The probable existence of at least one, and possibly two, now-lost manuscripts of the *Historia* further complicates the matter, but in the absence of more concrete information it would be unwise to use these hypothetical manuscripts as a basis for further speculation.

Utility

After the dedication Richer states that he embraces the task of writing because it is "supremely useful" *(summam utilitatem affert).* Evidently he expected his audience to be familiar with the reasons for this usefulness because he neglects to go into any further detail on the matter. The topos of utility is a cornerstone of classical and medieval historiography, but it is not clear how exactly Richer thought his history would prove useful.

Medieval historians tended to justify the writing of history on the grounds of its commemorative and moral-exemplary functions.[40] The most basic function of history was simply to preserve the memory of the past from being erased, particularly the memory of great and important actions.[41] Richer tells the reader that his particular goal in writing was "to recall to memory the frequent

39. See Hoffmann, "Die *Historien* Richers von Saint-Remi," 508–18. The fact that Frutolf of Michelsberg and Johannes Trithemius consulted the two-volume revision of the *Historia* at Bamberg, and the fact that this version was also dedicated to Gerbert, may offer some support for the idea that Richer had thrown in his lot with Gerbert and fled to Italy.

40. See Simon, "Untersuchungen zur Topik der Widmungsbriefe," 1.81–83, and 2.98–107.

41. Simon, "Untersuchungen zur Topik der Widmungsbriefe," 2.98, notes that the theme of preserving the past from oblivion was ubiquitous in histories, biographies, and saints' lives: "Beiläufig wird er in fast allen Vorworten angeführt." See also Goetz, "Die Gegenwart der Vergangenheit," 67. Herodotus, of course, famously cites the commemorative function of history in his prologue.

wars waged by the Gauls during the time of [their] kings, their various struggles, and the different reasons for their undertakings." Yet he does not state explicitly that he wishes to keep a record of these wars because of their importance, much less that the memory of the West Frankish kings ought to be preserved because they were heroic or worthy of imitation. Accordingly, he does not include one of the most common of historiographical topoi: that he will narrate events that are "worthy of memory" *(memoria digna).*[42]

Historiography could also fulfill a practical function, for a record of past events could serve as a guide for future action. In a very specific sense history could be a school for political and military leaders, and on a more general level it provided models of behavior to emulate and to avoid.[43] Thus Widukind of Corvey's *Saxon History* was intended to help his patroness Mathilda by holding up for imitation the deeds of her illustrious father and grandfather, Otto I and Henry the Fowler.[44] The moral-exemplary function is not entirely absent from the *Historia,* but neither is it particularly prominent. A few unabashed villains meet with deserved deaths, and there are several instances where traitors are punished for their treachery, but open authorial judgments are comparatively rare.[45]

42. For this topos, see Guenée, "Histoire, mémoire, écriture," 444. Cf. Isidore of Seville, *Etymologiae,* ed. W. M. Lindsay, 2 vols. (Oxford: Oxford University Press, 1957, 1962), 1.41.2: "haec disciplina [sc. historia] ad grammaticam pertinet, quia quidquid dignum memoria est litteris mandatur."

43. This didactic function was particularly characteristic of the historiography produced for the Frankish court in the ninth century. See Janet Nelson, "History-Writing at the Courts of Louis the Pious and Charles the Bald," in *Historiographie im frühen Mittelalter,* ed. Anton Scharer and Georg Scheibelreiter (Vienna: R. Oldenbourg, 1994), 435–42. Livy notes in his general preface that history provides models for the individual and for the state. See also Isidore of Seville, *Etymologiae* 1.43. For history as a storehouse of exempla, see Simon, "Untersuchungen zur Topik der Widmungsbriefe," 2.101ff.

44. *Res Gestae Saxonicae,* ed. Paul Hirsch and Hans Eberhard Lohmann, MGH SRG 60 (Hanover: Hahn, 1935), book 1, preface.

45. Winemar, the murderer of Archbishop Fulk of Rheims, dies of dropsy at *Historia* 1.18. Gislebert of Lotharingia drowns in the Rhine during the Battle of Andernach at 2.19. Count Heribert II of Vermandois is struck down by apoplexy at 2.37. For Richer's treatment of traitors, see the conclusion below.

Moreover, Richer's varying assessments of the West Frankish kings make it difficult to draw any general principles about kingship from the *Historia* aside from the obvious point that strong, legitimate kings were the best guarantor of security for the realm.

A potential clue to Richer's conception of the utility-topos comes at one of the most important points in the *Historia:* the convening of an assembly of West Frankish magnates at Senlis in 987 to discuss the royal succession after the death of King Louis V. Here Archbishop Adalbero of Rheims speaks in behalf of Hugh Capet and against the Carolingian candidate, Charles of Lotharingia. In his speech Adalbero refers to the didactic function of historiography:

> I am not unaware that Charles has supporters who argue that he is worthy to be king because of his ancestry. But if this is the issue, a kingdom is not acquired by hereditary right, nor should anyone be raised up to be king unless he is illuminated not only by nobility of body but also by wisdom of mind, unless he is fortified by faith and strengthened by greatness of spirit. I have read in annals that emperors of the most distinguished lineage have fallen from their high position because of their weakness of character, and that they have sometimes been succeeded by equals, sometimes by those who are inferior.[46]

Here Adalbero's reading of history provides support for the proposition that royal blood by itself does not qualify one to be king, an idea of central importance for the Capetian claim to the throne.[47] Is it possible that Richer saw his own history as useful in that, like the anonymous annals mentioned by Adalbero, it provided historical precedents in support of a particular political agenda?

46. *Historia* 4.11.

47. Cf. Archbishop Hincmar's use of historical precedents in his treatise on the divorce of Lothar and Theutberga and in his advice to the newly crowned Louis the Stammerer: *De divortio Lotharii regis et Tetbergae reginae, PL* 125.758: "successione etiam paterna quidam regnant, sicut de his omnibus in historiis et chronicis et etiam in libro qui inscribitur Vita Caesarum, invenitur," and 125.975–85: "Legimus in antiquis historiis quia saepe, quando reges constituti sunt, inter regni primores discordia orta est, quoniam aliqui sine aliorum consilio eius constitutionem vindicare sibi votuerunt." See J. M. Wallace-Hadrill, "History in the Mind of Archbishop Hincmar," in *The Writing of History in the Middle Ages,* ed. R. H. C. Davis and J. M. Wallace-Hadrill (Oxford: Clarendon Press, 1981), 43–70, esp. 56–61.

A case has certainly been made for the idea that Richer wrote with a pro-Capetian bias.[48] He does not hesitate to speak about the faults of the Carolingian kings (particularly Charles the Simple and Louis V), and Charles of Lotharingia is designated as a usurper *(tirannus)* after he takes up arms against the newly crowned Hugh Capet.[49] What makes such a theory ultimately untenable, however, is the way in which Richer voices his most direct criticism of the Carolingians from the perspective of the Capetians and their supporters. Adalbero's dismissal of Charles's claim to the throne does not necessarily tell us anything about Richer's views. Likewise, the use of the term *tirannus* to describe Charles later in book 4 reflects Hugh Capet's perspective, but not necessarily Richer's.[50] This is clear because a few chapters later, during an abortive confrontation between Charles and Hugh outside the walls of Laon, Hugh Capet is described as being conscious of having usurped the throne himself: "There was considerable hesitation on both sides, since Charles lacked a sufficient number of troops, while the king's conscience accused him of having acted unlawfully in despoiling Charles of his father's throne and usurping control of the realm."[51] Richer makes a conscious decision to represent the opinions of both sides in his account of the civil war between Hugh and Charles, and, indeed, this tendency is characteristic of all of the *Historia*. The focalization of competing political views from different perspectives makes it difficult to determine precisely where Richer's sympathies lay.[52]

As a result, we cannot assume that the lessons Adalbero draws

48. See Kortüm, *Richer von Saint-Remi,* 46–49.

49. Giese, *"Genus" und "Virtus,"* has the most detailed analysis of Richer's assessments of the West Frankish kings; for Charles the Simple, see 82–85; for Louis V, see 96–97. See also Bezzola, *Das Ottonische Kaisertum,* 114–17. In the *Historia* Charles the Simple alienates his nobles through his excessive affection for his Lotharingian favorite, Hagano (1.15–16), while Louis V is portrayed as dissolute and ineffective (3.95). For Charles of Lotharingia as a usurper, see *Historia* 4.18, 4.37. For discussions of the import of the word *tirannus* in Richer, see Giese, *"Genus" und "Virtus,"* 42–48 and 106–7, and Bezzola, *Das Ottonische Kaisertum,* 117–18.

50. Hoffmann, "Die *Historien* Richers von Saint-Remi," 478–79.

51. *Historia* 4.39.

52. See Hoffmann, "Die *Historien* Richers von Saint-Remi," 476–82.

from reading history reflect Richer's own opinions. While it is tempting to posit the inadequacy of the Carolingian royal line as a theme of the *Historia,* Richer does not make any attempt to justify the usurpations of the Robertian/Capetian dynasty. He designates Robert I, Hugh Capet's grandfather, as a *tirannus* and *regni pervasor* when he attempts to seize the throne from Charles the Simple, and he shows Hugh the Great, Robert's son, admitting in a speech to the assembled West Frankish magnates that his father had acted unjustly in ruling while Charles still lived.[53] Hugh the Great himself is repeatedly referred to as a usurper *(tirannus)* for opposing the legitimate king, Louis IV,[54] and in one of the last of the annalistic entries jotted down on the final folio of the manuscript Richer refers to the "perfidy" of King Robert the Pious.[55]

It is also important to note that Adalbero's speech at Senlis in support of Hugh's claim to the throne could have actually been a hindrance to the continuation of the Capetian dynasty in the future. If royal blood was not a sufficient qualification for the throne, then Hugh Capet's own son Robert would be vulnerable to the same kind of challenge that Hugh had posed to Charles of Lotharingia. Hugh himself was worried enough about the succession that he had Robert crowned co-ruler immediately after his own coronation, a move that met with some initial resistance from Adalbero.[56]

Because Richer does not express unambiguous support for either the Carolingian or the Robertian/Capetian houses, his history cannot be seen as politically useful to either side. In fact, the only kings whom Richer shows in a consistently favorable light are the Ottonian rulers of Germany. This might seem strange, but it

53. *Historia* 1.21, 1.45, 2.2.

54. See Bezzola, *Das Ottonische Kaisertum,* 118n57. Hugh is called a tyrant at *Historia* 2.22, 24, 26–28, 36, 48, 81, 82, 85, and 87.

55. *Historia* 4.109: "Gerbertus cum Rotberti regis perfidiam dinosceret, Ottonem regem frequentat et patefacta sui ingenii peritia, episcopatum Ravennatem ab eo accipit." Robert's "perfidy" was his decision to release Arnulf from captivity and reinstall him as archbishop of Rheims in 997.

56. *Historia* 4.12.

makes sense if we assume that he shared the views of his dedicatee or was astute enough to mimic support for those views in his work.[57] Gerbert owed his worldly success to the patronage of the Ottonian emperors, toward whom he maintained steadfast loyalty to the end of his life.[58] He met Otto I when he traveled to Rome as a young man in the company of his Spanish patrons, Count Borrell II of Barcelona and Bishop Hatto of Vich.[59] There Pope John XIII, astounded by Gerbert's knowledge of music, recommended him to the emperor, who in turn directed the pope to keep Gerbert in Rome. Thereafter he became a part of Otto's entourage and made lasting ties with members of the imperial household, serving as tutor to the future Otto II and probably witnessing his marriage to the Byzantine princess Theophanu.[60] After his triumph over the Saxon scholar Otric of Magdeburg in a disputation before Otto II at Ravenna, the emperor appointed him abbot of Bobbio.[61] Even after he abandoned Bobbio for Rheims, Gerbert remained in contact with Theophanu and Adelaide, the widow of Otto I.[62] When he fled Rheims in 997 in the face of increasing challenges to his position as archbishop, he sought refuge with Otto III, whom he tutored and for whom he wrote his dialectical treatise *De ratione et rationali uti*.[63] It was Otto III who ultimately appointed Gerbert to the archbishopric of Ravenna and to the papacy.[64]

57. See Bezzola, *Das Ottonische Kaisertum*, 123–27.

58. See Gerbert, letter 185, to Otto III (Riché and Callu, 2.478): "Tribus, ut ita dicam, seculi aetatibus, vobis, patri, avo, inter hostes et tela, fidem purissimam exhibui, meam quantulamcumque personam, regibus furentibus, populis insanientibus, pro vestra salute opposui."

59. *Historia* 3.43–45.

60. Riché, *Gerbert d'Aurillac*, 33.

61. *Historia* 3.57–65; Riché, *Gerbert d'Aurillac*, 57–65.

62. See Gerbert, letters 20, 52, 59, 128, 204, and 208.

63. *PL* 139:159–68.

64. For Gerbert's relationship with Otto III, see Bertrand Fauvarque "Le pape Gerbert et l'empereur Otto III," in *Gerbert: Moine, évêque et pape: D'un millénaire à l'autre: Actes des journées d'étude, Aurillac, 9–10 avril 1999* (Aurillac: Association cantalienne pour la commémoration du pape Gerbert, 2000), 271–84, and Gerd Althoff, *Otto III*, trans. Phyllis G. Jestice (University Park: Penn State University Press, 2003), 65–69.

As would be expected in a work dedicated to Gerbert, Richer includes little that could be construed as unfavorable to the Ottonians. The greatest source of tension for a West Frankish chronicler favorably disposed toward the German emperors was the conflict between the Carolingians and the Ottonians over Lotharingia, a territory that came under the control of the West Frankish kings in 911, but was lost to them in the early 940s.[65] Describing Otto I's campaign into Lotharingia in 939, Richer states explicitly that Charles the Simple (and thus by extension his son Louis IV, with whom Otto was contesting Lotharingia) had the better claim.[66] Yet after Otto's defeat of Gislebert of Lotharingia in 939 and his subsequent recovery of Lotharingia for the German kingdom, Richer treats Ottonian rule in this area as a fait accompli.[67] Nor does he express any support for Lothar's campaigns of 978 and 984. Richer does not appear to have viewed West Frankish claims of sovereignty in Lotharingia as sacrosanct.

The only real mark against Otto I in the *Historia* is his role in the assassination of the Norman duke William Longsword in 943.[68] Yet in Richer's telling Otto's responsibility is limited to a speech ad-

65. For an overview of West Frankish politics in Lotharingia in the tenth century, see Jean Dunbabin, "West Francia: The Kingdom," *New Cambridge Medieval History*, vol. 3, ed. Timothy Reuter (Cambridge: Cambridge University Press, 1999), 372–97.

66. *Historia* 2.18: "Otto interea Belgicos comperiens regis partes sustentare et a se penitus defecisse, Rheno transmisso Belgicam ingressus, eius loca plurima incendiis ac ingentibus predis devastat, eo quod ex collatione paterna princeps fieri Belgicis dedignantibus contenderet, cum eius pater Saxoniae solum propter Sclavorum improbitatem rex creatus sit, eo quod Karolus, cui rerum summa debebatur, adhuc in cunis vagiebat."

67. See *Historia* 3.67, where Richer states that Otto II was elected king "a Germanis Belgisque." Later in the same chapter he seems to confirm the legitimacy of Ottonian rule; at the very least he makes the Ottonian claims appear to be as strong as the Carolingian ones: "Etenim cum ab Ottone Belgica teneretur et a Lothario impeteretur, contra se dolos aut vires moliebantur, eo quod uterque et suum patrem eam tenuisse contenderet.... Nam et Ludovici patri Lotharii fuit, et eius post dono huius Ottonis pater Otto obtinuit." I do not think that this sentence should be taken as unambiguous evidence that Richer believed Lothar had the more valid claim to Lotharingia. Cf. *Historia* 3.81: "Belgicae pars quae in lite fuerat in ius Ottonis transiit."

68. *Historia* 2.30–31. For the assassination of William, see Jules Lair, *Étude sur la vie et la mort de Guillaume Longue-Épée Duc de Normandie* (Paris: A. Picard, 1893).

dressed to Hugh the Great and Count Arnulf of Flanders in which he laments the insult done to them by William and stresses the need to curb his insolence.[69] Hugh and Arnulf, not Otto, arrange the assassination in the next chapter, after Otto has gone back to Germany.[70] Subsequently Otto takes a leading role in defending Louis IV against the threat posed to him from Hugh the Great. Motivated in part by Louis IV's marriage to his sister Gerberga, Otto concludes a pact of friendship with him and arranges a reconciliation between Louis and Hugh.[71] Later, after Hugh rebels against the king and takes him into captivity, Otto sends a delegation to Hugo to insist that he restore Louis to the throne.[72] At the Synod of Ingelheim, which was convened in June 948 to adjudicate the ongoing dispute over the see of Rheims and to deal with Hugh's provocations against Louis, Otto even delivers a speech in Louis's behalf.[73]

Otto II appears as a paragon of good kingship. Richer calls him "a man of great intellectual ability and every virtue, distinguished for his knowledge of the liberal arts."[74] Before the disputation at Ravenna between Gerbert and Otric of Magdeburg, Otto delivers a speech in praise of the pursuit of knowledge.[75] Even the advisers of King Lothar, who bitterly contested Lotharingia with Otto, recognize the German emperor's merits.[76] Before Otto and Lothar conclude a peace treaty, Otto addresses the Franks in a formal oration in which he laments the discord between the two kingdoms and praises the benefits of peace.[77] Significantly, it is the collective

69. *Historia* 2.31.

70. *Historia* 2.32.

71. *Historia* 2.29.

72. *Historia* 2.49.

73. *Historia* 2.76. This speech is clearly Richer's invention. There is no evidence for it in Flodoard's *Annals* or other extant records of the synod. See Ernst-Dieter Hehl, ed., MGH Concilia 6.1 (Hanover, Hahn: 1987), 135–63.

74. *Historia* 3.67: "rem publicam strenue atque utiliter amministravit, vir magni ingenii totiusque virtutis, liberalium litterarum scientia clarus, adeo ut in disputando ex arte proponeret, et probabiliter concluderet."

75. *Historia* 3.58.

76. *Historia* 3.78: "A consultantibus tandem deliberatum est Ottonem in amiciciam regis revocandum, eo quod ipse vir virtutis esset, et per illum non solum dux mansuesci posset, sed et aliarum gentium tiranni subiugari utiliter valerent."

77. *Historia* 3.80.

West Franks *(Galli)* who first address Otto on the subject of reaching a truce, and not King Lothar, who comes off rather badly in comparison with his wise and well-spoken German rival.

Richer's varying assessments of Capetian and Carolingian kings, coupled with his largely favorable view of the Ottonians, argues strongly against the idea that he intended his history to bolster the claims of either of the competing West Frankish dynasties.[78] Indeed, the *Historia* has resisted all attempts to categorize it as useful to the Carolingians or Capetians because its only consistent political ideology is an indictment of feuding among the magnates *(dissidentia principum)* and an implicit criticism of the kings who failed to prevent it.[79] The absence of a more pronounced dynastic favoritism makes sense when we consider that his probable audience—the monks of Saint-Rémi and the clergy of Rheims—came from noble families who presumably held divergent opinions about the legitimacy of the Capetian succession.[80] The local perspective of the *Historia* also helps to clarify other aspects of the text. Richer's remarkably favorable portrait of Otto II, for example, may derive as much from the esteem in which he was held at Rheims as from a desire on Richer's part to praise one of Gerbert's patrons. Otto is included in the necrology of Saint-Rémi, and even in the midst of a campaign into West Francia he is reported to have donated generously to the monastery.[81]

In the end, Richer might have envisioned his work as useful because it attested to certain generally valid principles, the most obvious of which is the disastrous consequences of *dissidentia principum*. This theme would undoubtedly have met with approval from an audience composed of monks and secular clerics. On the other hand, he may not have been particularly interested in the question

78. A point made by Bezzola, *Das Ottonische Kaisertum*, 116–17.

79. Giese, *"Genus" und "Virtus,"* 107.

80. Simon MacLean, *History and Politics in Late Carolingian and Ottonian Europe: The Chronicle of Regino of Prüm and Adalbert of Magdeburg* (Manchester: Manchester University Press), 40–41, makes a similar point about Regino's *Chronicle* and the political opinions of the monks of Prüm.

81. Hoffmann, *Historiae*, 210n6; *Historia* 3.74.

of historical utility, at least as far as it pertained to his own work. He limits his discussion of usefulness to only four words *(quia summam utilitatem affert)* that form half of a subordinate clause offered to explain his enthusiasm for writing.[82] Skipping so lightly over the topos of utility in the prologue has the effect of decoupling the recollection of the past from its typical commemorative and moral-exemplary purposes. The same holds true for his treatment of the topos of *memoria.*

"The particular goal of this work," he writes, "is to recall to memory in writing the frequent wars waged by the Gauls during the time of [their] kings, their various struggles, and the different reasons for their undertakings." At first glance this statement of purpose appears similar to a common claim of medieval historians: that they wrote in order to commit certain important events to memory.[83] Robert Latouche even renders the phrase *ad memoriam reducere scripto* as "conserver par écrit la mémoire," a translation accepted by Bernard Guenée.[84] But *reducere ad memoriam* does not mean to "conserve in memory." It is not a synonym for phrases like *memoriae mandare, memoriae tradere,* or *litteris ad memoriam commendare.* Richer is not telling the reader that his particular goal is to preserve the memory of the past in writing; instead, his goal is to recall the past, literally, to lead it back to the mind of his audience.

Reducere ad memoriam is a common phrase in medieval Latin literature. It occurs twice in the Vulgate and frequently in patristic authors, and it crops up in the writings of many of Richer's contemporaries.[85] It often appears in contexts where an author stresses that

82. *Historia,* prologue: "Quam, quia summam utilitatem affert et rerum materia sese multiplex praebet, eo animi nisu complector, qua iubentis mira benivolentia pertrahor."

83. See Guenée, "Histoire, mémoire, écriture," 450.

84. Latouche, *Richer: Histoire de France,* 1.5; Guenée, "Histoire, mémoire, écriture," 450.

85. Isa. 43:26; Rom. 15:15. The phrase is used by Jerome, Augustine, John Cassian, Isidore of Seville, and Bede, among others. For its use by Richer's contemporaries, cf. Flodoard, *HRE* 3.27; Adso of Montier-en-Der, *Vita Basoli,* ed. Monique Goullet,

his audience should be mindful of the virtues of a saint, their own sins, or their duty to God. It always means "remember," "cause to be remembered," or "lead back to the memory," but never "preserve in memory" or "transmit to memory."

Is there really such a difference between preserving something in memory and recalling it to the memory? Certainly a historical text fulfills both functions, serving both as a documentary record of the past and a means of bringing that past to the mind of the reader or hearer.[86] But while these two functions go hand-in-hand, the fact that Richer mentions only one of them may be significant. *Tradere memoriae* and the phrases synonymous with it conjure up the image of the text as a kind of historical filing cabinet into which the author deposits an account of events too valuable to be abandoned to oblivion.[87] *Reducere ad memoriam,* by contrast, suggests an active presentation of history meant to achieve some kind of immediate effect. It is not surprising that this phrase occurs so commonly in contexts where it refers to the remembrance of sins or of the virtues of a saint. The act of reflecting on one's sins should lead to repentance, just as the proper appreciation of saintly virtues should lead one to live a more holy life.

The fact that Richer emphasizes the function of recalling rather than preserving makes sense when we consider that so many of the events recounted in the *Historia* had already been preserved in the *Annals* of Flodoard or in accounts of synods; they had already been "entrusted to memory." It is not surprising, then, that Richer says nothing about rescuing the memory of the West Frankish kings and their wars from oblivion. His own task was not to preserve events for posterity. Rather, it was to turn this historical data

---

Adsonis Dervensis Opera Hagiographica, CCCM 198 (Turnhout: Brepols, 2003), 220; Abbo of Fleury, *Vita S. Eadmundi,* in *Three Lives of English Saints,* ed. Michael Winterbottom (Toronto: Pontifical Institute for Medieval Studies, 1972), 84; Gerbert, letter 191 (Riché and Callu, 2.500).

86. See Melville, "Wozu Geschichte Schreiben?," 95–108.

87. Cf. Wipo, *Gesta Chuonradi imperatoris,* ed. H. Bresslau, MGH SRG 61 (Hanover: Hahn, 1915), 5: "cum primitiva auctoritas veteris testamenti ... novarum rerum frugem in memoriae cellario recondi debere praefiguret et doceat."

into a compelling narrative, to recall the past in such a way that it would spring to life in the mind of his audience.[88] To do so, he had to advance beyond the style of Flodoard's *Annals* and write a different kind of history.

Genre

In the prologue Richer says that his work begins with recent times *(initium a vicino ducendum existimavi)* because the events of the more distant past *(res multo ante gestae)* have already been treated sufficiently in the annals of Hincmar—that is, the *Annals of Saint-Bertin,* of which Hincmar wrote the final portion, covering the years 861–882. This statement raises two questions: first, to what degree did Richer view his work as a continuation of Hincmar's portion of the *Annals of Saint-Bertin,* and second, why did Richer rework Flodoard's *Annals* while leaving Hincmar's alone?

Richer does not say explicitly that he is writing a continuation of the *Annals of Saint-Bertin,* nor does he appear to conceive of his history as "annals." He never uses this term to refer to his own work, and early in book 1 he designates it as *historia.*[89] At the same time, he assumes that his work will be read in conjunction with Hincmar and even be copied into manuscripts directly after the *Annals of Saint-Bertin.* He states that the reader can find earlier events "by moving up from the beginning of my own work through his [Hinc-

88. Cf. the prologue to Henry of Huntington's *Historia Anglorum,* ed. and trans. Diana Greenway (Oxford: Oxford University Press, 1996), 4: "Historia igitur praeterita quasi praesentia visui repraesentat."

89. *Historia* 1.3: "Quorum quoque primus rex christianus Clodoveus fuisse traditur, a quo per succedentia tempora imperatoribus egregiis res publica gubernata fuisse dinoscitur, usque ad Karolum, a quo *historia*e sumemus initium." For the difficulty of assigning strict definitions to medieval terms like *historia, chronicon,* and *annales,* see Franz-Josef Schmale, *Funktionen und Formen mittelalterlicher Geschichtsschreibung* (Darmstadt: Wissenschaftliche Buchgesellschaft, 1985), 105–23. For one opinion on the genre of Richer's *Historia,* see Michel Sot, "Richer de Reims a-t-il écrit une Histoire de France?" in *Histoires de France, historiens de la France: Actes du colloque international, Reims, 14 et 15 mai 1993,* eds. Yves-Marie Bercé and Philippe Contamine (Paris: Librairie Honoré Champion, 1994), 47–58.

mar's] history." He then advises his audience to avoid confusing the various kings by the name of Charles and Louis that appear "in each of our works" *(in utroque opere).* Failure to do so will "throw into confusion the order of each work" *(ne ... operis utriusque ordinem turbet).* Thus, while Richer is conscious of the formal differences between Hincmar's annals and his own history, he clearly envisions his own work as in some sense a continuation of Hincmar.

The greater part of such a continuation, however, already existed in the form of Flodoard's *Annals,* which covered the years 919–966 in great detail. Richer adds only ten chapters of new material to account for the intervening years between the end of the *Annals of Saint-Bertin* in 882 and the beginning of Flodoard's *Annals* in 919.[90] One wonders why Richer didn't simply begin his history in 966/67. To put the question another way: Why did Richer treat Hincmar's contribution to the *Annals of Saint-Bertin* as untouchable, when he had no qualms about rewriting Flodoard's *Annals?*

Two factors probably influenced Richer's decision about what to treat as source material and what to treat as a finished product. First, and most important, he had to reckon with Hincmar's legacy. Hincmar was a figure of towering importance, and his shadow must have continued to loom large at Rheims more than a century after his death. Richer surely recognized that to rewrite Hincmar's contributions to the *Annals of Saint-Bertin* would have exposed him to charges of presumption and arrogance. It made better sense to link his own work to Hincmar's as a kind of continuation, perhaps in the hope that the two histories would be copied side-by-side in the future. Second, while both Flodoard and Hincmar wrote annals, their divergent styles may have led Richer to treat the two works differently. Flodoard limits himself to providing detailed, chronologically ordered entries for each year. He makes little effort to clarify the relationship between events.[91] One of Rich-

90. *Historia* 1.4–1.13, which covers the years 888–898. Chapter 1.14 is a description of the *mores* of Charles the Simple, and chapter 1.15 takes place in the year 920.

91. See Giese, *"Genus" und "Virtus,"* 48–58, and Sot, *Un historien et son église,* 86.

er's primary goals was to make these connections clear. Moreover, since Richer chose to focus on a limited number of themes during the years covered by the *Annals* (notably the *congressus Gallorum*), he could leave out much of Flodoard's annalistic miscellany and, by a process of deleting, editing, moving, and supplementing his source material, shape it into a true narrative history.

In contrast to Flodoard's rather conventional annals, the later entries of the *Annals of Saint-Bertin* transcend the usual characteristics of the genre. Rather than merely writing down information as it came to him, and thereby possibly obscuring the connections between events, Hincmar seems to have composed some of the entries for the late 860s and 870s at one sitting. In this way he could emphasize certain themes without letting a strict adherence to chronological order interfere with his narrative.[92] Thus, while Flodoard's *Annals* could provide Richer with abundant source material to develop a narrative history, Hincmar's portion of the *Annals of Saint-Bertin* already had a sophisticated narrative structure.[93]

While Richer saw himself as continuing a tradition of Rheims historiography, his decision to rewrite Flodoard shows that his ambitions extended beyond the composition of a series of annals that would supplement those of Hincmar and Flodoard. The form of Richer's history demonstrates that he made a conscious decision to depart from the conventions of Carolingian-era annalistic historiography.[94] Richer separates his material into books and chapters, not years. He does not include dates, and there is no one-to-one correspondence of chapter to year. In the prologue he refers to the potential confusion this lack of dates will cause and advises the reader to pay careful attention to the order of events *(rerum ordo)*. More-

92. See Marlene Meyer-Gebel, "Zur annalistischen Arbeitsweise Hinkmars von Reims," *Francia* 15 (1987): 75–108; Janet Nelson, *The Annals of St-Bertin* (Manchester: Manchester University Press, 1991), 13–14; Sot, *Un historien et son église*, 85–86.

93. See Wallace-Hadrill, "History in the Mind of Archbishop Hincmar," 52–55.

94. For the characteristic features of annals as a genre, see Michael McCormick, *Les annales du haut Moyen Âge*, Typologie des sources du Moyen Âge occidental 14 (Turnhout: Brepols, 1975), 11–21.

over, he follows classical historians like Orosius and Julius Caesar by beginning his work with a geographical and ethnographical excursus (1.1–3). Nor does he adopt the pose of the annalist, the largely invisible compiler and arranger of historical data. On the contrary, he can be an intrusive presence. We see this when he speaks to the reader in the first person to recount the adventures of his father, to narrate his own journey to Chartres, or to comment on one of Gerbert's speeches.[95]

Richer's history differs most from the annalistic genre, though, in its rhetorical superstructure. Only eleven chapters into the first book of the *Historia* the Frankish warrior Ingo, after murdering the Norman leader Catillus in cold blood during his baptism, delivers a formal oration in his own defense.[96] Fictional speeches like this one recall Livy and Sallust, not the annalistic tradition. Any reader who followed the procedure envisioned by Richer in his prologue and leafed back and forth between Hincmar's annals and Richer's *Historia* would have seen two quite different types of historiography ranged alongside one another. The very form of Richer's work called attention to itself.

"A Very Different Rhetorical Style"

Narrative style was an issue of primary importance for Richer. His incorporation of so much of Flodoard's *Annals* into his own history was only justifiable if this borrowed material was given a new and improved form. He makes an explicit statement about his stylistic originality in the prologue, in a passage that he added during a later stage of revision. But even apart from this claim, the prologue contains clues to Richer's preoccupation with the formal aspects of his history.

One important piece of evidence comes not from anything Richer says, but from what he leaves out. He forgoes entirely two

95. See *Historia* 2.87–90; 3.7–9 (Richer's father); 4.50 (Richer's journey to Chartres); and 4.73 (Richer commends Gerbert's speech at the Synod of Saint-Basle).

96. *Historia* 1.11.

different categories of topoi that are so prevalent in medieval prologues that their omission should put the reader on guard. First is the topos of hesitancy *(Verweigerungstopos),* in which the author expresses his reluctance to undertake the task of writing. A number of reasons were typically cited: inability or lack of education, unworthiness, lack of information or source material about the subject, wariness of writing about people who were still living, the need to deal with other pressing business, or continuing dissatisfaction with the text and a corresponding desire to improve it.[97] Closely linked to the topos of hesitancy is the modesty topos *(Bescheidenheitstopos),* in which the author expresses the various ways in which he is inadequate as a writer.[98] These commonplaces of affected modesty included the use of self-deprecating formulae (*mea parvitas, mea exiguitas,* etc.) and references to faulty style, lack of talent, lack of skill *(imperitia),* or lack of knowledge *(ignorantia, inscitia).* An author might also request corrections from the dedicatee, which served the dual purpose of expressing an appropriate degree of modesty and flattering the person for whom the work was intended.[99]

The topoi of hesitancy and modesty are ubiquitous among Richer's contemporaries. In the preface to his *Life of Saint Edmund,* Abbo of Fleury (ca. 945–1004) refers to himself as *mea parvitas* and *mea pusillitas* and beseeches his dedicatee, Dunstan of Canterbury, to find the time to correct the mistakes and supplement the gaps in his work.[100] Widukind of Corvey (d. after 973) prefaces his *Saxon History* with a dedication in which he calls himself *ultimus servulorum Christi* and *nostra humilitas.*[101] Thietmar of Merseburg (975–1018) deems himself "inferior to all of my predecessors" *(predecessorum*

97. Simon, "Untersuchungen zur Topik der Widmungsbriefe," 1.65–67.

98. See Simon, "Untersuchungen zur Topik der Widmungsbriefe," 1.108–19; Curtius, *European Literature and the Latin Middle Ages,* 83–84, 411–13; Curtius, "Mittelalterstudien," 247; Curtius, "Der Archipoeta und der Stil mittellateinischer Dichtung," *Romanische Forschungen* 54 (1940): 153–64.

99. Simon, "Untersuchungen zur Topik der Widmungsbriefe," 1.87–98; Janson, *Latin Prose Prefaces,*141–43.

100. *Vita S. Eadmundi,* 68: "suppliciter obsecro ut vel una die vertas michi tuum otium in honestum negotium, resecando hinc superflua, supplendo hiantia."

101. *Res Gestae Saxonicae,* book 1, preface, p. 1.

deterrimus meorum) and proclaims his history to be stylistically inadequate *(non ornatu splendent dictaminis ullo)*.[102]

Among the historians of Richer's period, however, it is Dudo of Saint-Quentin (ca. 960–1026), who takes the prize for exaggerated professions of humility. His *Gesta Normannorum* is a virtual primer in the topoi of modesty and hesitation.[103] In a lengthy dedicatory epistle to Bishop Adalbero of Laon, Dudo presents his book as the "insignificant and reprehensible draft of a poor little work," and one in need of severe editing.[104] He laments that the obscurities of the text must be brought to light by Adalbero, though he doubts whether he, "an indigent and inglorious author," is worthy of such a "noble corrector."[105] He goes on to claim that he did not undertake to write voluntarily, but at the request of Duke Richard I of Normandy.[106] Dudo's arsenal of topoi is by no means exhausted after the opening letter to Adalbero. Several introductory poems follow, the first of which is addressed to the book itself, which is characterized as entirely lacking in rhetorical polish.[107] The third poem *(futurae materiei trepidatio et dissuasio)* is a wearying meditation on Dudo's incompetence as a writer and his fear of making his work public.[108]

102. Thietmar of Merseburg, *Chronicon,* ed. Robert Holtzmann, MGH SRG n. s. 9 (Berlin: Weidmann, 1935), prologue, p. 3, line 5, and p. 5, line 37.

103. For the text of Dudo's history, see Jules Lair, ed., *De moribus et actis primorum Normanniae ducum* (Paris: Derache, 1861). Eric Christiansen has provided a translation and introduction to Dudo's work in *Dudo of St Quentin: History of the Normans* (Woodbridge, U.K.: Boydell Press, 1998).

104. *Gesta Normannorum, epistola panegyrica,* 118: "tantilli operis despectivam atque reprobabilem compositionem." All translations from Dudo are taken from Christiansen.

105. *Gesta Normannorum, epistola panegyrica,* 118: "Talem, et hujuscemodi honorem corde revolvo, et mente delibero, decere tantum patronum: ut quae in hoc codice suis tenebris obscura videntur, per te ad lucem referantur, quia non penuriosi et ingloriosi nomen compositoris, sed egregii correctoris laus acquiretur."

106. *Gesta Normannorum, epistola panegyrica,* 119: "certum te reddere volo, ut non rearis me huic operi haesisse voluntarie, nec illud spontanea voluntate coepisse."

107. *Gesta Normannorum, epistola panegyrica,* 120: "rhetorica ratione carens dulcaminis omni."

108. For this poem as an example of the topos of *trepidatio,* see Curtius, "Mittelalterstudien," 247.

Flodoard, too, deploys many of these conventions in his *Historia Remensis Ecclesiae*. The skillful self-deprecation of his prologue serves as a pointed contrast to the self-confidence of Richer:

> Spurred on by the frequent goading of your reminders, I have at last shaken off the torpor of my slothful idleness and abandoned the preoccupations of my various concerns, and I am turning over the fourfold work of my labor to the resourcefulness of your ardent devotion.... Do not wonder if I petition your lofty sanctity concerning this delay in complying [with your request], because I have been hindered by various duties, confined by the winter frost of an icy cold, and, in addition, hampered by a lack of scribes. Nor is it surprising that the delays in correcting my work are causing me considerable fear, because some previous writers are said to have spent more time in retractions than in making their work public. Yet not even now do I think that I have wholly eliminated all of my errors, and, if any of this writer's flaws are [still] to be found, your keen diligence will be able to expunge them. For I do not judge myself to be such a perfect seeker [after error] that I should not be willing to endure it if I found someone more thorough in removing mistakes. Therefore, because the love that belongs to your holiness has so profusely flowed up around my own [limited] capabilities, I have considered this fruit of my labor worthy to entrust to the protection of your patronage, so that what has been said in darkness by my own lowliness might be spoken in the light by the loftiness of your diligence.[109]

Flodoard lists a number of factors that have delayed the publication of his history. He begins with his own indolence and the other business in which he is engaged. He follows with excuses about cold weather and a lack of scribes. Finally, he mentions the delays caused by attempting to eliminate errors from his work, a task that he despairs of finishing. We have no reason to take Flodoard's words literally here. The quality and quantity of his writing—not to mention his active political career—surely absolve Flodoard from charges of sloth, and he had no reason to be worried about mistakes or stylistic inadequacy. On the contrary, his prologue is written in flawless Latin and decorated with stylistic ornaments

109. *HRE*, 57.

like the rhyming tricolon *prepediti ... obstricti ... coartati.* It is precisely this juxtaposition of sparkling prose with elaborate protestations of inadequacy that makes Flodoard's prologue such a masterpiece of disarming humility.

In contrast, Richer's prologue betrays no signs of hesitancy or modesty. Instead, he undertakes to write with a degree of enthusiasm equivalent to Gerbert's "marvelous goodwill" *(quam ... eo animi nisu complector, qua iubentis mira benivolentia pertrahor).* He does not seem to be concerned about the dangers of being tarred with charges of *impudentia* or *audacia.*[110] He does not invoke the aid of God or the saints, nor does he note the difficulty of the task before him.[111] And he assumes that his work will find an audience, twice mentioning future readers.[112] Aside from one reference to his work with the diminutive *opusculum,* Richer forgoes the modesty topos entirely.

We can only speculate about why Richer dispensed with these topoi. He may have been imitating classical historians, who rarely made such extravagant professions of humility and reluctance.[113] Or pride may have gotten the better of his sense of propriety.[114] Apart from the absence of humility topoi in the prologue, we have Richer's own words as evidence of his literary self-consciousness. Near the end of the prologue he refers explicitly to the originality of his own style in comparison with Flodoard:

Now if I am accused of being ignorant of the unknown past, I do not deny that I took some things from a certain book of Flodoard, a priest

110. A medieval author who appeared too eager to display his literary talents could expose himself to these charges. See Simon, "Untersuchungen zur Topik der Widmungsbriefe," 1.65–66, 85–86.

111. See Simon, "Untersuchungen zur Topik der Widmungsbriefe," 1.106–8, 113–14.

112. *Historia,* prologue: "Tantoque superiora lector ea inveniet ... prudens lector reges aequivocos pernotabit."

113. See Janson, *Latin Prose Prefaces,* 66–67. Classical historians tended to emphasize other themes, e.g., the value of history, the reasons for choosing a particular subject and time period, and the duty of impartiality.

114. Kortüm, *Richer von Saint-Remi,* 96, calls attention to the unusually self-confident tone of Richer's prologue, which, he asserts, prefigures the tendencies of later authors such as Otloh of St. Emmeram.

of Rheims, but the content of my work shows very clearly that I did not use the same words, but different ones, and that I employed a very different rhetorical style.[115]

This passage bears some resemblance to a subset of the humility topos: the author's admission of his own ignorance.[116] For a writer to reap the full reward of this kind of self-congratulatory humility, however, he had to admit to a lack of knowledge. Richer instead deflects the charge of *ignorantia* by raising the possibility that he will be accused of *ignorantia antiquitatis* without actually accepting the criticism. In fact, he may be having a joke at his imagined critics with a pun: the adjective *ignota* seems to implicitly criticize anyone who would fault Richer for factual errors *(ignorantia)* when writing about a past that is no longer fully knowable.

This passage was not part of Richer's first draft; it is written in a darker ink at the bottom of folio 1ʳ and keyed to the main body of the text. We can only speculate about why he decided to include it during the process of revision.[117] Possibly, after circulating an early draft of his history, he encountered criticism due to the inaccuracies in his work and added this passage in response.[118] If so, he chose a peculiarly ineffective way of responding to criticism.

Medieval historians sometimes disavowed responsibility for the truth of what they were writing on the basis of the unreliability of their sources.[119] A historian might present the reader with

115. *Historia,* prologue: "Sed si ignotae antiquitatis ignorantiae arguar, ex quodam Flodoardi presbyteri Remensis libello me aliqua sumpsisse non abnuo, at non verba quidem eadem, sed alia pro aliis longe diverso orationis scemate diposuisse res ipsa evidentissime demonstrat."

116. For *ignorantia* as a topos, see Simon, "Untersuchungen zur Topik der Widmungsbriefe," 1.111–12. Gerbert himself used this commonplace in the prologue to his *Acta* of the Synod of Saint-Basle, a work that Richer had studied carefully. See *Acta concilii Remensis,* prologue, 392: "Peto autem ab huius sacri conventus prelatis, si quod minus grave vel parum comptum expressero, non suae iniuriae, sed meae ascribi ignorantiae."

117. Glenn, *Politics and History,* 178–214, offers one hypothesis.

118. For an example of a monastic historian responding to criticism from his audience, see Roger Ray, "Orderic Vitalis and His Readers," *Studia Monastica* 14 (1972): 17–33.

119. See Marie Schulz, *Die Lehre von der historischen Methode bei den Geschichts*

two contradictory stories, for example, and then refuse to judge between them. Or he might include material of doubtful authenticity in his work with a caveat to the reader. More generally, the historian could shift the blame for untruths that remained in his own work to his sources. Since Flodoard's *Annals* are the most important source for the first part of the *Historia,* Richer could theoretically defend himself from criticism by claiming that the annals—and not his own ignorance—were responsible for any factual errors. Yet any critic who knew enough about the events recounted in both works to accuse Richer of ignorance would have been unimpressed with this defense. The liberties that Richer takes with Flodoard—rhetorical embellishments, changes to the order of events, and invention of army sizes and casualty statistics—are glaringly obvious. It is precisely to the degree that Richer departs from Flodoard that he exposes himself to justifiable criticism. He cannot, therefore, seriously claim that his source material is responsible for the historical inaccuracies that appear in his work. No critic of Richer would have found this line of defense in any way convincing.

Instead of reading the accusation of *ignorantia* as the actual or potential response of an informed reader to the inaccuracies in the *Historia,* we should view it as the reaction Richer imagined his audience might have when presented with the text: How did Richer himself know enough about the kings of the West Franks to write a history on the subject? The hypothetical critic envisioned here is not casting doubt on anything that Richer has actually written; he is instead questioning his qualifications to write history in the first place. It must have been obvious to some of his audience that Richer was borrowing from Flodoard, and he admits this, if somewhat grudgingly: *non abnuo … aliqua sumpsisse.* But he makes it clear that he borrowed only Flodoard's material, not his words: *at non verba quidem eadem, sed alia pro aliis.* This statement holds the key to understanding why Richer inserted this passage into

schreibern des Mittelalters, Abhandlungen zur Mittleren und Neuren Geschichte (Berlin: Walther Rothschild, 1909), 47–49.

his history to begin with: he wanted to stake a claim to his own stylistic originality. Not only does he use a "very different style" *(longe diverso orationis scemate)*, the difference is "very evident" *(res ipsa evidentissime demonstrat)*. Richer's tone here is assertive, verging on proud, but this statement is actually a milder version of his original claim. The manuscript shows very clearly that he originally wrote *prestantiore orationis scemate*. That is to say, his style was not merely "different," it was "superior."[120] He then thought the better of this claim and replaced *prestantiore* with *diversissimo* ("very different"), which he changed again, to *longe diverso*.

Richer was clearly interested in pointing out to his audience that he was departing from—and, implicitly, improving upon—Flodoard's *Annals*. But as we shall see, he could hardly claim to be improving upon Flodoard's Latin. He was adding something else, something vaguer: a *longe diversum orationis scema*. *Sc(h)ema orationis* means, approximately, "rhetorical style," but this translation does not account for the metaphorical sense of the expression. The phrase appears to be unattested before Richer, who probably coined it. *Sc(h)ema* could have a variety of meanings for a tenth-century monk. In rhetoric it was equivalent to *figura*, "a purposeful deviation in sense or language from the ordinary simple form."[121] *Sc(h)ema* was used generally to mean "shape" or "form," and Richer uses it on several occasions to describe geometrical figures.[122] It could also mean "appearance" or "attire," including the monastic habit, and it is therefore a word Richer would have associated with clothing.[123] It is probably the case that he is using *orationis scema*

120. Bamberg, Staatsbibliothek, MS Hist. 5 fol.1^r. Hoffmann's edition contains a facsimile of the manuscript.

121. Quintilian, *Institutio Oratoria*, ed. and trans. D. A. Russell, 5 vols. (Cambridge, Mass.: Harvard University Press, 2001), 9.1.14: "in sensu vel sermone aliqua a vulgari et simplici specie cum ratione mutatio." See also Lausberg, §499.

122. *Historia* 4.22: *longilatero scemate;* 1.29: *scemate lunae;* 3.105: *quadrato … scemate;* 4.22: *triangulo … scemate.*

123. See *Historia* 2.89, where Richer uses *scema* to refer to disguises worn by scouts loyal to Louis IV, who adopt the same dress *(eodem scemate)* as the stable-hands of the city of Laon.

metaphorically in this sense to imply that he will clothe the matter *(materia)* he has taken over from Flodoard in a very different type of rhetorical garb.[124]

This claim is certainly not without precedent. Monastic hagiographers could justify the revision and rewriting of saints' lives on the grounds that they were correcting the stylistic defects in the otherwise edifying matter handed down by their less cultivated predecessors. Richer is telling the reader that he will improve upon the annalistic style of Flodoard—that he will dress it in new rhetorical clothes. We already get a sense for Richer's modest opinion of Flodoard's *Annals* from his suggestion that his own history is intended to be a continuation of Hincmar's *Annals of Saint-Bertin*. Flodoard's *Annals* would function perfectly well in that capacity, but Richer mentions them only in passing and as part of his process of revision. For Richer, Flodoard's account of the years 919–966 was unsatisfactory because it was stylistically inadequate.

But what, specifically, does he mean by *longe diversum orationis scema?* Flodoard's *Annals,* while spare and unadorned, were not in need of orthographic or grammatical correction. Richer could not have been basing his claim to stylistic originality on the fact that he was revising the *incultus sermo* or *rusticitas* of his predecessor. We might, then, expect the *Historia* to differ significantly from Flodoard's *Annals* in diction, syntax, and overall prose style. The differences in these areas, however, turn out to be relatively minor.[125]

In general, Richer's diction differs from Flodoard's in two ways. First, he is more inclined to use classical vocabulary, preferring *res publica* to *regnum,* for example, and employing anachronistically Roman military terminology *(legio, cohors, centurio, testudo).*[126] He

124. Clothing metaphors were frequently used to describe the ornamentation of prose through the application of literary-rhetorical techniques. See, e.g., Cicero, *De oratore* 1.142; Julius Victor, *Ars Rhetorica,* Halm, p. 373, line 20.

125. See Hoffmann, "Die *Historien* Richers von Saint-Remi," 482–508, for an analysis of Richer's diction and style.

126. *Res publica* occurs twenty-three times in the *Historia,* while Flodoard uses it once in the *HRE* and not at all in the *Annals.*

demonstrates a greater familiarity with Caesar, Livy, Sallust, and Hegesippus than Flodoard, and his close knowledge of these authors provided him with a stock of words to draw upon when writing. Second, he draws upon a specialized vocabulary when dealing with subjects like siege engineering and medicine, subjects that do not appear in Flodoard's work.[127] His syntax is generally classical and he shows a clear preference for ending sentences with verbs; for example, every single sentence in the prologue ends this way. But the same largely holds true for Flodoard's *Annals.* Richer tends to avoid long periods and hypotaxis as much or even more than the *Annals,* so in this sense his style is not "very different." The differences in diction and syntax between the *Historia* and Flodoard's *Annals* are hardly enough to justify a claim to a *longe diversum orationis scema.* What really distinguishes Richer's history is neither elevated diction nor an elaborate prose style, but the amplification and embellishment of his source material. Richer adds detail, clarifies the relationships between events, and explains the motivations of characters.

By way of illustration it will be useful to compare a passage in the *Historia* to the entry from Flodoard's *Annals* upon which it is based. In book 2 Richer describes how King Louis IV sought William Longsword, duke of Normandy, as an ally against Hugh the Great and Heribert of Vermandois. Flodoard gives the following account:

Count Roger, after serving as an emissary for king Louis at the court of Duke William of the Normans, died there. William received Louis at Rouen in a manner befitting a king. William of Poitiers and the Bretons with their leading men also came to the king. The king, therefore, went with them to the Oise. But Hugh and Heribert, along with Otho, the duke of the Lotharingians, after destroying the bridges and carrying off the boats, encamped on the opposite side of the river with those whom they could carry; and after they disputed their differences through in-

127. E.g., Richer would have found relatively obscure words like *commissura, longurius,* and *sublica* in Caesar's *Bellum Gallicum.* See Hoffmann, "Die *Historien* Richers von Saint-Remi," 485–86.

termediaries a truce was finally agreed upon from the middle of September to the middle of November, and hostages were taken on both sides.[128]

Richer's treatment of the same events reads:

And so the king, taking counsel from good men, sent Roger, a person of distinction, to speak on his behalf with Duke William of the pirates. After carrying out this embassy at [William's] court on behalf of the king with great success, he departed from mortal affairs in that same place. Prior to this, however, he had succeeded in persuading the duke. For not long afterwards [William] sent some of his own men and summoned the king to him in good faith; he received him at Rouen and heaped large gifts on him in a very worthy fashion. The result of this was that others grew fearful and went over to the king's side in a more timely fashion. Thus, when Duke William of Aquitaine and Alan of Brittany learned that the pirates were taking the king's side, they hastened their approach and went to the king. They swore their loyalty and pledged military service to him. And so the king took these men and went to speak with the tyrants [Hugh and Herbert] near the river Oise. But the tyrants, since they were worried about the king's horsemen, went before them [to the Oise]; they destroyed the bridges and took all the boats in the area over to the other bank. And with that they set up camp with their men on the opposite bank of the river. The dispute between them was carried out by intermediaries, with just two small boats going back and forth from one side to the other. At last, after an exchange of hostages, they parted from one another in peace.[129]

128. Flodoard, *Annales*, s.a. 942, pp. 84–85: "Rotgarius comes apud Willelmum Nordmannorum principem functus legatione pro Ludowico rege ibidem defunctus est. Willelmus regem Ludovicum regaliter in Rodomo suscepit. Item Willelmus Pictavensis et Brittones cum suis principibus ad regem venerunt. Cum his ergo rex super Isaram venit. Hugo vero et Heribertus cum Othone duce Lothariensium destructis pontibus et ablatis navibus, cum his quoque quos habere poterant ex altera parte fluminis consederunt; et agitata inter eos per internuntios controversia dantur tandem indutiae a medio septembris usque ad medium novembris, et obsides accipiuntur utrimque."

129. *Historia* 2.28: "Etenim rex bonorum usus consilio, Rotgarium virum clarum Uuilelmo pyratarum principi pro se locuturum direxit. Qui apud eum pro rege optime functus legatione, ibi rebus humanis excessit. Ante tamen principi usque ad effectum suasit. Nam non multopost suorum legatione regem fideliter accersit, exceptumque Rodomi ingentibus donis dignissime accumulat. Unde et factum est

These two accounts vary little in syntax. Five of the six sentences in Flodoard end in verbs, while nine of ten in Richer end in verbs, and one ends in a participle. There is no particularly striking variance in sentence length or in the degree of hypotaxis. The vocabulary reveals a few noteworthy changes. Richer, as is his habit, changes Flodoard's *Nordmanni* to the more classical *piratae.*[130] He uses the dignified periphrasis *rebus humanis excessit* instead of the more workmanlike *defunctus est* to report the death of Count Roger of Laon. *Pace sequestra,* in place of Flodoard's *indutiae,* is a term that he may have borrowed from classical poetry—it occurs in both Virgil (*Aeneid* 11.133) and Statius (*Thebaid* 2.425). But what really sets the two passages apart is not a difference in syntax or diction, but Richer's addition of material not found in Flodoard. First, there is an increased use of adjectives and adverbs: *bonorum, clarum, optime, fideliter, ingentibus, dignissime, tempestivius.* These words are not merely ornamental; they reveal the attitudes of the characters toward one another and Richer's own judgments about their actions. They give us a sense of how Richer thought history should happen. Louis takes the advice of "good men" and sends a "distinguished" emissary to William's court at Rouen. William summons the king "in good faith" and the "large" gifts that he "very worthily" bestows on the king are an indication of his desire to make a public statement about his support for Louis. The fear of the other lords when they learn of this new alliance is emphasized by the "more timely" manner in which they hurry to

ut alii hinc formidantes, ad regem tempestivius sese contulerint. Uuilelmus itaque Aquitanorum dux Britannorumque Alanus piratas regiam rem curare comperientes, accessum maturant, regem adeunt, atque fidem pacti, miliciam iurant. His itaque rex collectis, predictis tirannis secus fluvium Isaram locuturus procedit. Tiranni regium equitatum suspectum habentes, prevenerunt atque pontes precipitaverunt, naves circumquaque in aliud litus abducentes. Sicque cum suis in adverso fluminis litore consederunt. Duabus tantum naviculis hinc inde cursantibus, per internuntios controversia inter illos agitata est. Tandem sub pace sequestra obsidum iure a sese discedunt."

130. Cf. *Historia* 1.48, 1.50, 1.51, 1.53, 1.56, 1.57, 2.20. *Piratae* is Richer's standard term for the Normans.

the king to pledge their fealty. Richer's use of descriptive terms is not always intended to express interior motivations; the fact that the negotiators travel in "just two small boats" *(duabus tantum naviculis)* is a picturesque touch, but probably nothing more. But in general, these kinds of qualifiers help the reader understand the relationships between characters.

Richer also uses a series of meaningful conjunctions *(etenim, tamen, nam, unde et, itaque* [twice], *sicque)* to clarify the connection between sentences. In contrast, Flodoard uses the comparatively weak conjunctions *item, vero,* and *et.* He uses *ergo* once, but far from clarifying the connection between the two clauses, it reveals only that the connection is clear to Flodoard: Duke William of Aquitaine and the Bretons come to the king; *therefore* he goes with them to the Oise. The reason for the king's departure with his new allies is not spelled out in any more detail than this.

Most important, Richer explains the motivations of his characters. The king decides to ally himself with William Longsword of Normandy because he has consulted with good advisors. William goes over to the king's side because he is convinced by the arguments of the king's emissary, Count Roger of Laon. William of Aquitaine and Alan of Brittany join the royal party because they fear this new alliance. The king and his allies go the Oise because they want to meet with Hugh and Heribert to pressure them to make peace. Hugh and Heribert destroy the bridges across the river and confiscate all the boats in the area because they fear the power of the king's horsemen. Richer brings into sharper relief the connections between events that he finds in Flodoard, and he teases out these connections when they are only implicit in the *Annals.* This passage is representative of the ways in which Richer reworks Flodoard's *Annals.* At a basic level, he increases in the level of detail and clarifies the motives *(rationes)* of historical actors. In many places, however, his changes are much more substantial. Rather than simply fleshing out his annalistic source material, he uses Flodoard as a starting point to develop dramatic scenes filled with dialogue, speeches, and highly embellished descriptions.

Truth and Plausibility

At the end of the prologue Richer states that he thinks the reader will be satisfied if he has arranged everything "plausibly, clearly, and concisely" *(probabiliter atque dilucide breviterque).*[131] Plausibility, clarity, and brevity were the three "virtues of narrative" *(virtutes narrationis)* recommended by the rhetorical handbooks of antiquity.[132] By invoking them as stylistic ideals Richer shows that he viewed his history as a *narratio* governed by the rules of rhetorical invention, and thus gives us a valuable window into how he conceived of his task.[133] But what exactly does Richer mean by *probabiliter*? This word is typically rendered "plausibly," but a more accurate translation might be "readily believable."[134] However we choose to translate it, the important thing is to determine how Richer himself defined the word, and what distinction existed in his mind between the readily believable *(probabile)* and the verifiably true *(verum).*

In classical rhetoric the *narratio*—the statement of the facts of a case—was the second component of a speech (after the *exordium*), in which the orator presented to his audience a selective version of events calculated to win them over to whatever point of view he was advocating. *Narratio* as a rhetorical term of art was not limited to narratives within speeches, however. In the *De inventione* Cicero enumerates three categories of *narratio,* two of which involve "public issues" *(civiles causae)* and one of which does not.[135] This third category was subdivided into narratives organized principally around events and narratives organized prin-

131. *Historia,* prologue: "Satisque lectori fieri arbitror, si probabiliter atque dilucide breviterque omnia digesserim." The virtues are explained at *De inventione* 1.20.28–1.21.29 and *Rhetorica ad Herennium* 1.9.14–1.9.16.

132. *Rhetorica ad Herennium* 1.9.14; *De inventione* 1.20.28; Quintilian, *Institutio Oratoria* 4.2.31; Marius Victorinus, *Explanationes in Ciceronis Rhetoricam* 1.20, p. 88; Martianus Capella, *De nuptiis* 5.551.

133. See Lake, "Truth, Plausibility, and the Virtues of Narrative at the Millennium," *Journal of Medieval History* 35 (2009): 221–38.

134. The translation used by Eleonore Stump.

135. *De inventione* 1.19.27: "Tertium genus est remotum a civilibus causis quod delectationis causa non inutili cum exercitatione dicitur et scribitur."

cipally around people.[136] The former category contained three subdivisions: *fabula,* a narrative that was untrue and could not have happened; *argumentum,* a narrative that was fictional but could have happened; and *historia,* a narrative of actual events that took place in the distant past.[137] Cicero thus conceived of history both as an account of true events and as a *narratio* that required the application of the techniques of rhetorical discovery *(inventio).* A historical narrative, therefore, needed to possess the three virtues of narrative mentioned previously: clarity, brevity, and plausibility *(narratio aperta, narratio brevis, narratio probabilis).*

To secure the appropriate degree of plausibility, the speaker or writer had to account for a number of different factors. Cicero offers a comprehensive list in the *De inventione:*

> The narrative will be plausible ... if the proper qualities of the character are maintained, if reasons for their actions are plain, if there seems to have been ability to do the deed, if it can be shown that the time was opportune, the space sufficient and the place suitable for the events about to be narrated; if the story fits in with the nature of the actors in it, the habits of ordinary people and the beliefs of the audience.[138]

Similarly, the anonymous author of the *Rhetorica ad Herennium* states that a plausible narrative *(verisimilis narratio)* will account for "the length of time" *(spatia temporum),* "the standing of the persons involved" *(personarum dignitates),* "the motives in the planning" *(consiliorum rationes),* and "the advantages offered by the scene of action" *(locorum opportunitates).*[139] In his commentary on the *De inventione,* Marius Victorinus uses a diagram to summarize the seven elements necessary for securing plausibility in the narration:

136. *De inventione* 1.19.27: "Eius partes sunt duae, quarum altera in negotiis, altera in personis maxime versatur."

137. *De inventione* 1.19.27: "Fabula est in qua nec verae nec veri similes res continentur ... Historia est gesta res, ab aetatis nostrae memoria remota.... Argumentum est ficta res, quae tamen fieri potuit."

138. *De inventione* 1.21.29, trans. H. M. Hubbell, Loeb Classical Library (Cambridge, Mass.: Harvard University Press, 1949), 61.

139. *Rhetorica ad Herennium* 1.9.16, trans. H. M. Caplan, Loeb Classical Library (Cambridge, Mass.: Harvard University Press, 1954), 29.

person *(persona)*, deed *(factum)*, cause *(causa)*, place *(locus)*, time *(tempus)*, method *(modus)*, and means *(facultas)*. Each one of these narrative elements corresponded to a question: *quis, quid, cur, ubi, quando, quemadmodem*, and *quibus adminiculis*, respectively.[140] He then notes that Cicero rightly added an eighth element, opinion *(opinio)*, which Victorinus subdivides into the opinion of the speaker and his client, the opinion of the public, and the opinion of the judges.[141] A speaker who did not take into account each of these aspects of narrative risked undermining the credibility of his account.

Of course the historian who constructed his narrative based upon the rules of rhetorical invention was hardly ever in a position to have access to accurate information about every circumstance of the events that he was describing. In these situations rhetorical "discovery" *(inventio)* tended to become outright invention, as the author was compelled to supplement his account with conjectures or plausible fictions. This procedure was not only unavoidable, it was entirely licit. For the rules of rhetorical *inventio* did not demand that a narrative be true, only that it appear to be true.[142] Hence the demand that a narrative be "readily believable" *(probabilis)* rather than true. In the *De inventione* Cicero defines the *probabilis* as "that ... which for the most part usually comes to pass, or which is a part of the ordinary beliefs of mankind, or which contains in itself some resemblance to these qualities, *whether such resemblance be true or false*."[143] This is the standard that Richer adopted for himself in the *Historia*.

There is one potentially serious objection to this hypothesis, however, because in several places Richer uses the word *probabiliter* to describe types of discourse that appear to be actually aiming

140. *Explanationes in Ciceronis Rhetoricam* 1.21, p. 94: "in his septem omnis ad fidem argumentatio continetur."

141. Ibid.

142. *De inventione* 1.7.9: "Inventio est excogitatio rerum verarum aut veri similium quae causam probabilem reddant."

143. *De inventione* 1.29.46: "Probabile autem est id quod fere solet fieri aut in opinione positum est aut quod habet in se ad haec quandam similitudinem, sive id falsum est sive verum" (trans. Hubbell).

at truth instead of the mere plausibility envisioned by Cicero in the *De inventione*.[144] In his account of the contest of medical knowledge between Charles the Simple's court physician Derold and an anonymous Salernitan in book 2, for example, he states that Derold, the winner of the contest, answered the problems that were set for him *probabiliter*.[145] In the disputation at Ravenna Gerbert defends his taxonomy of the branches of knowledge *(divisio philosophiae)* against his critics and claims that he had recently demonstrated it *probabiliter dilucideque*. Upon Otto II's accession to the throne, Richer praises the emperor for his wisdom, and particularly for his skill in disputation, noting that "he could state propositions in accordance with the rules of the art and draw conclusions *probabiliter*."[146] In each of these cases the word *probabilis* or *probabiliter* seems to denote something much closer to truth than mere plausibility or ready believability, and if that is the case, we must concede the possibility that Richer is using the word in the same way in the prologue. What these three passages have in common, however, and what distinguishes their use of the word *probabiliter* from the way it is deployed in the prologue, is that they all describe a process of dialectical argumentation. Definition, division, and deduction are all parts of dialectic, and plausibility as a *terminus technicus* of dialectic differed in important ways from plausibility as a virtue of narrative. Specifically, it came much closer to truth.

The reasons for this are twofold. First, in dialectic, plausibility was a quality of the arguments themselves; it was not established through a process of creative invention like that used by orators. The practitioner of dialectic sought to find arguments and draw conclusions that were "readily believable," but this did not involve the fictional generation of circumstantial details demanded by nar-

144. The following is an abbreviated version of the more detailed argument made in Lake, "Truth, Plausibility, and the Virtues of Narrative," 229–32.

145. *Historia* 2.59: "Deroldus quidem utpote litterarum artibus eruditus, probabiliter obiecta diffiniebat."

146. *Historia* 3.67: "Vir magni ingenii totiusque virtutis, liberalium litterarum scientia clarus, adeo ut in disputando ex arte et proponeret et probabiliter concluderet."

rative plausibility. Second and more importantly, plausibility, not truth, was the highest degree of certitude that could be achieved in dialectical disputation. Boethius, whose corpus of logical works formed the basis for instruction in dialectic in the early Middle Ages, spells this out explicitly, drawing a distinction between *demonstratio,* which uses necessarily true premises and draws necessarily true conclusions, and *dialectica,* which uses readily believable premises and draws readily believable conclusions.[147] The participant in a dialectical disputation only sought to make his answers readily believable, because that was the highest truth value to which he could aspire. This is why Richer uses the word *probabiliter* to describe Derold's definitions of medical terms, Gerbert's division of the branches of knowledge, and Otto's deductions, even though it looks like he means something like "accurately" or "correctly." Their arguments may indeed have been true, but that was outside the scope of dialectic. Richer, who had been thoroughly trained in both rhetoric and dialectic, clearly understood the difference between plausibility as predicated of a dialectical argument and plausibility as predicated of a historical narrative. When he uses the word *probabiliter* in the prologue, it is accompanied by brevity and clarity, which marks it out as a virtue of narrative; it thus clearly points to the *De inventione,* and for that reason we should understand it as defined by Cicero in that text.

In laying claim to the Ciceronian virtues of narrative for his history, Richer was implicitly categorizing his work as a *narratio* composed according to the criteria for rhetorical invention laid out in handbooks like the *De inventione.* By holding up "ready believability" as a stylistic virtue, he implies that his audience could expect a history that met the requirements for narrative plausibility, but not necessarily one that was true. This is a remarkable claim for a historian to make, and it represents a significant departure from standard medieval practice. For while historians in the Middle Ages were almost invariably compelled to incorporate plausible fictions

147. *De topicis differentiis, PL* 64.1181–82.

into their work, it was highly unusual for them to admit to doing so. In fact I have been unable to find a single example of a medieval historiographer prior to Richer who claimed to write *probabiliter.*[148]

For this reason we cannot simply dismiss Richer's invocation of the virtues of narrative as an empty rhetorical topos. To the contrary, the *Historia* itself shows quite clearly that he understood exactly what the word *probabiliter* meant, and that it accurately describes his historical methodology. The criterion of the readily believable—as opposed to the verifiably true— is central to Richer's whole approach to writing history. He eschews the scrupulous excerpting of documents favored by Flodoard and follows one of the central doctrines of classical rhetoric: a speech or a narrative must inspire trust *(fides)* in its audience. It need not be true, but it must have the appearance of truth.[149]

It is important to note that in the passage mentioned earlier where Richer defends himself against a potential accusation of *ignorantia,* he does not explicitly defend the truth value of the events he depicts. Nor does he voice any apprehension that he will be accused of writing falsehoods, a frequent concern of medieval historians.[150] He does not even include a traditional disclaimer to be writing the truth, a topos particularly common in works of narrative history.[151] He almost seems exasperated with pedantic quibbling about the details of the "unknown past." Richer's prologue is a signal to his audience that they should expect a certain kind of

148. Dudo of Saint-Quentin, who wrote at the beginning of the eleventh century, also lays claim to the narrative virtue of plausibility in the preface to book 3 of the *Gesta Normannorum* (Lair, 177–78). The anonymous author of the *Chronicon S. Michaelis* in the eleventh century and Richard of Poitiers in the twelfth both claimed to incorporate plausible or verisimilar material in their histories. See Lake, "Truth, Plausibility, and the Virtues of Narrative," 225n20, 234–36.

149. Cicero, *De inventione* 1.21.29: "Probabilis erit narratio, si in ea videbuntur inesse ea quae solent apparere in veritate"; *Rhetorica ad Herennium* 1.9.16: "si vera res erit, nihilominus haec omnia narrando conservanda sunt; nam saepe veritas, nisi haec servata sint, fidem non potest facere"; Cicero, *Partitiones oratoriae* 31: "narratio est rerum explicatio et quaedam quasi sedes et fundamentum constituendae fidei."

150. See Simon, "Untersuchungen zur Topik der Widmungsbriefe," 1.96.

151. See Simon, "Untersuchungen zur Topik der Widmungsbriefe," 2.89, and Schulz, *Die Lehre von der historischen Methode,* 5–14.

history. He is not cobbling together a series of excerpts from earlier written sources and eyewitness accounts. Instead, he is making a conscious attempt to compose a history based on the rules of classical rhetoric, a history in which he will embellish his sources to make his narrative convincing to the reader. Unlike many late antique and medieval authors who stressed the edifying message of their work while apologizing (disingenuously or not) for stylistic defects, Richer signals the importance of the form of his history.[152]

Richer's claim that he would be satisfied if he wrote *probabiliter* does not ipso facto imply that he was abandoning the criterion of factual accuracy, however. Nor can it necessarily be interpreted as an admission to his audience that his history was a tissue of plausible fictions. For in the classical rhetorical tradition to which Richer was heir it was possible for a history to be "true" in spite of the fact that it contained a great deal of material that was merely plausible.

Rhetorical doctrine, as we have seen, held that plausibility was as important as truth to the composition of a convincing *narratio*. At the same time, the narrative genre of *historia* dealt with actual events.[153] As a result, the historian was faced with conflicting obligations: to record information that was factually accurate, while at the same time amplifying and embellishing it to make it "readily believable" to its audience. To our way of thinking, any attempt to reconcile these two obligations is bound to fail; for the criterion of truth is ultimately incompatible with the criterion of plausibility. A historian might very well choose to include plausible fictions in his work, but he could not *admit* to doing so without undermining any claim to truthfulness. The apparent contradiction between the standards of truth and plausibility did not present an insuperable dilemma to historians influenced by the doctrines of classical rhetoric, however.[154] For in the classical historiographical tradition, truth and plausibility were separate and distinct standards that ap-

152. See Kortüm, *Richer von Saint-Remi*, 95.

153. *De Inventione* 1.19.27: "Historia est gesta res, ab aetatis nostrae memoria remota"; Isidore, *Etymologiae* 1.44.5: "Historiae sunt res verae quae factae sunt."

154. Lake, "Truth, Plausibility, and the Virtues of Narrative," 232–34.

plied to different parts of a historical work. A history was truthful if it was founded on a basis *(fundamenta)* of well-attested facts (dates, people, places, and events) and if it recounted these facts without partisanship or bias.[155] The narrative virtue of plausibility, on the other hand, applied not to the foundation of a historical work, but to the rhetorical superstructure built atop it, the *exaedificatio.*

The earliest and most influential discussion of the distinction between *fundamenta* and *exaedificatio* is found in book 2 of Cicero's *De oratore,* in a speech delivered by the orator Marcus Antonius that is generally thought to reflect Cicero's own opinions about history writing.[156] Antonius famously refers to what he calls the "first law of history," that one should say nothing that is false and keep quiet about nothing that is true.[157] But while this statement appears at first glance to be an endorsement of modern standards of historical writing, the rest of Antonius's speech makes it clear that the Ciceronian standard of narrative truth was considerably less strict than our own. Antonius (and thus Cicero) construes truth and falsehood primarily as a matter of avoiding partiality and bias rather than factual accuracy. Antonius also implies that this historical law applies only to the basic framework of narrative history, the *fundamenta.* The rhetorical superstructure *(exaedificatio)* built atop this framework of fact was judged according to a different standard, that of plausibility. The same idea is implicit in the *De inventione,* where Cicero defines *historia* as "an account of actual occurrences," while at the same time categorizing it as a type of *narratio* subject to the rules of invention according to the standard of "ready believability."[158] In both texts Cicero assumes that history will be "true" while simultaneously endorsing the use of plausible fictions.[159]

155. Cicero, *De oratore* 2.53.

156. See esp. Woodman, *Rhetoric in Classical Historiography,* 70–116.

157. *De oratore* 2.62: "Nam quis nescit primam esse historiae legem, ne quid falsi dicere audeat? Deinde ne quid veri non audeat, ne qua suspicio gratiae sit in scribendo, ne qua simultatis."

158. *De inventione* 1.19.27: "Historia est gesta res, ab aetatis nostrae memoria remota" (trans. Hubbell).

159. *De inventione* 1.19.27; *De oratore* 2.51–64.

Both the *De oratore* and the *De inventione* were copied at Rheims at Gerbert's behest in the late tenth century, and while we cannot prove that Richer was familiar with the former, his debt to the *De inventione* is clear.[160] It is important, therefore, that we understand his use of the word *probabiliter* as both he and Gerbert would have—as a *terminus technicus* of classical rhetoric. It was not an admission that he was abrogating the historian's traditional obligation to tell the truth, nor was it a meaningless invocation of a standard prefatory topos. It was an attempt to lay claim to the Ciceronian virtues of narrative for his work, a sign that he was making a conscious break from the annalistic mode of historiography represented by Hincmar and Flodoard in order to write a history that satisfied the Ciceronian requirements for plausible narrative.

If certain aspects of Richer's prologue are ambiguous and admit of more than one interpretation, this much can be said with confidence: it is the statement of purpose of a self-consciously literary historian. Indeed, much of it can be read as an effort on Richer's part to explain his methodology in rhetorical terms. He explicitly divides his text into an *exordium* and a *narratio*, and given the opportunity to revise it, he might well have brought all of his chapter titles together into a table of contents that would have served as a *partitio*.[161] He alludes to three of the five parts of rhetoric—

160. Erlangen, Universitätsbibliothek, MS 380, a manuscript that contains the *De oratore*, was copied for Gerbert by a monk named Ayrard between 983 and 991, the period in which Gerbert was assembling a new rhetorical library. See Hoffmann, *Bamberger Handschriften*, 23. Richer himself may have been one of the scribes of Bamberg, Staatsbibliothek, MS Class. 25, a manuscript copied around the year 1000 that contained both the *De inventione* and the commentary by Marius Victorinus. See Hoffmann, *Bamberger Handschriften*, 22–23 and 27–28. For Richer and the *De inventione*, see chap. 4 below.

161. The prologue itself is a kind of *exordium*, but Richer also appears to have envisioned a separate *exordium* after his geographical and ethnographical chapters. Thus, at the end of the prologue he notes that "I will begin the *exordium* to the work as a whole once I have briefly made a division of the world and divided Gaul into its parts." Richer's use of rhetorical terminology to label his text corresponds to Notker Labeo's statement that the *partes orationis* are found in the works of historiographers; Notker equates the prologue, chapter headings, and text of written history with the *exordium*, *partitio*, and *narratio* of a speech. See *De arte rhetorica*, ed. James C. King and Petrus W. Tax, *Notker der Deutsche: Die kleineren Schriften*, vol. 7

inventio (statements about material, sources, and the virtues of narrative),[162] *dispositio* (remarks on the need for a proper *ordo*),[163] and *elocutio (at non verba quidem eadem, sed alia pro aliis longe diverso orationis scemate)*[164]—and while his professed goal to "recall to memory" the wars of the West Frankish kings does not refer directly to oratorical *memoria* as one of the five parts of rhetoric, it recalls Cicero's recommendation that the orator should remind the audience of his arguments in the peroration of a speech.[165] Moreover, when he asks that his inclusion of material unconnected with the West Frankish kings be excused due to "incidental reasons that could not be avoided," he is alluding to the distinction that Martianus Capella draws between the principal and incidental questions *(quaestiones)* that make up a case (5.443), and the corresponding principal and incidental narratives in a speech.[166] Most importantly, Richer implies that this history will adhere to the standard of the readily believable as opposed to the verifiably true. As a consequence he seems to have put a low premium on some of the traditional duties of the historian: the gathering of eyewitness testimony, the reproduction of documents, and the critical evaluation of sources. The bulk of his energy is devoted instead to the embellishment and amplification of his source material—to the creation of a "very different rhetorical style."

(Tübingen: Max Niemeyer Verlag, 1996), 121: "iste tres partes orationis ab oratoribus acceptae etiam apud hystoriographos inveniuntur: Prologus, capitula, textus."

162. *Historia,* prologue: "materia sese multiplex praebet ... ex quodam Flodoardi presbyteri Remensis libello me aliqua sumpsisse non abnuo."

163. *Historia,* prologue: "Ubi enim rerum ordo non advertitur, tanto nitentem error confundit, quanto a serie ordinis errantem seducit." Cf. *De inventione* 1.7.9: "dispositio est rerum inventarum in ordinem distributio."

164. *De nuptiis* 5.442: "elocutio, quae arripit verba vel propria vel translata, quaeque nova facit vetera componit"; *De inventione* 1.7.9: "elocutio est idoneorum verborum ad inventionem accomodatio."

165. *De inventione* 1.52.98.

166. *Historia,* prologue: "Si qua vero aliorum *efferantur,* ob *incidentes* rationes quae vitari non potuerunt id evenisse putetur." Cf. *De nuptiis* 5.433 and 5.551: "Narrationum aliae sunt ipsius causae et negotii, aliae incidentes. Ipsius causae sunt, sine quibus res quae agitur intellegi non potest; *incidentes,* quae aut probationis gratia aut exempli aut augendi aut invidiae aut voluptatis extrinsecus *afferuntur.*" (*Efferuntur* is a variant reading here. See the *apparatus criticus* in Willis, 193.)

[TWO]

Rewriting History

RICHER AND HIS WRITTEN SOURCES

AT DIFFERENT POINTS in the *Historia* Richer refers to each one of his four most important written sources: Flodoard's *Annals* and *HRE,* and Gerbert's *Acta* of the synods of Saint-Basle and Mouzon.[1] Because each one of these texts is extant, and because so much of the *Historia* is a reworking of them in one way or another, we are in a remarkably good position to understand the methods by which Richer excerpted and refashioned his written source material. The survival of Richer's autograph manuscript is a further stroke of good luck. Bamberg, Staatsbibliothek, MS Hist. 5, with its numerous corrections, expunctions, and erasures, offers us an unusually revealing glimpse of a medieval historian at work. At the same time, Frutolf of Michelsberg's *Chronicon* and Johannes Trithemius's *Annales* preserve fragments of a later redaction of the *Historia,* so that in some cases we have access to three different phases of composition: the first draft and revisions contained in Richer's autograph, and the modifications made in the subsequent two-book recension used by Frutolf and Trithemius.

Comparing passages in the *Historia* to the sources upon which they are based, analyzing the revisions within the manuscript, and studying the subsequent changes in the hypothetical lost redaction can give us valuable insight into Richer's historical methodology. For anyone wishing to use the *Historia* as a source for the political

1. *Historia,* prologue (Flodoard's *Annals*); 1.19 *(HRE)*; 4.73 (*Acta* of the Synod of Saint-Basle); 4.101 (*Acta* of the Synod of Mouzon).

history of the tenth century, the picture that emerges from such an analysis is not necessarily an encouraging one. Richer demonstrates a notable indifference to chronological accuracy, occasionally appears to misunderstand his sources, advances dubious political claims, and allows himself broad artistic license. Yet if the investigation that follows is not likely to inspire confidence in Richer as a reliable mediator of historical data, it will nonetheless provide some understanding of why he chose to write in the way that he did, and it will show that behind the manipulation of his written source material lay specific and consistent literary goals.

Selection

Among the most basic of the historian's tasks is the determination of what is to be included in his work. Richer's written sources presented him with a wealth of information (a circumstance to which he alludes in his prologue), but the greater part of this material had to be excluded in order to maintain focus on his principal themes, the wars of the West Frankish kings and the fortunes of the church of Rheims.[2] He employs the *HRE* selectively, mostly for information about events before 921, and his pattern of usage suggests that he consulted it on an ad hoc basis without ever fully absorbing and mastering its contents. His principles of selection with regard to Flodoard's *Annals,* his chief source from 1.15 to 3.21, are generally clear. He leaves out all miracles and most portents, information about foreign kingdoms such as Italy and Byzantium, and much of the complicated political maneuvering in West Francia that was only marginally relevant to his main narrative threads. By way of simplifying the narrative and keeping the focus on the principal historical actors, he also occasionally reduces the number of people involved in an event.[3]

2. *Historia,* prologue: "quia ... rerum materia sese multiplex prebet."

3. See, e.g., *Historia* 2.28, where no mention is made of Count Otho of Verdun in Louis's negotiations with Hugh the Great and Heribert of Vermandois. Cf. Flodoard, *Annales,* s.a. 942, p. 85.

The criteria upon which he bases his decisions about what to include are not always obvious, however. All of the events for the year 933 in the *Annals* are passed over in silence, for example, including seemingly relevant ones such as the bringing back of the archiepiscopal *pallium* from Rome for Artald, a synod held at Rheims, the Norman duke William Longsword's submission to King Radulf, and Radulf's capture of the stronghold of Château-Thierry from Heribert of Vermandois.[4] In some cases it is difficult to be certain of Richer's motives. He neglects to mention several events that reflect poorly on Charles the Simple and his allies during the year 922, including Charles's plundering of *villae* that belonged to the church of Rheims and his attack on the city of Rheims itself during Pentecost Sunday.[5] He might have excluded this material out of sympathy for Charles, but it is equally possible that he simply wanted to avoid overburdening his narrative with unnecessary detail. For in fact he leaves out all of the maneuvering between Charles's and Robert's armies during the summer of 922, not just the material prejudicial to Charles. We face a similar difficulty in assessing Richer's motives in his account of the synod of Mouzon at the end of book 4. He mentions that a letter sent from Pope John XV to the synod was read out before the bishops, but he chooses not to include the text on the grounds that he was striving for brevity and did not find it very useful.[6] The real reason that he declined to include the letter, however, may have been that it contained arguments hostile to Gerbert.[7]

4. Flodoard, *Annales*, s.a. 933, pp. 54–57.

5. Flodoard, *Annales*, s.a. 922, pp. 8–9. Every mention of Charles's favorite Hagano in reference to the Battle of Soissons is also excised. The reader of the *Historia* would not know that Hagano accompanied Charles when he departed Laon for Lotharingia in the face of Hugh the Great's advance on the city, that some of Hagano's allies were attacked by Hugh the Black of Burgundy as they prepared a raid on *villae* in the diocese of Rheims, or that Hagano's own private treasure was seized by Robert's forces when he captured Laon.

6. *Historia* 4.100: "Et statim protulit scriptum atque in aures considentium recitavit, quod quia brevitati studemus et nobis minus fuit accommodum nostris scriptis inserere vitavimus."

7. Alternatively, he might simply have had a hard time getting hold of the letter,

In other cases the nature of the material that Richer excluded strongly suggests that he was attempting to influence the audience's perception of the historical figures about whom he was writing. Thus, Heribert of Vermandois is left out of King Radulf's campaigns against the Vikings in 925 and 926 to deny him any of the glory associated with the king's victories,[8] and no mention is made of William Longsword's alliance with Otto I during the German king's invasion of Lotharingia in 939, or his participation in attacks on the royal cities of Rheims and Laon in 940, after he had pledged fealty to Louis.[9]

Richer also takes care to excise material prejudicial to the archbishops of Rheims (save for Hugh, son of Heribert of Vermandois, and Arnulf). This seems to be the motive behind a curious omission in book 2. In the year 940 Flodoard reports that Louis and Artald conducted a successful military operation against the stronghold of Châtillon-sur-Marne, which was being used as a base of operations from which a certain Hervey was raiding *villae* that belonged to the diocese of Rheims.[10] After receiving hostages, Flodoard reports, Louis went to the monastery of Saint-Rémi, where "he committed himself to the intercession of this saint, promising with sureties that he would give a pound of silver every year, and he gave to the monks of this same place a precept of immunity for this same stronghold."[11] This extract shows Louis and Artald acting swiftly and decisively to aid the church of Rheims, and it involves gifts and a confirmation of privileges to Saint-Rémi. It is not at all obvious, therefore, why Richer chose not to include it in his history. His reasoning only becomes clear when we realize that the Hervey against whom the operation was directed was the nephew and namesake of Archbishop Hervey of Rheims. We know

since it is not found in Gerbert's *Acta* of the synod, and the words *nobis minus fuit accommodum* could also be taken to mean "it was not readily available to us."

8. Flodoard, *Annales*, s.a. 925–26, pp. 28–33. See below.

9. Flodoard, *Annales*, s.a. 939, p. 73; s.a. 940, pp. 76–77. Richer also leaves out Louis's attack on William earlier in 939 (p. 71)

10. Flodoard, *Annales*, s.a. 940, p. 76.

11. Flodoard, *Annales*, s.a. 940, p. 76.

from the *Historia Remensis Ecclesiae* that Archbishop Hervey had enriched both his nephew and his brother Odo with property belonging to the church of Rheims, and that this property had been confiscated from them when they refused to support the consecration of Hervey's successor, Seulf, in 922.[12] The nephew Hervey's construction of a stronghold and his raiding of *villae* belonging to the diocese of Rheims were presumably part of an attempt to stake a claim to his lost possessions. Richer, for his part, clearly felt no need to dwell on Archbishop Hervey's gifts of church property to family members or the feud between his nephew and later archbishops. Seven years after this incident Hervey reappears in Flodoard's *Annals,* again plundering the estates of the church of Rheims from the stronghold at Châtillon-sur-Marne.[13] This time when he emerges from his fortified position to attack soldiers who have interfered with his raiding, he is killed. Not surprisingly, Richer ignores this incident as well.

Richer's silence has the effect of shielding Archbishop Hervey from potential criticism about the alienation of church land to relatives. But was that his primary intention? Flodoard's *Historia Remensis Ecclesiae,* a document whose purpose was the glorification of the church of Rheims and its archbishops, does not shrink from recounting these events involving Hervey's nephew; indeed, it is our primary source for them.[14] That Richer should have omitted this information while Flodoard did not is a sign that his goal may not have been primarily political (i.e., the creation of a falsified version of the past in order to improve Hervey's reputation), but literary. The portrait of Hervey that emerges in the *Historia* is that of a vigorous defender of the possessions of his see (1.19), and an eloquent and brave advocate for Charles the Simple (1.22–23). To include references to his nephew's quarrels with Seulf and Artald

12. *HRE* 4.18, p. 410. See also Friedrich Prinz, *Klerus und Krieg im früheren Mittelalter: Untersuchungen zur Rolle der Kirche beim Aufbau der Königsherrschaft* (Stuttgart: Anton Hiersemann, 1972), 156.

13. *Annales,* s.a. 947, pp. 105–6.

14. *HRE* 4.18, p. 410; 4.33, p. 426.

would have been a distraction from the simplicity of this narrative. Thematic simplicity, by contrast, was not one of the goals of the *Historia Remensis Ecclesiae,* which was more a monument to the church of Rheims than a literary *narratio.* As we shall see, there are many other similar instances in the *Historia* where the selective omission of material derives from an attempt to create thematic clarity. In every case there is a political dimension to the simplification of history, and the political and literary aspects of Richer's approach to his source material cannot be neatly disentangled. But we should not always assume that these kinds of changes were primarily made with polemical intent.

Causation

One of the most fundamental and immediately recognizable differences between Richer's *Historia* and Flodoard's *Annals* is their contrasting approach to causality, a difference that stems from the divergent methods and purposes of their respective genres. The narrative historian, if his work was to make any sense at all, was obliged to provide a convincing explanation for why things happened and why people acted as they did. The annalist, by contrast, could content himself with providing a chronological record of significant occurrences (wars and political developments, but also disasters, meteorological phenomena, and portents) without necessarily drawing connections between them. Implicit in this approach was the assumption that even the most random concatenation of seemingly unrelated events served as a record of divine providence and thus made sense *sub specie aeternitatis.*[15] In Flodoard's case, he may also have expected that his *Annals* would be used primarily as an *aide-mémoire,* and that anyone consulting them at Rheims would be familiar enough with the events recounted therein to be

15. For the generic features of annals, see Herbert Grundmann, *Geschichtsschreibung im Mittelalter: Gattungen, Epochen, Eigenart* (Göttingen: Vandenhoeck & Ruprecht, 1965), 24–28, and McCormick, *Les annales du haut Moyen Âge.*

able to fill in the missing details. Of course this assumption is precisely what makes a work like Flodoard's *Annals* so bewildering to a modern reader. From our perspective the motivations of the actors who populate its pages are hardly ever self-evident.

If Richer was to turn Flodoard's *Annals* into a cohesive narrative that made sense on its own terms, he had to elucidate the causes and motivations that were absent in it. He signals his intention to do this in the prologue by declaring that he will examine the "various motives for action" *(diversas negotiorum rationes)* of the Gauls. Elsewhere his constant efforts to clarify the internal reasoning of his characters can be perceived from the frequency of explanatory conjunctions (*cum, quia, eo quod,* etc.) and verbs like *arbitrari, putare, cogitare, reri,* and *meditari.* Because Richer had to invent the *rationes* that were absent in his source material, his attribution of motives to characters gives us interesting insights into his way of thinking.

A useful example of the way in which Richer draws out the motives left unmentioned in Flodoard's *Annals* is his account of the capture of Charles the Simple by Heribert of Vermandois. On June 15, 923, the armies of Charles and the rebel king Robert of Neustria met at the Battle of Soissons.[16] Although Robert was killed in the fighting, Charles was forced to flee, and a short time later he was lured to a meeting and taken prisoner by Heribert.[17] Flodoard's account of Charles's capture reads as follows:

> Count Heribert sent his cousin Bernard, along with other envoys who were reportedly unaware of the plan that was being carried out through them, to Charles. Having been persuaded by their oaths, Charles set out to meet Heribert with a few men. Heribert received him in his fortress of Saint-Quentin, on the Somme. Then, after those who had come with him had been sent away, he had Charles taken to a stronghold of his called Château-Thierry on the river Marne.[18]

16. *Historia* 1.44–46; Flodoard, *Annales,* s.a. 923, p. 13.
17. Flodoard, *Annales,* s.a. 923, p. 15.
18. Flodoard, *Annales,* s.a. 923, p. 15.

What is most obviously missing from this account is an explanation of why Charles agreed to meet Heribert, and why he came to him with only "a few men." Richer fills in these gaps in his account of the episode at 1.47:

> Heribert, who was responsible for such great wickedness [i.e., the coronation of Radulf], disguising his complicity, sent envoys to invite king Charles to come to him. He claimed that he had tried to oppose these disgraceful acts, but that the multitude of conspirators had forcefully restrained him. At that time there had been no opportunity for him to offer counsel, but now he had discovered the best way to make it up to him. Hence, Charles should hasten quickly to meet with him—but with just a few men, since if they both came in the company of large retinues, the enmity between the two sides might result in open fighting. And if Charles so desired, he could ask the envoys themselves to swear an oath guaranteeing his safe passage. Taken in by these words, he had the envoys swear an oath guaranteeing their good faith, and without giving his advisers a chance to consider the matter he went at once to meet his betrayer.

The actions of Heribert and Charles in this episode are consistent with the way in which Richer has previously characterized them. At 1.14 Charles is described as *ingenio simplici* ("lacking in guile"), and he has previously been portrayed as resistant to counsel and demonstrated a headstrong refusal to listen to advice from the magnates.[19] Here he naively accepts Heribert's proposal and fails to give his counselors an opportunity to think it over. Heribert is naturally devious, but his reason for asking Charles to come without a larger entourage (namely, the possibility that their followers might come to blows) and Charles's acceptance of that stipulation make sense in the context of an incident earlier in the *Historia* in which a quarrel breaks out between the youthful retainers of Charles and Henry the Fowler of Germany (who are in fact allies at the time).[20] Flodoard's *Annals* contains a report of a similar brawl

19. *Historia* 1.14: "Corpore prestanti, ingenio bono simplicique"; 1.24: "Scio enim quam difficile et arduum sit ei consilium dare, cum sua inconstantia, tum suorum invidia." Charles refuses to heed warnings to rid himself of his favorite Hagano at 1.15, 1.16, and 1.21.

20. *Historia* 1.20.

on Easter Sunday between the soldiers of King Radulf and those of Bishop Ingramnus of Laon, "during which many of the laity as well as clergy were wounded or killed."[21] The potential for armed violence between retinues suspicious of one another, therefore, was very real, and although Heribert's use of that explanation is disingenuous in this case, we can see why the gullible Charles might have gone along with his proposal. Richer thus provides clarity on two important points—why Charles agreed to Heribert's proposal, and why he came with so few men—through a process of historical inference based on his understanding of the actors involved and his assumptions about the kinds of things that could be expected to happen in a given situation.

The same process is on display in virtually every chapter of the *Historia* based on an entry in Flodoard's *Annals.* In the year 940, for example, Flodoard reports that Archbishop Artald of Rheims besieged the stronghold of Chausot, and that after King Louis arrived on the fifth day of the siege they captured and destroyed it together.[22] Richer, evidently misreading his source, mistakenly assumed that the king was away in Burgundy at the time, and he offers an explanation of why Artald would undertake such an offensive without help from the king: "lest anyone should think his resources wanting" *(ne suae rei putaretur inopia).*[23] The assumption is probably wrong, since Louis actually arrived to help Artald within the week, but it provides a minor insight into Richer's view of how bishops had to act, namely, that they needed to create the perception of military strength to prevent neighboring landowners from encroaching on their territory. As these and subsequent examples will confirm, Richer was a strategic thinker who assigned realistic motivations to his characters based on his understanding of human psychology. His inferences may be incorrect, but they have the merit of giving us a window into the mentality of a tenth-century thinker.

21. *Annales*, s.a. 935, p. 61.

22. *Annales*, s.a. 940, pp. 75–76.

23. *Historia* 2.21.

Chronology

In the prologue Richer refers specifically to the confusion that could arise if proper attention were not paid to chronology: "For when the sequence of events is not attended to, error confuses the struggling reader to the degree that it leads him astray from the proper order."[24] Ironically, keeping the events of his own history within an accurate chronological framework does not seem to have been a high priority. By failing to keep material drawn from different sources in sync, making simple errors in calculating the passage of time, and deliberately distorting the chronology of Flodoard's *Annals* to suit his own purposes, he introduced a number of errors into his work.

The first problem is largely localized to book 1, where for most of the reigns of Odo (888–898) and Charles the Simple (898–923) Richer lacked a source like Flodoard's *Annals* that could furnish him with both a detailed record of events in West Francia and an overarching chronological framework. As a result, his account of Odo's reign is spotty and incomplete, although some of the information that he provides about the early years of Odo's rule is corroborated elsewhere and probably derives from a now-lost written source.[25] The date that he gives for Odo's coronation (February 29, 888) is also found in the *Lesser Annals of Saint-Germain*.[26] The *Annals of Saint-Vaast* confirm that West Francia was stricken with a severe famine in 892 and that Odo spent that winter in Aquitaine.[27] Richer's claim that there was scarcely any wine to be had in

24. *Historia*, prologue: "Ubi enim rerum ordo non advertitur, tanto nitentem error confundit quanto a serie ordinis errantem seducit."

25. See Édouard Favre, *Eudes, comte de Paris et roi de France* (882–898), Bibliothèque de l'École des Hautes Études, Sciences philologiques et historiques 99 (Paris: É. Bouillon, 1893), 230–33.

26. For the date of Odo's coronation, see Ernst Dümmler, *Geschichte des Ostfränkischen Reiches*, vol. 3 (Leipzig: Duncker & Humblot, 1887–1888), 316n2.

27. *Annales Vedastini*, ed. B. de Simson, MGH SRG 12 (Hanover: Hahn, 1909), s.a. 892, p. 72; *Annales Vindocinenses*, ed. Louis Halphen, Recueil d'annales angevines et vendômoises (Paris: Picard, 1903), s.a. 892, p. 55.

the kingdom at this time is also consistent with a report in the *Annals of Vendôme*,[28] and the specific prices given for commodities during the famine bear the hallmark of an annalistic source.[29] The account of Odo's victory over the Viking warlord Catillus at the Battle of Montpensier and Catillus's subsequent murder at 1.6–11 is distorted by unreliable oral traditions and heavily supplemented with invented material, yet it may ultimately derive from an actual battle that Odo fought with William the Pious of Aquitaine in 893.[30] Moreover, Richer's statement that Odo's victories over the Vikings spanned "about five years" *(hoc fere per quinquennium)* is accurate if we take the Battle of Montpensier in 892/893 as representing the end of that period. The manuscript shows that *quinquennium* is a correction for *biennium*, so this may be a case where Richer was attempting to shore up the chronology of his narrative during the editing process.[31]

Curiously, Richer passes over the entire period between Charles's coronation on January 28, 893, and Odo's death in January 898 in silence, leaving out any mention of the sporadic civil war waged between them from 893 to 897. *Historia* 1.12–13 gives the mistaken impression that Odo died shortly after his return from Aquitaine in 893 and that Charles, who had been crowned in his absence, immediately assumed the throne without a struggle. It is possible that

28. *Historia* 1.5. Cf. *Annales Vindocinenses*, s.a. 892, p. 55.

29. *Historia* 1.5: "Iam enim mensura frumenti quae sedeties ducta modium efficit decem dragmis venibat. Gallinatius quoque quatuor dragmis. Ovis vero tribus unciis, atque vacca iabo tollebatur."

30. Christian Lauranson-Rosaz, *L'Auvergne et ses marges (Velay, Gévaudan) du VIIIe au XIe siècle: La fin du monde antique?* (Le Puy-en-Velay: Les Cahiers de la Haute-Loire, 1987), 63–66. Richer may have heard the story of Ingo, the king's standard-bearer at Montpensier and the murderer of Catillus, during his visit to Chartres in 991. At *Historia* 1.11 Ingo is given the castle of Blois and the castellan's widow as a reward for his bravery, making him the legendary ancestor of the counts of Blois and Chartres. See Ferdinand Lot, "L'origine de Thibaud le Tricheur," *Le Moyen Age* 20 (1907): 181–83.

31. See Bamberg, Staatsbibliothek, MS Hist. 5, folio 2^V, line 19. The phrase *et hoc fere per biennium* is also used at 3.94 and 4.79, and may simply be a meaningless piece of filler used to create the impression of temporal precision. See Latouche, "Un imitateur de Salluste," 304.

Richer lacked sources for the second half of Odo's reign, but it would be surprising if he were genuinely unaware of their conflict. Alternatively, he may have avoided mentioning the four-year struggle between Odo and Charles because he viewed them both as legitimately crowned kings and was disinclined to linger on the strife between them.[32] He makes a point of justifying the decision to elect Odo in 888, noting that the West Frankish magnates did so "not as traitors, but as men indignant against their enemies" (i.e., the Vikings). These chapters generally cast Odo in a positive light, depicting both his vigor *(strenuitas)* and boldness *(audacia),* but a passage that was subsequently expunged casts aspersions on his nonroyal blood. "After Odo was made king," Richer writes, "he carried out all of his tasks energetically and successfully, except that when armed violence broke out, he had limited power to settle the disputes."[33] The expunged passage explains that Odo was unable to keep the peace "because the *milites* sometimes scorned to be subject to a person of middling status."[34] Richer may well have struck this passage because he deemed it impolitic to question the origins of Hugh Capet's ancestors at a time when Gerbert was still on good terms with Hugh and Robert the Pious.[35] The fact that he chose to include it in the first place, however, should make us suspicious of his claim to have undertaken the *Historia* at Gerbert's request, for Gerbert would not have been interested in seeing Hugh's claim to the throne undermined after his appointment as archbishop.

Although Richer's account of Odo's reign is incomplete, it does not contain any obvious chronological errors. His treatment of the period between Charles's accession in 898 and the Battle of Soissons in 923 (1.13–1.46), by contrast, is considerably more confused. Chapter 14 begins in the immediate aftermath of Odo's death.

32. For Richer's conception of royal legitimacy, see Bezzola, *Das Ottonische Kaisertum*, 117–23.

33. *Historia* 1.5: "Creatusque rex, strenue atque utiliter omnia gessit, preter quod in militari tumultu raram componendi lites potestatem habuit."

34. Fol. 2^{V}, lines 16–17.

35. See Hoffmann, "Die *Historien* Richers von Saint-Remi," 479.

Richer reports that Charles appointed Odo's brother Robert to be *dux Celticae,* giving him independent control over Neustria.[36] The *Historia* gives the impression of a smooth transfer of power from Odo to Charles, with Robert peacefully accommodating himself to the new king and—initially at least—forgoing any claim to the throne. There is no hint that Charles's formal recognition of Robert as marquis of Neustria was actually part of an agreement negotiated in 897 that cleared the path for Charles to succeed to the throne upon Odo's death.[37] There is, however, a passing allusion to a possible falling out between the two men. Richer states that Charles "followed [Robert's] advice for about four years and became very familiar with him."[38] It is not clear where he derived the period of four years, but the words *fere per quadriennium* are a correction for *plurimum.*[39] That is, Richer originally wrote that Charles "relied heavily on [Robert's] counsel" *(eius plurimum consilio utens),* but subsequently changed this to "employed his counsel for about four years" *(eius fere per quadriennium consilio utens).* Left unsaid is what happened at the end of this period. Assuming that the correction is based on something more than Richer's imagination, it may be a reference to a tradition found in the *Annals of Saint-Vaast* according to which Robert left Charles's court in 900 after Manasses, a *fidelis* of Duke Richard the Justiciar of Burgundy, made disparaging remarks about Robert in the presence of the king.[40] Robert only returned to Charles in 903, after which he appears to have remained faithful to him until 918.[41] Of

36. Historians have traditionally referred to Robert as margrave of Neustria. In the *Historia, Gallia Celtica* is defined as the territory between the Marne and the Garonne (1.2), while Neustria is the area bounded by the Seine and the Loire (1.4).

37. Geoffrey Koziol, "Charles the Simple, Robert of Neustria, and the *Vexilla* of Saint-Denis," *Early Medieval Europe* 14, no. 4 (2006): 361; Yves Sassier, *Hugues Capet: Naissance d'une dynastie,* 61.

38. *Historia* 1.14: "Quem etiam rex Celticae ducem preficit, ac in ea omnium gerendorum ordinatorem concedit, eius fere per quadriennium consilio utens, eique admodum consuescens."

39. Bamberg, Staatsbibliothek, MS Hist. 5, fol. 6^{r}, line 2.

40. *Annales Vedastini,* s.a. 900, p. 82.

41. Auguste Eckel, *Charles le Simple* (Paris: Émile Bouillon, 1899), 57–58. Koziol,

course this incident occurred two years after Charles's accession to the throne, not four, but given the imprecision of Richer's chronology for the first two decades of Charles's reign, it is possible that this is the incident to which he is alluding.

Charles is subsequently led throughout Neustria by Robert, who receives him in his cities and strongholds *(urbibus atque oppidis)*. There is no other evidence to corroborate this journey, but we find similar royal tours at 1.12, where Charles is welcomed in the cities and strongholds of *Belgica*, and at the beginning of book 3, when the newly crowned Lothar is escorted through Neustria by Robert's son, Hugh the Great.[42] It is likely, therefore, that Richer invented the story of Charles's tour of Neustria because it accorded with his views about what should have happened at the beginning of his reign.

Afterwards Charles departs for Saxony, where he appoints Henry the Fowler duke:

> After he had conferred Celtic Gaul on Robert, he departed for Saxony. He made a circuit through the cities, royal estates, and strongholds of this region, taking control of them without any resistance. And there he also appointed Henry, a Saxon distinguished by his royal ancestry, as duke over all of the inhabitants.[43]

Both the tradition and the chronology here are inaccurate. Henry became duke of Saxony after the death of his father, Otto, in 912, not at the beginning of Charles's reign. Nor did he owe his position to Charles, whose rule never extended into East Francia. It is impossible to say whether Richer invented this story outright or if some version of it was circulating at Rheims, but the effect is not merely to advance a West Frankish/Carolingian claim to suzerainty over East Francia (whose last Carolingian king, Louis the Child,

"Charles the Simple," argues convincingly that the relationship between Robert and Charles was considerably more strained during this period.

42. *Historia* 3.3.

43. *Historia* 1.14: "Et sic Rotberto Gallia Celtica collata, in Saxoniam secedit. Cuius urbes sedesque regias lustrans cum oppidis nullo renitente obtinuit. Ubi etiam Heinricum, regio genere inclitum, ac inde oriundum, ducem omnibus preficit."

died in 911), but to suggest that Charles actually wielded power east of the Rhine. The chapter ends with the astounding claim that Charles "held the Slavs [*Sarmatae*] in peaceful submission" and "bound the English and other peoples from across the sea to himself."[44] This is followed by a chronological note added in the margin—"but scarcely for ten years" *(vix tamen per decennium)*—referring, presumably, to Charles's alleged lordship over East Francia and the lands beyond. There is a possibility here that *vix per decennium* is not simply a stab in the dark in a chapter otherwise characterized by chronological vagueness. If Richer actually knew that Louis the Child died in 911 and that Henry was made duke of Saxony in 912, he might have dated Charles's supposed visit to Saxony to this period. It would then be possible to read *vix per decennium* as implying that Charles's rule in Saxony lasted only from the time of Louis's death in 911 until his own control over West Francia unraveled between 920 and 922. There is a further possibility that Richer is simply misremembering Charles's acquisition of Lotharingia—rather than Saxony—in 911, when, after the accession of Conrad to the East Frankish throne, the Lotharingian nobility recognized Charles as king, after which he crossed over the Meuse and asserted his control over this territory.[45]

More light could be shed on this passage if we could determine the original reading of the manuscript with certainty. In the excerpt just cited, the underlined sections were not part of the first draft; Henry's appointment as duke was added later at the bottom of the folio, and the word *Saxoniam* is actually a correction for a word beginning with "B."[46] Pertz suspected that the expunged word was *Belgicam*,[47] which, if correct, would mean that the origi-

44. *Historia* 1.14: "Sarmatas absque prelio subditos habuit. Anglos quoque ac reliquos transmarinorum populos mira benivolentia sibi adegit." The text originally read *militare adegit*, emphasizing the vassal status of these lands. See fol. 6^r, line 12.

45. Eckel, *Charles le Simple*, 93–101.

46. Fol. 6^r, line 9. The appointment of Henry as duke is also found in Frutolf, *Chronicon*, 181, lines 44–45, which demonstrates that it survived into Richer's revised draft.

47. *Richeri historiarum libri IIII*, 573, note m.

nal reading accurately reported Charles's acquisition of Lotharingia in 911.[48] The reading *Belgicam,* however, is doubtful both on palaeographical and contextual grounds. Hartmut Hoffmann, the most recent editor of the manuscript, posits that the expunged word is actually *Baioariam* (Bavaria).[49] *Belgicam* actually makes little sense in light of what Richer has previously written, as we can see if we look at the passage in context:

> Returning home after taking control of everything, he made for Belgica and honored Saint Remigius with outstanding gifts. After he had conferred Celtic Gaul on Robert, he departed for Saxony.[50]

It would scarcely be possible for Charles to "depart" into Belgica if he were already there! Hoffmann's reading of this passage is therefore to be preferred. Richer is consistent in his view that Charles exercised dominion over both Lotharingia and Germany, and we need not treat the revisions here as evidence of a later attempt on his part to emphasize Henry's subordinate status.[51]

Chapter 14 ends ominously, with the statement that "perhaps [Charles] would have remained supremely fortunate throughout, had he not erred so grievously in one matter."[52] The error to which Richer refers is his unseemly devotion to Hagano, a nonnoble *(mediocris)* of Lotharingian origin whom Charles promotes to a position of prominence above any of the leading men of the realm (1.15). At 1.16 Charles holds a council at Soissons, attended by Robert and magnates from all over Gaul. There the excessive deference shown to Hagano by the king provokes the ire of Robert, who leaves the council along with many of the other magnates and begins plotting to seize the crown for himself. This part of the chapter is clear-

48. Eckel, *Charles le Simple,* 91ff.

49. *Historiae,* 50, note i.

50. *Historia* 1.14: "Inde quoque omnibus obtentis rediens, Belgicam repetit ac sanctum Remigium donis egregiis honorat. Et sic Rotberto Gallia Celtica collata, in Saxoniam secedit."

51. Hoffmann, "Die *Historien* Richers von Saint-Remi," 470–71.

52. *Historia* 1.14: "Et forte felicissimus per omnia fuisset, si in uno nimium non errasset."

ly based on the 920 entry for Flodoard's *Annals,* which reports that "almost all of the counts of Francia abandoned Charles at Soissons because he refused to dismiss his counselor Hagano."[53] At the end of 1.16, as part of his effort to seize the throne, Robert schemes to get rid of Archbishop Fulk of Rheims (who had crowned Charles during Odo's absence in Aquitaine and remained his most stalwart supporter), and he subsequently enters into talks with Count Baldwin II of Flanders (d. 918) to detach him from the king. Fulk, however, died in the year 900, twenty years before the council of Soissons. Thus, while according to Richer's own prior statement at least ten years of Charles's reign had elapsed at this point, Robert's rebellion is now linked to an event that took place in 900, during the third year of his reign.

Chapter 17 continues to narrate events that happened in the year 900. When Charles learns of Baldwin's treachery, he besieges and captures the castle of Arras and the abbey of Saint-Vaast, which he turns over to Archbishop Fulk. In his anger at the loss of these possessions, Baldwin plots to kill the archbishop and dispatches one of his vassals, Winemar, to carry out the assassination. After Fulk's murder (1.17) and Winemar's excommunication and death (1.18), Hervey (900–922) is promoted to the see of Rheims (1.19). The newly elected archbishop then mounts a successful campaign to retake the stronghold of Mézières from Count Erlebald of Châtresais. Hervey's capture of Mézières is recorded in Flodoard's *Annals* for the year 920, so Richer has now skipped over the twenty years between his consecration as archbishop and his campaign against Erlebald without alerting the reader.

Richer's confusing intermingling of events from the year 920 (Charles's abandonment at Soissons, Robert's plot to win the throne, Hervey's campaign against Erlebald) with others that happened twenty years earlier (Baldwin's plot to assassinate Fulk, Hervey's succession to the see of Rheims) stems from the difficulty that he encountered when trying to reconcile the chronology of Flodoard's

53. *Annales,* s.a. 920, p. 2.

HRE with that of the *Annals*. The *HRE* is his sole source for the events of the year 900, but it does not assign them a date. Presumably Richer could have discovered the year of Fulk's death in the archives at Rheims, but even if this were not the case, by looking ahead in the *HRE* he could have seen that the abandonment of Charles at Soissons took place after the archbishop's murder, and not before it.[54]

In Flodoard's *Annals* Erlebald now proceeds to King Charles, who was "delaying in the county of Worms, encamped against Henry, the Transrhenish *princeps*."[55] While there, he is slain by unnamed enemies of the king. Flodoard's version of events is characteristically terse. No reason is given for Charles's sudden arrival in the county of Worms, Erlebald's visit to the king, or his murder. Richer fills in the *rationes negotiorum* that are missing in his source, but in the process he gives Erlebald's murder a significance that it does not otherwise possess. At 1.20 Charles withdraws into the county of Worms to speak with Henry, who is depicted as a loyal servant of the West Frankish king. *Sedens contra*, the phrase used by Flodoard to describe Charles's posture in relationship to Henry, is ambiguous enough that Richer may actually have thought that Charles was encamped across the Rhine in order to speak with a vassal rather than to engage in a military campaign, whereas the latter was in fact the case.[56] Erlebald arrives "to complain about his monstrous treatment at the hands of the archbishop of Rheims," that is, to seek relief from the king for Hervey's capture of Mézières. Subsequently a violent quarrel breaks out between some German and Frankish youths, and as Erlebald

54. *HRE* 4.15.

55. *Annales*, s.a. 920, p. 3: "Qui Erlebaldus profectus ad regem, qui tunc morabatur in pago Warmacensi sedens contra Heinricum principem Transrhenensem." The translation is drawn from Bachrach and Fanning, *The Annals of Flodoard of Reims*, 4.

56. See Adalbert of Magdeburg's continuation of the *Chronicle* of Regino of Prüm: *Reginonis abbatis Prumiensis Chronicon cum continuatione Treverensi*, ed. F. Kürze, MGH SRG 50 (Hanover: Hahn, 1890), s.a. 923, p. 157. Although the annalist dates this campaign to 923, it must have happened in 920, as Flodoard reports. See Georg Waitz, *Jahrbücher des deutschen Reichs unter König Heinrich I* (Leipzig: Duncker & Humblot, 1885), 49–50, and note 4; Eckel, *Charles le Simple*, 112; MacLean, *History and Politics*, 237n25.

tries to put an end to the melee, he is killed by the combatants.[57] Henry, suspecting treachery, flees to his ships and is forced to cross back over the Rhine by the king's attendants, who suspect that it is Henry who has come to the meeting with treacherous intent. The chapter ends with an explanation of the importance of this episode: "From that time forward [Henry] was reported to be hostile to Charles."[58] In the next chapter (1.21) Robert of Neustria allies himself with Henry and conspires with other leading men to depose Charles. Richer has thus taken the notice of Erlebald's death in Flodoard's *Annals* and used it to explain the falling out between Charles and Henry, who up to this point had been depicted as a loyal vassal of the West Frankish king.

Charles now retires to Soissons, where a second assembly is held. Robert's partisans once again try to persuade Charles to dissociate himself from Hagano, but they do so in a deliberately half-hearted manner, hoping that he will refuse to heed their admonitions so that they will thereby acquire legitimate grounds for opposing him.[59] If, as seems likely, Richer invented this second council at Soissons and the second warning from Robert to Charles, it may be because he wanted to emphasize both Charles's stubbornness and Robert's awareness that open opposition to a sitting king required extraordinary justification. A marginal comment added later at 1.16 suggests that he wished to present Robert's rebellion not simply as the rash undertaking of a disloyal subject, but as a calculated reaction to two major affronts to his honor: Charles's deference to Hagano and his own exclusion from the royal succession. The note states that "although [Robert] supported the king, he nonetheless envied him his kingdom not a little, since it seemed to him that he ought to have inherited it after the death of his brother."[60]

57. Flodoard, *Annales*, s.a. 920, p. 3, reports only that Charles was "camped opposite to Henry" *(sedens contra Heinricum)*. Richer, *Historia* 1.20, says that Henry was "attending to administrative matters before the king with the utmost fidelity" ("Heinricus apud regem de rerum dispositionibus fidelissime satagebat").

58. *Historia* 1.20.

59. *Historia* 1.21.

60. Fol. 6v: "Quamvis etenim regi faveret, non mediocriter tamen ei regnum invidebat, cum sibi post fratrem hereditandum magis videretur."

Dissatisfaction with this confusing and unnecessary duplication of councils at Soissons evidently prompted Richer to make a change in his revised draft. Frutolf of Michelsberg, in a passage in which he claims to be quoting Richer directly, reports that after Charles's grant of *Gallia Celtica* to Robert and his appointment of Henry as duke of Saxony, he celebrated Easter at Aachen.[61] It was Aachen, rather than Soissons, to which "the leading men from all of Gaul flocked," and it was here that the first signs of dissatisfaction with Charles's devotion to Hagano manifested themselves.[62] In this version of the story it is Henry, not Robert, who warns the king of the consequences that await him if he does not remove Hagano from his inner circle.[63] And just as Robert storms out of the council at Soissons "unbidden" *(iniussus)* at 1.16, here Henry departs the council "without consultation" *(inconsulto).* In Frutolf's *Chronicle* this dispute at Aachen, rather than the fracas at Worms, leads to the falling out between Henry and Robert, which suggests that the account of Erlebald's death at 1.20 was either left out or changed significantly in the process of revision.[64]

We encounter similar narrative redundancy and further difficulty in reconciling the chronology of different sources at chapters 1.28–33, which narrate Robert of Neustria's victory over the Viking warlord Rollo and the subsequent conversion of Rollo's followers to Christianity. Richer's description of the battle (1.28–30) appears

61. Frutolf, *Chronicon,* 181, lines 39–47: "Est autem alius quidam hystoriographus tempora Karoli huius, cuius memoriam pre manibus habemus, suorumque successorum digerens, qui scribit eundem Giselbertum filiam Heinrici duxisse priusquam rex fieret, dum adhuc ducatum amministrasset, ipsumque Heinricum a Karolo ducatum Saxonicum accepisse, et eum ac Ruotpertum, qui postea rex factus est, inter principes, qui a rege propter Haganonem, ut predictum est, defecerant, primos fuisse. *Sic enim dicit:* 'Gallia Celtica Ruotperto collata, Karolus Saxoniam secedit. Cuius urbes sedesque regias perlustrans, nullo resistente obtinuit, ibi quoque Heinricum, regio genere inclitum ac inde oriundum ducem, omnibus donat.' Et post pauca: 'Interea Galliarum urbibus ac oppidis firmiter obtentis, cum paschalis sollemnitas immineret, Aquisgrani palatio rex sese recepit.'"

62. Frutolf, *Chronicon,* 181, lines 47–53.

63. Frutolf, *Chronicon,* 181, lines 50–52.

64. Frutolf, *Chronicon,* 181, lines 52–54.

to incorporate traditions about the famous Battle of Chartres, at which Robert and Richard the Justiciar, duke of Burgundy, defeated Rollo and his men,[65] and his account of the conversion of Rollo's followers by archbishops Witto of Rouen and Hervey of Rheims (1.31–33) draws heavily on the *HRE*, which presents the conversion as a direct result of the battle.[66] The Battle of Chartres is usually dated to 911, and the conversion and settlement of Rollo's men took place in the years immediately following, but Richer locates the battle in the year 921,[67] apparently taking his cue from an unrelated passage in Flodoard's *Annals* in which Robert lays siege to the Normans on the Loire for five months.[68] Flodoard does not provide dates for either the Battle of Chartres or the conversion of Rollo and his followers in the *HRE*, so Richer's erroneous dating of these events appears at first glance to be understandable. Had he compared the *HRE* more carefully with the *Annals*, however, he would have recognized that the events he describes at 1.28–33 could not have taken place after the year 920. The next two chapters of the *HRE* report on Charles's abandonment at Soissons (4.15) and the death of Count Erlebald of Châtresais (4.16), events that Richer knew from Flodoard's *Annals* took place in the year 920. With a minimum of effort, therefore, he could have seen that the Norman conversion he describes at 1.31–33 should have taken place before the council of Soissons at 1.16 and Erlebald's death at 1.20. He thus appears to have deliberately or accidentally conflated the Battle of Chartres with a less important military action that took place ten years later, and once again to have drawn upon Flodoard's *HRE* as a source without realizing —or caring—that the ma-

65. Hoffmann, *Historiae*, 65, chap. 28, note 1; Walther Vogel, *Die Normannen und das fränkische Reich bis zur Gründung der Normandie (799–911)* (Heidelberg: Karl Winter, 1906), 397n2.

66. *HRE* 4.14.

67. *Historia* 1.28 begins with the words *dum haec gerebatur*; the previous two chapters report on a synod held at Trosly-Loire (1.26), the death of Bishop Rodulf of Laon (1.26), and Charles's campaign against Count Ricuin of Verdun (1.27), all events that took place in 921. See Flodoard, *Annales*, s.a. 921, pp. 5–6.

68. Flodoard, *Annales*, s.a. 921, p. 6.

terial he excerpted was not in sync chronologically with the rest of his narrative.[69]

Not only is Richer's account of the Norman conversion at 1.31–33 out of order chronologically, it also duplicates his own previous mention of that conversion. In the *HRE* Flodoard makes it clear that Rollo and his followers were granted the territory around Rouen—the core of what would become the duchy of Normandy—as a result of their agreement to accept Christianity after the Battle of Chartres.[70] The work of converting them was then undertaken by Archbishops Witto and Hervey, and it is this conversion that Richer describes at 1.31–33. Yet earlier in the *Historia* he presents the Norman settlement as having occurred prior to the reign of Odo. At 1.4 the Viking raids that convince the West Frankish magnates to crown Odo rather than the eight-year-old Charles are said to have taken place after the Vikings had already been granted Rouen and the six cities of Bayeux, Avranches, Évreux, Sées, Coutances, and Lisieux. This means that the Norman settlement would have had to have taken place before February of 888.[71] Richer obviously recognized this discrepancy, because at 1.31–33 he ignores any mention of the Norman settlement and treats the conversion of Rollo's followers as a separate and unrelated event. Like the two councils at Soissons, the two conversions of the Normans at 1.4 and 1.31–33 are an unnecessary doublet brought about by Richer's failure to reconcile Flodoard's *Annals,* the *HRE,* and whatever oral traditions he was relying upon.

By the end of the reign of Charles the Simple, as Richer was able to rely more heavily on Flodoard's *Annals* and less on traditions about events that were difficult to date accurately, these kinds of large-scale chronological errors disappear. Yet simple mistakes in the reckoning of time continued to bedevil him. These are particularly noticeable in the obituary notices of Louis IV and Lothar.

69. Carl von Kalckstein, *Geschichte des französischen Königthums unter den ersten Capetingern,* vol. 1 (Leipzig: T. O. Weigel, 1877), 151n2.

70. *HRE* 4.14.

71. *Historia* 1.4.

Richer states that Louis IV died at the age of thirty-six, in the eighteenth year of his reign.[72] Earlier he makes Louis fifteen at his coronation,[73] which is correct since Louis was born in 921 or late 920. But of course if Louis was fifteen years old in 936, then at his death in 954 he would have been thirty-three, not thirty-six. Even greater confusion attends the death of Lothar, which Richer reports as follows:

> And so, having outlived Otto by ten years, in the thirty-seventh year after he had succeeded to the throne upon his father's death, in the forty-eighth year after he had taken up the crown and scepter of rule from his father the king, and in the sixty-eighth year of his life, he died and yielded to nature.[74]

All of this information is incorrect. Lothar died in the year 986, which means that he did not outlive either Otto I (d. 973) or Otto II (d. 983) by exactly ten years. Louis IV died in 954, so that Lothar died in the thirty-second year after he had succeeded to his father's throne, not the thirty-seventh. And Lothar was born in late 941, making him forty-four (not sixty-eight) when he died, ruling out the possibility that he had been crowned by his father forty-eight years earlier. Indeed, if Lothar was sixty-eight when he died, he would have been born in 918, three years before the birth of his own father!

More interesting than these examples of simple carelessness are the cases in which Richer deliberately changes the order of events in Flodoard's *Annals* or draws connections between otherwise unrelated events by eliding the passage of time between them. He reports, for example, that after the Battle of Soissons (June 15, 923) an earthquake struck the county of Cambrai and knocked down a number of houses.[75] "This was a forewarning of the disaster to come," he continues, "when the king was unlawfully taken

72. *Historia* 2.103. The manuscript shows that the number eighteen is a correction from seventeen, and thirty-six a correction from twenty-two. See fol. 31^{V}, lines 11–12.

73. *Historia* 2.4.

74. *Historia* 3.109.

75. *Historia* 1.46.

captive and thrown into prison, there to remain until the end of his days."[76] In fact, Flodoard reports that the earthquake struck Cambrai in 922, a year before the Battle of Soissons.[77] Richer evidently moved the earthquake to the immediate aftermath of the battle in order to make it serve as a premonition of Charles's fate, and perhaps implicitly as a sign of divine displeasure.

He takes similar liberties with a series of portents that appeared in the sky above Rheims in October 934. Flodoard reports that streaks of fire were seen darting across the sky, followed by a pestilence that "afflicted mortal bodies with various sicknesses."[78] A year later, in the fall of 935, King Radulf fell ill, leading to his death in the spring of 936.[79] There is no connection between the pestilence of 934 and Radulf's illness in the *Annals.* In the *Historia,* by contrast, the fiery portents in the sky lead to an outbreak of disease (in this case, erysipelas), and "not long after this" *(nec multopost)* King Radulf falls ill and dies.[80] Richer links together these events despite the fact that he must have known that Radulf did not actually get sick in 935 from a seasonal outbreak of disease a year earlier.[81]

In these two passages Richer manipulates his source material to serve the dramatic interests of the narrative, linking dire portents with events to which they actually had no temporal relationship. In other cases the liberties that he takes with Flodoard's chronology have a political dimension. A case in point is his account of Heribert of Vermandois's irregular acquisition of the see of Rheims for his son Hugh in 925. In that year Flodoard's *Annals* report that "the see of Rheims was entrusted to Count Heribert in the name of his son Hugh, a young boy who was, it was said, not yet five years old."[82] The *HRE* gives a more detailed report: after

76. *Historia* 1.46.
77. Flodoard, *Annales,* s.a. 922, p. 11.
78. Flodoard, *Annales,* s.a. 934, p. 59.
79. Flodoard, *Annales,* s.a 935, p. 62; s.a. 936, p. 63.
80. *Historia* 1.65.
81. *Historia* 1.65. Cf. Flodoard, *Annales,* s.a. 934, p. 59; s.a. 935, p. 62.
82. Flodoard, *Annales,* s.a. 925, pp. 32–33.

the death of Archbishop Seulf, who was rumored to have been poisoned by Heribert's men, Heribert went to Rheims and compelled the clergy and laymen of the city to elect Hugh bishop, a decision that King Radulf subsequently ratified.[83] Richer, on the other hand, presents Hugh's election as the product of a reconciliation between Heribert and King Radulf. The *Historia* says that a quarrel arose between them because "Heribert was making unreasonable demands of the king, while the king refused to grant them, on the grounds that nothing would satisfy him."[84] Heribert subsequently took Charles the Simple out of captivity and tried to reestablish him on the throne as a way of threatening Radulf.[85] When this plan fell through, he reconciled with Radulf at the urging of Hugh the Great, and as a demonstration of his loyalty he returned Charles to captivity at Péronne. In return, he asked Radulf for a reward and was duly granted the see of Rheims for his son.[86]

The problem with Richer's account of these events is that Hugh was consecrated bishop in 925, whereas the quarrel between Heribert and Radulf described at *Historia* 1.52–54 took place between 927 and 928.[87] Between the end of 1.54, therefore, when Charles is put back in prison, and the beginning of 1.55, when Hugh is elected bishop, we leap back in time three years, from 928 to 925. Richer's language follows Flodoard's closely enough to suggest that he had a copy of the *Annals* before him as he wrote.[88] He cannot, therefore, have been unaware of the chronological inaccuracy in his own account. One possible explanation, given his sparing use of the *HRE* and general clumsiness in exploiting it as a source, is that, overlooking the more detailed account of Hugh's election found there, and finding the one-sentence notice in the *Annals* insuf-

83. *HRE* 4.19–20, p. 411.

84. *Historia* 1.52.

85. *Historia* 1.52–54.

86. *Historia* 1.54–55.

87. Flodoard, *Annales*, s.a. 927–28, pp. 37–43. According to Flodoard, Radulf and Heribert were quarreling over the county of Laon.

88. Cf. *Historia* 1.55: "Unde et ab rege donari petens, episcopium Remense *sub optentu filii sui adhuc pueri* ab eo accepit," and *Annales*, s.a. 925, pp. 32–33: "Episcopatus Remensis Heriberto comiti commissus est *sub obtentu filii sui Hugonis, admodum parvuli*, necdum, seu ferebatur, quinquennis."

ficient, he decided to explain Heribert's acquisition of the see by linking it with the reconciliation of Heribert and Radulf. Alternatively, Richer may have sought to further undermine the legitimacy of Hugh's election by denying that the clergy and laymen of Rheims agreed to it, presenting it instead as the result of a royal command. It is significant that no mention is made of the consent of the clergy and the laity to Hugh's appointment at the time. Later, when Radulf falls out with Heribert again and seeks to have Hugh deposed, the townsmen of Rheims remind him that they accepted Hugh on his orders *(regio iussu)*.[89] The king subsequently admits that he erred in foisting Hugh off upon them and asks them to consider the advantages of being ruled by "a good pastor."[90]

A similar motivation underlies Richer's subtly altered account of the restoration of Archbishop Artald to the see of Rheims after the death of Heribert of Vermandois in 943. Artald had been installed as archbishop in 931, after King Radulf had captured Rheims and expelled Hugh,[91] but he lost control of the see nine years later when Heribert and Hugh the Great retook the city.[92] Artald was then induced by threats to relinquish his office and retire to the monastery of Saint-Basle.[93] In Flodoard's *Annals* Artald abandons Saint-Basle immediately after Heribert's death in 943 and returns to Louis, who promises to restore the see of Rheims to him.[94] Richer, however, locates Artald's return to Louis (2.36) prior to Heribert's death (2.37). If we rely on Flodoard's account, the impetus for Artald's reconciliation with Louis appears to have been pure self-interest: with Heribert no longer around, and Hugh the Great less invested in protecting his former ally's nephew, Archbishop Hugh, Artald saw an opportunity to recover his see. In the *Historia*, by contrast, Artald looks less like a calculating opportunist than a loy-

89. *Historia* 1.59.
90. *Historia* 1.60.
91. Flodoard, *Annales*, s.a. 931, p. 51; *Historia* 1.61.
92. Flodoard, *Annales*, s.a. 940, pp. 76–77.
93. Flodoard, *Annales*, s.a. 940, pp. 76–77.
94. Flodoard, *Annales*, s.a. 943, p. 87.

al subject rallying to the king's side at the first opportunity. "When he learned that the king had arrived," Richer writes, "he immediately abandoned whatever had been left to him by [Heribert] and returned to the king, preferring to remain with him and be content with little rather than be held hostage by the gifts of an insatiable tyrant."[95] That Richer made this change with the intention of concealing Artald's self-serving behavior is confirmed by the fact that he also covers up an earlier instance of the archbishop's disloyal backsliding. In his entry for the year 940, Flodoard reports that shortly after giving up the see of Rheims in exchange for the abbeys of Saint-Basle and Avenay (940), Artald left Saint-Basle and joined King Louis, abandoning any pretence of loyalty to Hugh and Heribert.[96] A year later (941) he was still with the king when Louis's army was caught by surprise and destroyed as he was attempting to raise Hugh and Heribert's siege of Laon. Rather than remaining loyal to Louis after this defeat, however, Artald abandoned him and reconciled with Hugh and Heribert, swearing an oath to them and receiving back the abbeys of Saint-Basle and Avenay, along with the manor of Vendresse.[97] No mention of this episode is found in the *Historia*.

Bias and Plot Formation

Calculated silence was one of several techniques that Richer used to mediate between his sources and his audience. Just as he had no qualms about altering the chronology of his sources to advance the dramatic interests of his narrative, he was also more than willing to amplify, embellish, and selectively edit these sources to create a version of history that accorded with his own views about the past. Not surprisingly, with the exception of Hugh and Arnulf, the *Historia* paints an almost wholly positive portrait of the arch-

95. *Historia* 2.36.

96. Flodoard, *Annales*, s.a. 940, p. 77.

97. Flodoard, *Annales*, s.a. 941, p. 82. See also Lauer, *Le règne de Louis IV d'Outre-Mer* (Paris: É. Bouillon, 1900), 71.

bishops of Rheims. Inconvenient facts like Artald's wavering loyalty to Louis IV, Hervey's granting of church lands to his brother and nephew, and Seulf's role in inviting Radulf into West Francia to replace Charles the Simple, are ignored;[98] Fulk is portrayed as a martyr, and Hervey as the heroic rescuer of Charles, while Adalbero and Gerbert are both praised in panegyrical terms. Richer's treatment of the West Frankish kings is more nuanced. His belief in the legitimacy conferred by Carolingian blood jostles up against an appreciation for the effectiveness and consensual governance of Odo, Radulf, and Hugh Capet, while even Robert's rebellion against Charles is presented in such a way that his grounds for opposing the king are made to seem reasonable. The principle according to which Richer reworked Flodoard in recounting the reigns of the West Frankish kings, therefore, was not so much partisan bias as the desire to highlight certain themes.

The most striking aspect of Richer's treatment of the reign of Charles the Simple is his advancement of dubious and unhistorical claims about the extent of his power, chief among them that Charles exercised suzerainty over the lands east of the Rhine. Shortly after his elevation to the throne, Charles is said to have made a tour of Saxony, where he appointed Henry the Fowler duke over all the inhabitants.[99] As we saw earlier, in this passage the word *Saxoniam* was actually a correction for a word beginning with the letter "B," and Charles's appointment of Henry as duke was not part of his original draft, but was added later at the bottom of the folio. At the same time that Richer made these two revisions, he edited another passage dealing with Charles's relationship to Henry. At 1.20, the chapter in which Erlebald of Châtresais comes to visit Charles at Worms, Richer originally wrote that Henry was "busying himself intently establishing friendship" between himself and Charles *(de amicicia inter se habenda plurimum satagebat)* when the fight broke out that killed Erlebald. Subsequently, howev-

98. For Seulf's role in welcoming Radulf, see Flodoard, *Annales,* s.a. 923, p. 14.
99. *Historia* 1.14.

er, he edited the text to say that Henry "was busying himself with administrative matters before the king with the utmost fidelity" *(de rerum dispositionibus fidelissime satagebat).*[100]

On the surface both sets of revisions appear calculated to emphasize Henry's vassal status. A similar agenda has been suspected as the impetus for a series of revisions at 1.22–24 that have prompted exasperated reactions from scholars convinced of Richer's bad faith and proto-nationalist partisanship for the West Frankish Carolingians.[101] At 1.22 Charles, having been rescued from captivity at the hands of Robert's supporters by Archbishop Hervey, sends him to summon Henry the Fowler in the hopes of arranging a reconciliation. The corrected text of the *Historia* reads as follows:

> The king, employing the good counsel of his men, sent Archbishop Hervey of Rheims to summon Duke Henry, who was foremost among everyone in Saxony. For having been persuaded by Robert, he had abandoned the king with the others.[102]

What Richer originally wrote, however, is quite different:

> The king, employing the counsel of Archbishop Hervey of Rheims, sent envoys to summon Gislebert, who was more powerful than everyone in Belgica. For having been persuaded by Henry, he had abandoned the king along with a number of others.[103]

Here it is Hervey (rather than the king's men) who advises the king, and Henry the Fowler (rather than Robert) who works to undermine Charles. More importantly, it is Duke Gislebert of Lothar-

100. Fol. 7v, lines 12–13.

101. See in particular Walther Kienast, *Deustschland und Frankreich in der Kaiserzeit (900–1270),* vol. 1 (Stuttgart: Anton Hiersemann, 1974), 487–91. For the various approaches taken to these chapters, see Giese, *"Genus" und "Virtus,"* 10–16; Bezzola, *Das Ottonische Kaisertum,* 130–33; Hoffmann, "Die *Historien* Richers von Saint-Remi," 450.

102. *Historia* 1.22: "At rex, bono suorum usus consilio, per Heriveum metropolitanum ducem Heinricum, qui in Saxonia omnibus preerat, accersit. Hic enim ab Rotberto persuasus, cum aliis ab rege discesserat."

103. Fol. 8r, lines 26–29: "At Remorum metropolitani Herivei consilio usus, Gislebertum, qui in Belgica omnibus potior erat, per legatos accersit. Hic enim ab Heinrico persuasus, cum aliis nonnullis ab rege discesserat."

ingia—making his first appearance in the *Historia*—rather than Henry the Fowler with whom Charles seeks to reconcile. A related change is made in the next chapter (1.23), a persuasive speech delivered by Hervey. In the revised text of the manuscript Hervey addresses his interlocutor, Henry, as "best of the Germans," and reports that Charles wants him to "be foremost among those who are known to inhabit Germany."[104] Originally, however, the embassy was addressed to Gislebert, who is addressed as "the best of the men of Belgica" *(Belgicorum optime)* and whom, it is said, Charles wishes to rule over "those who are known to inhabit Belgica."[105] In the following chapter the marginal title has also been changed, and the name *Gislebertus* had been replaced by *Heinricus.*[106]

The substitution of Gislebert's name with Henry's at 1.22–24 has been interpreted as an attempt to emphasize Henry's subordinate status, since Charles does not go to meet him at the boundary between their territories, but instead summons him to his court.[107] Georg Heinrich Pertz declared that the change was made "so that [Richer] could pretend that Germany was subject to Charles at that time,"[108] and Wilhelm Wattenbach cited the revised text of these chapters as an example of Richer's willingness to corrupt his own text in order to satisfy a "pathological national vanity."[109] In contrast, Georges Bardot took the position that Richer had purely formal reasons for making the changes.[110] In going back over what he had written, Bardot reasoned, Richer became aware of several inconsistencies in his narrative: he had left Charles and Henry as

104. *Historia* 1.23.

105. Fol. 8^{V}, lines 7 and 13.

106. Fol. 8^{V}, line 16. *Heinricus* has also been added above the line, and over an erasure, at line 26.

107. *Historia* 1.22: "per Heriveum metropolitanum ducem Heinricum, qui in Saxonia omnibus preerat, accersit." See Giese, *"Genus" und "Virtus,"* 10–16.

108. *Historiarum libri IIII*, 564.

109. *Deutschlands Geschichtsquellen im Mittelalter bis zur Mitte des dreizehnten Jahrhunderts*, vol. 1 (Berlin: Wilhelm Hertz, 1893), 415.

110. "Remarques sur un passage de Richer," in *Mélanges carolingiens*, eds. G. Bardot, Ph. Pouzet, and A. Breyton, Bibliothèque de la Faculté des Lettres de Lyon 7 (Paris: Ernest Leroux, 1890), 1–39.

enemies after their dispute at Worms (1.20) despite the fact that Flodoard's *Annals,* in the entry for 921, refers to a treaty between them and a subsequent confirmation of that peace;[111] he had depicted a mending of relations between Charles and Gislebert at 1.23–24, when there was no mention earlier of any dispute between them; and he had shown Gislebert warring against Charles (1.37–38) and then making peace with him through the agency of Henry (1.39), who was presumably still hostile to Charles and who—in the unrevised draft—had incited Gislebert to revolt in the first place (1.22).[112] The same logic also explains why Richer expunged three lines dealing with a visit that Charles paid to Gislebert during an expedition into Lotharingia at 1.27.[113]

Bardot's thesis is persuasive, but it does not explain why Richer also expunged two other mentions of Gislebert that do not create any narrative inconsistency. Chapter 1.28 describes a raid into Neustria led by the Norman warlord Rollo, followed by Robert's mustering of an army to deal with the invaders. Richer originally wrote that four cohorts were sent from Belgica by Gislebert, but he subsequently changed *ab Gisleberto* to *ab rege.*[114] Later in the chapter the words *duce Gisleberto* are expunged as well.[115] Similarly, at 1.30, which describes the battle between the armies of Robert and Rollo, the phrase *Gislebertus cum Belgis inprovisus prosequitur* has been changed to *Belgae inprovisi prosequuntur.*[116] The logic behind Richer's removal of Gislebert's name in these chapters only becomes clear when we look ahead in the manuscript. At 1.34 he reports on the death of the Lotharingian magnate Reginar Longneck (d. 915) and the accession of his son, the aforementioned Gislebert, to his *honores.* These events occur at the beginning of folio 10, which, along with folio 11, seems to have been inserted into

111. Flodoard, *Annales,* s.a. 921, p. 6.

112. "Remarques sur un passage de Richer," 5–6.

113. Fol. 9^r, lines 19–21: "Quid sibi in animo sit Gisleberto demonstrans, habita apud eum conquestione de quibusdam. Eius quoque consilio militum copias colligit, ire volens hostiliter in eos qui nulla penitentia ducti ad sese non redierunt."

114. Fol. 9^r, line 33.

115. Fol. 9^r, line 38.

116. Fol. 9^v, lines 12–13.

the second quire after it was already complete, and may have been part of a prior draft of the *Historia.*[117] The rest of folio 10 contains a hostile description of Gislebert (1.35); Gislebert's plotting against the king (1.36); Charles's subversion of Gislebert's Lotharingian allies (1.37); the siege of the stronghold of Harburc and Gislebert's flight to the court of Henry the Fowler (1.38); Gislebert's temporary reconciliation with Charles and subsequent attempts to enlist Henry as an ally against him (1.39); and Gislebert's alliance with Robert of Neustria (1.40). None of this material is found in Flodoard's *Annals,* and it must have derived from other sources, including, possibly, a written source.[118] The introduction of folio 10 into the second quire created problems of inconsistency with the text that went before it. Specifically, Gislebert's sudden introduction at 1.34 necessitated removing any trace of him from the previous chapters. Thus, the substitution of Gislebert for Henry at 1.22–24 and the removal of Gislebert's name at 1.27, 1.28, and 1.30 appear to be the result of Richer's clumsy attempt to harmonize different sources, rather than a conscious effort to diminish the status of Henry.[119]

Setting aside the changes to the manuscript that resulted from the introduction of folio 10, we are still left with the apparently tendentious edits at 1.14 and 1.20. Upon closer scrutiny, however, neither of these changes is actually as significant or as politically charged as it first appears. In the first place, Richer was consistent in his belief that East Francia belonged by rights to Charles the Simple; this was not a novel claim introduced via the revision at 1.14 in which Charles entered into Saxony and appointed Henry duke.[120] Nor was his reluctance to grant Henry the title of king simply the product of proto-nationalist sentiment or partisanship

117. Waitz, *Richeri Historiarum Libri IIII,* 23, note f; Glenn, "The Composition of Richer's Autograph Manuscript," 167–71; Glenn, *Politics and History,* 143–44; Hoffmann, "Die *Historien* Richers von Saint-Remi," 449–50.

118. Hoffmann, *Historiae,* 3.

119. Wittich, "Richer über die Herzoge Giselbert von Lothringen und Heinrich von Sachsen," 137–38.

120. Hoffmann, "Die *Historien* Richers von Saint-Remi," 470–71.

for Charles. Flodoard, who betrays no obvious bias toward any party in the *Annals,* consistently refers to Henry as *princeps* and only accords him the title of *rex* upon his death at 936.[121] Second, in explaining the appointment of Henry as *dux,* Richer notes that he was "distinguished by royal birth" *(regio genere inclitum).*[122] This statement was not, strictly speaking, true, and it was not the kind of claim that he would have added if his goal was to diminish Henry's status. To the contrary, the attribution of royal blood to the founder of the Saxon royal line implicitly served to justify the rule of Henry's son and successor, Otto I. The revision at 1.20, whereby Henry goes from negotiating with Charles to serving him as a loyal vassal, is simply a consequence of the revision at 1.14: if Charles had already appointed Henry as duke of Saxony, it would make little sense for the two of them to be establishing a relationship of *amicitia* a short time later. Moreover, the fact that in the revised version of the chapter Henry is reported to have been conducting himself "very faithfully" *(fidelissime)* before the king makes his expulsion by Charles's retinue after the fracas that kills Erlebald look all the more unjust. Indeed, in later chapters Henry is depicted as the more sober and mature of the two. Archbishop Hervey, for example, praises Henry for his prudence, generosity, and loyal service to his lord, and is compelled to apologize for Charles's immature behavior (1.23).

Richer's sympathy toward Charles and his erroneous belief that he held sway over the lands east of the Rhine cannot, therefore, be interpreted as part of a broader program to delegitimize Ottonian rule. The most important proof of this is that Richer abandons West Frankish claims to dominion over both Germany and Lotharingia over the course of books 2 and 3. At 2.16 he still appears to treat *Germania* as an area that belonged to Louis IV,[123]

121. *Annales,* s.a. 936, p. 64. Before this Flodoard refers to Henry as *princeps Transrhenensis* and *Germaniae princeps.*

122. Bezzola, *Das Ottonische Kaisertum,*132.

123. *Historia* 2.16: "Comperto vero contra regem illorum neminem stare, ipsumque regem in partes Germaniae prosperum secessisse, mari remenso ad propria remeat." See Hoffmann, "Die *Historien* Richers von Saint-Remi," 471.

but at 2.18 he grudgingly recognizes that Henry had been elected king of Saxony, and although he apparently revoked the royal title from him in his revised draft,[124] he does not call into question the rights of Henry's descendants to undisputed rule in Germany.[125] Otto I is first accorded the title of *rex* at 2.29. He is referred to as *rex Saxoniae* in the next chapter, and subsequently given the titles *rex Germanorum* (2.49, 3.67), *rex Transrhenensium* (2.49), and *rex Germaniae et Italiae* (3.44).[126] Otto II is referred to as *augustus* or *caesar augustus* throughout the disputation at Ravenna,[127] and at 3.67 Richer reports that he was elected king "by the Germans and the Lotharingians" *(a Germanis Belgisque).*

Richer's tendentious claims about the extent of Charles the Simple's power were not intended to undermine the legitimacy of the Ottonian emperors, who were, after all, Gerbert's patrons. His conviction that Charles presided over an empire that included not only Lotharingia and Germany, but also the territories of the Slavs and the lands across the English Channel, seems to have sprung from nostalgia and wishful thinking as much as anything else.[128] At the beginning of the *Historia* he refers to Charles's grandfather and namesake, Charles the Bald, as "the celebrated emperor of the Germans and the Gauls," although Charles's rule over a unified empire was limited to the brief period between his coronation on Christmas Day of 875 and his death less than two years later.[129] Richer evidently granted the same imperial rights to Charles the Simple, ignoring the fact that Carolingian rule persisted in East

124. Frutolf, *Chronicon,* 186, lines 27–30.

125. For Richer's perspective on the Ottonian kings, see Bezzola, *Das Ottonische Kaisertum,*123–37, and Bernd Schneidmüller, "Widukind von Corvey, Richer von Reims und der Wandel politischen Bewußtseins im 10. Jahrhundert," in *Beiträge zur mittelalterlichen Reichs- und Nationsbildung in Deutschland und Frankreich,* ed. Bernd Schneidmüller and Carlrichard Brühl (Munich: R. Oldenbourg, 1997), 97–99.

126. At 2.61 Richer originally referred to Otto I as *rex Belgicae* before expunging this word. See fol. 25^r, line 12.

127. *Historia* 3.56–60, 3.65.

128. See Bezzola, *Das Ottonische Kaisertum,* 132.

129. *Historia* 1.4. Richer incorrectly refers to Charles the Bald as Charles the Simple's great-grandfather.

Francia under Arnulf (887–899) and his son Louis the Child (900–911).[130] His belief that Charles was the legitimate heir to the whole Carolingian empire also explains his erroneous claim that Charles was crowned at Saint-Rémi by the archbishops of Mainz, Cologne, and Trier.[131]

Although Richer promoted an entirely unhistorical view of Charles's power, he was hardly blind to the king's faults. From the beginning of Charles's reign it is implied that he lacks the necessary qualities to be an effective king. He is first described as *ingenio bono simplicique*—"of good and sincere character." *Simplicitas*—naïveté or guilelessness—was a quality ill-suited to a king in the brutal and treacherous world of the early tenth century, and in Richer's telling it leads directly to Charles's downfall when he foolishly lends credence to the promises of Heribert of Vermandois and goes to meet him without a large retinue (1.47).[132] In pointed contrast to Odo, who is described as "a vigorous warrior" and "a daring and violent man," and whose reign is characterized by military successes over the Vikings culminating in his triumph at Montpensier, Charles was "not particularly accustomed to military training."[133] He was, moreover, "conspicuous for a lack of self-control over his bodily lusts, and a certain degree of negligence in carrying out judgments."[134] Charles is thus depicted as frivolous and irresponsible, unable to subordinate his own desires to the responsibilities of office.[135]

These defects might not have been fatal had Charles placed himself in the hands of capable advisors. Instead, he ignores the advice of his counselors, and rather than seeking consensus from the leading men, a prerequisite for successful kingship, he dishon-

130. Arnulf was the bastard son of Charles the Fat's elder brother Carloman (d. 880).

131. *Historia* 1.12.

132. On the sobriquet *simplex*, sometimes translated as "straightforward," see Geoffrey Koziol, "Is Robert I in Hell? The Diploma for Saint-Denis and the Mind of a Rebel King (Jan. 25, 923)," *Early Medieval Europe* 14, no. 3 (2006): 238n14.

133. *Historia* 1.14. For Odo, see 1.5.

134. *Historia* 1.14.

135. *Historia* 1.24.

ors them by promoting his Lotharingian favorite Hagano to the role of chief counselor (1.15), a move rendered all the more foolish by the fact that it alienates Robert of Neustria, whose support he could ill afford to lose.[136] Robert leaves the king's council disgusted by Charles's frivolity *(levitas)*, the same vice that later characterizes his great-grandson, Louis V, the last king of the Carolingian line.[137] In a sense Charles's reign plays out as a tragedy in the *Historia*: a basically virtuous king *(ingenio bono)* who lacks both guile and experience in military matters rules successfully for several years *(vix tamen per decennium)* but commits a fatal error that sets in motion a series of events leading to his downfall and the dissolution of a united Carolingian empire.

Richer's desire to impose a tragic structure on Charles's life and career may also help to explain his curiously distorted account of the Battle of Soissons, Charles's final, failed attempt to take back his kingdom from Robert. In Flodoard's *Annals*, Robert's son Hugh and Heribert of Vermandois force Charles and his Lotharingian supporters to flee, after which they take control of the battlefield and seize spoils; Flodoard states unequivocally that Robert's allies were victorious.[138] Richer, by contrast, presents the battle as a stalemate, with both sides declaring themselves the victors.[139] He claims that Hugh did not stay on the field long enough to seize spoils, and that while Charles could have done so, he was not tempted by greed and thought it potentially dangerous to do so with Robert's army still lurking about.[140] Nor, in his version of events, is Charles compelled to flee. Instead, he departs for Lotharingia in good order, intending to return later in force.[141] Charles subsequently musters a larger army and prepares to lead it into West Francia, striking fear into his rebellious subjects and causing

136. In the *Historia*—and in Flodoard's *Annals*—Charles's promotion of Hagano drives away an otherwise faithful Robert. The reality was more complicated. See Koziol, "Charles the Simple, Robert of Neustria, and the *Vexilla* of Saint-Denis."

137. *Historia* 1.16.

138. *Annales*, s.a. 923, p. 13.

139. *Historia* 1.46.

140. *Historia* 1.46.

141. *Historia* 1.46.

them to adopt a more submissive demeanor.[142] When news reaches him that Radulf has been crowned by the magnates, however, he allows himself to be lured to the fateful meeting with Heribert of Vermandois. Richer's account of the battle and its aftermath suggests that Charles came within a hair's breadth of keeping his kingdom, and that it was only Heribert's treachery that undid him.

One of the tools that Richer uses to create the impression that the Battle of Soissons was a draw rather than a Robertian victory is the invention of army sizes and casualty statistics. Like all medieval chroniclers, Richer was forced to estimate when it came to providing numbers for the sizes of armies or the number of men killed in a battle. Yet the nonchalance with which he alters the figures found in Flodoard's *Annals* or invents his own numbers when Flodoard is silent is nonetheless striking. For the Battle of Soissons he cites a figure of 10,000 men for Charles's army, making it half the size of Robert's, but the multiple revisions in the manuscript make it clear that he was pulling these numbers out of thin air.[143] Even more egregious is his attribution to Flodoard of casualty figures that he himself invented. He reports that 7,118 men died on Charles's side and 11,349 men on Robert's, citing Flodoard as his source despite the fact no such figures are found in either the *Annals* or the *HRE.*[144]

The trend of fabricated numbers continues with a series of encounters between Viking raiders and kings Radulf (923–936) and Louis IV (936–954). Flodoard's account of a battle between the forces of the Viking warlord Ragenold and a group of Burgundian magnates at Chalmont in January 925 reports that more than 800 of the Vikings were killed, but Richer changes the number of Viking dead to 950.[145] In response to Ragenold's raids, Radulf led an

142. *Historia* 1.46.

143. *Historia* 1.44. Fol. 11^{r}, line 22, of the manuscript shows that he originally wrote 5,000, which he crossed out and replaced with 6,000, before changing it to 10,000.

144. *Historia* 1.46.

145. Flodoard, *Annales,* s.a. 925, p. 27: "plus quam DCCC sternunt." Two of the manuscripts used by Lauer read *DCCCC.* The battle actually took place on Dec. 6, 924. See Hoffmann, *Historiae,* 84n8.

army against a Viking camp on the Seine. According to Flodoard, a number of Vikings were killed by the royal army, but the survivors managed to escape from their camp with the connivance of some of the king's forces, who failed to establish a siege.[146] Richer, by contrast, describes a rout in which the king's forces set fire to the Viking camp, kill 3,000 of the enemy in a pitched battle, and force the rest to flee to the coastal stronghold of Eu.[147] Flodoard's *Annals* report that in 926 1,100 Vikings were killed in a battle with King Radulf at Faucembergues; Richer inflates the number of casualties to 8,000.[148] At 2.35 Richer gives a detailed description of a battle between King Louis IV and the Viking leaders Sihtric and Turmod near Rouen in 943. While Flodoard gives no figures for the size of the armies or the number of those slain, Richer reports that Louis brought 800 men into battle and killed 9,000 of the enemy (!)—a correction for his original figure of 4,000.[149]

Although Richer's method of devising army sizes and casualty statistics is disconcertingly casual, it is not arbitrary; in most cases his inventions or amplifications have a discernible purpose. Inventing huge army sizes magnified the importance of a battle, while increasing the number of enemy casualties (e.g., the 9,000 Vikings killed by Louis near Rouen, or the 8,000 by Radulf at Faucembergues) served to aggrandize the victor and glorify his achievement. Suspiciously precise numbers like the casualty figures at the Battle of Soissons must have been designed to lend credibility to his account. After all, who would bother to provide such an exact figure unless he had a legitimate source? In every case Richer's goal was to increase the dramatic impact of his narrative. Thus, he inevitably increases the numbers he finds in Flodoard, and when he changes his own figures, he almost always revises them upward.[150]

146. Flodoard, *Annales,* s.a. 925, pp. 28–29.

147. *Historia* 1.49.

148. *Historia* 1.51. Cf. Flodoard, *Annales,* s.a. 926, p. 33.

149. Fol. 20^{v}, line 28. Cf. Flodoard, *Annales,* s.a. 943, p. 88.

150. An exception to this rule is found at fol. 9^{r}, line 33 (*Historia* 1.28), where Richer changes the nine cohorts sent by Gislebert of Lotharingia to aid Robert into four cohorts sent by King Charles.

Richer's fictitious account of the destruction of the Viking camp on the Seine and his magnification of the victory at Faucembergues are consistent with his largely favorable portrayal of Radulf. This is not necessarily to be expected from an author sympathetic to Charles, for Radulf was invited into West Francia and crowned in the immediate aftermath of the Battle of Soissons, when Charles retained some hope of recovering his kingdom and was still attempting to persuade the magnates to come back to him.[151] Richer, however, places the blame for Radulf's elevation to the throne squarely on the shoulders of the magnates, foremost among them his bête noir Heribert of Vermandois.[152] He portrays Radulf as an unwilling replacement for Charles,[153] ignoring Flodoard's statement that Radulf hurried to come to the magnates with a large band of troops as soon as he was summoned.[154] After his coronation Radulf continues to manifest admirable qualities. He visits Charles in prison and humbly seeks his pardon, not out of political expediency, but "in order to demonstrate the rectitude with which he lived his life."[155] When he captures Rheims from Heribert and expels the boy-bishop Hugh, he delivers a speech to the townsmen in which he admits to having erred more seriously in foisting Hugh off upon them than they did in refusing him access to the city.[156] Elsewhere he is shown governing with the consent of the

151. Flodoard, *Annales,* s.a. 923, p. 14: "Karolus dehinc Heribertum comitem, Seulfum archiepiscopum, ceterosque regni primates multis legationibus ut ad se revertantur exorat."

152. *Historia* 1.47: "Galli a pertinatia nullatenus quiescentes, Rodulfum Richardi Burgundionis filium accitum, apud urbem Suessonicam eo licet satis reclamante regem sibi prefecerunt...Quod Heribertus tantorum malorum incentor sese velle dissimulans, Karolum regem per legatos accersit." See also the revised version in Frutolf, *Chronicon,* 181, lines 15–18, where Hugh and Heribert conspire together to bring Radulf in as king.

153. *Historia* 1.47: "eo licet satis reclamante."

154. Flodoard, *Annales,* s.a. 923, p. 14: "pro Rodulfo in Burgundiam transmiserunt, qui ocius cum multa suorum manu illis occurit." Richer also conspicuously fails to mention that Archbishop Seulf of Rheims was one of the magnates complicit in bringing in Radulf to replace the still-living Charles.

155. *Historia* 1.55.

156. *Historia* 1.60.

magnates,[157] giving generously to the monastery of Saint-Rémi,[158] and dealing swiftly and successfully with the Viking incursions that occupied him for much of the first half of his reign.[159]

In order to aggrandize Radulf's victories over the Vikings while simultaneously depriving Heribert of any of the credit, Richer plays down the level of cooperation between the two men and studiously excises all mentions of Heribert from Radulf's early campaigns. He leaves out Heribert's participation in Radulf's punitive expedition against the Viking war band that had devastated Burgundy in 925,[160] and he gives Radulf sole credit for the successful assault on the Viking stronghold of Eu later that year, although it is clear from Flodoard's *Annals* that Heribert and Arnulf of Flanders led the attack, whereas Radulf was actually at Beauvais.[161] In the following year Radulf and his troops destroyed a Norman army in the county of Arras; Flodoard reports that Radulf and Heribert together besieged the Normans, who were trapped in a wooded area, and that when the Normans broke out and attacked the king's camp at night, Heribert prevented Radulf from being captured.[162] In Richer's version of events no mention is made of Heribert, and Radulf receives all the credit for the victory.[163] As was the case with Odo, the picture of Radulf that emerges in the *Historia* is that of a vigorous and effective king whose ability to exercise control over the magnates is nonetheless undermined by doubts about the legitimacy of his rule. At the beginning of book 2, Hugh the Great declares that Radulf was unable to quell *discordia* because of the lack of respect for his nonroyal birth.[164] This statement recalls the expunged passage early in book 1 in which Richer notes that Odo was unable to prevent violent quarrels from breaking out because "the *milites* sometimes scorned to be subject to a person of middling status."[165]

157. See *Historia* 1.48–49.

158. *Historia* 1.49.

159. In 924 Radulf levied a tribute to be turned over to the Vikings to secure peace; he fought battles against Viking war bands in 925, 926, and 930.

160. *Historia* 1.49. Cf. Flodoard, *Annales*, s.a. 925, p. 28.

161. *Historia* 1.50. Cf. Flodoard, *Annales*, s.a. 925, pp. 31–32.

162. *Annales*, s.a. 926, p. 33.

163. *Historia* 1.51.

164. *Historia* 2.2.

165. Fol. 2^{v}, lines 6–17.

Not surprisingly it is Radulf's successor Louis IV, the king whom Richer's father served, toward whom he demonstrates the most overt favoritism. A comparison of the *Historia* with Flodoard's *Annals* shows that Richer adapted his source with an eye toward improving Louis's image, amplifying, distorting, and editing Flodoard to burnish Louis's reputation and shift the blame for the failures of his reign onto Hugh the Great. Ironically, it is Hugh, a constant thorn in Louis's side for most of his reign, who at the beginning of book 2 convinces the other magnates to recall Louis from exile and crown him king. Flodoard gives no explanation for Hugh's surprising decision not to seek the crown for himself, stating matter-of-factly that "Count Hugh sent across the sea to summon Louis, the son of Charles, to take up the throne."[166] In accordance with his stated intention of elucidating *rationes negotiorum,* Richer seizes the occasion to provide an explanation for Hugh's motives. In a speech delivered to the assembled West Frankish magnates, Hugh admits that his father committed a crime by ruling while the true king lived, and suggests that bringing a non-Carolingian to the throne would lead to contempt for the royal office and civil strife. The speech is one of the high-water marks of the *Historia:* a convincing exposition of how Hugh might have publicly justified his refusal of the throne delivered with true literary artistry.

In much the same way that Robert of Neustria initially accommodated himself to the rule of Charles the Simple (1.14), Hugh serves Louis as a devoted follower at the beginning of his reign. In a gesture signifying his submission to the king-designate, he brings a horse for Louis to mount upon his arrival in Francia and subsequently serves as Louis's squire *(armiger),* carrying his arms and going before him until he is relieved by the other magnates.[167] After his coronation, Louis yields to Hugh's urging and makes a tour of Burgundy, visiting "royal cities and residences" and receiv-

166. *Annales,* s.a. 936, p. 63.

167. *Historia* 2.4. An expunged passage at fol. 15^{v}, lines 25–27, specifies that Heribert and Arnulf served as *armigeri* after Hugh.

ing oaths of fidelity from the magnates of the region.[168] There he defeats the lone holdout against his authority, Hugh the Black (the late King Radulf's brother), by besieging and capturing the city of Langres, after which he returns to Paris with the duke in triumph. The royal tour described by Richer in these chapters bears little resemblance to what we find in the *Annals,* however. In Flodoard's version of events the sole purpose of the expedition is to recapture Langres from Hugh the Black, who had seized it after the death of Radulf.[169] Instead of Louis asserting his authority over the region with Hugh's assistance, Hugh the Great and Hugh the Black divide the duchy of Burgundy between themselves.[170] Whereas Richer portrays Hugh as a loyal follower of the king and the king himself as the undisputed master of Burgundy, Flodoard's account gives the impression that Hugh was simply using Louis to advance his own claims in the area.[171]

Richer's decision to represent the expedition as a successful assertion of royal authority on Louis's part colors his explanation of the king's subsequent decision to remove himself from Hugh's supervision. Flodoard says only that "the king withdrew himself from the oversight of Duke Hugh," but the natural conclusion is that he resented being used as a pawn to help Hugh take control of Burgundy.[172] Richer claims instead that Louis, "puffed up by the success of his good fortune, decided that his affairs could be managed without the duke's oversight."[173] Louis's rash decision to rule without the advice and consent of Hugh, the most powerful nobleman in his realm, recalls Charles the Simple's foolish alienation of Robert of Neustria, and Richer uses similar language to describe the disastrous consequences of their actions.[174] He subsequently excuses Louis's failure to take any action against the Hungarians during the devastating invasion of 937, although he was at Laon

168. *Historia* 2.5.

169. *Annales,* s.a. 936, p. 64.

170. Flodoard, *Annales,* s.a. 936, p. 65.

171. Lauer, *Le règne de Louis IV,* 16–17.

172. Lauer, *Le règne de Louis IV,* 18.

173. *Historia* 2.6.

174. *Historia* 2.6: "Quod etiam fuit non minimae [originally *magnae*] labis seminarium." Cf. 1.15: "Quod etiam multam regi intulit labem."

and could have led an army against them, on the grounds that the king had been deserted by his followers.[175] To the degree that he had lost the support of the magnates, however, it was because he had dismissed Hugh and taken control of the administration of military affairs earlier that year.[176]

After the falling out between Louis and Hugh, Richer emphasizes Hugh's recalcitrance, deceitfulness, and cruelty. From this point on he frequently refers to Hugh as a "tyrant" *(tirannus)*[177] and makes subtle, and not-so-subtle, alterations to Flodoard's *Annals* to justify and illustrate this epithet.[178] His account of Hugh's efforts to secure Louis's release after his capture by the Viking warlord Harald in 945 is a case in point. Flodoard says that Hugh worked to secure the king's release, and that after the Normans demanded Louis's sons as hostages, a message was sent to Queen Gerberga to request that she turn them over.[179] No account is given of Hugh's motives, although when he hands the king over to his vassal Theobald le Tricheur it becomes clear that it was self-interest rather than loyalty that made him eager to secure his release.[180] Richer spells out what is only implicit in Flodoard. He states explicitly that Hugh went to Bayeux to thank the Normans for capturing Louis; that he negotiated the king's release so that he could have him in his power; and that he concealed the king's captivity from Queen Gerberga when he sent to ask her for her two sons.[181] For good measure, he advances the claim that Hugh's intention was to do away with the royal line by getting rid of Louis and his sons.[182]

175. *Historia* 2.7. See Lauer, *Le règne de Louis IV*, 26–27.

176. *Historia* 2.6.

177. Prior to Hugh's estrangement from the king, Richer never refers to him as a tyrant. It subsequently becomes one of his standard epithets. See *Historia* 2.22, 2.24, 2.26, 2.27, 2.28, 2.36, 2.81, 2.82, 2.85, and 2.87.

178. It is perhaps not accidental that Richer leaves out examples of Hugh's cruelty before his disagreement with Louis. See, e.g., the executions and maimings he carries out after capturing the *castrum* of Saint-Quentin: Flodoard, *Annales*, s.a. 933, p. 57.

179. Flodoard, *Annales*, s.a. 945, p. 99.

180. See Lauer, *Le règne de Louis IV*, 134–35.

181. *Historia* 2.48.

182. *Historia* 2.48.

Other examples of tendentious changes to Flodoard are not hard to find. Richer makes no mention of Hugh's successful campaign in Normandy in 943,[183] but amplifies considerably the brief notice about Louis's victory over the Viking chiefs Turmod and Sihtric that same year.[184] While Flodoard reports that in 947 Hugh was persuaded "by certain people" to attack the city of Rheims during the king's absence,[185] in the *Historia* it is Hugh who convinces his men to undertake the siege as part of a calculated affront to the king.[186] In the *Annals* Hugh lays siege to the city of Soissons in the summer of 948, prior to his excommunication at the Synod of Trier later that year.[187] Richer pushes the excommunication back to an assembly of bishops held at Laon before Hugh's campaign, which allows him to claim that Hugh greeted the anathema issued by the bishops with contempt.[188] In Flodoard's account of Hugh's attack on the village of Cormicy, near Rheims, in the summer of 948, he says that Hugh's "brigands" *(praedones)* killed about forty people while plundering the church.[189] Richer claims that Hugh himself, "showing no mercy to the throngs of the poor," was responsible for burning more than 560 people to death inside the churches.[190]

In addition to adapting the *Annals* to emphasize Hugh's villainy, Richer leaves out a considerable amount of material that had the potential to reflect poorly on Louis. This includes an attack on his own vassals,[191] acts of treachery committed by his *fideles*,[192] depredations inflicted upon the city of Rheims and the surround-

183. Flodoard, *Annales*, s.a. 943, p. 88.

184. *Historia* 2.35.

185. Flodoard, *Annales*, s.a. 947, p. 104.

186. *Historia* 2.62.

187. *Annales*, s.a. 948, pp. 117, 119.

188. *Historia* 2.85. Richer displaces the events of the Synod of Trier to the council at Laon. See *Historia* 2.82, and Flodoard, *Annales*, s.a. 948, pp. 116, 118–20.

189. *Annales*, s.a. 948, p. 117.

190. *Historia* 2.85.

191. Lauer, *Le règne de Louis IV*, 107n2.

192. Flodoard, *Annales*, s.a. 944, p. 91: Louis's *fideles* capture the stronghold of Montigny-Lengrain through treachery; s.a. 944, p. 92: Rodulf betrays the *munitio* of Clastres to the sons of Heribert of Vermandois.

ing area by his armies,[193] a plot by his men against Otto I when the two kings were at peace,[194] and Otto's humiliating expulsion of Louis's envoys in response to reports that Louis was slandering him behind his back.[195] While the exclusion of any one of these episodes could be explained on the grounds of its marginal relevance to the overall thrust of the narrative, taken together, they suggest that Richer was consciously skipping over material that did not accord with the picture of Louis that he was trying to create.

A similar impulse informs Richer's subtly altered portrayal of the last years of Louis's reign. Flodoard reports than in 950 Louis went to his brother-in-law, Otto I of Germany, and sought his help in arranging a peace agreement with Hugh. Otto in turn promised to send Duke Conrad the Red of Lotharingia, along with some Lotharingians, to see to it.[196] Conrad, accompanied by "certain bishops and counts," subsequently went to speak with Hugh, after which Louis and Hugh came to opposite sides of the Marne River and negotiated through intermediaries (the dukes Conrad and Hugh the Black of Burgundy, and the bishops Adalbero of Metz and Fulbert of Cambrai). As a result of the negotiations Hugh agreed to become Louis's vassal, to reconcile with Count Arnulf of Flanders and Artald of Rheims, and to return Laon to Louis.[197] In Richer's account Hugh's sudden desire to reconcile with Louis is not the result of pressure from Otto and Conrad (whose mission is not mentioned), but of warnings from the bishops of Gaul

193. Flodoard, *Annales,* s.a. 944, p. 93: royal *milites* plunder the diocese of Rheims, taking vengeance against the sons of Heribert for the capture of Clastres; s.a. 945, p. 96: The area around Rheims is devastated by Louis's army during the siege of the city. See also *HRE* 4.31.

194. *Annales,* s.a. 943, p. 90.

195. Flodoard, *Annales,* s.a. 944, pp. 92–93, reports on a contentious meeting at Aachen between Otto, the Lotharingians, and envoys from Hugh and Louis. Otto is initially hostile to Hugh's envoys, but one of them, Manasses, reveals certain *mandata* from Louis that criticized Otto and accused him of being a perjurer. After this Otto expels Louis's envoys and welcomes those of Hugh. None of this is included in the *Historia,* where after the treaty of 942 Louis and Otto remain firm allies.

196. *Annales,* s.a. 950, p. 126.

197. *Annales,* s.a. 950, p. 127.

about the folly of persecuting one's lord and the threat to his soul posed by excommunication.[198] Chastened by their admonitions, Hugh "humbly requests" to be reconciled with the king and promises to make satisfaction to him.[199] In this way a turn of events that in Flodoard's *Annals* looks like a political maneuver orchestrated by Otto becomes an act of genuine submission and repentance on Hugh's part.

Afterward, Richer reports, Louis and Hugh "cherished one another in friendship with a devotion equal to the hostility with which they had assailed one another in the past."[200] With this statement the storyline of Hugh and Louis, which has occupied almost all of book 2, comes to an end. Rheims and Laon are both back in Louis's possession, and Hugh is subject (at least nominally) to the king's authority once more. Flodoard's *Annals* show that the peace between them was short-lived, however. Later that same year Hugh took advantage of Louis's illness to gain entrance to Amiens (which was held by Arnulf of Flanders, an ally of the king with whom Hugh had made peace on the Marne), and from that point relations between the two men deteriorated until a "confirmation" of their previous peace (really a new treaty) was agreed to three years later.[201] The misrepresentation involved here is comparatively minor: Louis did end his reign reconciled to Hugh, if not exactly in the manner recounted in the *Historia*. It is nonetheless important, because it allows Richer to bring Louis's reign to a close on an unambiguously triumphal note. The untidy series of events from 950 to 953 in Flodoard's *Annals* is swept away, replaced by a simplified version of the past that sees Hugh and Louis return to the harmony that prevailed between them before the Burgundian expedition of 936.

Richer's goal in this case was not to deflect all criticism from Louis, but to present a particular narrative of his reign, that of a

198. *Historia* 2.96.

199. *Historia* 2.97.

200. *Historia* 2.97.

201. Flodoard, *Annales*, s.a. 950, p. 127. See Lauer, *Le règne de Louis IV*, 209–10, 214–15, 223.

capable and legitimate king who, after making a serious error in judgment by alienating Hugh the Great, is subsequently undermined and abandoned by him, but is restored to power through the combined intervention of secular and religious authorities (Otto I of Germany, on the one hand, the papacy and the West Frankish bishops, on the other). Richer never directly criticizes Louis, but he alludes to his mistakes, which are manifestations of the same character flaws that undid his father: stubbornness, naïveté, and self-pity. Charles's foolish refusal to give up Hagano is paralleled by Louis's rash decision to remove himself from the supervision of Hugh the Great.[202] Charles's failure to listen to his counselors is analogous to the complaint of the Lotharingian magnates that Louis did everything without seeking advice first.[203] As Charles delivered himself unsuspectingly into the hands of Heribert of Vermandois, Louis falls into a trap set for him by Harald, the Norman ruler of Bayeux.[204] And whereas Charles complains to his men about his abandonment by the West Frankish magnates, Louis complains in public and in private about his treatment at the hands of Hugh the Great.[205] Unlike Charles, Louis is a brave and vigorous warrior, but like his father he is ultimately abandoned, betrayed, and imprisoned, left to appeal to outside help to regain his throne.

Richer's approach to Louis's reign is characteristic of his methodology as a whole. He does not simply produce an amplified version of Flodoard's *Annals*: he brings into relief particular plot lines and themes and then uses amplification, selective editing, and occasionally distorted chronology, to make them as clear as possible. We can see this process at work elsewhere. Charles's reign, as previously mentioned, unfolds like a tragedy: he rules successfully over a united empire until a single error, after which he is aban-

202. *Historia* 2.6.

203. *Historia* 2.16. Significantly, the chapter title is *Belgicorum querimonia apud regem super eius levitate.*

204. *Historia* 2.47.

205. *Historia* 2.52, 2.73.

doned and loses his throne. In the case of Odo and Radulf, thematic clarity is probably a more accurate term than plot to describe the manner in which Richer gives unity to their reigns. Both are presented as vigorous *(strenuus)* rulers and successful warriors whose ability to rule is undermined by concerns about their legitimacy.

Evidence for this same tendency toward thematic simplification can be discerned even when Richer was no longer using written sources that can serve as a point of comparison. The brief reign of Louis V (986–987) is characterized by immaturity and weakness.[206] Hugh Capet embodies the vigor of his Robertian forebears but also must deal with questions of legitimacy, which gnaw at his conscience.[207] Thematic unity is more difficult to find in Richer's account of Lothar's reign, which revolves around three conflicts: his attempt to seize Lotharingia from Otto II (3.67–81), his dispute with Hugh Capet (3.82–90), and a renewed attempt to assert control over Lotharingia during the minority of Otto IIII (3.99–108). Because the Lotharingian campaigns pitted Lothar against Gerbert's Ottonian patrons and Adalbero's Lotharingian relatives, while Hugh was responsible for Gerbert's appointment to the see of Rheims, Richer's tone in these chapters is, for the most part, studiously neutral, and the portrait of Lothar that emerges is ambiguous.[208] There is, however, a turning point in the narrative, a secret peace treaty negotiated between Lothar and Otto II at Margut-sur-Chiers in the late spring or early summer of 980.[209] Richer reports that after the treaty Lothar could no longer rely on the duke, "since, because of the peace that had been obtained through treachery [*dolo*], he was more than a little mistrustful of him." Hugh, in other words,

206. *Historia* 3.95, 4.1–4.

207. *Historia* 4.39.

208. Giese, *"Genus" und "Virtus,"* 95. Note in particular the way that Richer talks about Adalbero's relatives at 3.103: "Belgicae dux Teodericus, necnon et vir nobilis ac strenuus Godefridus, Sigefridus quoque vir illustris, Bardo etiam et Gozilo fratres clarissimi et nominatissimi." Duke Thierry I of Upper Lotharingia was Adalbero's cousin; Godfrey, count of Verdun, was his brother; Siegfried, count of Luxemburg, was his uncle. Bardo and Gozelo, count of Bastogne, were Adalbero's nephews.

209. *Historia* 3.81; Lot, *Les derniers Carolingiens,* 118–19, 121n1.

had been cut out of the deal with Otto, which had been conducted without consulting him, and a number of people took umbrage on his behalf.[210] The word *dolus,* used here to describe the manner in which Lothar sought and obtained the peace from Otto, is highly charged. Richer always uses *dolus* or *dolosus* to describe the use of cleverness or trickery by those of whom he disapproves (e.g., Arnulf of Flanders, Heribert II of Vermandois, and Adalbero of Laon),[211] whereas admirable figures (Louis IV, Richer's father) act *ingeniose* or *per astutiam.*[212] Ferdinand Lot pointed out that after Lothar's act of *dolus* at Margut Richer begins to take a more sympathetic attitude toward Hugh Capet. Lothar becomes increasingly associated with *doli,* whereas Hugh is never referred to as a *tirannus* even when he is up in arms against the legitimate king.[213] Lothar's death in 986, while he is plotting yet another campaign into Lotharingia, is presented as something of a relief: "But God, who assigns limits to all earthly things, brought peace to the men of Belgica and an end to Lothar's reign."[214]

It is reasonably clear that Richer structured his depiction of the reigns of each of the West Frankish kings around some preconceived notion of its principal theme or plotline. But can any overarching plot be discerned in the *Historia* as a whole? One might point to the exhaustion of the Carolingian line, whose last two representatives are the dissolute Louis V and the rebellious Charles of Lotharingia, as the point toward which the last hundred years of West Frankish history had been leading.[215] Yet Hugh is described as haunted by doubts about his legitimacy in his war with Charles, and Richer quickly abandons his earlier support for Robert the Pious when the king allows Arnulf to resume control over the see

210. *Historia* 3.81.

211. Heribert of Vermandois: 1.47, 2.7; Arnulf of Flanders: 2.11; Adalbero of Laon: 4.41, 4.42, 4.47.

212. *Historia* 2.9, 2.87, 2.89.

213. Lot, *Les derniers Carolingiens,* 121n1; Giese, *"Genus" und "Virtus,"* 94.

214. *Historia* 3.108.

215. See, e.g., Giese, *"Genus" und "Virtus,"* 97: "Die Karolinger sind unfähig geworden, die Herrschaft auszuüben; sie haben keine 'virtus' mehr."

of Rheims in 997.[216] Thus, to read this—or any other overarching plot—into the *Historia* would require a selective reading of the text. There is no cause for assuming a unified political view beyond a conventional preference for strong, legitimate kings who ruled by consensus and who deferred to the clergy when necessary. Richer took a comparatively cautious approach to writing about the recent past, one that balanced a belief in Carolingian legitimacy with an acceptance of the virtues of Hugh Capet and his predecessors.

The Synod of Saint-Basle

Richer's task when exploiting Flodoard's *Annals* as a source was to select the relevant information, draw clearer connections between events, amplify this material to make it both credible and interesting, and give coherence to the narrative by developing certain themes and plotlines. In the case of Gerbert's *Acta* of the Synod of Saint-Basle he faced a different sort of challenge: to reduce his source text down to a summary that would preserve its essential details without allowing the key point—the legitimacy of Arnulf's deposition—to be obscured by lengthy orations and citations of papal letters and conciliar decrees.[217]

The synod met on June 17 and June 18 of 991 at the monastery of Saint-Basle-de-Verzy, in the diocese of Rheims, to decide the fate of Archbishop Arnulf. Two and a half months earlier Arnulf and his uncle Charles, duke of Lower Lotharingia, had been betrayed and captured by Adalbero, the bishop of Laon, after which they were turned over to Hugh Capet and confined to captivity.[218] Charles had begun to plot against Hugh Capet soon after his coronation in July 987 and had taken control of Laon through treach-

216. *Historia* 4.39, 4.109.

217. For the synod, see Lot, *Études sur le règne de Hugues Capet,* 31–81; Riché, *Gerbert d'Aurillac,* 126–40; Kortüm, *Richer von Saint-Remi,* 68–78; Carozzi, "Gerbert et le concile de Saint-Basle"; Hehl, *Die Konzilien Deutschlands und Reichsitaliens 916–1001,* 2.380–83.

218. *Historia* 4.47.

ery the following year.[219] Arnulf swore fidelity to Hugh Capet and his son Robert in a written document prior to his election as archbishop in 989, but he betrayed the city of Rheims to Charles later that year.[220] Hugh and Robert convened the synod in response to the complaints of Arnulf's friends and defenders, who were indignant about his capture and were issuing written tracts and collections of canons in his behalf.[221] Thirteen bishops from the ecclesiastical provinces of Rheims, Bourges, Lyon, and Sens assembled in the church of the monastery of Saint-Basle.[222] Siguin of Sens was chosen president of the synod, and Arnulf of Orléans oversaw conciliar procedure and served as arbiter of the proceedings.[223] The council was stacked with bishops loyal to Hugh and Robert, and Arnulf had no chance of an acquittal.[224] In the face of damning testimony against him, and with his defenders cowed into submission, he retired to the crypt of the church with a small group of bishops, where he confessed his guilt and asked to be released from office.[225] Shortly after the conclusion of the proceedings (possibly on the following Sunday), Gerbert was elected archbishop of Rheims in his place.[226]

In convening a provincial synod to try Arnulf, Hugh and Robert were violating a long-standing precedent according to which accused bishops could only be judged by the pope, not by regional councils.[227] This violation of papal prerogative was one of the primary arguments advanced by Arnulf's defenders, and it rendered

219. For Charles's rebellion, see *Historia* 4.15–47, and Lot, *Les derniers Carolingiens*, 220ff.

220. *Historia* 4.33–36. For Arnulf's *libellus fidelitatis*, see *Acta concilii Remensis*, chap. 8, p. 399.

221. *Historia* 4.51.

222. *Acta concilii Remensis*, chap. 1, pp. 394–95.

223. *Acta concilii Remensis*, chap. 1, p. 395.

224. Lot, *Études sur le règne de Hugues Capet*, 32, points out that all of their sees were under the control of Hugh.

225. *Acta concilii Remensis*, chap. 30, p. 434; chap. 40, pp. 440–41.

226. Lot, *Études sur le règne de Hugues Capet*, 79; Gerbert, letter 179 (Riché and Callu, 2.446–51).

227. Lot, *Études sur le règne de Hugues Capet*, 31.

the decision of the synod to depose Arnulf null and void in the eyes of the papacy and many other observers, including the German court and the bishops under its influence.[228] In an attempt to settle the question of the validity of Arnulf's deposition in a manner satisfactory to Rome, the papal legate, Leo, abbot of Saint-Boniface-and Alexis, convened a synod at the Lotharingian abbey of Mouzon on June 2, 995. In response to the summoning of this synod Gerbert drew up his own *Acta* of the synod of Saint-Basle to defend the legitimacy of the proceedings and justify his own occupancy of the see of Rheims.[229] In the prologue he addresses the bishops who took part in the synod and others who were in attendance, asking them to correct any errors or stylistic infelicities in his account.[230] The primary intended audience for the *Acta*, however, was not the thirteen bishops who had deposed Arnulf, but those who had not been present, and whose opinion could still weigh in Gerbert's favor. We know from the letters that Gerbert sent to Wilderod of Strasbourg and Notker of Liège that the *Acta* were targeted specifically at the bishops of Lotharingia, none of whom had been present at the synod of Saint-Basle, and some of whom had called into question the validity of the oath of fidelity that had been demanded of Arnulf.[231]

Richer's redaction of Gerbert's *Acta* (which appears, along with the account of his journey to Chartres in mid-March of that same year, on the bifolium 49/50 and the scrap 51) is a slimmed-down and considerably abbreviated version of the synod that maintains dramatic tension without getting lost in a sea of technical legal arguments. He reduces the almost 19,000 words of his source text to about 2,800 words, making his abridgement less than 15 percent the length of the original; the contents of thirty-five of the fifty-five

228. For reaction to the decision of the synod, see Lot, *Études sur le règne de Hugues Capet*, 82ff. For Arnulf's defenders, see *Acta concilii Remensis*, chap. 19, p. 408, and chap. 23, pp. 416–17; Lot, *Études sur le règne de Hugues Capet*, 52–53.

229. Lot, *Études sur le règne de Hugues Capet*, 96; Carozzi, "Gerbert et le concile de St-Basle," 662.

230. *Acta concilii Remensis*, prologue, 392.

231. *Acta concilii Remensis*, chap. 7, p. 399; *Historia* 4.31.

chapters of the *Acta* are dispensed with entirely.[232] The scope of the abridgement suggests that we should be careful about reading too much into the exclusion of any single chapter or passage. Bishop Arnulf of Orléans's notorious diatribe against the papacy, a speech of some 3,000 words that receives no mention in Richer's account of the synod, is one such example.[233] Its omission has been cited as evidence that Richer wrote his redaction of Gerbert's *Acta* after the accession of Pope Gregory V in May 996, since Gregory was a cousin of Otto III, Gerbert's patron, and thus someone whose office Richer would not have wished to denigrate.[234] An equally likely possibility, however, is that the speech's excessive length and marginal relevance to the question of Arnulf's guilt made it a target for exclusion.[235]

Richer adapted those portions of the *Acta* whose contents he chose to include through a combination of paraphrase, rewriting, and amplification, sometimes merely rephrasing Gerbert's words, sometimes changing their meaning entirely. The end result of this editing process is an abridgement that for the most part remains faithful to the spirit of the original, which is not surprising given that Gerbert was the dedicatee of the *Historia*. This makes it all the more puzzling, however, that on several occasions Richer's version of events differs markedly from the *Acta*.

The first such deviation appears in the response to the opening address of Arnulf of Orléans at 4.54–55. In the *Acta* the first of the bishops to reply to Arnulf is Archbishop Siguin of Sens, who demands that the accused, Arnulf of Rheims, be granted a remission from punishment in the event that he is convicted by the synod (a virtual certainty in this case), citing in support of his position the thirty-first chapter of the Fourth Council of Toledo (633).[236]

232. Richer draws directly on chaps. 1–7, 9, 11–13, 17–19, 23, 30, 50, and 53–55 of the *Acta*.

233. *Acta concilii Remensis*, chap. 28, pp. 420–30.

234. *Acta concilii Remensis*, chap. 28, pp. 420–30. See Carozzi, "Gerbert et le concile de St-Basle," 663; Lot, *Études sur le règne de Hugues Capet*, 56n3: "Richer n'ose le reproduire."

235. See Latouche, *Richer: Histoire de France*, 2.259n4.

236. *Acta concilii Remensis*, chap. 3, p. 396.

Archbishop Daibert of Bourges speaks next, showing even greater unease with the prospect of Arnulf's conviction. "It is a very grave matter," he declares, "to put oneself forward as a judge in extraneous (i.e., secular) matters, so that when you convict the guilty party, you are brought down with him, and when you pass judgment, you depart having been condemned yourself."[237] Daibert's concern was that if the bishops participated in a treason trial where the guilt of the accused was all but foreordained, they would be complicit in a death sentence, which would violate the clerical prohibition against shedding blood.[238] Bishop Hervey of Beauvais then challenges Daibert's point, claiming that an even greater danger confronted the bishops—the possibility that if they failed to enforce the law, the clergy would be hauled up before secular courts in the future.[239]

Richer's account of these speeches differs in significant ways from his source. He preserves the sense of Siguin's objection, but Daibert's reply bears no relation at all to what we find in the *Acta*. Rather than calling attention to the danger of holding a treason trial in an ecclesiastical court, Daibert instead questions the necessity of a remission from punishment for Arnulf:

> Since it is evident that a crime has been committed, and there is no argument about what to call it or how serious it is, I cannot understand why it should be thought necessary that the defendant receive a pardon. And yet necessity is thought to apply here, since judgment is not to be rendered unless the defendant is first granted remission from punishment in the event that he is found guilty. But if we look to secular law, then whatever crime anyone has committed is subject to a punishment the severity of which is based upon on the gravity of the act.[240]

237. *Acta concilii Remensis,* chap. 4, p. 397.

238. See the thirty-first chapter of the Council of Toledo cited by Siguin, *Acta concilii Remensis,* chap. 3, p. 396. See also the remarks of Godesmann of Amiens, *Acta concilii Remensis,* chap. 6, p. 398: "Non est enim aequum nos fieri auctores effundendi sanguinis, qui debemus esse auctores salutis."

239. *Acta concilii Remensis,* chap. 4, p. 397.

240. *Historia* 4.54.

Hervey of Beauvais's response to Daibert is similarly altered. In the *Acta* Hervey warns the bishops that they will expose themselves to the danger of being tried before secular courts if they fail to discipline Arnulf. Here, Hervey argues that even if Arnulf is granted remission from punishment, he will still suffer the consequences of his actions in the event that he is found guilty.

We should be very careful not to compare divine laws to the laws of the courtroom. There is a great difference between them, because divine laws apply to matters concerning the church, while secular laws apply to worldly affairs. The former are superior to the latter to the same degree as the latter are inferior to the former. Wherefore the honor accorded to divine laws must be preserved in every instance. If, then, our brother and fellow bishop Arnulf is found guilty of treason, I do not deny that he ought to receive some degree of leniency from our most serene kings out of respect for his priestly status and because of his blood relations. Nonetheless, if he is shown by his own confession to be unworthy of the priestly office, then there is no way that he will escape the judgment of this court.[241]

There are three possible explanations for Richer's departures from the *Acta* in these two chapters. He might have had access to a different account of Daibert and Hervey's speeches,[242] he might have misunderstood the *Acta*,[243] or he might have deliberately changed the content of their remarks. The first possibility is unlikely for a number of reasons. There is no evidence that Richer was present at the synod,[244] and even if he was, no reason to think that he retained an accurate memory of events that took place at least four years before he drafted his version of the proceedings. In theory he could have consulted Gerbert's notes or spoken to other participants, but the fact that he otherwise relies entirely on the

241. *Historia* 4.55.

242. See Carozzi, "Gerbert et le concile de St-Basle," 663.

243. Gabriel Monod, "Études sur l'histoire de Hugues Capet," 252; Lot, *Études sur le règne de Hugues Capet*, 44n2–3; Latouche, *Richer: Histoire de France*, 2.239n2.

244. The *Acta* mention only bishops, abbots, and clergy: *Acta concilii Remensis*, chap. 1, pp. 394–95. Richer may well have been in Chartres at the time. See *Historia* 4.50.

Acta,[245] coupled with his general carelessness in adapting his other written sources, makes it unlikely that he took the time and effort to research an alternative account of Daibert and Hervey's remarks—assuming that one even existed.[246] The second possibility warrants closer consideration because there are several points in the *Historia* where Richer does misread his sources, but Gerbert's Latin is not particularly cryptic here, and it is hard to explain the wholesale changes to these speeches as the product of a misunderstanding.[247] The most likely explanation, therefore, is that he deliberately rewrote Daibert and Hervey's speeches.

What, then, was his motive? To answer this question we have to consider the nature of the material that he expunged. Daibert's concern in the *Acta* about the danger of bishops participating in a treason trial is replaced in the *Historia* by a wholesale endorsement of Arnulf's guilt.[248] Hervey of Beauvais's warning that a failure to rule on the matter would expose the bishops to judgment in secular courts is replaced by an assurance that divine and secular law could be reconciled in this particular case, since Arnulf would be punished by the secular arm of the law, but his blood would not be spilled out of respect for his priestly office and his noble birth (Arnulf was the bastard son of King Lothar). Richer was evidently uninterested in the potential danger that sitting in judgment on Ar-

245. He cites the *Acta* explicitly at *Historia* 4.73.

246. See Carozzi, "Gerbert et le concile de St-Basle," 663, who overestimates the reliability of Richer's redaction.

247. Examples of Richer misreading his sources include *Historia* 2.82, where he conflates a council held at the church of Saint-Vincent at Laon in the summer of 948 to excommunicate Theobald le Tricheur (Flodoard, *Annales,* s.a. 948, p. 116) with the Synod of Trier in October of that year (See *MGH Concilia* 6.1.164–70); 3.6, where Duke Boleslav I of Bohemia is depicted as an adversary of King Otto, whereas Boleslav actually fought with Otto against Hungarian invaders (cf. Flodoard, *Annales,* s.a. 955, p. 141); *Historia* 3.17, where Pope John XII (955–964) is referred to as the successor of Octavian, whereas Octavian was actually the pope's given name; and *Historia* 2.68, where Marinus, bishop of Bomarzo, is referred to as the bishop of Ostia.

248. *Historia* 4.54*: "Cum constet factum, et de nomine facti dubitatio nulla sit, quantum quoque facinus perpendatur, quomodo ex necessitate reo sit indulgendum penitus non adverto."

nulf posed to the ecclesiastical *ordo,* a supposition confirmed by the fact that he deliberately removes three subsequent references to this issue in later chapters.[249] The most obvious explanation for his disinterest is that the issue had become largely irrelevant by the time he was writing. Arnulf's life was ultimately spared by Hugh and Robert, and the criticisms leveled against the proceedings at Saint-Basle by Gerbert's opponents focused instead on the right of a provincial synod to depose a bishop without papal authority. In the interest of streamlining his account of the synod, it may have seemed easier to Richer simply to remove any mention of this subject.

At the same time, he also seems to have been intent on quickly disposing of any grounds for disagreement among the bishops so that he could depict a synod whose participants were essentially in agreement with one another. The end result is a subtle, but persistent, tendency to undermine any arguments that might work in Arnulf's favor. In the *Acta,* for example, Ratbod of Noyon asks that Arnulf's written oath of fidelity *(libellus fidelitatis)* to Hugh and Robert be brought forth and read aloud so that the bishops can deliver their opinion of its validity as evidence against him:

> "Because," declared Bishop Ratbod of Noyon, "I hear many of our brothers saying that the written oath of fidelity that Arnulf put forth in the form of a chirograph is sufficient to condemn him, while rumor has it that certain of the Lotharingians are raising objections to this document, I should like to hear the judgment of such worthy fathers and learn what we are to make of it."[250]

Richer rewrites the speech so that instead of asking for the advice of his fellow bishops, Ratbod professes his belief that the *libellus* is sufficient to convict Arnulf, and he dismisses the objections of the Lotharingian bishops as groundless:[251]

249. *Acta concilii Remensis,* chap. 5, p. 397; (Bruno of Langres), chap. 6, p. 398 (Godesmann of Amiens), chap. 6, p. 398 (Bruno of Langres).

250. *Acta concilii Remensis,* chap. 7, p. 399.

251. The chapter title is even more direct: "Demonstratio Ratbodi, quod libellum *infidelitatis* episcopi Lothariensium perperam calumnientur."

Bishop Ratbod of Noyon addressed them: "If it pleases you, reverend fathers, I think that you should now examine the written pledge of fealty that Arnulf formerly gave to the kings to guarantee his loyalty. For it seems to me that this alone should suffice to condemn him, inasmuch as through the sacrilege of perjury he has completely violated the pledge that he made under oath and confirmed in his own handwriting. There is still something that gives pause, however, namely the fact that the Lotharingian bishops are said to be raising an argument against it. They wrongly claim that it was written, read out, and stored away in contravention of the divine laws. And so, if it pleases you, let the document be brought forward so that you may examine it."[252]

Whereas in the *Acta* Ratbod contrasts the arguments of "many of our brothers" with those of "certain of the Lotharingians," here he assumes the validity of the *libellus* as evidence against Arnulf from the outset, using the loaded word *calumniantur* to describe the objections of the Lotharingian bishops.

The reaction to the reading of the *libellus* is similarly one-sided in the *Historia*. In the *Acta,* after the oath of fidelity has been read out, Arnulf of Orléans, in keeping with his assigned role as the administrator of the synod and the interpreter of the business conducted there *(ordinis custos ac omnium gerendorum interpres),* offers his opinion of the document:

When the document had been read out, Arnulf, the venerable bishop of the church of Orléans, replied: "In my opinion this document possesses great power to convict; at the same time it also has subtle powers of defense, if we take into account the people involved. For its author, Arnulf, is hateful because on account of his enormous ambition to obtain office he left behind this detestable memorial to himself, one unheard of in an earlier age. Those who contrived it appear to have done something useful and necessary, since if he ever wished to renounce the faith that he had sworn, this document would exist as a witness against him, and if he deviated from it, running afoul of his sworn statement and his subscription, he would deprive himself of the office. And lest by chance after sinning he should be protected any longer by the title of archbishop, he himself as archbishop openly called down a sentence

252. *Historia* 4.59.

of damnation against himself. But because the priest [Adalger] has arrived, I will bring my speech to a close so that he may have an opportunity to speak."[253]

Arnulf's reference in this speech to the "subtle powers of defense" possessed by the *libellus* has been the occasion of some debate. Ferdinand Lot proposed that Arnulf intended to explain what he meant in the second half of his speech, but was interrupted by the arrival of the priest Adalger and prevented from doing so.[254] Claude Carozzi has suggested instead that Arnulf did intend to impute powers of defense to the *libellus fidelitatis,* namely, that such an oath would never have been demanded from a weak or unworthy person.[255] Carozzi bases his argument on the version of the speech in the *Historia,* founded on his assumption that Richer understood the meaning of the words that Gerbert attributed to Arnulf in the *Acta.* Unlike the speeches of Daibert and Hervey, however, Gerbert's words *are* cryptic here, and Richer seems to have faced the same difficulty that we do in explaining exactly what Arnulf meant by *subtiles vires defensionis.* While his version of the speech is no clearer than Gerbert's, it appears, contra Carozzi, to deliberately rule out the possibility that the *libellus fidelitatis* could offer any support to Arnulf's defenders:

After the document had been read aloud, the synod enquired into whether it contained the power to convict or defend anyone. The venerable bishop Arnulf then spoke, since he had been entrusted with the task of interpreting: "In itself this document contains partly a defense, and it partly lends support to the accusers. Arnulf, the author of this document, was himself responsible for the fact that it was drawn up. Because he was suffering overmuch from the sickness of hateful avarice, he committed an act worthy of censure, in that he did not preserve the fidelity that he swore. For this he is subject to reproach. And the fact that wise and good men saw to it that the document was drawn up in order to oppose the trickery and guile of a most debased man provides

253. *Acta concilii Remensis,* chap. 9, p. 400.
254. *Études sur le règne de Hugues Capet,* 46n3.
255. "Gerbert et le concile de St-Basle," 671–72.

a forceful and steadfast defense against those who raise objections. But whatever the case, it must still be corroborated by testimony. Let the priest Adalger present himself.[256]

Here the "subtle powers of defense" referred to by Arnulf of Orléans do not defend Arnulf of Rheims, but rather the document itself. That is, Richer seems to be arguing that because the *libellus fidelitatis* had been drawn up by wise and good men, it was therefore unimpeachable and had to be accepted as evidence against Arnulf. Rather than helping to defend Arnulf, it provided a defense against those who questioned the validity of the document, in this case the Lotharingian bishops who had misgivings about the propriety of demanding an oath in which the Eucharist was taken to confirm the threat of damnation.[257] Ferdinand Lot may well have been right to suggest that Richer had difficulty making sense of the *Acta* here. In that case, his interpretation of *subtiles vires defensionis* simply reflects his best guess as to what Arnulf of Orléans could have meant. Whatever the meaning of Arnulf's comments in the *Acta,* however, and whether or not Richer understood them, it is significant that his version of the speech removes any possibility that the *libellus* could be used to argue against the validity of Arnulf of Rheims's deposition.

Richer's other most significant departures from *Acta* can similarly be explained as the result of his desire to present a unified front among the bishops and deny Arnulf any effective line of defense. In chapter 11 of the *Acta* the priest Adalger testifies before the synod, describing his role in helping Arnulf turn the city of Rheims over to Charles of Lotharingia. He is followed in chapter 12 by Bishop Odo of Senlis, who recalls to the synod the anathema that Arnulf disingenuously issued against those who had sacked the city of Rheims

256. *Historia* 4.61.

257. *Historia* 4.30–31; *Acta concilii Remensis,* chap. 7, p. 399. Carozzi, "Gerbert et le concile de St-Basle," 672, following Latouche, *Richer: Histoire de France,* 2.249, translates *querulos* as "les accusateurs," but that cannot be correct here. It must instead refer to those who are complaining about the use of the *libellus fidelitatis* as evidence, namely, the Lotharingian bishops.

in 989.[258] Richer's version of Adalger's testimony is abbreviated, but not noticeably different. The speech that follows Adalger's in the *Historia,* however, is delivered by Wido of Soissons rather than Odo of Senlis and bears little relation to Odo's speech in the *Acta:*

> Wido, the bishop of Soissons, now spoke: "It is clear in this case from the testimony of this man that two people are bound by a single share of guilt. For although Adalger says that he was the one who carried out this wicked deed, nonetheless his lord, who urged him to do it, is not guiltless, because he made himself responsible for the crime. Therefore, since clear evidence shows that both men are involved in this affair—one urging on the deed and the other carrying it out—the judgment to be meted out does not escape you, reverend fathers."[259]

The point of this change is to emphasize that although Adalger actually gave Charles the key to the city, Arnulf was equally guilty of the crime. At 4.65 Odo of Senlis delivers a speech unrelated to anything in the *Acta* in which he urges the bishops to render their verdict because, as he puts it, "There is no need to allot more time for differences of opinion to be presented, when the facts are so clear and the grounds for reaching a judgment are so plainly apparent."[260] Richer ends up allotting one chapter to the arguments of Arnulf's defenders (4.67), but each of their arguments is summarily dismissed, whereupon they immediately abandon their effort to defend him (4.68–69).

The discrepancies between Richer's account of the synod of Saint-Basle and Gerbert's *Acta* stem from the different audiences for which their works were intended and the different purposes of the authors. Gerbert composed his *Acta* in order to explain and justify the circumstances surrounding Arnulf's deposition to other bishops, particularly those from Lotharingia.[261] For this reason

258. *Acta concilii Remensis,* chap. 12, pp. 401–2.

259. *Historia* 4.63.

260. *Historia* 4.65.

261. See Lot, *Études sur le règne de Hugues Capet,* 96. He sent copies of the *Acta* to the bishops Wilderod of Strasbourg (Riché and Callu, 2, *Annexe* 1, 582–651) and Notker of Liège (letter 193, Riché and Callu, 2.510–13). See Hehl, *Acta concilii Remensis,* 381; Riché, *Gerbert d'Aurillac,* 155–59.

he presents a version of events that is, on the surface at least, even-handed, in that it accords ample space to the arguments of his opponents.[262] Richer, on the other hand, wrote for Gerbert and the monastic and clerical communities at Rheims. His intention was to flatter and defend his dedicatee. Hence, there was no point in dwelling on anything other than Arnulf's guilt and the justice of his deposition. Richer's changes to Gerbert's *Acta* were intended to simplify the proceedings and preserve dramatic tension. He accomplished this by eliminating superfluous material such as conciliar canons and papal letters and by keeping the narrative moving at a quick pace. There is certainly no reason to think that he was trying to effect an ideological shift in Gerbert's account of the synod.[263] To the contrary, he was advocating Gerbert's position, only with less subtlety.

If we can draw an overarching conclusion about Richer's methodology from the foregoing investigation of his written sources, it is that he was prepared to sacrifice fidelity to his sources in order to achieve particular narrative goals. The most important of these were thematic clarity (i.e., the bringing into relief of particular themes and plotlines from his written sources), and the explication of motives (the construction of a narrative where events were fully explicable in terms of human causality). Of equal importance was his desire to transform his annalistic source material from the narrative mode to the dramatic, a topic that will be considered in the next chapter.

262. *Acta concilii Remensis*, chap. 20–22, pp. 409–16. See also Lot, *Études sur le règne de Hugues Capet*, 33–34, on the reasons to trust the basic accuracy of Gerbert's account.

263. Cf. Glenn, *Politics and History*, 125–27. Such a hypothesis is even less likely given the fact that Richer explicitly directs the reader's attention to the *Acta* at 4.73.

[THREE]

Narratio Probabilis and the Techniques of Dramatization

IN COMPOSING THE FIRST HALF of the *Historia* Richer had two principal tasks: to take the large and unwieldy mass of information in Flodoard's *Annals* and select from it the events that would form part of his own history, and to transform the resulting framework of annalistic notices into a narrative history by supplementing it with outside sources (when possible) and by giving it a new and different rhetorical form.[1] At a basic level this new *orationis scema* demanded that careful attention be paid to all of the elements required to secure narrative plausibility, particularly the reasoning that led people to act as they did *(rationes negotiorum).* At the same time, Richer envisioned his task as a historian as extending beyond the process of amplification and explication. He states in the prologue that his intention was to recall the events of his history to memory through writing *(ad memoriam reducere scripto)*—that is, to bring them back to the mind of the reader.

To achieve this goal he had to do more than augment and embellish Flodoard's *Annals*; he had to breathe life into the events of his history. He did so by interlacing the narrative sections of the *Historia* with dramatic scenes. Such scenes were a characteristic feature of classical historiography, and countless examples could be found in the works of Richer's historiographical models: Sallust,

1. Richer deals with the entire period from 888 to 920 in eleven chapters, from *Historia* 1.4 to 1.14; he begins to use Flodoard's *Annals* as a source at 1.15. At 3.22, when the *Annals* can no longer serve as a source, the narrative jumps from 965 to 969.

Caesar, Livy, and Hegesippus. That most, if not all, of the specific details of any scene had to be freely invented was expected. For classical historians the construction of a literary edifice *(exaedificatio)* atop the foundation *(fundamenta)* of historical data was made possible by the fact that history, as a type of *narratio,* was governed by the rules of rhetorical composition, and thus by the doctrine of the "readily believable."[2] History as a narrative form comprised both events that were known to have happened and those that were of the sort to have happened.[3] The gaps in the historical record had to be filled in through rhetorical *inventio,* the "discovery" of readily believable material.[4]

The inclusion of dramatic scenes remained a feature of literary historiography throughout the Middle Ages. Of course it was not always the historian's imagination—tempered by a sense of the plausible—that served as the basis of composition. Often the dramatic scene was not so much the product of rhetorical invention as the literary deposit of oral-traditional storytelling.[5] At many points in the first two books of the *Historia* we can detect the presence of oral-traditional material.[6] Richer's account of Odo's reign, although probably dependent in part on an annalistic source, is mostly legendary in nature.[7] Charles the Simple's campaign against Gislebert of Lotharingia (1.37–40) is not found in Flodoard, and Richer's information may derive ultimately from Gerberga, Gisle-

2. *De inventione* 1.19.27; *De oratore* 2.53; see Woodman, *Rhetoric in Classical Historiography,* 70–116.

3. *De inventione* 1.19.27: "Narratio est rerum gestarum aut ut gestarum expositio."

4. *De inventione* 1.7.9: "Inventio est excogitatio rerum verarum aut veri similium quae causam probabilem reddant"; Marius Victorinus, *Explanationes in Ciceronis rhetoricam* 1.7, p. 45: "Inventionem esse dicit ad negotii fidem aut verarum rerum aut veri similium excogitationem; sed orator in veri similibus maxime versatur. Duo enim genera sunt argumentorum, necessarium et probabile; necessarium in veris rebus est, probabile in veri similibus."

5. The foundational work on this topic is Joaquín Martínez Pizarro, *A Rhetoric of the Scene: Dramatic Narrative in the Early Middle Ages* (Toronto: University of Toronto Press, 1989).

6. Lauer, *Le règne de Louis IV,* 267–76; Hoffmann, *Historiae,* 6–7; Kortüm, *Richer von Saint-Remi,* 22–25; Latouche, "Un imitateur de Salluste," 292–93.

7. Favre, *Eudes, comte de Paris et roi de France,* 230–31.

bert's first wife, possibly through Richer's father.[8] The account of the Battle of Soissons in the *Historia* (1.45–46) contains legendary elements, some of which are also found in the *Chronicon* of Ademar of Chabannes. Richer's narrative of the events surrounding the murder of William Longsword (2.30–33) clearly drew on oral traditions; Flodoard provides next to nothing on the subject, and different versions of the story appear in other contemporary sources.[9] Louis IV's arrival in West Francia, where he tames a wild horse without using a stirrup, has epic overtones, and the two anecdotes in the middle of book 2 about a group of young men who steal boats for King Louis's army (2.57) and the rivalry between Derold of Amiens and the doctor of Salerno (2.59)—were clearly orally circulating stories.[10] Finally, when Richer narrates the exploits of his father (2.87–90, 3.7–9) he must have been retelling tales that he had heard during his youth.

In these cases, where there are no written sources known to us that Richer could have been using, we can posit the influence of oral tradition with confidence. Yet it is not always possible to distinguish clearly between material derived from oral report and material devised through the process of rhetorical invention. This is especially true in the case of dramatic scenes based on events found in Flodoard's *Annals.* Any attempt to separate out these two types of material involves a certain degree of speculation, but certain criteria can assist us.

In the first place, oral tradition and rhetorical invention are different kinds of discourse that serve different purposes. Oral traditions are propagated for a reason: they serve an explanatory or legitimizing purpose.[11] The same may not necessarily be true of material invented to satisfy the demands of *narratio probabilis.*

8. Hoffmann, *Historiae,* 7. For Richer's father and Queen Gerberga, see *Historia* 3.7–9.

9. See Lair, *Étude sur la vie et la mort de Guillaume Longue-épée.*

10. For Richer's use of epic motifs, see Kortüm, *Richer von Saint-Remi,* 24–25.

11. Jan Vansina, *Oral Tradition: A Study in Historical Methodology,* trans. H. M. Wright (Chicago: Aldine Publishing Co., 1965), 77: "Every testimony and every tradition has a purpose and fulfils a function. It is because of this that they exist at all." The

Second, certain formal characteristics of the scene may indicate the use of oral tradition as a source. In his groundbreaking study of the dramatic scene in early medieval historiography, Joaquín Martínez Pizarro describes the development of a "new narrative mimesis" characterized by specific features derived from traditional oral storytelling: the effacement of the narrator, the designation of specific time and place for characters, the use of direct speech, and the role of gesture, posture, and objects.[12] Martínez Pizarro's work provides a useful starting point for analyzing dramatic scenes in the *Historia.*

Third, the internal evidence of the text can assist us. Specifically, there are a number of instances in which Richer recycles descriptive elements, language, or motifs from one scene to another, a practice that should make us suspicious about his access to genuine oral traditions about the events in question. While the ephemeral nature of oral culture makes it impossible to make precisely grounded judgments about what is and what is not an artifact of oral tradition, our access to Richer's most important written sources at least allows us to see what he is adding to Flodoard. In most cases it will become clear that even when oral tradition provided the seed for Richer's reworking of his source material, rhetorical invention based on the standard of the readily believable played the more important role.

Dramatic Narrative on a Small Scale: The Siege of Rheims and the Death of Heribert

Battles and deaths are two of the most common themes for rhetorical amplification in the *Historia.*[13] Because these scenes tend to

bibliography on the subject of oral tradition and early medieval history is large and expanding rapidly. See in particular James Fentress and Christopher Wickham, *Social Memory* (Oxford: Blackwell, 1992), 144–72, and Matthew Innes, "Memory, Orality, and Literacy in an Early Medieval Society," *Past and Present* 158 (1998): 3–36.

12. *A Rhetoric of the Scene,* esp. 8–15.

13. This is generally true of narrative historiography in the high and later Middle Ages. See Ruth Morse, *Truth and Convention in the Middle Ages: Rhetoric, Representation and Reality* (Cambridge: Cambridge University Press, 1991), 118–19.

be relatively formulaic, and because they draw on identifiable written sources for many of their details, they offer a good entry point into Richer's techniques of scene composition.

In May 945 Archbishop Hugh of Rheims refused to allow King Louis IV, recently returned from a campaign in Normandy, to enter the city. As a result, the king gathered an army of Norman troops and a group of loyal counts and laid siege to Rheims.[14] Flodoard summarizes the battle between the forces of the king and the archbishop in one sentence:

> Whenever there was fighting at the gates or near the walls many men were wounded on each side, and some were even killed.[15]

Richer describes the same battle in considerably more detail:

> During the initial assault there was heavy fighting. For archers had been deployed in various locations, and the men defending the walls were wounded by their arrows. Yet as soon as they withdrew, fresh troops stepped in to take their place and keep up the fight. Outside the walls many men were struck by projectiles and rocks hurled from above and forced to retreat. There were repeated clashes and frequent hand-to-hand combat at the gates and at the wall. The men on both sides fought ruthlessly and showed no signs of backing down, and they never would have yielded until they had both been wiped out, had the siege not been broken off through the entreaties of intermediaries.[16]

Two features of this scene are noteworthy. First, the particular events of the battle described here are almost certainly fictional. Richer was not present at the siege of Rheims in 945, and nothing suggests that he based his account on the testimony of reliable witnesses. The events of the battle are generic, and the vocabulary is drawn from classical authors and the Old Testament. His account describes not so much a particular siege as the kinds of things that usually happened during sieges. It was standard practice for Richer to flesh out battle scenes with details that he invented or borrowed

14. *Historia* 2.44. For the political context, see McKitterick, "The Carolingian Kings and the See of Rheims," 236–37.

15. *Annales*, s.a. 945, p. 96.

16. *Historia* 2.44.

from Caesar, Livy, or Hegesippus, and both the language and the details of this siege reappear with minor variations in other parts of the *Historia*.[17] Second, the depiction of the battle is dramatic. Richer does not merely summarize the results of the combat; he sets out the stages by which it unfolds over time, from the first assault, to the replacement of wounded troops on the walls, the repeated fighting at close quarters, and finally the abandonment of the siege. He describes actions taking place simultaneously in different places—on the walls, outside the city, and at the gates—and he emphasizes the ferocity and duration of the fighting through the figure of anaphora *(Sepe tumultus reparantur, sepe ad portas, sepe ad murum comminus congressi).* These sorts of details are lacking in Flodoard, who summarizes battles rather than dramatizing them. Battles are mentioned as a typical theme for the *descriptio,* one of the twelve elementary rhetorical exercises described in Priscian's *Praeexercitamina,* a standard textbook that may have been used at Rheims, and it is possible that the style of amplification we see here derives ultimately from this sort of rhetorical school exercise.[18]

Two years before Hugh was besieged at Rheims, his father, Count Heribert II of Vermandois, died. Flodoard reports on this event in his *Annals,* but pays no special attention to it. In keeping with his terse and dispassionate style, he dispenses with Heribert's death and burial in ten words:

Count Heribert died, and his sons buried him at Saint-Quentin.[19]

17. E.g., "Quibus amotis, alii intacti succedunt" mirrors 2.83: "At aliis fatigatis, alii intacti succedunt." Both may derive from Livy 43.18: "intermissione interdiu noctuque alii aliis succedentes."

18. Priscian, *Praeexercitamina,* chap. 10 (Halm, 558). Although there is no evidence of a manuscript of the *Praeexercitamina* at Rheims in the tenth century, Gerbert's abbey of Bobbio possessed one, and he could have had a copy made after his return to Rheims. See Michele Tosi, "Il governo abbaziale di Gerberto a Bobbio," in *Gerberto, scienza, storia e mito,* 206n446, and Becker, *Catalogi bibliothecarum antiqui,* 69n430. In addition to military *descriptiones,* the *Historia* contains a *descriptio* of Gislebert of Lotharingia at 1.35 and a short account of the city of Verdun at 3.101 that may reflect training in ecphrastic exercises such as the *laus urbium.*

19. *Annales,* s.a. 943, p. 87.

Richer takes this meager account of Heribert' death and transforms it into a dramatic scene:

> In the meantime, Heribert was plotting all manner of mischief and making detailed arrangements for the ruin of certain people. While he was sitting among his men, dressed in his finery and holding forth to them with an outstretched hand, he was struck by a severe apoplexy caused by an excess of humors, and at the very moment when he was giving orders, his hands contracted and his sinews grew tight, his mouth twisted up to his ear, he shuddered and his hair stood up on end, and right in front of his men he unexpectedly dropped dead. He was taken up by his men and buried at Saint-Quentin.[20]

The decision to dramatize this particular incident presumably stemmed from the ill repute that still clung to Heribert's name five decades after his death. Richer portrays Heribert as ambitious, treacherous, and unscrupulous—a fomenter of civil discord, a thorn in the side of the kings of West Francia, and a long-standing source of grief for the church of Rheims. Heribert makes his first appearance in the *Historia* at the Battle of Soissons, leading Robert's son Hugh on to the battlefield to rally the forces of his slain father and deny Charles the victory.[21] In the aftermath of the battle he lures Charles to a meeting and takes him captive, allowing Radulf to become king without opposition.[22] Later he turns against Radulf and exacts the archiepiscopal see of Rheims from the king as the price of his loyalty.[23] By engineering the highly irregular election of his five-year old son Hugh as archbishop in 925 he proceeds to lay the groundwork for a protracted conflict over the occupancy of the see, and after the death of Radulf in 936 he continues to challenge the authority of Louis IV.[24] Heribert was a driving force behind much of

20. *Historia* 2.37: "His ita sese habentibus, cum Heribertus quaeque pernitiosa pertractaret ac de quorundam calamitate multa disponeret, cum inter suos in veste preciosa sederet atque apud illos extensa manu concionaretur, maiore apoplexia ob superfluitatem humorum captus, in ipsa rerum ordinatione constrictis manibus nervisque contractis, ore etiam in aurem distorto, cum multo horrore et horripilatione coram suis inconsultus exspiravit. Susceptusque a suis, apud sanctum Quintinum sepultus est."

21. *Historia* 1.46.

22. *Historia* 1.47.

23. *Historia* 1.54–55.

24. *Historia* 2.7, 2.22, 2.23.

the strife that afflicted West Francia between Charles's deposition in 922 and his own death in 943, and the artistic license that Richer exercised in composing his death scene was the product of a desire to create a fitting end for a treacherous and rapacious magnate who had rebelled against three different kings and usurped control over the see of Rheims.[25]

Richer's description of Heribert's death differs in significant ways from two other roughly contemporary accounts. According to Folcuin of Lobbes (d. 990), Heribert was plotting to kill Louis IV while hunting, but he was betrayed by one of his accomplices and executed.[26] Rodulf Glaber reports that Heribert was being questioned about the state of his soul and the future arrangements for his property, when he died after a long period of illness, still muttering, "There were twelve of us who swore to betray Charles."[27] These conflicting accounts show that stories about Heribert's death were circulating orally in the late tenth and early eleventh centuries, so we cannot rule out the possibility that Richer's version is also based on oral tradition. Yet there are reasons to be skeptical. In the first place, it was standard practice for Richer to invent fictional mortal illnesses for his characters, so the odds are good that he also invented Heribert's cause of death and the particulars of this scene.[28] Apart from this, the differences between Richer's account and those of Folcuin and Rodulf Glaber are important. Both Folcuin and Glaber explicitly link Heribert's death to treason

25. For Heribert, see Helmut Schwager, *Graf Heribert II. Von Soissons, Omois, Meaux, Madrie sowie Vermandois (900/06–943) und die Francia (Nord-Frankreich) in der ersten Hälfte des 10. Jahrhunderts*, Münchener historische Studien, Abteilung Mittelalterliche Geschichte 6 (Kallmünz and Opf: Lassleben, 1994).

26. *Gesta abbatum S. Bertini Sithiensium*, ed. O. Holder-Egger, MGH SS 13 (Hanover: Hahn, 1881), 626.

27. *Historiae* 1.3.

28. See *Historia* 1.11 (Ingo); 1.13 (Odo); 1.18 (Winemar); 1.56 (Charles the Simple); 2.103 (Louis IV); 3.14 (Artald of Rheims); 3.96 (Otto II); 3.109 (Lothar); 4.24 (Adalbero of Rheims); 4.94 (Count Odo I of Blois and Chartres). See L. C. MacKinney, "Tenth-Century Medicine as Seen in the *Historia* of Richer of Rheims," *Bulletin of the Institute of the History of Medicine* 2 (1934): 347–75, for discussions of these death scenes.

against the king, in the former case his attempt to murder Louis IV, in the latter his betrayal of Charles the Simple. Moreover, in Folcuin's version Heribert's plot is revealed through the agency of God, and his execution is explicitly characterized as a divine punishment.[29] Both of these oral traditions serve a function: they explain Heribert's death as the punishment due to a traitor, in the first case stating explicitly, and in the second implying, that God was responsible for his miserable end. The same is not true of Richer's version. Visually, it is arrestingly vivid. But it offers no explanation for, or explicit legitimization of, Heribert's death, and for this reason it is less likely to have survived as an independent oral tradition.

Richer's account, unlike the other two, also bears obvious traces of rhetorical invention and literary amplification. The symptoms preceding Heribert's death are derived in part from the description of *apoplexia* found in a medical textbook that he had studied at Chartres.[30] The sentence structure is more artificial and more complex than we would expect if this scene were an artifact of oral tradition. It begins with a series of subordinate clauses: two balanced *cum*-clauses, then a perfect participle *(captus)*, and then two chiastically arranged ablatives absolute *(constrictis manibus nervisque contractis)* underscored by the rhetorical figure of homoeoteleuton. There follow two prepositional phrases *(cum multo horrore et horripilatione/coram suis)*, in one of which Richer deploys the rhetorical figure of *derivatio (horrore et horripilatione)*, and a predicate adjective *(inconsultus)*.[31] Only in the last word of the sentence—*exspiravit*—does Heribert finally die. There is a performative aspect to this passage as well. The oral elements of alliteration *(his ita sese*

29. *Gesta abbatum S. Bertini Sithiensium*, chap. 102, p. 626: "Deo illi dignam pro factis compensationem reddente.... Hoc autem consilium, Deo miserante, non potuit latere.... Deo autem illi iustam retributionem pro factis reddente."

30. Chartres, Bibliothèque municipale, MS 62, which he almost certainly read during his journey to Chartres in 991 at the request of his friend Heribrand (for which see *Historia* 4.50). See MacKinney, "Tenth-Century Medicine," 366 and note 49.

31. For *derivatio* as etymologizing stem repetition, see Lausberg § 648.

habentibus cum Heribertus; pernitiosa pertractaret; horrore et horripilatione), assonance *(ore etiam in aurem distorto),* and homoeoteleuton *(constrictis manibus nervisque contractis)* suggest that the scene may have been composed with an eye toward oral recitation.

The dramatic particulars of the scene—the count's malicious plotting with his counselors, his expensive finery, and the sudden stroke of apoplexy that strikes him down in the middle of his address to his men, as well as the theatrical elements of Heribert's death—the shuddering, the bristling hair, and the twisted grin—are all specifically calculated to leave the image of this sudden, terrible death impressed in the reader's mind. At the same time, there is no obtrusive authorial commentary. The circumstances of Heribert's demise may offer an implicit moral lesson, but Richer's tone is not openly didactic. He does not directly address the reader to comment on the action, nor does he ascribe Heribert's death to divine judgment. This willingness to let events speak for themselves suggests that rhetorical amplification is being employed in the service of a literary goal as much as an ethical or political one. It is just possible that the kernel of this story—that Heribert dropped dead while addressing his henchmen—was circulating orally at Rheims. But the scene as we have it here—with its rhetorical polish, absence of dialogue, and lack of explanatory force—is not the literary deposit of an orally circulating story.

These two passages exemplify on a small scale Richer's use of rhetorical invention to flesh out his source material. The embellishments in these scenes are comparatively minor, but they demonstrate his adherence to the historiographical standard of the readily believable as opposed to the verifiably true. And it is not a very great step from inventing a disease or adding realistic details to the account of a siege to writing dialogue and speeches for historical actors and dramatizing important events over the course of multiple chapters. Adopting the standard of plausibility gave Richer a great deal of compositional freedom.

Hagano and the Desertion of Charles the Simple

The abandonment of Charles the Simple by the magnates in 920 was the turning point of his reign and an event that Richer invested with tremendous significance. His explanation and dramatization of the events surrounding Charles's downfall is thus of considerable interest. Flodoard, as usual, provides only a tantalizing outline of what happened. His entry in the *Annals* for the year 920 begins as follows:

> In the year of Our Lord 920 almost all of the counts of Francia abandoned their king, Charles, at the city of Soissons, because he refused to dismiss his counselor Hagano, whom he had raised up from those of middle rank to a position of power. Hervey, the archbishop of Rheims, received the king after everyone had deserted him and brought him to his own residence at the manor of Chacrise. The next day they went to Crugny, a manor belonging to the see of Rheims, and they remained there until they went to Rheims. And so he accompanied the king for nearly seven months, until he restored his leading men to him and him to his kingdom.[32]

This is all we learn about the abandonment of Charles the Simple. When Flodoard next mentions Charles, he is at Worms meeting with Henry the Fowler. Hervey, meanwhile, leaves Rheims to besiege Erlebald of Châtresais. Erlebald subsequently flees to Worms to plead his case before the king, where he is killed by his enemies. At this point Flodoard moves on to discuss other matters.

Richer takes this concise account and expands it into a dramatic narrative over the course of several chapters. He sets the stage for Charles's desertion with the ominous declaration that "perhaps he would have remained supremely fortunate throughout, had he not erred so grievously in one matter."[33] He then proceeds to dramatize Hagano's unseemly familiarity with the king and Charles's refusal to heed the warnings of the unhappy magnates:

32. *Annales,* s.a. 920, p. 2.

33. *Historia* 1.14: "Et forte felicissimus per omnia fuisset, si in uno nimium non errasset."

For although he treated the nobles with great generosity, he had particular affection for Hagano, whom he had raised up from those of the middle rank to a position of power, so much so that while each one of the nobles kept their distance, Hagano alone clung to the king's side. On a number of occasions he even took off the king's hat in public and put it on his own head, which in the end proved disastrous for the king. For the nobles thought it degrading, and they went to the king and complained bitterly that this man of obscure birth was detracting greatly from the royal dignity, sitting as he did beside the king like a counselor, as though there were a shortage of noblemen. If he did not give up this excessive familiarity they would depart the king's council altogether. But the king paid no heed to their admonitions, nor did he abandon his favorite.[34]

On a purely formal level, Richer includes many more adjectives and adverbs than Flodoard *(multa, precipua, longe, solus, sepissime, multam, satis, multum, penitus, minime)* and uses conjunctions *(nam, cum, tamen, adeo ut, etiam, etenim, cum, nisi)* that are both more frequent and more charged with explanatory force than Flodoard's *autem, vero,* and *sicque.* In this case, however, he goes further by expanding Flodoard's annalistic notice into a dramatic scene with vivid visual elements (Hagano clings to the side of Charles while the indignant nobles stand off to the side) and a significant gesture (Hagano plucks off the king's hat and puts it on his own head). He also fleshes out the motivation of the rebellious magnates by developing the theme of resentment *(indignatio)* that is only implicit in Flodoard's account: the nobles bristle at the king's displays of affection for an inferior *(mediocris).* Even more galling is the fact that Charles dotes on Hagano in public, in a way that detracts from his

34. *Historia* 1.15: "Nam cum multa benignitate principes coleret, precipua tamen beatitudine Haganonem habebat, quem ex mediocribus potentem effecerat, adeo ut magnatibus quibusque longe absistentibus, ipse regio lateri solus haereret, pilleum etiam a capite regis sepissime sumptum, palam sibi imponeret. Quod etiam multam regi intulit labem. Etenim primates id ferentes indignum, regem adeunt ac apud eum satis conqueruntur hominem obscuris parentibus natum regiae dignitati multum derogare, cum acsi indigentia nobilium ipse tamquam consulturus regi assistat. Et nisi a tanta consuetudine cesset, sese a regis consilio penitus discessuros. Rex dissuasionibus his minime credulus, a dilecto non cessit."

own prestige *(regia dignitas),* and, implicitly, their own. Ultimately, it is *indignatio,* one of the characteristic emotional states of the aristocracy in the *Historia,* that will lead them to abandon the king.

Richer continues this theme in the next chapter, given the marginal title *Indignatio Rotberti in Haganonem* ("The Resentment of Robert against Hagano"). Robert, marquis of Neustria, had every reason to be offended at the preferential treatment given to Hagano. As the most powerful nobleman in Charles's kingdom and the brother of the late king Odo, he had a reasonable expectation that Charles would defer to him as the most important of his counselors. Just as Richer dramatized Charles's "excessive affection" *(nimia dilectio)* for his favorite through Hagano's removal of Charles's hat, here he encapsulates Robert's grounds for resentment *(indignatio)* against the king in a gesture. Charles is holding a royal audience at Soissons, to which noblemen from all over Francia have come:

> Robert supposed that he, among them all, was held in particular esteem by the king, since he had made him the duke over all of Celtic Gaul. Yet when the king was seated in his palace, he ordered that the duke should sit at his right hand, while Hagano at the same time should sit at his left. Duke Robert quietly resented that a person of no stature should be considered equal to himself and preferred to the magnates. Yet he controlled his anger and hid how he felt, scarcely speaking to the king. After a while he got up and took counsel with his own men. After conferring with them, he sent messengers to inform the king that he could not stand for Hagano to be treated as an equal to himself and honored before the chief men. Indeed, he thought it disgraceful that a man of this sort should cling to the side of the king while the noblest men of the Gauls kept their distance. If the king did not reduce him back to his middling status, he would have him strung up and hanged without mercy. The king could not abide these insults to his favorite and replied that he would rather do without the advice of all of his counselors than his friendship with Hagano. This infuriated Robert, who departed unbidden for Neustria with the majority of the magnates and installed himself at Tours, where he vented his resentment at the king's immaturity.[35]

35. *Historia* 1.16: "Inter quos cum Rotbertus in maiore gratia apud regem sese haberi putaret, utpote quem ducem in Celtica omnibus prefecerat, cum rex in pala-

In this case the significant gesture, and the source of Robert's *indignatio,* is Charles's decision to seat Robert and Hagano next to him at the same time.[36] Richer hammers home the idea of resentment without subtlety, using forms of *indignus, indignari,* or *indignatio* five times in the chapter. He repeats himself in other ways as well: *personam mediocrem sibi aequari magnatibusque preponi* is echoed three lines later in *Haganonem aequari primatibusque anteferri.* Similarly, *regi haerere et Gallorum nobilissimos longe absistere* mirrors a construction one chapter earlier *(magnatibus quibusque longe absistentibus ipse regio lateri solus haereret).* Richer makes the reasoning of his characters as clear as possible through these repetitions, and establishes beyond doubt the reason for Charles's abandonment: the nobles, and particularly Robert, could not bear the repeated public affronts to their status brought about by Hagano's public appearances with the king. Charles's faults are *nimia dilectio,* on the one hand (the same flaw ascribed to Arnulf of Rheims in relation to his uncle, Charles of Lotharingia, in book 4), and immaturity, or frivolity *(levitas),* on the other.[37]

Perhaps as a result of his focus on the theme of Charles's immaturity, Richer leaves out one of the principal motivations that Robert and his son Hugh had for being angry with Hagano. Flodoard mentions in his entry for the year 922 that Hugh entered the terri-

---

tio sedisset, eius iussu dux dexter, Hagano quoque ei levus pariter resedit. Rotbertus vero dux tacite indignum ferebat personam mediocrem sibi aequari magnatibusque preponi. At iram mitigans, animum dissimulabat, vix regi pauca locutus. Celerius ergo surgit ac cum suis consilium confert. Quo collato, regi per legatos suggerit sese perferre non posse sibi Haganonem aequari, primatibus anteferri. Indignum etiam videri huiusmodi hominem regi haerere et Gallorum nobilissimos longe absistere. Quem nisi in mediocritatem redigat, sese eum crudeli suspendio suffocaturum. Rex dilecti ignominiam non passus, facilius se omnium colloquio quam huius familiaritate posse carere respondit. Quod nimium Rotbertus indignatus, cum optimatibus plerisque iniussus Neustriam petit, ac Turonis sese recipit, multam ibi de regis levitate indignationem habens."

36. Hugh still had the more prominent position on the king's right. See Heinrich Fichtenau, *Living in the Tenth Century: Mentalities and Social Orders,* trans. Patrick J. Geary (Chicago: University of Chicago Press, 1991), 28.

37. The marginal title of 4.32 is "Quod amplius iusto Karolum Arnulfus dilexerit."

tory of Laon "on account of the aforementioned Hagano, to whom the king had granted the abbacy of Chelles, which belonged to Rothilde, who was [the king's] aunt, but Hugh's mother-in-law."[38] By making Hagano lay abbot of Chelles, Charles had robbed Hugh of an inheritance to which he was entitled and helped to undermine the arrangements that Robert had made to secure his son's position.[39] It is possible that Richer dispensed with this detail out of a desire for narrative simplicity, but more likely that he chose to exclude it because it ran counter to the portrait of Charles that he was trying to evoke in the *Historia.* Charles is depicted as naive *(ingenio simplici),* fickle *(inconstans),* immature *(levis),* and headstrong, but never as ruthless, unjust, or calculating. To mention his confiscation of the abbey of Chelles would have transformed the nature of his error from foolish loyalty to an undeserving favorite (a frequent source of criticism for medieval kings, and one that helped to displace the blame for their errors onto their counselors) to the deliberate and unjust dispossession of a leading magnate, complicating Richer's earlier assessment of Charles's character and making Robert and Hugh more sympathetic in the process.[40]

The story of Hagano and Charles the Simple culminates in the second, redundant, audience at Soissons, where another dramatic scene unfolds.[41] Noblemen loyal to Robert attempt once more to persuade the king to abandon Hagano, but this time it is only to provide Robert with a pretext to seize the throne. Charles once more refuses to heed the admonitions of his nobles, who now "judged that they would have very just grounds for resentment *(indignatio)* against him."[42] Charles's stubborn refusal to part ways with Hagano leads to an attempt by Robert and his allies to kidnap the king, a plan that is thwarted only by the timely intervention of

38. *Annales,* s.a. 922, p. 8.

39. See Koziol, "Charles the Simple," 358.

40. For royal counselors, see Geneviève Buhrer-Thierry, "Le conseiller du roi: Les écrivains carolingiens et la tradition biblique," *Médiévales* 12 (1987): 111–23.

41. *Historia* 1.21.

42. *Historia* 1.21.

Archbishop Hervey of Rheims, who arrives to rescue Charles from captivity. Flodoard says nothing about an attempt to imprison the king, merely reporting that Hervey "received the king when everyone else had deserted him and brought him to his own residence at the manor of Chacrise."[43] Again, Richer uses an entire chapter to dramatize this incident:

> Surrounded by armed men, [Hervey] entered the traitors' council, as they all looked on in astonishment. He took on a frightening aspect: "Where, I ask, is my lord the king?" Out of so many men, only a few could summon up the nerve to respond, reckoning that they had been completely foiled. When they had recovered their courage, they replied: "He is inside, taking counsel with a few men." The archbishop applied force to the locked door, broke open the bolts, and found the king sitting with a few men (for they had consigned their captive to a prison cell and put guards over him). The archbishop took him by the hand and said, "Come, my king, and avail yourself of your own men." And with that Charles was led from the midst of the traitors by the archbishop.... After his departure the traitors were confounded with shame and resentful that they had been outwitted.[44]

Richer dramatizes Hervey's rescue of the king through dialogue and vivid gestures: bursting into the council room of the traitors, breaking open the locked door, and leading the king out while his captors look on in astonishment. Again, a word central to the theme of the chapter is repeated, as Richer uses forms of the word "traitor" *(desertor)* six times, and once more similar phrases occur in close proximity.[45] We can compare Richer's technique here to Flodoard's own reworking of the story in the *Historia Remensis Ecclesiae:*

> After nearly all of the Frankish nobles had completely abandoned King Charles, deserting him at the city of Soissons because of Hagano, his counselor, whom he had chosen from among those of the middle rank

43. Flodoard, *Annales,* s.a. 920, p. 2.

44. *Historia* 1.21

45. "intro cum paucis consultat ... cum paucis sedentem repperit;" "desertores pudore confuis ... confusique ad Rotbertum redeunt."

and whom he listened to and honored above all of the leading men, this bishop [Hervey], who was always faithful, devout, and brave in the face of danger, fearlessly took the king from this place and brought him to his own dwelling; and from there he led him to the city of Rheims. He followed him and kept him company for nearly seven months, until he restored his counts to him and him to his kingdom.[46]

This version of the story is an aesthetic improvement upon the account in the *Annals*. Flodoard avoids repetition and creates *variatio* by interchanging the terms *optimates, principes,* and *comites,* and adds emphasis by using the adverbs *penitus* and *semper.* He employs adjectives *(fidelis, pius, robustus, intrepidus)* to characterize the hero of this portion of his history, archbishop Hervey. A relative clause *(quem de mediocribus...)* is included to offer a clearer explanation for the abandonment of Charles. Finally, he expands the four distinct clauses of the *Annals* into one long and well-balanced period. But nothing here compares to the drama that unfolds in Richer's account. While Flodoard is primarily interested in burnishing Hervey's reputation, Richer sets out to explain the causes and motivations of his characters.

What conclusions, if any, can we draw about the interplay between oral tradition and rhetorical invention in the foregoing scenes? The anecdote about Hagano removing the king's hat and putting it on his own head has the ring of an authentic oral tradition. It contains a significant gesture (one of the features of oral-traditional storytelling enumerated by Martinez Pizarro), it serves an explanatory purpose that would justify its continued oral transmission (it symbolizes the reason for the *indignatio* of the nobles), and there is no antecedent to it in any of Richer's classical sources. The seating of Hagano beside Charles at Soissons does have a clas-

46. *HRE* 4.15, p. 408: "Cum pene cuncti Francorum optimates apud urbem Suessonicam a rege suo Karolo desciscentes propter Haganonem, consiliarium suum, quem de mediocribus electum super omnes principes audiebat et honorabat, eum penitus reliquissent, hic pontifex fidelis et pius atque robustus in periculis semper existens, regem intrepidus ab eodem loco suscipiens ad metatum suum deduxit indeque secum ad urbem Remensem perduxit, et per septem fere menses eum prosecutus atque comitatus est, donec illi comites suos eundemque regno restituit."

sical parallel, namely, a quarrel about seating precedence between Jugurtha and Hiempsal in chapter 11 of Sallust's *Jugurthine War.* This is a story that Richer must have known well, since it occurs immediately after a speech that he used as a model, but we cannot say with certainty whether it influenced the seating-precedence motif in the *Historia.*[47] Hervey's entrance into the council of the traitors is not found in Flodoard and contains both a dramatic gesture (breaking down the door leading to the king's cell) and some dialogue. It also serves a legitimizing function, emphasizing the heroism of the archbishop. Indeed, it is the kind of story that we might expect to be circulating in clerical circles at Rheims.

What is most striking, however, is how faint the oral-traditional footprint is in this series of scenes. In no case do we appear to have anything like the literary record of an oral-traditional tale as it was actually narrated. Direct dialogue is absent from every scene save for Hervey's entrance into the council of traitors, and as we will see, there is some cause to be suspicious about the authenticity of the putative oral tradition underlying this scene. The only elements of the previous scenes that hint at oral tradition are Hagano's removal of Charles's hat and the seat that he occupies at Charles's table (if this is not simply a variation on a theme from Sallust). Otherwise Richer is mostly concerned with explicating people's reasons for acting as they did. Although detailed stories about Charles and Hagano must have been circulating at the time when Richer was writing, comparatively little of that oral-traditional material seems to have made it into the *Historia.*

Arnulf and the Capture of Montreuil

A recurring type of dramatic scene in the *Historia* is the betrayal of a city or stronghold.[48] Among the most detailed of these is Count Arnulf of Flanders's plot to seize the stronghold of Montreuil-sur-

47. *Historia* 2.51.

48. 1.63 (Noyon), 2.7 (Château-Thierry), 2.11–12 (Montreuil-sur-Mer), 3.11 (Dijon), 4.16 (Laon), 4.47 (Rheims), and 4.75–76 (Melun).

Mer, which occupied a strategically important position on a promontory near the mouth of the Canche River, from Count Erluin in 939.[49] Flodoard describes the events with characteristic brevity:

Count Arnulf captured a seaside fortress of Erluin's called Montreuil after a certain traitor handed it over, and he sent Erluin's wife across the sea, along with his children, to King Aethelstan [of England]. Not long afterwards, having assembled a sizable band of Northmen, Erluin took back the fortress in battle. Some of Arnulf's soldiers whom he found inside he killed, and some he kept in order to get his wife back.[50]

What is most obviously missing from this account is the reason for Arnulf's decision to seize Montreuil, the circumstances of the betrayal of the stronghold, and an explanation of how Erluin was able to retake it. Richer fills in all of these gaps and expands this brief passage to cover five chapters. He begins his account of the attack on Montreuil by assigning a motive to Arnulf: the income that came into the port from trade:

Count Arnulf of Flanders devised a plot to capture Montreuil, a coastal fortress that belonged to Erluin, intending to take possession of it because of the great profits that it brought in from maritime traffic.[51]

He then develops three words in Flodoard—*tradente quodam proditore*—into a chapter-length dramatic scene. Some of Arnulf's men meet secretly with a guard named Robert and attempt to persuade him to betray Montreuil:

At last they sighed and said, "Alas, Robert, alas, Robert! (for this was his name) How many misfortunes you have escaped! How many dangers you have been rescued from! And what is more, how much success and good fortune are owed to you!" And they immediately set before him two rings, one made of gold, and the other of iron. "Take note," they said, "of what these things mean." When he professed his ignorance, they continued: "Imagine in the gold ring splendid gifts, in the iron the chains of a prison. For the time is at hand when this stronghold, too, must pass under someone else's control."[52]

49. See Lauer, *Le règne de Louis IV*, 38–39.
50. *Annales*, s.a. 939, p. 72.
51. *Historia* 2.11
52. *Historia* 2.11

Here the scene is focused not upon a gesture, but upon important objects (another indicator of oral-traditional storytelling): the gold and iron rings that symbolize Robert's dilemma. Ultimately he reasons that he has little choice. He is presented with a fait accompli, since Arnulf's messengers assure him that Montreuil will fall. By joining Arnulf's party now he can not only save his own life, but also get rich in the bargain. Richer briefly recounts his internal struggle:

> Driven by greed, he hesitated over this betrayal. He wavered, at a loss for what he should do. At last he decided that the dishonor of this treachery could be excused by the fact that he knew that all the members of the garrison were soon going to be exiled or put to death. Therefore, he promised to betray [the stronghold] and pledged his faith by swearing an oath.[53]

In the next chapter Arnulf arrives to take the city. Here Richer sets the stage for another scene:

> The sun had now set. The traitor had sent a few men out through the gate, under the pretext that they were going to attend to some useful business. He himself stood on the wall and held up a burning torch, ostensibly to provide light for the servants whom he had dispatched, though in fact he had given notice through the envoys that the light would be the signal for them to approach. Arnulf and his knights charged forward and entered the stronghold through the open gate.[54]

Just as Arnulf had arranged it, the city falls quickly. Erluin's wife and children are captured, but Erluin himself escapes in disguise, and in the next chapter (2.13) he goes before the Norman duke William Longsword to plead for help. Erluin's complaint *(conquestio)* before the duke forms the next scene in this drama. Richer voices Erluin's complaints in indirect discourse: he has been deprived of his stronghold, his soldiers, and his family, so that all that is left to him is his own body. Yet while the possibility of recapturing Montreuil will always remain, the loss of his wife and children presents "a disaster with no ending" *(calamitatem interminabilem)*. If they are

53. *Historia* 2.11.

54. *Historia* 2.12.

killed, Erluin's grief will forever torment him; if they remain alive as hostages, he will be haunted by a vain hope of recovering them. As is so often the case in the *Historia*, the speech convinces its audience. William dispatches some of his men to help Erluin. At 2.14 Erluin recaptures Montreuil and at 2.15 he defeats a plundering expedition sent against him by Arnulf.

Richer expands Flodoard's brief account of the dispute over Montreuil in a similar fashion to the episode of Hagano. Motivation—in this case the greed *(cupiditas)* of both Arnulf and Robert—is stated explicitly. He stresses the theme of treachery through the repetition of a few key words—*dolus, proditio, proditor*—but makes no attempt to create variation through synonyms or periphrasis. The drama unfolds in a succession of scenes. At 2.11 Arnulf's men attempt to persuade Robert to throw in his lot with them and betray Montreuil; at 2.12 Robert, having turned traitor, signals to Arnulf and his men to enter the city; at 2.13 Erluin appears before William Longsword and pleads for assistance. The perspective then widens to include two accounts of battles between Arnulf and Erluin's men. Richer explains the actions of Arnulf, Robert, and Erluin by drawing out their motives. Dialogue (between Robert and Arnulf's men) and indirect discourse (Robert's internal debate and Erluin's *conquestio*), as well as significant objects (the iron and gold rings and the torch Robert uses to signal to the invaders) add a sense of dramatic immediacy. Persuasive speech is central to the course of events. Arnulf's men persuade Robert to consider betraying the city; Robert convinces himself in an interior monologue that he has no choice but to turn traitor; and Erluin's speech convinces William Longsword to lend him aid.

The betrayal of Montreuil was clearly an event that was still remembered in the late tenth century because Dudo of Saint-Quentin also recounts it, although his version differs markedly from Richer's.[55] The most important potential indicators of an underlying oral tradition in Richer's account—dialogue, significant objects, and the

55. *Gesta Normannorum* 3.59–60, pp. 203–5.

name of the castellan—all occur in chapter 11. The statement that Erluin was at Montreuil when the stronghold fell and escaped in disguise (2.12) is not found in Flodoard. This could be a case where Richer had access to additional knowledge, but more likely it was an attempt to explain how Erluin ended up at the court of William Longsword after the fall of Montreuil. Erluin's complaint to William (2.13) is clearly an authorial invention, as is Robert's interior monologue (2.11). As usual, Richer pays close attention to the motives and psychology of the actors. In his account Arnulf seeks to capture Montreuil because of the income it brought in from maritime trade. While this explanation may seem self-evident to modern readers, it represents a contrast with the motives ascribed to Arnulf by Dudo. Dudo prefaces his account of the capture of Montreuil with a lengthy description of the machinations of the devil, who poisons the minds of the Franks against William Longsword and stirs up cruelty, greed, and injustice throughout the realm.[56] In his version of events it is diabolically induced madness, rather than a rational strategic calculation, that leads Arnulf to seize the stronghold from Erluin.

> And so this venom was deeply instilled by means of the devil's agents and went about more and more cruelly with hostile rage, and grew abominably stronger through the iniquity of evil-doers; and justice was defiled throughout the whole realm.... For this reason a prince named Arnulf, the much-famed margrave of the Flemish region, who had been deeply tainted with this foul poison, stole the castle which is called Montreuil from count Erluin.[57]

The motive ascribed to Arnulf here is typical. In the *Gesta Normannorum* the actions of those who oppose the Norman dukes are typically attributed to frenzy, madness, or poison dripped into the hearts of men by the devil or his agents. Richer, by contrast, never uses diabolical influence as an explanation for the actions

56. *Gesta Normannorum* 3.59, p. 203.

57. *Gesta Normannorum* 3.59, p. 203; translation in Christiansen, *Dudo of St. Quentin*, 79.

of his characters. Baldwin of Flanders decides to kill Archbishop Fulk because he is angry at losing the Abbey of Saint-Vaast, not because he is driven to do it by the devil.[58] Arnulf betrays the city of Rheims to Charles of Lotharingia out of family loyalty, not supernatural prompting.[59] Even Gislebert of Lotharingia and Heribert of Vermandois, about whom Richer has nothing good to say, act purely out of self-interest, and never as a result of diabolical agency. Richer's attribution of purely secular motives to historical actors is a defining feature of his methodology, a product both of his conscious desire to imitate the historians of classical antiquity and his knowledge of and appreciation for political and military strategy.[60]

Oral Tradition and Rhetorical Invention

The four groups of scenes just examined provide a useful inventory of the ways in which Richer reworked and amplified Flodoard's *Annals*. On a formal level he uses intensifying adjectives and adverbs to create emphasis, employs descriptive vocabulary to shape the reader's opinion of characters and their actions, and clarifies the connections between events by linking sentences together with explanatory coordinating conjunctions as opposed to the weaker conjunctions characteristic of annals. He also accounts for the elements required to secure narrative plausibility—person *(persona)*,

58. *Historia* 1.17.

59. *Historia* 4.32.

60. We find a similar distinction in the motives ascribed to historical actors in competing accounts of the betrayal of Melun to Count Odo I of Blois and Chartres in 991. Richer explains Odo's desire to seize the fortress in terms of its strategic importance: he lacked control of a secure crossing over the Seine and wanted a place where he could bring troops across the river (4.74). In contrast, Odo of Saint-Maur, writing in the 1050s, attributes Odo's seizure of the castle to the instigation of the devil. See *Vita Burchardi comitis*, ed. Charles Bourel de la Roncière, *Vie de Bouchard le Vénérable, comte de Vendôme, de Corbeil, de Melun et de Paris (Xe et XIe siècles) par Eudes de Saint-Maur* (Paris: Alphonse Picard, 1892), 18: "Huic venerando comiti, instigante humani generis inimico, infestus atque inimicus existebat valde Odo comes eiusque bonis invidebat actibus quia illum in aula regis sibi preponi atque honorari et diligi a cunctis conspiciebat."

deed *(factum)*, cause *(causa)*, place *(locus)*, time *(tempus)*, method *(modus)*, and means *(facultas)*. Thus, while Flodoard merely reports that Heribert died and was buried at Saint-Quentin by his sons, Richer gives us a specific time and place (Heribert's council chamber, while he was addressing his men), a means of death (apoplexy), and a cause ("superfluity of humors"). Similarly, whereas Flodoard's *Annals* report that the stronghold of Montreuil was betrayed to Arnulf "by a certain traitor," Richer gives us a specific person (Robert), a cause *(cupiditas)*, a time and place for the betrayal (at sundown, as Robert stood on the walls), and explanations of how the surrender and recapture of the city took place.

Was Richer consciously rewriting Flodoard with the requirements of plausible narrative in mind? There is some indication that this is the case. If we examine the *Historia* in terms of the elements required by Cicero and Marius Victorinus to secure narrative plausibility, we find that in general terms it accounts for all of them.[61] Because the *Historia* is written in a loosely annalistic framework and comprises a series of smaller mini-narratives rather than the single master narrative envisioned by classical rhetoricians, each of the Ciceronian elements of narrative is not fully developed in every scene or chapter. Yet Richer attempts in most cases to flesh out his source material by introducing precisely those circumstances that were needed to create a sense of verisimilitude.

Of course any dramatic scene had to account for person, deed, time, place, method, and means. What distinguishes Richer's scene construction is the careful attention that he pays to causes and motivations. Charles the Simple's *levitas* and the *indignatio* of his most prominent subjects are responsible for his abandonment and Robert's usurpation of the throne. Greed drives Arnulf of Flanders to attack Montreuil, and the same greed entices the guard Robert to betray the city. Richer set himself the task to write history that explained the *rationes negotiorum* of the actors, and because plausibility, not factual accuracy, was the goal of *narratio probabilis*, these

61. *De inventione* 1.21.29.

motivations could be freely invented as long as they corresponded to the beliefs of the audience.[62] Richer's audience would no doubt have found the motivations that he ascribes to his characters to be convincing. Civil discord among the nobles *(dissidentia principum)* is a prominent theme in the *Historia,* and resentment *(indignatio)* and greed *(cupiditas)* were the engines that drove this discord. Any monk or secular cleric of Richer's day would have been well acquainted with these unsavory characteristics of the nobility, and in that sense his narrative could not have been more plausible. The explicit exposition of motives is a requirement of *narratio probabilis,* but not a common feature of orally transmitted stories, where the nonpresence of the author is the rule. Thus, while other aspects of Richer's scene construction cannot be definitively tied to an attempt to satisfy the rhetorical requirements for narrative plausibility, his attention to *causae* and *rationes* probably can.

The requirements of *narratio probabilis* gave Richer both the license and the obligation to invent material to embellish his sources, and in some cases there is reason to suspect that material that appears to derive from oral tradition may actually be the product of *inventio,* either outright "invention," or else the recycling of certain types of narrative motifs. Consider, for example, the scene in which Robert of Montreuil negotiates with Arnulf's henchmen to betray the stronghold. Certain aspects of Richer's account—dialogue, the name of the castellan, the gold and iron rings—suggest oral tradition, and indeed, we know that the story was in general circulation because Dudo of Saint-Quentin discusses it at some length. At the same time, Richer's account of the betrayal of the stronghold strongly resembles other accounts of treachery in the *Historia,* all of which follow a common pattern.

At 2.7, for example, Heribert of Vermandois persuades Walo, the castellan of Château-Thierry, to hand the fortress over to him.[63]

62. *De inventione* 1.19.27: "Probabilis erit narratio, si in ea videbuntur inesse ea quae solent apparere in veritate."

63. For Walo, see Schwager, *Graf Heribert II,* 390–91. He was castellan of Heri-

This betrayal follows the pattern seen in the capture of Montreuil: the castellan is tricked by a persuasive speech, there is a promise of a material reward, a swearing of oaths, and a time appointed for the betrayal. Finally, when the time comes to let the enemy's troops into the city, the traitor pretends to set the men under his command an important task, leaving the stronghold undefended. In both cases Richer expands upon a passing notice in the *Annals* and in both cases he invents a scene with similar elements to dramatize the betrayal. An analogous case occurs at 1.63 where an unnamed cleric who wants to become bishop of Noyon convinces Adelelm, the count of Arras, to take the city by force. Richer adds a number of elements missing from Flodoard's bare outline of events.[64] There is an explicit mention of treachery, a persuasive speech that convinces Adelelm, and the promise of a reward.[65] Likewise, at 3.11, Robert of Troyes, Heribert's son, plots to capture the royal castle of Dijon. Flodoard's account is limited to two brief sentences, whereas Richer spells out Robert's motivation in detail and emphasizes his greed.[66] Robert sends messengers to corrupt the castellan. There is an explicit promise of reward and a persuasive speech in indirect discourse.[67] Then the castellan gives over to greed, the messengers promise a specific monetary reward, and they swear an oath to Robert.

A final example is the story of the capture of Melun at 4.74–75. In this case Count Odo I of Blois and Chartres decides that he wants to take the castle of Melun, consults with his men, and then sends one of them to corrupt the castellan. Again, there is treachery, a promise of faithfulness, and an oath. Instead of a sin-

---

bert's fortress of Château-Thierry when it fell to King Radulf in 933, after which he swore allegiance to Queen Emma. Later that same year some of the men Walo had set to guard the fortress betrayed it to Heribert. See Flodoard, *Annales*, s.a. 933, pp. 55–57.

64. *Annales*, s.a. 932, p. 52. See also Olivier Guyotjeannin, *Episcopus et comes: Affirmation et déclin de la seigneurie épiscopale au nord du royaume de France (Beauvais-Noyon, Xe–début XIIIe siècle)* (Geneva: Librairie Droz, 1987), 37–38.

65. *Historia* 1.63.

66. *Annales*, s.a. 959, p. 147; s.a. 960, p. 148. Cf. *Historia* 3.11.

67. *Historia* 3.11.

gle speech of persuasion there follows a dialogue in which Odo's man tries to persuade the castellan to betray the stronghold to his master. Faced with a similar situation, Robert of Montreuil first weighed the prospect of a reward against the dishonor he was likely to incur and ultimately excused his actions by reasoning that he had no real choice in the matter.[68] Similarly, the castellan of Melun asks Odo's man how he can exculpate himself from the guilt and dishonor that will accompany a betrayal of his charge. In Robert's case greed and cowardice moved him to turn traitor, but it was necessary to cloak these baser motivations in casuistic reasoning. The same process occurs here. The castellan of Melun lets himself be persuaded by the arguments of Odo's messenger (that Odo is favored by fortune, while the king is weak and unworthy of support), but it is really greed that motivates his betrayal. In the end, both the unlucky castellan and his wife are hanged when kings Hugh and Robert retake Melun shortly thereafter (4.78).

In this case Richer is not drawing on Flodoard for the outline of the story, so there is no way to determine exactly how much of it he had heard and how much he invented. Yet we can be fairly sure that a significant portion of the account is the product of his own imagination. The betrayal of Melun to Odo is mentioned in two other near-contemporary accounts, a life of Count Burchard of Vendôme written by Odo of Saint-Maur in the 1050s, and the early eleventh-century *Historia Francorum Senonensis.* Both of these sources give the name of the castellan as Walter, and both report that he was hanged along with his wife. But neither includes the story of the negotiations between Walter and Odo's messenger.[69] We are left with the question of whether Richer had more information than Odo of Saint-Maur or the author(s) of the *Historia Fran-*

68. *Historia* 2.11.

69. Both accounts of the betrayal of the city are very short. See *Vita Burcardi comitis,* chap. 7, p. 18: "Qua de re seductione quadam atque traditione castrum Milidunum ei furatus est"; *Historia Francorum Senonensis,* ed. G. Waitz, MGH SS 9 (Hanover: Hahn, 1851), 369: "In ipso anno tradidit Walterius miles et uxor eius castellum Milidunum Odoni militi." The capture of Melun is incorrectly assigned to the year 999 in this source.

corum Senonensis. It is possible, since Richer visited Chartres in March 991, and the betrayal of Melun took place in the summer or early fall of that year.[70] At the same time, the dialogue is clearly the product of Richer's invention, and the other elements of the betrayal follow the same pattern seen elsewhere in the *Historia.* Richer seems to have developed a certain idea of how strongholds were betrayed and then reprised this sequence of events, with some modification, in different places. When we take this into account, very little about the betrayal of Montreuil looks original—only the name of the castellan and the gold and iron rings. Even the dialogue, as we shall see, bears the heavy imprint of rhetorical invention.

The recurrence of dramatic motifs occurs in other places as well. Archbishop Hervey's dramatic entrance into the council of traitors at 1.22, for example, looks very much like a scene at 2.30 where William Longsword bursts into the council chamber of Louis IV and accosts King Otto I of Germany for seating himself above the king. In both cases someone makes a violent entrance into a council chamber, delivers an angry harangue, humiliates his target, and dies shortly thereafter. At 1.22 Hervey breaks open the doors *(Metropolitanus ostio obserato vim infert),* takes Charles by the hand and tells him to come with him *("veni … tuisque potius utere").* The traitors *(desertores)* taking part in the council are covered in shame *(pudore confusi)* and indignant that they have been outwitted *(illusos sese indignabantur).* Hervey dies soon after the coronation of Robert in 922.[71] At 2.30 William breaks open the doors of the council chamber *(foribus clausis vim intulit),* tells Louis to rise *("surge … ..paululum, rex"),* and rebukes Otto *(Quapropter oportere Ottonem inde amoliri),* who is stricken with shame *(pudore affectus).* Otto complains about this treatment and plots William's murder at 2.31–32. William is then killed a short time later (2.33).

William's angry reaction to being shut out of the council cham-

70. See Hoffmann, *Historiae,* 283n1. We do not know when Richer left Chartres; he may or may not have been there when Melun was captured.

71. *Historia* 1.41.

ber in turn resembles the account of Charles's council at Aachen preserved in Frutolf's *Chronicle*.[72] In this scene, which evidently replaced the first of the two duplicative councils at Soissons (1.16) in the revised version of the *Historia,* Charles is celebrating Easter at Aachen and provokes the anger of some of the magnates—most notably, Henry the Fowler of Saxony—by shutting them out of his chamber for several days:

> Every day they waited outside the doors of the royal bed-chamber; every day they expected the king's exit from the inner chamber of the palace. But when no response was given to them from the king for four days, Henry, taking it very badly, reportedly claimed that either Hagano would someday rule with Charles, or Charles would be reduced to middling status with Hagano.[73]

Henry's reaction here recalls both 2.30, where William Longsword waits indignantly outside the doors of Louis's council chamber without being called *(Diucius ergo afforis exspectans, cum non vocaretur, rem animo irato ferebat)* and 1.16, where Robert of Nesutria angrily threatens to have Hagano hanged if the king does not reduce him back to his former middling status *(Quem nisi in mediocritaem redigat, sese eum crudeli suspendio suffocaturum).* Richer introduces Henry's warning to Charles with the words *dixisse fertur* ("he is reported to have said"), which implies that he was drawing upon an established oral tradition for this scene. But if that is the case, and he did not simply make it up, it is odd that he neglected to include it in the first draft of the *Historia,* where the falling out between Charles and Henry is instead presented as the result of the fracas at Worms that resulted in the death of Erlebald of Châtresais (1.20). The significance of Erlebald's death in the revised version of the *Historia* must in turn have been diminished, since the purpose of the story that he was killed by quarreling German and Gaulish youths—which is inconsistent with Flodoard's *Annals*—was to explain the origin of the hostility between Charles

72. Frutolf, *Chronicon,* 181, lines 39–47, and see chap. 2 above.
73. Frutolf, *Chronicon,* 181.

and Henry after the council of Soissons, a role now served by Henry's exclusion from Charles's chambers at Aachen.[74]

The replacement of Robert with Henry here as the agent who threatens Charles if he does not reduce Hagano back to his middling status is similar to the replacement of Gislebert of Lotharingia with Henry at 1.23 and 1.24 as the recipient of the embassy from Hervey of Rheims. It is hard to imagine that either of these revisions could have been based on Richer's sudden acquisition of new and more accurate information. Instead, in both cases, he was trying to create a more plausible version of history, and in doing so, he felt no compunction about changing around the characters in these scenes. These kinds of revisions are a strong indication that some of the material in the *Historia* that appears to be derived from oral tradition may actually be the product of rhetorical invention.

The same suspicion arises when we examine Richer's detailed accounts of two important military engagements: the Battle of Soissons in 923 (1.46), and Louis IV's victory over the Viking army of Sihtric and Turmod in 943 (2.45). We have already seen that Richer directly contradicts Flodoard on several important aspects of the Battle of Soissons (presenting the battle as a draw rather than a victory for the Robertian party, denying that Robert's allies occupied the battlefield and seized spoils, and depicting Charles's retreat as an organized withdrawal) and that he invents casualty statistics for the battle which he disingenuously attributes to Flodoard. Some of the discrepancies between the two accounts may be linked to a pro-Carolingian oral tradition about the battle, a tradition that also appears to be reflected in the confused version of events found in the *Chronicle* of Ademar of Chabannes.[75] Richer provides a considerable amount of information not found

74. Flodoard, *Annales*, s.a. 920, p. 3, says that Erlebald was set upon and killed by "enemies of the king" at Worms.

75. Ademar, *Chronicon*, ed. P. Bourgain, CCCM 129 (Turnhout: Brepols, 1999), 143. See also Patrick Geary, *Phantoms of Remembrance: Memory and Oblivion at the End of the First Millennium* (Princeton, N.J.: Princeton University Press, 1994), 151–52.

in Flodoard that must have been derived from popular legend. He mentions the names of two of Charles's captains, for example: Fulbert, who commanded 6,000 soldiers (and who is also attested in Ademar's *Chronicle*), and Harald, who was appointed to command the 4,000 men whom Charles originally intended to lead into battle before he was persuaded to remain on the sidelines.[76] Richer also describes Robert's death in a scene that is redolent of heroic epic: he ranges over the battle incognito until he is discovered by a band of warriors who have been sworn to kill him. In true heroic fashion, Robert does not shrink from revealing his identity:[77]

> Showing no fear, he immediately uncovered his beard and revealed who he was, whereupon he struck a tremendous blow with his sword at Count Fulbert. Having been dealt a mortal wound, Fulbert was knocked to Robert's right. This enabled him to strike him with his spear through the armhole of his hauberk, wounding him grievously in the side, and driving the point of his spear through his liver, his lung, and the left side of his abdomen, all the way to his shield. Robert was then surrounded by others, and after receiving seven more spear wounds, he collapsed to the ground and lay there, unmoving.[78]

Robert's beard is also mentioned in Ademar's account of the battle, although in this case he wears it flowing over his armor, which allows him to be recognized.[79] Richer's description of the battle, therefore, appears to be a blend of actual oral traditions and partisan deformations of Flodoard. When we look ahead to Louis's victory over the Vikings Sihtric and Turmod in book 2, however, we encounter an incident suspiciously similar to Robert's death at Soissons:[80]

76. *Historia* 1.46. Cf. Adhemar, *Chronicon,* 143.

77. *Historia* 1.43, 1.46.

78. *Historia* 1.46.

79. Ademar, *Chronicon,* 143: "Rotbertus autem ipse vexillum sibi ferebat, dejecta barba canitiae plena extra loricam, ut cognosceretur."

80. On Louis's battle with Sihtric and Turmod and its possible relationship to epic sources, see Ferdinand Lot, *Études sur les légendes épiques françaises* (Paris: H. Champion, 1958), 181–82.

Turmod, for his part, was still in the thick of battle, fighting with all of his might, when he was struck head-on by Louis's charging horse and thrown down to the ground. The king careened past him without recognizing who he was, whereupon he was set upon by his foes, but he stood his ground and fought them hand-to-hand. Turmod, surrounded by his men, came up from behind him, flanked him on the right side, and struck him with his spear through the armhole of his hauberk, delivering a blow that reached almost as far as his left lung. The king, whose attention had been briefly diverted from this attack by the slaughter around him, turned to look at the man who had just wounded him. Then he struck a blow crosswise to his right and cut off the head and left arm of his attacker.[81]

The curious similarity between Louis's wound here and Robert's wound at 1.46 suggests either an outright invention on Richer's part or else the recycling of a legendary motif. If we accept its validity as an oral tradition in at least one of the two battles, then Soissons is by far the more likely candidate. The idea that Louis received a spear strike that passed through the right side of his body (presumably perforating his liver, as it had in Robert's case) and almost reached his left lung is contradicted by Flodoard's *Annals,* which report that Louis returned to Compiègne after the battle and say nothing about a period of convalescence necessary to recover from such a wound.[82] Indeed, Richer himself has Louis return to Compiègne in good order and says nothing about Louis's recovery from his injury.

Richer's invention of dubious casualty statistics for the battle (9,000 Viking slain versus 800 of Louis's men) should already make us skeptical about his sources for the account. His claim that the king received an almost-mortal wound, decapitated Turmod in one blow, and then returned to Compiègne without stopping to recover beggars belief. Nor is Louis's wound the only element in the battle recycled from elsewhere in the *Historia.* Richer reports that after the king's troops broke through the Viking formation, Sihtric

81. *Historia* 2.35.

82. Flodoard, *Annales,* s.a. 943, p. 88. See also Lauer, *Le règne de Louis IV,* 101.

fled and hid in some thorn bushes, where he was caught and run through with three spear thrusts.[83] This episode mirrors Catillus's flight at the Battle of Montpensier in book 1, where he too hides in thorn bushes and is discovered by men ranging over the field of battle. Although Catillus himself is spared, the men hiding with him are put to the sword.[84]

Unlike precise numbers of casualties, specific numbers of wounds need not be the product of rhetorical invention, since this is exactly the kind of detail that would have circulated in oral traditions about a battle. Yet even in these cases we have reason to doubt the authenticity of what Richer tells us. The ten wounds said to have been received by Count Warnerius of Troyes at the Battle of Chalmont, for example, have the ring of oral tradition, yet the fact that Richer otherwise took all of his information about the battle directly from Flodoard, who nowhere mentions such a number, all but rules out this possibility.[85] The same is true of his description of the murder of Archbishop Fulk by Baldwin's henchman Winemar at 1.17, an amplified version of the account given by Flodoard in the *Historia Remensis Ecclesiae.* Richer makes a number of dramatic changes to the battle between Winemar's men and the archbishop's, among them the claims that Winemar himself (rather than the undefined "they" of Flodoard's version) struck Fulk down, and that he ran him through with seven spear thrusts.[86] This happens to be precisely the same number of spear wounds that Robert of Neustria received in Richer's account of the Battle of Soissons, so once more we appear to be dealing with a recycled legendary motif.

In the quest to separate out oral tradition from authorial invention, analyzing the nature of speech in dramatic scenes is a potentially useful tool. Joaquín Martínez Pizarro has identified sev-

83. *Historia* 2.35.

84. *Historia* 1.9.

85. *Historia* 1.49: "Warnerus vero equo occiso quo vectus ferebatur X vulneribus perfossus interierit." Cf. Flodoard, *Annales,* s.a. 925, p. 27: "Warnerius comes, ibi equo cui sedebat occiso, captus et interemptus est."

86. *Historia* 1.17. Cf. *HRE* 4.10, p. 402.

eral features of dramatic dialogue adapted from oral storytelling, namely, "brevity, syntactical and lexical simplicity, [and] the coordination of speech with action and physical expression."[87] When we find these features in a dramatic scene in the *Historia,* therefore, there is good reason to suspect the influence of oral tradition.

It turns out that very little of the speech in the *Historia* is truly informal in the way that that designation is used by Martínez Pizarro. One major category of nonoratorical speech in the *Historia* is the significant utterance or brief exchange of dialogue in a scene that contains no other speaking. This kind of speech is artificial rather than naturalistic. It is not an attempt to mimic the way real historical actors would have spoken to one another, but a means of drawing attention to certain moments in the narrative. Rather than enhancing verisimilitude, it crystallizes the essential dramatic element in a scene. Early in book 1, for example, Ingo, a stable officer of King Odo, offers to carry the king's standard into battle when none of the magnates is willing to do so:

> I, a stable officer of the king from among those of middle rank, will carry the royal standard through the enemy lines if it does not detract from the honor of my superiors. Nor do I fear the uncertain outcome of the battle, since I know that I shall [only] die once.[88]

The purpose of this monologue is to dramatize Ingo's heroism. There is no back-and-forth debate between Ingo and the king, nor any sense that a battle is raging in the background. Odo accepts the offer with a similarly brief and rhetorically self-conscious reply: "By virtue of my dispensation and the will of the leading men, you shall be my standard-bearer."[89] Richer probably heard this story about Odo, the legendary founder of the house of Blois, while he was at Chartres reading medical manuscripts in 991. The dialogue

87. Martínez Pizarro, *A Rhetoric of the Scene,* 87.

88. *Historia* 1.9: "Ego ex mediocribus regis agaso, si maiorum honori non derogatur, signum regium per hostium acies efferam. Nec fortunam belli ambiguam expavesco, cum semel me moriturum cognosco."

89. *Historia* 1.9: "Ad haec Odo rex, 'Nostro,' inquit 'dono, ac principum voluntate signifer esto.'"

itself, however, is formal and artificial. It is more likely to be an authorial composition than the record of an oral tradition circulating in the region around Chartres.

In a later scene King Charles mourns the death of Count Reginar Longneck (d. 915) with an oratorical flourish at his tomb:[90]

> "Alas," he said, "Once high, he is now brought low, once mighty, he is most narrowly confined," signifying with the first statement the man and with the other his tomb.[91]

This passage does not form part of a larger scene—Richer adds no other dialogue or description. Nor does it serve a legitimizing or explanatory function that could explain its survival as an independent oral tradition. Charles's lament serves instead as a kind of dramatic foreshadowing of the grief that Reginar's son Gislebert will cause the king.[92] Richer introduces Charles's dramatic utterance with the words *dicitur ... dixisse,* implying that he had received it from oral report, yet the similarity of these words to a passage in Augustine's *Ennarrationes in Psalmos* should at least arouse the suspicion that he invented them himself.[93]

A final example of the use of isolated speech as a dramatic tool is Heribert of Vermandois's sneering rebuke to Walo, the castellan of Château-Thierry, after he has betrayed the fortress to Heribert.[94] Walo was serving as castellan for Heribert in 933, when King

90. For Reginar, see Rüdiger E. Barth, *Der Herzog in Lotharingien im 10. Jahrhundert* (Sigmaringen: Jan Thorbecke, 1990), 15–38.

91. *Historia* 1.34: "'O,' inquiens, 'ex alto humilem, ex amplo artissimum,' altero personam, altero monumentum significans."

92. Gislebert rebelled against Charles in 919 and was made *princeps* by the Lotharingians in 920, after which he opposed Charles's interests in the region. See Flodoard, *Annales,* s.a. 920, p. 4, and Kienast, *Deustschland und Frankreich in der Kaiserzeit,* 1.51, and note 105.

93. Augustine, *Ennarrationes in Psalmos,* eds. E. Dekkers and J. Fraipont, CCSL 38–40 (Turnhout: Brepols, 1956), 101, *sermo* 1.19: "ex alto factus est humilis." Cf. *Analecta hymnica medii aevi,* vol. 27, ed. Clemens Blume and Guido M. Dreves (Leipzig: O. R. Reisland, 1897), 70: "Tu mundi constitutor es,/ Tu septimo throno sedes, / Iudex, ex alto humilis, / Venisti pati pro nobis" (both cited by Hoffmann, *Historiae,* p. 70, chap. 34, note 5).

94. *Historia* 2.7.

Radulf besieged and captured Château-Thierry.[95] After the fortress fell, Walo abandoned Heribert and pledged his loyalty to its new master, Queen Emma, but later in the same year some of the men he had appointed to guard the stronghold betrayed it back to Heribert.[96] Then, in the spring of 934, King Radulf and Hugh the Great laid siege to Château-Thierry once again. This time Walo and some of his men climbed the walls at night while the guards slept and captured part of the stronghold, which soon thereafter reverted to the control of the king.[97] The fact that Walo had abandoned his fidelity to Heribert and gone over to King Radulf's party in 933, and had fought actively on the king's behalf the next year, helps to explain Heribert's actions when he retakes Château-Thierry in 937. Rather than rewarding Walo as he had promised, he has him put in chains, remarking sarcastically:

> "Do you suppose," he said, "that this stronghold is to remain under your control?"[98]

The *Historia* makes no mention of Walo's previous disloyalty, which makes Heribert's duplicity here seem like an arbitrary act of betrayal rather than a prudent necessity. Richer assigns these words to Heribert in order to dramatize his faithlessness, and perhaps also to make a point about the rewards due to traitors. He makes no attempt to conjure up a scene unfolding in a real time and place, however. Heribert's statement has the ring of authentic speech, but the lack of any descriptive elements or other dialogue in the scene robs it of realism. This kind of speech act is unlikely to be the literary record of an oral tradition about the betrayal of Château-Thierry, an event about which Richer surely had no more information than Flodoard. Rather, it is artificially composed speech *(sermocinatio)* intended to make a dramatic point.

In certain cases these kinds of dramatic utterances make up

95. Flodoard, *Annales,* s.a. 933, pp. 55–56.
96. Flodoard, *Annales,* s.a. 933, p. 57.
97. Flodoard, *Annales,* s.a. 934, p. 58.
98. *Historia* 2.7: "'Putasne,' inquit, 'tuae curae oppidum hoc reservandum?'"

part of more fully developed scenes that include specific time and place, dramatic gestures, and significant objects. When Archbishop Hervey of Rheims storms into the chamber occupied by nobles holding King Charles captive, for example, he asks a brief question: "Where, I ask, is my lord the king?" *("Ubi, inquam, est dominus meus rex?").* The conspirators respond with the brief reply: "He is taking counsel with a few men inside" *("Intro cum paucis consultat"),* whereupon the archbishop breaks down the door and gives the king a short command: "Come, my king, and avail yourself of your own men instead" *("Veni ... rex, tuisque potius utere").*[99] The scene contains enough specific elements—dialogue, dramatic gestures, and the precise number of men (1,500) that Charles took with him to Rheims after he left captivity—that one is inclined to attribute it to an oral source. Yet we have reason to be suspicious. Flodoard recounts the germ of the story in the *HRE,* a work specifically intended to glorify the church of Rheims, but includes none of the dramatic elements.[100] The dialogue is not naturalistic and informal—as we would expect if it derived from oral storytelling—but artificial and dramatic, intended to focus the reader's attention on the heroism of the archbishop.[101] More suspiciously, the number 1,500 crops up one chapter earlier in the *Historia Remensis Ecclesiae,* where it refers not to the number of men who accompanied Charles when he left Soissons, but to the number of soldiers that Archbishop Hervey led against the Hungarians the previous year.[102]

Similarly, the scene in which Arnulf's men persuade Robert to betray Montreuil to their lord contains direct speech, significant objects, and gestures. Yet not only is it strikingly similar to other

99. *Historia* 1.22.

100. *HRE* 4.15, p. 408.

101. A similar scene unfolds at *Historia* 2.30 when William Longsword, duke of Normandy, storms into the room where Otto I of Germany, Hugh the Great, and Arnulf, count of Flanders, are meeting with King Louis IV. As is the case with Hervey's forced entrance into the council of traitors, the onlookers sit by in stunned silence while William rebukes Otto, leaving the words of the speaker to resound in the ears of the audience.

102. *HRE* 4.14, p. 407.

scenes of betrayal in the *Historia,* the language used by Arnulf's men is more artificial and rhetorically polished than we would expect if it were the record of an oral tradition. Note, for example, their opening salvo:

> "Alas, Robert, alas, Robert!" (for this was his name) "How many misfortunes you have escaped! How many dangers you have been rescued from! And what is more, how much success and good fortune are owed to you!"[103]

After their address to Robert, the messengers employ a florid tricolon marked by anaphora and rounded out with a phrase borrowed from Hegesippus *(secundarum rerum … successus),* an author with whom Arnulf's vassals were unlikely to have been acquainted.[104] This is, in fact, a hallmark of Richer's style: variants on a tricolon made up of rhetorical questions appear in the *Historia* on several other occasions.[105] One similar instance is a complaint delivered by Louis IV to his men concerning his persecution at the hands of Hugh the Great, in which the king opens his speech with two clauses exactly parallel to those used by Arnulf's men:

> In their presence the king delivered a complaint in these words, saying "Alas, Hugh, Alas, Hugh. How many of my possessions have I been deprived of by you! How many evils have I been afflicted with! And in what misery am I now held captive!"[106]

103. *Historia* 2.11: "'Eia te,' inquiunt, 'Rotberte, eia te Rotberte' (sic enim vocabatur); 'quantis malis elapsus, quantis periculis exemptus es, et quanti insuper secundarum rerum tibi debentur successus.'"

104. *Bellum Iudaicum* 1.35.1: "tanto rerum secundarum successu levatus."

105. Cf. *Historia* 2.73 (Louis's address to the synod of Ingelheim): "'Quanto,' inquiens, 'Hugonis instinctu, quantoque eius impulsu conqueri cogor, testis est ille, cuius gratia vos hic congregatos paulo ante relatum est'"; 2.77 (a letter addressed by the Synod of Ingelheim to Hugh the Great): "Quantis malis, quantaque persecutione vexaveris illam venerabilem Remorum metropolim, quanta quoque crudelitate debacchatus sis in dominum tuum regem, ora omnium locuntur"; 4.97 (Adalbero of Laon is rebuked by followers of Hugh Capet): "Et o summae divinitatis miserationem inestimabilem, quantis miseriis erepti, quanto ludibrio subtracti sumus."

106. *Historia* 2.52: "Apud quos etiam rex his verbis conquestus est. Et 'Eia tu,' inquiens, 'Hugo, eia tu Hugo. Quantis bonis a te privatus, quantis malis affectus, quanto etiam merore nunc detineor.'"

That Richer composed these nearly identical tricola himself is confirmed by the fact that he uses a similar construction to address the reader during his account of his journey to Chartres:

> How great my agitation was at that moment, and how great my anxiety, those who have ever undergone similar misfortunes can judge from their own experiences.[107]

It is noteworthy that the phrase *perpendere valere* used here is also found earlier in the mouths of Arnulf's messengers (2.11: "*Et vide,*" *inquiunt,* "*quid in his perpendi valeat*"). All of this suggests that their speech to Robert cannot be a direct record of a circulating oral tradition. The scene that Richer describes at 2.11 thus appears to consist of the kernel of an oral tradition heavily overlaid with authorial embellishment.

The same holds true for Richer's account of the murder of William Longsword, which unfolds over four chapters at 2.30–33. This is clearly a case where Richer was drawing on oral-traditional material as his primary source; the existence of stories about William's death in other contemporary sources confirms that accounts of murder of the Duke of Normandy circulated in the late tenth and eleventh centuries.[108] Nonetheless, the dialogue in these scenes bears the imprint of rhetorical composition, suggesting that he was not merely translating oral-traditional material into Latin, but that he was using it as a springboard for his own rhetorically ornamented narrative.

For example, when William enters the room where King Louis is meeting with Otto, Hugh the Great, and Arnulf of Flanders, he

107. *Historia* 4.50: "Quanta tunc fuit perturbatio, quanta anxietas, illi perpendere valent, qui casus similes aliquando perpessi sunt, et ex similibus similia colligant."

108. See Lair, *Étude sur la vie et la mort de Guillaume Longue-Épée.* The most important accounts contemporary with Richer are Dudo's *Gesta Normannorum* and an anonymous *Planctus.* For the latter, see Phillipp August Becker, "Der planctus auf den Normannenherzog Wilhelm Langschwert (942)," *Zeitschrift für französische Sprache und Literatur* 63 (1939): 190–97. Flodoard, *Annales,* s.a. 943, p. 86, offers only the scantiest information: "Arnulfus comes Willelmum Nordmannorum principem ad colloquium evocatum dolo perimi fecit."

rebukes the king's counselors for their lack of deference to the king and their failure to include him in the meeting:

> William could not bear this insult to the king. "Was I not to be included?" he asked. "Have I ever been stained by the dishonor due to a traitor?" He drew near angrily and said, "Rise up a little, my king."[109]

This encounter does not occur in any other contemporary account of the William Longsword legend. Certain aspects of the dialogue mark the scene out as part of Martínez Pizarro's new narrative mimesis and suggest oral transmission: the sentences are short, syntactically simple, and coordinated with physical expression.[110] At the same time the dialogue is more Latinate in syntax and more consciously rhetorical than one would expect if Richer was simply translating a vernacular story into Latin. The two questions *An his interesse non debui?* and *Desertorisne dedecore aliquando sordui?* are marked by end-rhyme, parallelism, and alliteration. If Richer borrowed the scene from an oral tradition, he was not simply translating the vernacular directly into Latin.

Richer's authorial presence makes itself more evident in the next chapter (2.31), where he describes Otto's resentment at his public humiliation by William. Otto's lament to his men is presented as a *conquestio,* a category of classical rhetoric with its own forms of argument, rather than as a spontaneous and informal outburst. Rhetorical and dialectical terminology in the chapter *(colores verborum, rationibus determinatis)* and phrases recycled from elsewhere in the *Historia* (*ultra aequum et ius* at 2.31 mirrors *preter ius et aequum* at 1.43) suggest authorial composition as well. Moreover, both the *conquestio* delivered by Otto at 2.31 and the *deliberatio* between Hugh the Great and Arnulf of Flanders in the next chapter about the advisability of murdering William are in *oratio obliqua,* a type of speech not typically associated with orally transmitted

109. *Historia* 2.30: "Uuilelmus regis iniuriam non passus, 'An,' inquit, 'his interesse non debui? Desertorisne dedecore aliquando sordui?' Fervidus propinquans, 'Surge,' inquit, 'paululum, rex.'"

110. *A Rhetoric of the Scene,* 87.

scenes. The style of these chapters indicates that, whether or not Richer had heard the kernel of this story from someone else, he had reworked it to a large degree. We are some distance from the "rhetoric of the ordinary" described by Martínez Pizarro.

While Richer's authorial hand has always been recognizable in the highly artificial orations he writes for his characters, it should now be evident that he supplemented both Flodoard and his oral-traditional material in other ways. He certainly wrote dialogue into these stories, and he may have invented many of the core elements of episodes that appear to derive from oral tradition. At the very least, he recycled certain narrative motifs, whether they were drawn from folklore and rumor (the betrayal of cities, the *indignatio* of nobles) or from classical historiography (the battle, the burial of a king, or rhetorical set pieces like the *conquestio* and the *deliberatio*). The use of these sorts of narrative motifs is part of the process of rhetorical *inventio,* which was not the "invention" of material out of thin air, but the "discovery" of the right kinds of material to use. Folklore and oral tradition could have served Richer as one particularly rich source of material. Because Richer clearly had no problem creating "readily believable" (i.e., fictional) diseases, speeches, motivations, accounts of battles, and letters, in the absence of evidence to the contrary, we should be cautious about assigning all of the new material that he incorporates into the *Historia* to authentic oral traditions. Apart from his father, Richer never discloses the sources of his oral information, nor does he ever make reference to witnesses to confirm the truth of what he is saying. This stands in stark contrast to his explicit mention of all his principal written sources.

It is surprising how meager the oral-traditional elements in the first half of the *Historia* really are. Rather than the retelling of oral tales in *toto,* in most instances we have fragments of oral tradition heavily overlaid with rhetorical amplification. In this respect the *Historia* differs from earlier histories like Notker the Stammerer's *Gesta Karoli Magni* or Agnellus of Ravenna's *Liber pontificalis ecclesiae Ravennatis.* Richer was writing at a point when the new narrative mimesis described by Martínez Pizarro was petering out, giving way to a different style of rhetorically self-conscious historiography that took root in northern Francia in the late tenth and early eleventh centuries, a style whose leading exponents were Aimoin of Fleury, Dudo of Saint-Quentin, and Richer himself.[111] This development was a direct result of the increased attention given to Ciceronian rhetoric in the schools of northern Francia in the late tenth century, and it is to the influence of this type of rhetorical training on Richer that we will now turn.

111. Christiansen, *Dudo of St. Quentin*, xx–xi.

[FOUR]

Rhetoric and the *Historia*

THE PREVIOUS CHAPTERS have examined Richer's historical methodology and explored the theoretical foundations of his approach to writing history. His stylistic self-consciousness, comparative indifference to factual accuracy, and fanciful amplification of his sources are best explained as the result of a conscious decision to write history according to the rhetorical conventions of classical historiography. Like the classical and late antique historians whom he took as models, he employed the precepts for the composition of an oratorical *narratio* as guidelines for writing history. Latin rhetorical handbooks required that the *narratio* be rendered readily believable *(probabilis)* through the discovery *(inventio)* of material that was either true *(verum)* or similar to the truth *(verisimile)*. In accordance with this doctrine, Richer wove his history together from two separate strands: events that had actually happened *(gesta)* and those that could have happened *(ut gesta)*.[1] Each type of material required a different kind of authorial activity. On the one hand he had to accumulate, select, and organize material from oral and written sources to create a basic historical framework, and on the other to expand and embellish this material through rhetorical *inventio*.

The free rein that Richer gave to invention in the *Historia* may have diminished the reputation of his work among modern scholars, but it belongs to a long historiographical tradition. The fictional speeches, conversations, and dramatic scenes that he composed

1. *De inventione* 1.19.27.

have impeccable antecedents in the histories of Livy, Sallust, and Hegesippus, while the requirement that a narrative be plausible, if not necessarily true, was articulated by Cicero and the anonymous author of the *Rhetorica ad Herennium* in the first century B.C. and perpetuated in subsequent commentaries and rhetorical handbooks.[2] Although the *Historia* contains a substantial amount of dubious or demonstrably false material, Richer's historical imagination is actually restrained when compared to that of Dudo of Saint-Quentin in the early eleventh century or Geoffrey of Monmouth in the twelfth. Considered against the background of the full range of medieval historical writing, the level of artistic license that Richer exercises in the *Historia* is hardly unusual.

Nevertheless, his conception of history as a rhetorical exercise is an innovation in the tradition of historical writing at Rheims. The role that *inventio* plays in the *Historia* sets it apart from the sober annals of Hincmar and Flodoard, and from the careful archival research and documentary precision of Flodoard's *HRE.* In the prologue Richer more or less tells the reader that he is doing something different from his predecessors by claiming that he will use a style distinct from that of Flodoard's *Annals (longe diversum orationis scema)* and discuss causes and motivations *(diversas negotiorum rationes)* as well as events. His deployment of rhetorical artifice and his authorial self-consciousness point to a shift in the function of historiography at Rheims from the preservation of a true account of the past in the collective memory to a literary evocation of that past in which the writer himself takes center stage.

What explains this change? A lack of documentation about the schools at Rheims and the literary community that existed there in the second half of the tenth century hinders our ability to answer this question with as much confidence as we would like. Two things are clear, however. First, Adalbero and Gerbert were responsible for a cultural and intellectual revival at the cathedral school of Rheims and the surrounding monasteries beginning in

2. *De inventione* 1.20.29; *Rhetorica ad Herennium* 1.9.16.

the early 970s. Second, and more immediately relevant to this inquiry, Gerbert put the study of classical rhetoric at Rheims on a new footing by overhauling the curriculum and assembling a new library of rhetorical texts, among which the works of Cicero represented some of his most prominent acquisitions. It is not a coincidence that a work with the literary-rhetorical aspirations of Richer's *Historia* first appears at Rheims in the immediate aftermath of these educational reforms.

Richer and the Rhetorical Curriculum at Rheims

While it is often assumed that Richer was a student of Gerbert at the cathedral school of Rheims, there is no direct proof of this.[3] Nonetheless, so many aspects of his intellectual training bear the imprint of Gerbert's influence that we are probably justified in talking about him as Gerbert's student in some sense. Richer echoes all seven of the classical authors whose works Gerbert used to teach the figures of speech,[4] displays a solid command of dialectic (as evidenced by his account of the *disputatio* at Ravenna at 3.57–65), and knew enough about arithmetic, geometry, music, and astronomy to describe Gerbert's curriculum in the *quadrivium* (3.49–54) in precise detail. He shared Gerbert's interest in medicine and his belief in the power of persuasive speech,[5] and

3. See, e.g., Riché, *Gerbert d'Aurillac,* 40, where the author unaccountably claims that Richer must have entered Saint-Remi near 980, "puisqu'il dit avoir été son élève en 991." Oscar Darlington, Uta Lindgren, and, most recently, Hélène Gasc, also assume that Richer was a student of Gerbert.

4. These were Virgil, Statius, Terence, Juvenal, Persius, Horace, and Lucan (*Historia* 3.47). For Richer's allusions to these authors, see the index of citations in Hoffmann, *Historiae,* 315–25.

5. For Richer's knowledge of medicine, see MacKinney, "Tenth-Century Medicine as Seen in the *Historia* of Richer of Rheims." Gerbert's interest in medicine is revealed in his correspondence. In two different letters, one written in 983 to an otherwise unknown abbot named Gisalbert, and another to Rainard, a monk of Bobbio, in 988, Gerbert requests a copy of the *Ophthalmicus* of Demosthenes Philalethes. See letter 9 (Riché and Callu, 1.18–19) and letter 130 (2.318–21). In a letter written in

his vocabulary mirrors that of his dedicatee often enough to suggest direct influence. While we cannot determine the precise nature of the relationship between the two, Richer appears to have looked upon Gerbert as an intellectual mentor. He describes him admiringly as "a man of great intellectual ability and marvelous eloquence sent by God himself."[6] One of Gerbert's letters sheds some light on the kind of intellectual relationship that may have existed between them. Writing to Evrard, the abbot of Saint-Julien at Tours, Gerbert states that "Both when I am at leisure and when I am occupied, I teach what I know, and I learn what I do not know."[7] The letter implies that teaching was a part of Gerbert's daily existence, not an activity limited to the classroom, and it is quite possible that he had a relationship with Richer in which he served as a kind of scholarly mentor, quite apart from any formal instruction.[8] We get a glimpse of similar intellectual friendships in Gerbert's correspondence with Constantine of Fleury and Adalbold of Utrecht, and with his former students Ayrard of Saint-Thierry and Remi of Metlach.[9]

The starting point for any attempt to reconstruct the rhetorical curriculum at Rheims in the 970s and 980s is Richer's description

February 989 to an anonymous correspondent seeking advice on treating kidney stones, Gerbert states that he has always sought to acquire knowledge of medicine, though he has avoided its practice. See letter 151 (2.372).

6. *Historia* 3.43.

7. Letter 44 (Riché and Callu, 1.108): "Proinde in otio, in negotio, et docemus quod scimus, et addiscimus quod nescimus."

8. On the relationship between Gerbert and his students, see Jason Glenn, "Master and Community in Tenth-Century Rheims," in *Teaching and Learning in Northern Europe, 1000–1200,* ed. Sally N. Vaughn and Jay Rubenstein (Turnhout: Brepols, 2006), 51–68.

9. For Gerbert's correspondence with Constantine, see letters 86, 139, 143,191, and Riché and Callu, volume 2, *annexe* 5, letter 1 (rules for using the abacus and for multiplication and division), letter 2 (a defense of the study of numbers), letter 3 (a description of how to construct a hemisphere with sighting tubes for observing the heavens), letters 4 and 5 (explanations of passages in Boethius's *De musica*), and letter 6 (explanation of a passage in Boethius's *Institutio arithmetica).* His letter to Adalbold on finding the area of a triangle is *annexe* 5, letter 7. For Ayrard of Saint-Thierry, see letter 7, and for Remi of Mettlach, see letters 134, 148, 152, and 162.

of Gerbert's teaching at *Historia* 3.46–54.[10] He begins his account by enumerating the texts Gerbert used to teach dialectic: Porphyry's *Isagoge* and its Boethian commentary, Aristotle's *Categories* and *On Interpretation,* Cicero's *Topics,* also with a commentary by Boethius, and several logical works either by Boethius, such as *On Differential Topics, On the Categorical Syllogism, On Hypothetical Syllogisms,* and *On Division,* or thought to be by him, as is the case with *On Definition.*[11] After this list he moves on to discuss Gerbert's course in rhetoric:

> After they had toiled over these texts, he wanted to promote his students to the study of rhetoric, but he was concerned that the art of oratory could not be learned without prior knowledge of the modes of expression, which are to be learned in the poets. For this reason he introduced them to the poets with whom he thought they ought to be made acquainted, expounding and teaching the poets Virgil, Statius, and Terence, the satirists Juvenal, Persius, and Horace, and the historian Lucan. When they had been acquainted with these authors and instructed in the modes of

10. For Gerbert's pedagogy in general, see Pierre Riché, "L'enseignement de Gerbert à Reims dans le contexte européen," in *Gerberto, scienza, storia e mito,* 51–69; Oscar Darlington, "Gerbert, the Teacher," *American Historical Review* 52 (1946–1947): 456–76; and Hélène Gasc, "Gerbert et la pédagogie des arts libéraux à la fin du dixième siècle," *Journal of Medieval History* 12 (1986): 111–21. For his instruction in the *quadrivium,* see Uta Lindgren, *Gerbert von Aurillac und das Quadrivium: Untersuchungen zur Bildung im Zeitalter der Ottonen,* Sudhoffs Archiv 18 (Wiesbaden: Franz Steiner Verlag, 1976). For the cathedral school of Rheims, see Riché, *Les écoles et l'enseignement dans l'Occident chrétien de la fin du Ve siècle au milieu du XIe siècle* (Paris: Aubier Montaigne, 1979), 179–81. For a discussion of the cathedral school of Rheims in the context of other schools in France and Germany, see Joachim Ehlers, "Dom und Klosterschulen in Deutschland und Frankreich im 10. und 11. Jahrhundert," in *Schule und Schüler im Mittelalter. Beiträge zur europäischen Bildungsgeschichte des 9. bis 15. Jahrhunderts,* ed. M. Kintzinger, Sönke Lorenz, and Michael Walter (Cologne: Böhlau Verlag, 1996), 39–41.

11. Richer states that Gerbert used Marius Victorinus's translation of Porphyry's *Isagoge,* but this work is no longer exstant and was almost certainly not available at Rheims. He must instead be referring to Boethius's translation of the *Isagoge,* the first edition of which contained many quotations from Victorinus's translation. See Pierre Hadot, *Marius Victorinus. Recherches sur sa vie et ses oeuvres* (Paris: Études Augustinienes, 1971), 20, 367–69; and Hoffmann, *Historiae,* 193n3. *On Definition* was for a long time attributed to Boethius but was actually written by Marius Victorinus. See John Marenbon, *Boethius* (Oxford: Oxford University Press, 2003), 13–14, and 184n18.

expression, he brought them over to the study of rhetoric. After they had been instructed in this art, he brought in a sophist with whom they practiced *controversiae*; and they conducted themselves according to this art in such a way that they seemed to act without any art at all, which is the greatest achievement for an orator. But this is enough about logic.[12]

Given the detail with which Richer describes Gerbert's curriculum in dialectic, this is a surprisingly insubstantial summary. We are presented with only two pieces of information: that before students were promoted to the study of rhetoric proper, they completed a preliminary course in the "modes of expression" (literally, the tropes, but this probably also included the figures of speech), and that the capstone of their instruction was participation in *controversiae*—practice debates on hypothetical, and usually highly convoluted, legal scenarios—before a "sophist."[13] The meagerness of this account, which tells us only about the beginning and end of the course of study, means that the content of the curriculum itself has to be divined from other sources. Gerbert's letters and the remains of his personal book collection, the manuscript holdings of the cathedral of Rheims and the monastery of Saint-Rémi, and the text of the *Historia* itself all help to fill in the picture of the rhetorical curriculum at Rheims in the late tenth century, allowing us to form an idea of Gerbert's contribution to the study of rhetoric and to see how his innovations influenced Richer and his history.[14]

12. *Historia* 3.47–48.

13. The use of the term *sophista* to describe a teacher of practice in speaking probably derives from Victorinus, *Explanationes in Ciceronis rhetoricam* 1.1, p. 7.

14. For a reconstruction of the holdings of the library of the cathedral at Rheims from the mid-ninth to mid-tenth centuries, see Carey, "The Scriptorium of Reims during the Archbishopric of Hincmar," and Sot, *Un historien et son église,* 67–77. For Hincmar's libraries, see Devisse, *Hincmar Archevêque de Reims,* 3.1469–1512. No catalogue from the monastery of Saint-Rémi survives, but François Dolbeau has produced both a minimum estimate of the size of the monastery's holdings in the thirteenth century and a tentative reconstruction of part of the library catalogue. See Dolbeau, "Un catalogue fragmentaire des manuscrits de Saint-Rémi de Reims au xiiie siècle," *Recherches augustiniennes* 23 (1988): 223–43. For Gerbert's personal library, see Riché, "La bibliothèque de Gerbert d'Aurillac"; Mütherich, "The Library of Otto III"; and Hoffmann, *Bamberger Handschriften,* 22–30.

Gerbert refers specifically to his instruction in rhetoric in a letter that he wrote to Bernard, a monk at his home monastery of Aurillac, in March 987:

> Furthermore, when autumn was over, out of love for [my students] I constructed a certain table of the rhetorical art, arranged on twenty-six sheets of parchment fastened together in the shape of an oblong, made of two sheets by thirteen sheets—a work truly wonderful for the ignorant, and useful for the studious for comprehending the fleeting and very obscure materials of the rhetoricians and for fixing them in the mind.[15]

This thirteen-by-two sheet rectangle of parchment probably contained a series of schematic tree diagrams of the categories and subdivisions of the art of rhetoric: the three *genera* (judicial, deliberative, and demonstrative), the five parts of rhetoric (invention, arrangement, expression, memory, and delivery), the four types of *status* (conjectural, definitional, qualitative, and translative), the parts of a speech (exordium, narrative, partition, confirmation, refutation, digression, and peroration), the figures of speech and topics, and all of the various divisions and subdivisions that fell under these headings. Smaller-scale versions of such diagrams can be found in (for example) Bamberg, Staatsbibliothek, MS Class. 25, a manuscript of the *De inventione* with the Victorinus commentary copied at Rheims at Gerbert's request, and in Munich, Bayerische Staatsbibliothek, Clm 14436, a manuscript assembled by Hartwic of Saint-Emmeram that contains several rhetorical treatises and may reflect Gerbert's influence.[16] The purpose of memorizing this

15. Letter 92 (Riché and Callu, 1.220). Translation in Lattin, *The Letters of Gerbert,* 140–41.

16. For Bamberg, Staatsbibliothek, MS Class. 25, see Hoffmann, *Bamberger Handschriften,* 22–23; Friedrich Leitschuh and Hans Fischer, *Katalog der Handschriften der Königlichen Bibliothek zu Bamberg* (Bamberg, 1887–1912; reprint, Wiesbaden: Harrassowitz, 1966), 27–28. The manuscript also contains the anonymous short treatise *De attributis personae et negotio.* For Munich, Bayerische Staatsbibliothek, Clm 14436 and its possible connection to Gerbert, see Harriet Pratt Lattin, "The Eleventh Century MS Munich 14436: Its Contribution to the History of Coordinates, of Logic, of German Studies in France," *Isis* 38 (1948): 205–25.

detailed technical apparatus was twofold: it gave students the tools to organize and generate speech through the *partes orationis* and the topics, and it allowed them to assign points of contention in legal disputes to the correct *status,* which in turn facilitated the discovery of appropriate arguments.

The most likely sources for Gerbert's diagram were the standard late-antique and early medieval compilations of rhetorical lore: The *Ars rhetorica* of Fortunatianus, Cassiodorus's *Institutiones,* Martianus Capella's *De nuptiis Philologiae et Mercurii,* and Isidore of Seville's *Etymologiae,* all four of which are attested at Rheims in the tenth century.[17] These were also the texts that probably served as the foundation for the rhetorical curriculum. Richer's language in the *Historia* indicates that the *De nuptiis* played a role in his own training, and this corresponds well to what we know was going on in other tenth-century schools.[18] His reference in the prologue to the "incidental reasons" *(incidentes rationes)* that might divert him from the principal theme of the West Frankish kings and their wars echoes Martianus Capella's distinction between the principal and incidental questions that make up a case and the principal and incidental narratives in a speech.[19] The terminology that he uses to refer to the figures of speech and thought also points to the *De nuptiis.*[20] Textual evidence outside of the *Historia* confirms that the text was a familiar one at Rheims.[21] More-

17. Reims, Bibliothèque municipale, MS 975 contains book 2 of Cassiodorus's *Institutiones.* Gerbert's copy of the *De nuptiis,* with the gloss by Remigius of Auxerre, is found in London, British Library, MS Royal 15A.XXXIII. Isidore's *Etymologiae* are found in Rheims, Bibliothèque municipale, MS 425. Hincmar of Rheims had access to Fortunatianus's *Ars rhetorica* in Berlin, Staatsbibliothek, MS Lat. Qn. 687. See Devisse, *Hincmar, archevêque de Reims,* 3.1493.

18. For the circulation of the *De nuptiis,* see Claudio Leonardi, "I codici de Marziano Capella," *Aevum* 33 (1959): 434–89 (1), and 34 (1960): 1–99, 411–524 (2). See also Cora E. Lutz, "Martianus Capella," in *CTC,* vol. 2 (Washington, D.C.: The Catholic University of America Press, 1971), 368.

19. Cf. Martianus Capella, *De nuptiis* 5.443, 551.

20. Richer's use of the phrase *simulationis color* (4.42, 4.47) points to *De nuptiis* 5.523.

21. An anonymous panegyric to Constantine of Fleury written at Saint-Rémi in the 980s (incipit "Constantine, meis opus est non promere verbis") uses the phrase

over, two tenth-century manuscripts attest to its use at Rheims. Bamberg, Staatsbibliothek, MS Class. 39, a codex of the *De nuptiis* that probably came from Fleury, was glossed at Rheims in this period, and may have become part of Gerbert's personal library.[22] London, British Library, MS Royal 15A.XXXIII, which contains Remigius of Auxerre's commentary on the *De nuptiis*, was owned by the monastery of Saint-Rémi, and jottings on the first folio indicate that Gerbert had read it.[23]

The *De nuptiis,* along with the works of Cassiodorus, Isidore, and Fortunatianus, contained a convenient survey of the principal elements of classical and late-antique rhetoric. Yet while the breadth and comprehensiveness of these works made them ideal for schoolroom instruction, they could not provide an in-depth treatment of *inventio,* the means of discovering material appropriate for a speech, sermon, or narrative. For this reason, in the late tenth and eleventh centuries scholars began to devote increasing attention to two treatises that came to exercise an enormous influence over rhetorical education in the Latin West: Cicero's *De inventione* and the pseudo-Ciceronian *Rhetorica ad Herennium.*

Gerbert and Richer both appear to have been familiar with the *Rhetorica ad Herennium,* but we have no proof that there was a copy at Rheims during the tenth century, and nothing suggests that it played a prominent role in rhetorical education.[24] If it was

---

panegyricus ductus in a way that recalls both *De nuptiis* 5.470 and Fortunatianus, *Ars rhetorica* 5 (Halm, 84, line 24). A shorter poem (incipit "Convenio signis quem convenisse loquelis") that comes next in the manuscript (Bern, Burgerbibliothek, MS 394) refers to the dedicatee, Bovo, as a "friend of the Muses" who has been "pastured on the fields of blessed Capella." Szövérffy, 1.125–26, suspects that the two poems are by the same author. Manitius, 2.507, recognizes the possibility of single authorship but does not make any definitive claim.

22. See Riché, "La bibliothèque de Gerbert d'Aurillac," 98; Leonardi, "I codici de Marziano Capella," 1.6–7; and Leitschuh, *Katalog,* 40–41. Hoffmann, *Bamberger Handschriften,* 23, points out that there is no proof that this manuscript was at Rheims, or in Gerbert's hands, in the late tenth century. It might have left Rheims earlier.

23. See Hoffmann, *Bamberger Handschriften,* 26–27. Dolbeau, "Un catalogue fragmentaire," 223, provides evidence for two additional sets of glosses on Martianus Capella at Rheims.

24. Gerbert's use of the words *amaros exitus* in letter 185 (Riché and Callu,

taught at all, it probably had subordinate status. There can be little doubt about the importance of the *De inventione,* however. Both Cicero's text and the detailed commentary by the fourth-century Neoplatonist (and later Christian) scholar Marius Victorinus were read and copied at Rheims in this period, and Gerbert evokes his own Ciceronianism in language borrowed from the *De inventione.*[25] What role the *De inventione* played in the educational curriculum at the cathedral school of Rheims or at the monastery of Saint-Rémi remains murky. Nothing hints at the presence of the text at Rheims prior to Gerbert's arrival in 972, and his rather loose quotation from it in a letter he wrote for Adalbero in March 984 cannot be adduced as proof that he was teaching the *De inventione* this early.[26] We do know that two different commentaries on the *De inventione*—those of Marius Victorinus and the obscure late antique grammarian Grillius—were copied at Rheims at the end of the tenth century.[27] Moreover, we can trace the series of events that brought the Victorinus commentary to Rheims.

In a letter to Abbot Evrard of Saint-Julien at Tours written in January 985, shortly after his return from Bobbio, Gerbert declared that he was diligently assembling a library to aid in teaching rhetoric.[28] Then in September 988 he wrote to the monk Rainard of Bobbio, requesting among other texts a copy of *Victorius de re-*

2.478) echoes *Rhetorica ad Herennium* 4.15.21. Richer's use of the phrase *ut a principio exordiar* at *Historia* 2.73 recalls *Rhetorica ad Herennium* 3.4.7 *(exordiri licebit . . . a principio).* Neither Flodoard nor Hincmar quote from the *Ad Herennium.*

25. Letter 44 (Riché and Callu, 1.108): "Nam et apposite dicere ad persuadendum . . . summa utilitas."

26. Letter 27 (Riché and Callu, 1.56): "mementote illius Tulliani: stultum est ab eis fidem exigere a quibus multociens deceptus sis." Cf. *De inventione* 1.39.71: "Summa igitur amentia est in eorum fide spem habere quorum perfidia totiens deceptus sis." There are no allusions to the *De inventione* in Hincmar or Flodoard, suggesting that there may not have been a copy of the text at Rheims until Gerbert arrived, or, at the very least, that it was not studied until then.

27. See Hoffmann, *Bamberger Handschriften,* 22. Bamberg, Staatsbibliothek, MS Class. 24 contains Grillius's *In Ciceronis librum de inventione.* While Grillius's commentary was widely used in the Middle Ages, it breaks off at 1.22 of the *De inventione,* making it decidedly less useful than Victorinus.

28. Letter 44 (Riché and Callu, 1.108).

thorica, that is, the commentary on the *De inventione* by Marius Victorinus.[29] A passage in Aimoin's *Life* of Abbo of Fleury appears to confirm that the Victorinus commentary was not available at Rheims prior to Gerbert's arrival. Aimoin states that in his youth Abbo went to Rheims to study rhetoric, but having made no progress, he returned to Orléans, where he read Victorinus independently.[30] Abbo visited Rheims around 970—during the time of Adalbero and Gerannus, but before Gerbert.[31] Gerbert, therefore, would not have found Victorinus's commentary at Rheims when he arrived. He would have had to acquire it from somewhere else, and he clearly knew that his former abbey of Bobbio possessed a copy.[32] We do not know if Gerbert ever obtained this manuscript from Rainard, but some time around the year 1000, Victorinus's commentary, along with the full text of the *De inventione,* was copied at Rheims in Bamberg, Staatsbibliothek, MS Class. 25.[33]

Three aspects of the *De inventione* had a clearly perceptible influence on Richer's approach to history writing: its idealistic conception of the power of eloquence, its detailed apparatus of rules for devising material in speeches, and its theoretical conception of history as a type of rhetorical *narratio.* In the opening chapters Ci-

29. Letter 130 (Riché and Callu, 2.320). Claude Carozzi, *Adalbéron de Laon: Poème au roi Robert* (Paris: Les Belles Lettres, 1979), xv, has suggested that the reference here may be to the *Ars rhetorica* of Julius Victor. The limited transmission of this work, however, and an entry in a tenth-century library catalogue from Bobbio that reads *Marii Victoris de rethorica,* makes it more likely that it was Victorinus's text to which Gerbert was referring. See Tosi, "Il governo abbaziale di Gerberto," 205n399, and Becker, *Catalogi bibliothecarum antiqui,* 69n388.

30. *Vita Abbonis,* chap. 3, *PL* 139.390.

31. Pierre Riché, *Abbon de Fleury: Un moine savant et combatif* (Turnhout: Brepols, 2004), 27.

32. Two of the three texts that Gerbert requested from Rainard—Victorinus's commentary on the *De inventione (Victorius de rethorica)* and the ophthamological treatise of Demosthenes Philalethes *(Demosthenis optalmicus)* are found in the Bobbio library catalogue. See Tosi, "Il governo abbaziale di Gerberto," 205n399 and 409. Lattin, *The Letters of Gerbert,* 169n5, speculates that Gerbert had a copy of this library catalogue with him at Rheims.

33. See Hoffmann, *Bamberger Handschriften,* 22–23, and Leitschuh, *Katalog,* 27–28.

cero argues for the indispensable role of eloquence in creating and sustaining civil society (1.1–5) and defines the nature, function, end, materials, and parts of rhetoric (1.5–9). He designates rhetoric as a part of civic, or political, knowledge; its function *(officium)* is to speak appropriately so as to persuade *(dicere apposite ad persuasionem),* and its end *(finis)* is to persuade through speech *(persuadere dictione).*[34] For Cicero the art of eloquence was more than a set of rules governing spoken and written expression; it was a powerful tool capable of bringing uncivilized men together into communities and instructing them in civic virtue.[35] This conception of eloquence as a practical, politically oriented body of knowledge was adopted enthusiastically by Gerbert, who alludes to Cicero's definition of the function of rhetoric in his letter to Evrard, writing that "[the ability] to speak appropriately in order to persuade … is supremely useful."[36] The same belief in the power of persuasive speaking pervades the *Historia,* a text in which oratory is central to all forms of political decision making.[37] There is not merely a great deal of speech in the *Historia;* there is a great deal of speech that issues in tangible results. In Richer's vision of the past it is Hugh the Great's oration to the assembled West Frankish magnates, rather than any shadowy political machinations, that leads to the decision to recall Louis IV from England.[38] Similarly, when another council of leading men meets at Senlis to determine the royal succession after the death of Louis V in 987, Adalbero of Rheims delivers a speech that is instrumental in Hugh Capet's election.[39] Speeches do more than explain causes and motivations in the *Historia;* eloquence itself is a powerful motive force. Archbishop Hervey of Rheims provides a memorable encapsulation of Richer's belief in the power of eloquence when, in a speech to Henry the Fowler of Germany, he poses

34. *De inventione* 1.5.6.

35. *De inventione* 1.2.2–1.2.3.

36. Gerbert, letter 44 (Riché and Callu, 1.108): "Nam et apposite dicere ad persuadendum et animos furentium suavi oratione ab impetu retinere, summa utilitas."

37. Kortüm, *Richer von Saint-Remi,* 98.

38. *Historia* 2.2. Tellingly, when Hugh decides to send for Louis, he dispatches *legatos oratores* across the English Channel.

39. *Historia* 4.11.

the rhetorical question: "What is there that a persuasively composed oration cannot accomplish?"[40]

The importance of the *De inventione* as an educational tool extended beyond its exalted view of the role that rhetoric had to play in society. Unlike the *De nuptiis,* with its comparatively limited treatment of rhetorical invention, the *De inventione* provided a systematic set of guidelines for devising material to be included in speeches, and it contained a detailed exposition of *status*-theory, the branch of rhetoric that organized different types of disputes into categories and found suitable arguments for both sides. As we will see, Richer was trained to find arguments based on *status*-theory, but both he and Gerbert seem to have used the *De inventione* more as a means of categorizing speech than of devising it.

Finally, and perhaps most importantly, the *De inventione* defined history as a type of rhetorical *narratio* and thus made historiography subject to the rules of rhetorical invention.[41] Marius Victorinus emphasizes this connection between rhetoric and history in his remarks on the virtues of narrative:

> Therefore these three virtues can apply to the narrative in a speech and to the narrative outside the scope of civil cases. For history should be concise in exposition, clear, and readily believable, just as Sallust ascribed all of these [attributes] to himself in his *Catiline.*[42]

Cicero's most sophisticated discussion of the relationship between history and rhetoric is actually found in the *De oratore,* which explains in more depth how *inventio* was to be applied to historical texts. Here Marcus Antonius discusses the role that rhetoric should play in historiography and draws a celebrated distinction between mere annalists *(tantummodo narratores)* and literary historians *(exornatores rerum).*[43] It is tempting to suppose that Richer envisioned himself as the *exornator* of Flodoard's *Annals* based on

40. *Historia* 1.23: "Quid enim suasorie digesta non efficit oratio?"

41. *De inventione* 1.19.27.

42. *Explanationes in Ciceronis rhetoricam* 1.20, p. 88.

43. *De oratore* 2.54. Cf. Victorinus, *Explanationes in Ciceronis rhetoricam* 1.1, p. 10: "haec monumenta dupliciter accipiamus, aut annales aut historias: primo enim annales fuerunt, post historiae factae sunt."

his knowledge of this passage. The *De oratore* had a limited transmission in the Middle Ages, but we know that Gerbert managed to obtain a copy. The colophon of Erlangen, Universitätsbibliothek, MS 380, a composite manuscript that contains the *De oratore,* indicates that it was copied for Gerbert by a monk named Ayrard between 983 and 991—during the period when he was assembling his rhetorical library at Rheims.[44] In the absence of any definitive proof that Richer himself had read the *De oratore,* it is not unreasonable to suppose that some of its doctrines may have trickled down to him via Gerbert.

Oratory in the *Historia*

Richer's embrace of the Ciceronian conception of historiography explains several of the most characteristic features of his history: a preference for the appearance of truth *(verisimile)* over strict factual accuracy *(verum),* an interest in elucidating the motives that led people to act as they did *(rationes negotiorum),* and an emphasis on his stylistic superiority to Flodoard's *Annals.* In Cicero's view the narrative historian was required to take the foundation *(fundamenta)* of names, dates, and facts from his sources and build atop them a rhetorical superstructure *(exaedificatio)* in which the intentions of historical figures *(consilia),* their deeds *(acta),* and the results of their deeds *(eventus)* were described in detail and explained in terms of causes and motivations.[45] This is precisely what Richer did in reworking Flodoard's *Annals.*

One of the essential components of *exaedificatio* was the composition of fictional speeches. Speech served both to embellish and

44. See Reynolds, *Texts and Transmission,* 102–9, and Hoffmann, *Bamberger Handschriften,* 23 and note 59. Hoffmann points out that this was almost certainly not the Ayrard of Aurillac mentioned in Gerbert's letters 17, 45, 91, and 163, but probably the Ayrard charged by Gerbert in letter 7 with copying a number of manuscripts at Orbais and Saint-Basle. Since these monasteries are in the vicinity of Rheims, and Erlangen MS 380 was written in the scriptorium at Rheims, this Ayrard must have been a monk at Rheims, not Aurillac.

45. *De oratore* 2.62–64.

to expound, allowing the author to demonstrate his rhetorical ingenuity, explain the motivations of characters, and add dramatic immediacy to his narrative. Despite the importance of formal oratory in the narrative historiography of the Middle Ages, we are not particularly well informed about how medieval historians learned to write speeches. Lacking explicit authorial statements on the subject, we are left to assume that they acquired the necessary skill in oratorical composition from several interrelated practices: training in school exercises such as Priscian's *Praeexercitamina,* the study of prescriptive rhetoric from textbooks like the *De inventione* and the *Rhetorica ad Herennium,* and practice in imitating classical and late antique authors. Learning to write speeches thus involved both *ars,* the conscious application of the precepts of classical rhetoric, and *imitatio,* the imitation of model authors.

In Richer's case we are well positioned to draw some conclusions about his methods of oratorical composition.[46] He was a prolific writer of speeches, so there is a large sample to examine. Moreover, his frequent citations of classical authors provide a useful inventory of the historians whom he used as models. In addition, three narrative histories roughly contemporary with the *Historia*—Widukind of Corvey's *Res gestae Saxonicae* (ca. 967–973), Aimoin of Fleury's *Gesta Francorum* (ca. 997–ca. 999), and Dudo of Saint-Quentin's *Gesta Normannorum* (ca. 996–ca. 1020)—provide a point of comparison, helping us to determine what is distinctive and what is conventional about his speeches. As we will see, while Richer was capable of employing the specific precepts of the *De inventione* to furnish lines of argument for his characters, more often than not he used Cicero's rhetorical terminology while devising his own arguments or borrowing from classical historians. In that sense the theoretical influence of the Ciceronian rhetorical corpus may have been more important to him than the specific instructions for discovering arguments.

46. Kortüm, *Richer von Saint-Remi,* 97–104, provides a brief but important analysis of Richer's speech writing by analyzing the forms of *conquestio* and *deliberatio* in the speeches of Ingo at 1.11, Charles of Lotharingia at 4.9, and King Radulf at 1.60.

The Genus Iudiciale, Conquestio, and *Indignatio*

Richer signals the appearance of speeches in his history in the chapter titles that appear in the margins of the manuscript. On almost every occasion when a formal oration is delivered, he alerts the reader by including a title that describes the speech to follow, using terms such as *oratio* (2.2, 3.73, 3.79, 3.82, 4.2, 4.11, 4.26, 4.42), *oratio suasoria* (1.60), *oratio suasorie habita* (1.11), *prolocutio* (2.51), *conquestio* (1.23, 2.13, 2.31, 2.73, 4.9, 4.14, 4.74), *responsio* (1.24, 3.80, 4.27), *querimonia* (2.16, 2.52), *deliberatio* (2.32, 4.49), *indignatio* (2.50), *declamatio* (3.83), and *purgatio* (4.6).[47] Richer's practice of labeling his speeches mirrors the way in which speeches were identified in manuscripts of model authors like Sallust; this in turn suggests the possibility that he may have intended his own orations to be used as models.[48] For our purposes these marginal chapter headings are useful because, when coupled with Richer's use of specific verbs like *conqueri, deliberare,* and *indignari* to describe the action of speakers, they allow us to separate the speeches in the *Historia* into different categories and analyze them on that basis.

The first speech in direct discourse in the *Historia* is delivered by the Frankish warrior Ingo, who carries King Odo's standard

47. All of these examples are taken from speeches delivered outside of church synods. The synodal speeches are similarly titled: for example, *praelocutio* (2.71, 4.53), *responsio* (2.72, 2.75, 4.58), *conquestio* (2.73), *oratio* (2.74, 2.76), and *indignatio* (4.56, 4.64).

48. Beryl Smalley, "Sallust in the Middle Ages," in *Classical Influences on European Culture, A.D. 500 to 1500,* ed. R. R. Bolgar (Cambridge: Cambridge University Press, 1971), 165–75, notes that the speeches in the *Bellum Catilinae* and the *Bellum Iugurthinum* attracted the greatest attention of glossators, who added rubricated titles and marginal notes to point them out. See also Carmen Cardelle de Hartmann, "Sallust in St. Emmeram: Handschriften und Kommentare in der Bibliothek des Klosters St. Emmeram (Regensburg)" *Journal of Medieval Latin* 18 (2008): 10, for the identification of speeches from the *Bellum Iugurthinum* (*ORATIO ATHERBALIS, ORATIO MEMMII, ORATIO MARII*) in Munich, Bayerischen Staatsbibliothek, Clm 14477, an eleventh-century manuscript copied at Hersfeld and later brought to the monastery of Saint-Emmeram at Regensburg.

into battle against the Vikings at Montpensier (1.9). In the aftermath of his victory Odo brings the captured enemy chieftain, Catillus, to Limoges with him to be baptized. After Catillus has been immersed in the baptismal font three times, Ingo steps forward and plunges his sword into him, killing him on the spot (1.10). Furious, Odo orders his men to seize and execute his treacherous retainer, but Ingo throws away his sword, grasps the altar of Saint Martin, and begs leave to address the king and his men. He then proceeds to deliver a formal oration in his own defense:

I appeal to God, who is privy to my intentions, that nothing was dearer to me than your safety. It was love for you that drove me to this. It was for your safety that I cast myself down into these misfortunes. For the sake of all of [your] lives I did not fear to undergo so great a danger. Certainly it is a serious deed that has been done, but its utility is greater still. I do not deny that I have offended against the sovereignty of the king, but I maintain that many advantages have been realized through this criminal act. The intent of the agent should be considered, and the future utility of the crime should be taken into account. I realized that the tyrant, after he was captured, asked to be baptized out of fear, and that after he was released he would requite the many wrongs [done to him] and exact the severest vengeance for the slaughter of his men. I turned my sword against him because I perceived that he would be the cause of future calamity. This was the reason for my crime. This is what drove me to wickedness. This I did for the salvation of the king and his men. And would that through my death the liberty of our fatherland and peace in our affairs would follow! But if I am put to death, it will be clear that I died in order to save the king and the leading men. Let each man now consider whether he should undertake to serve the king in return for a reward of this sort, and whether one should be subject to this sort of punishment in return for his loyalty. Behold the recent wounds to my head, my chest, and my side! The scars of the past are plain to see; bruises are spread throughout the remaining limbs of my body. Debilitated by unceasing pain from these [wounds], I await nothing after so many evils except death, the end of misfortunes.[49]

49. *Historia* 1.11.

Not surprisingly given the impact of formal oratory in the *Historia*, Ingo's eloquence wins him a reprieve:

> With this lament he moved some to be well-disposed to him and drove others to tears. As a result, some of the king's retainers, acting on his behalf, mollified the king and persuaded him to be merciful and have pity, declaring that it was of no benefit to the king if one of his own men should die. To the contrary, he should rejoice in the tyrant's death, because if he had died as a believer then he had been given over to life, and if he had undergone baptism as a trick then his schemes had failed utterly. At this the king tempered his anger, and after the barbarian had been buried, he took Ingo back into his favor.[50]

In his discussion of this passage, Hans-Henning Kortüm observes that Richer conceived of Ingo's speech as a *conquestio* in the Ciceronian sense, that is, "a passage seeking to arouse the pity of the audience."[51] Ingo succeeds in his lament through repetition and pathetic personal appeals, capping off his speech with a maxim borrowed from the *Distichs of Cato,* a widely diffused school text and a rich source of sententious wisdom.[52] In terms of *status*-theory, the defense adopted by Ingo falls under the heading of *comparatio,* or "comparison," a strategy in which the defendant admits to committing a crime but argues that a just and advantageous outcome was thereby made possible.[53]

In its use of the *conquestio* form and the defensive technique of *comparatio,* Ingo's speech reflects Richer's knowledge of the *De inventione* and confirms the influence of this text in the scholarly community at Rheims after Gerbert's arrival. This speech is detailed enough to let us take Kortüm's analysis further, however, and examine the degree to which Richer employed the detailed argumentative strategies, or topics, appropriate for both the *con-*

50. *Historia* 1.11.

51. *De inventione* 155.106, trans. Hubbell, 157. For Ingo's speech, see Kortüm, *Richer von Saint-Remi,* 99–100.

52. *Disticha Catonis,* ed. Marcus Boas and H. J. Botschuyver (Amsterdam: North-Holland Publishing Co., 1952) 3.22: "Fac tibi proponas mortem non esse timendam, quae bona si non est, finis tamen malorum est."

53. *De inventione* 1.11.15, trans. Hubbell, 33.

questio and the *comparatio.* We can frame the inquiry as a question: In composing this speech, how closely was Richer following the technical precepts found in the *De inventione,* and how much was he using the basic definitions of the *conquestio* and *comparatio* as a framework on which to hang his own arguments? It turns out that in the case of *comparatio* he consciously employed some of the topics mentioned by Cicero, while for the *conquestio*—a type of oration that appears several times in the *Historia*—he was generally content to rely on his own sources of argument.

The use of *comparatio* as a defensive technique reveals that Richer assigned Ingo's speech to the qualitative status *(constitutio generalis).* In this type of legal issue the defendant admitted to committing the act in question and accepted the definition of the act by the prosecution, and instead based his defense on some potentially exculpatory aspect or quality of the act.[54] The qualitative status was divided into two subheadings: the equitable *(iuridicalis)* and the legal *(negotialis).* The former was subdivided into two more categories. In the "absolute" division *(qualitas absoluta)* an action could be excused in and of itself; in the "assumptive" division *(qualitas assumptiva)* the justification of an action could only be completed by adducing one or more external circumstances.[55] One of the four subheadings of the *qualitas assumptiva* was the *comparatio,* in which the defendant admitted to a crime but argued that it enabled the accomplishment of a greater good. In Ingo's case the crime was the murder of Catillus; the greater good that followed was the preservation of the king and the leading men. In a sense, the act was committed for the sake of what did not happen next: a future catastrophe *(futura clades)* that would occur when Catillus and his men took revenge for the defeat inflicted upon them at Montpensier.

Cicero includes a detailed discussion of the strategy of *compa-*

54. *De inventione* 1.8.10, 1.9.14–15. Issues of fact fell under the conjectural status *(constitutio coniecturalis).* Disputes over the definition of an act fell under the definitional status *(constitutio definitiva).*

55. See Lausberg § 171–96.

ratio in book 2 of the *De inventione,* providing both an example and a list of appropriate topics *(loci communes).*[56] For the defendant these included first of all "that no deed should be judged inexpedient or base, or for that matter advantageous or honorable, unless it is known with what intent [*quo animo*], at what time [*quo tempore*] and for what reason [*qua de causa*] it is done."[57] The time of the deed is not at issue in Ingo's speech, but he refers specifically to both his intention and his reason for committing the crime, using language that reflects knowledge of the relevant passage from the *De inventione.* Ingo first reminds his audience that "the intent [*animus*] of the agent should be considered and the future utility of the deed should be taken into account."[58] He then states that concern for the safety of the king and his men drove him to kill Catillus, giving his point emphasis through parallelism and anaphora:

> This was the reason for my crime. This is what drove me to wickedness. This I did for the salvation of the king and his men.[59]

Next in the list of topics for the *comparatio* is the amplification of the positive effects of the deed, "in which the magnitude of the service performed is demonstrated and enlarged upon by reference to the advantage or honor or necessity [*utilitas*] of the deed."[60] Ingo also employs a version of this topic, reminding his audience that "It is a serious deed that has been done, yet the utility of the deed is greater still" *(Grande quidem est gestum negotium, sed maior est negotii utilitas).*

Richer's deployment of the specific topics of the *comparatio* shows that he was not only familiar with the detailed body of lore associated with rhetorical *status*-theory, but that he attached some importance to it. This is confirmed by his recommendation of Gerbert's *Acta* of the Synod of Saint-Basle because of its usefulness for

56. *De inventione* 2.24.72–2.26.79.

57. *De inventione* 2.26.77, trans. Hubbell, 243.

58. *Historia* 1.11: "Consideretur auctoris animus, animadvertatur etiam futura facinoris utilitas."

59. *Historia* 1.11: "Haec est mei facinoris *causa.* Haec me ad scelus impulit. Hoc ob regis suorumque salutem peregi."

60. *De inventione* 2.26.77, trans. Hubbell, 243.

those familiar with rhetorical *status*.[61] Gerbert had a thoroughgoing knowledge of this branch of rhetorical doctrine and must have promoted its study in the schools of Rheims. His use of *status*-theory as a means of classifying disputed issues is evident in the long letter of self-defense that he sent to Wilderod of Strasbourg in the summer of 995 to accompany his *Acta* of the Synod of Saint-Basle.[62] The letter itself is subdivided into the different parts of a speech *(exordium, narratio, partitio, confirmatio et reprehensio, epilogus)*, and the division *(partitio)* begins by mentioning the need to identify the *status* of the dispute between himself and Arnulf, using terminology from the *De inventione*.[63] It is not surprising that this facet of classical rhetoric should have received particular scrutiny in an ecclesiastical center as important as Rheims, since the ability to define the issue at stake in a judicial proceeding and devise a suitable defense would have had concrete practical applications for monks and secular clerics taking part in the proceedings of synods.

Richer's recommendation of Gerbert's *Acta* to students of rhetoric appears to have been more than calculated flattery. The content of Richer's speeches suggests that he had learned how to deploy arguments derived from *status*-theory from Gerbert's teaching. Ingo's speech, in fact, closely echoes one of Gerbert's speeches from the *Acta* of the Synod of Saint-Basle. Early in the synod the priest Adalger, an accomplice of Arnulf who took the keys to the city of Rheims from him and opened the gates of the city to Charles's men, is brought before the tribunal to speak in his own defense.[64] Adal-

61. *Historia* 4.73: "Qui [liber] non solum sinodalibus causis, sed et status rethoricae cognoscentibus utillimus habetur." Further confirmation of Richer's knowledge of *status*-theory can be seen in the speech of Daibert of Bourges at 4.54.

62. See letter 217 (Riché and Callu, 2.582–651). See also Lattin, *The Letters of Gerbert*, 259–60, for the historical context. Gerbert sent copies of the letter, which summarized material in the *Acta* of the Synod of Saint-Basle, to Wilderod and to Notker of Liège in preparation for a synod to be held at Ingelheim in early 996, at which the dispute over the archbishopric of Rheims was to be discussed.

63. Letter 217 (Riché and Callu, 2.590).

64. *Acta concilii Remensis*, chap. 11, pp. 400–401. For Adalger's role in the betrayal of Rheims, see also *Historia* 4.34. Richer refers to him as Algerus.

ger does not deny helping to betray the city of Rheims to Charles, but he shifts the responsibility for his actions onto Arnulf:

> It was love for him, and his command, that cast me down into these misfortunes.[65]

This appeal is strikingly similar to a passage in Ingo's speech:

> It was love for you that drove me to this. It was for your safety that I cast myself down into these misfortunes.[66]

In admitting his actions but shifting the blame to his superiors, Adalger adopts as his defense a subset of the qualitative status related to, but distinct from, the *comparatio* employed by Ingo. In addition to *comparatio,* the assumptive division *(qualitas assumptiva)* of the equitable part *(pars iuridicalis)* of the qualitative status *(constitutio generalis)* contained three other strategies: *concessio* ("confession and avoidance"), *remotio criminis* ("shifting the charge"), and *relatio criminis* ("retort of the accusation").[67] Here Adalger, in implicating his superiors in order to absolve himself of guilt, uses the technique of *remotio criminis.*[68] He admits giving the sacraments to the traitor Charles and opening the gates of the city of Rheims to his forces, but he repeats several times that he was only obeying Arnulf's orders:

> And so that this deed should be concealed under the guise of honorable conduct, I offered my hands together with the sacraments to Charles, but at his command; I took the keys to the city, but from his hand; I opened the gates, but under his instructions.[69]

While Adalger presumably said something like this at the Synod of Saint-Basle, the words and the manner of expression are clearly Gerbert's. Gerbert tells the reader as much in the prologue to the

65. *Acta concilii Remensis,* chap. 11, p. 401, lines 10–11: "Eius amor, eius imperium me in has precipitavit miserias."

66. *Historia* 1.11: "Vester amor ad hoc me impulit. Ob vestram salutem in has me miserias precipitavi."

67. *De inventione* 1.11.15, trans. Hubbell, 31.

68. *De inventione* 1.11.15.

69. *Acta concilii Remensis,* chap. 11, p. 400, lines 15–17. Cf. *Historia* 4.34.

Acta, where he explains that it will be necessary to employ three types of interpretative techniques *(triplex genus interpretationis)* in order to reduce the speeches of the various participants to a satisfactory literary form. In some cases he will translate word-for-word from the vernacular into Latin. In others the "gravity of thought" and the "worthiness of expression" will be made to conform to the type of speech *(genus dicendi).* Finally, there will be occasion for "hidden things to be investigated and for the sentiments themselves to be brought clearly into the light," a statement that suggests that Gerbert felt licensed to practice the same kind of amplification in writing speeches that Richer did.[70] We can be confident, therefore, that the speech as we have it is Gerbert's composition. Adalger may well have uttered a few sentences of no particular eloquence in which he denied being guilty of anything more than loyalty to Charles and Arnulf. Gerbert then took this material and shaped it into a formal oration in which he clarified the rhetorical status (the *constitutio generalis*) and the strategy of defense *(remotio criminis).*

The similarity between these two passages could actually be taken as a clue to help in dating the composition of the *Historia.* For if Richer composed Ingo's speech only after reading Gerbert's version of Adalger's statement in the *Acta*, it would move the *terminus post quem* of the *Historia* to the date when Gerbert wrote the *Acta,* probably some time in the spring of 995.[71] This would have significant implications for our understanding of the *Historia,* for it would imply that Richer began writing at the precise point when Gerbert's position as archbishop was becoming seriously threatened. Arguments against the 995 *terminus post quem* have already been presented on practical and codicological grounds, and the

70. *Acta concilii Remensis,* prologue, 392.

71. Gerbert redacted his version of the synod's proceedings as a response to the convocation of a synod at Mouzon on June 2, 995. The *Acta* were in the hands of the papal legate, Abbot Leo of Saint-Boniface-and-Alexis, by June 9. See *Leonis abbatis et legati ad Hugonem et Rotbertum reges epistola.* The *Acta* must have been redacted some time before the synod itself. See Carozzi, "Gerbert et le concile de Saint-Basle," 662, and Lot, *Études sur le règne de Hugues Capet,* 96.

similarity between the two passages may be the product of Richer's tendency to adopt Gerbert's stylistic proclivities rather than a direct borrowing. The phrase *praecipitare in miserias* crops up in a letter that Gerbert wrote on behalf of Queen Emma to her mother Adelaide in 986,[72] and the related *praecipitare in mala* occurs in Sallust's *Bellum Iugurthinum,* one of Richer's primary sources for quotations and stylistic embellishment, in a chapter that he cites multiple times in the *Historia.*[73] A possible explanation for the similarity between the two passages is that they both derive from a scenario that Gerbert developed to teach the qualitative *status* in the classroom.

Status-theory demanded the use of specific arguments based on the strategies adopted by the parties to a *controversia,* so once Richer framed Ingo's self-defense as a form of *comparatio,* it followed naturally that he would employ the appropriate topics. When it came to the rhetorical form of the *conquestio,* however, he was content to use the term to denote speeches of complaint without adhering strictly to the topics enumerated by Cicero to win the pity of the audience.[74] These included the comparison of the speaker's former prosperity to his present misfortunes, the graphic presentation of the speaker's woes, and an appeal to the audience to consider their own loved ones. Above all, Cicero declared, the topics of the *conquestio* should demonstrate the power of fortune and the weakness of men.[75] Scrutinizing Ingo's speech, one is hard-pressed to find evidence that Richer employed any of the sixteen topics recommended in the *De inventione.*

Given the frequency of speeches of complaint in the *Historia,* it is perhaps surprising that Richer did not make greater use of the

72. Letter 74 (Riché and Callu, 1.180): "O amara dies … quae me in has miserias praecipitavit."

73. *Bellum Iugurthinum* 14: "has quae me premunt aerumnas cum anima simul amisisti. At ego infelix in tanta mala praecipitatus ex patrio regno rerum humanarum spectaculum praebeo." Cf. *Historia* 2.52 (where this precise passage is cited), 1.17, 3.95, 4.2, 4.9, and 4.14.

74. *De inventione* 1.55.107–1.56.109.

75. *De inventione* 1.55.106.

apparatus of argumentative strategies from the *De inventione*.[76] Ingo's speech, as Kortüm points out, is short on argumentative ingenuity and long on pathos.[77] The most memorable and, from the audience's standpoint, the most affecting, aspect of the speech is the speaker's baring of the wounds he had received in the king's service. This was not a topic derived from the rhetorical handbooks of antiquity, however, but a theme that Richer borrowed from classical historiography. In similar fashion, the other *conquestiones* in the *Historia* tend to abound with pathetic elements and motifs drawn from model authors, while avoiding specific rhetorical topics. After his abandonment by the magnates, for example, Charles the Simple delivers a speech to his remaining counselors in which he argues that death would be preferable to the loss of his kingdom:

> He said that he would be more wretched if this disaster befell him than if he closed his eyes at the final moment of death, because in the former case his griefs would only increase, but in the latter they would be taken away. It was preferable that he should be slain by the sword rather than deprived of his kingdom by a usurper. For after the loss of his kingdom all that remained was for him to be sent away into exile.[78]

Charles invokes here the same theme that brought Ingo's speech to a close, namely, that death is the end of all misfortunes.[79] Erluin of Montreuil lodges a similar complaint to William Longsword after Arnulf of Flanders captures his stronghold and his family:

> Erluin was scarcely out of danger of death when he went before Duke William of the Northmen and poured out a long tale of woe about his misfortunes, declaring himself a miserable wretch because now that he had been dispossessed of his stronghold and his fighting men, and

76. There are twelve speeches that Richer either designates as a *conquestio* in the chapter title or in which he uses the verb *conqueri* to describe the action of the speaker. See *Historia* 1.11, 1.23, 1.42, 2.13, 2.16, 2.31, 2.52, 2.73, 4.2, 4.9, 4.14, 4.74. Five of these (1.42, 2.13, 2.16, 2.31, 4.74) are in indirect discourse.

77. Kortüm, *Richer von Saint-Remi*,101.

78. *Historia* 1.42.

79. *Historia* 1.11: "nihil post tot mala nisi mortem malorum finem exspecto."

robbed of his wife and children, he possessed nothing but his own body. He was not quite as distraught about losing Montreuil, for there remained some hope of recovering it, since land was immovable and the stronghold was not going anywhere. But the loss of his wife and children seemed to spread before him an endless source of misery, because if they died, he would be oppressed by continual grief, whereas if they lived but remained under someone else's power, he would be the prey of idle hopes.[80]

The *conquestiones* of Charles and Erluin develop in similar ways. Both begin with *sese inquiens* and a comparative adjective (although in the second example *infeliciorem* has only emphatic, not comparative force).[81] Both Charles and Erluin explain the hopelessness of their case by enumerating the possibilities open to them: for Charles it is death or exile, unless someone comes to his aid; for Erluin it is either the death of his family or perpetual uncertainty about their fate. In these and the other laments in the *Historia* it is difficult to find any unambiguous references to Cicero's topics of the *conquestio.* Erluin's complaint about the loss of his family is similar to the twelfth topic, in which the speaker laments his separation from friends or loved ones.[82] Yet even here we cannot be certain that Richer took the idea from the *De inventione,* since Cicero stresses the separation *(disiunctio)* from those with whom the speaker has lived with great joy, while Erluin focuses on the mental torment occasioned by his uncertainty over the fate of his wife and children.

In another of Richer's *conquestiones* a theme that appears to derive from the *De inventione* is in fact a borrowing from Hegesippus. Shortly after the coronation of Hugh Capet, Charles of Lotharingia delivers an embittered complaint to his friends in which he emphasizes the sorry lot of his children:

80. *Historia* 2.13.

81. Cf. *Historia* 1.42: "miseriorem sese inquiens si hac urgeatur calamitate quam si oculos claudat suprema morte," and 2.13: "sese inquiens infeliciorem, cum oppido et militibus privatus, uxore filiisque orbatus, nihil preter corpus possideat."

82. *De inventione* 1.55.109.

I see myself growing older, and with every passing day I am deprived of more and more of my patrimony. I cannot look upon my little ones, the offspring of an unfortunate father, without tears, for to them I am the source of griefs to come rather than future honors. I have been a most ill-fated father who was scarcely ever able to be at the side of my children. You at least, my friends, should show sympathy for a grieving father and come to the aid of a destitute parent. Provide support for children who even at a very young age have come to know suffering. Make provision for those who have been reduced to humble circumstances and who are destined to meet with misfortunes that may prove to be irreversible. Let yourself be swayed, at the very least, by the common tie of blood that you share, by their nobility, which should not be disregarded, and by the recompense that will be returned to you with profit many times over.[83]

Charles's lament appears to echo the fifteenth topic of the *conquestio,* in which the speaker complains of the ill fortune that has befallen his loved ones.[84] In this case, however, Richer did not take the theme of the father lamenting for his children from the *De inventione;* he borrowed it and the words with which to express it from a speech in the *Bellum Iudaicum* in which Herod the Great, after arranging for the murder of his sons Alexander and Aristobulus, cynically complains about the misfortunes his orphaned grandchildren must now face.[85]

Despite the profusion of *conquestiones* in the *Historia,* therefore, Richer appears to have made little effort to incorporate the Ciceronian topics appropriate to the genre into his speeches. The reasons for this neglect are probably not hard to determine. The complaint is a universal means of expression, and a writer of Richer's ability hardly needed to consult a list of stock themes when envisioning what a king abandoned by his retainers or a nobleman deprived of his land and his family would say. While the proper use of *status*-theory required the speaker or writer to memorize the various types of rhetorical issues and their corresponding arguments, the author

83. *Historia* 4.14.

84. *De inventione* 1.56.109.

85. *Bellum Iudaicum* 1.42.3.

writing a complaint did not necessarily need a technical apparatus of rhetorical precepts.

The number of speeches labeled with the term *conquestio* in the *Historia* is noteworthy, because this word was not commonly used to refer to an independent speech at the time that Richer was writing. None of the many speeches in the histories of Widukind, Aimoin of Fleury, or Dudo of Saint-Quentin is designated as a *conquestio,* for example, although some of their speeches are similar in tone to Richer's *conquestiones.*[86] This may stem from the fact that in classical rhetoric the *conquestio* was not a speech in and of itself, but rather one element of a larger speech. In the *De inventione* the *conquestio* is one of the three elements of the peroration *(conclusio)* of a speech, along with the *enumeratio* (summing-up) and the *indignatio* (rousing of indignation).[87] Richer appears to have adopted the use of *conquestio* to denote a speech of complaint—as opposed to an element of the peroration—from Gerbert, who uses the term twice in his *Acta* of the Synod of Saint-Basle. In one instance he notes that the case made in support of Arnulf was not so much a defense *(defensio)* as a complaint *(conquestio).*[88] *Conquestio* also appears in the chapter headings to designate a speech delivered by Bruno, the bishop of Langres (980–1016).[89] Bruno was a nephew of Charles of Lotharingia and a cousin of Arnulf who had vouched for Arnulf's future good conduct when suspicions were raised about him prior to his election to the see of Rheims.[90] In his speech

86. Cf. Dudo, *Gesta Normannorum* 2.20, p. 160: At a gathering of the Franks Charles the Simple laments that Rollo is plundering his land. Dudo uses the verb *condolere;* Aimoin, *Gesta regum Francorum* 2.18, *PL* 139.679: Clotild, the widow of Clovis, goes to the tomb of Saint-Martin at Tours and offers a tearful prayer to the saint, asking him to secure a peace between her sons. Aimoin also uses the word *condolere* to describe her address; *Gesta regum Francorum* 3.12, *PL* 139.700–701: The Austrasians complain to Sigebert that they have been deprived of the opportunity for plunder by virtue of his peace treaty with his brothers Chilperic and Guntram. The speech is designated a *querela.*

87. *De inventione* 1.52.98.

88. *Acta concilii Remensis,* chap. 49, p. 446, lines 8–12.

89. *Acta concilii Remensis,* 392: *Conquestio Brunonis episcopi.*

90. Charles and his brother King Lothar were half-brothers of Bruno's mother,

at the synod Bruno laments his role in helping Arnulf to secure the archbishopric and his own credulity in believing that his kinsman would live up to the oath he swore to Hugh Capet. Richer includes a version of Bruno's speech in the *Historia*. Although he does not change its tone or import, he assigns it the title of *indignatio* rather than *conquestio* in the marginal chapter heading.[91] Richer seems to have viewed the terms *conquestio* and *indignatio* as to some degree interchangeable, as evidenced by another speech in the *Historia* in which Otto I of Germany vents his displeasure at being dishonored by William Longsword.[92] Otto's speech—delivered to Hugh the Great and Arnulf of Flanders in indirect discourse—is called a *conquestio* in the chapter title and is introduced in the body of the text by the word *conquerebatur*.[93] The manuscript shows, however, that Richer crossed out an earlier sentence in which he referred to Otto's speech as an *indignatio*.[94]

Theoretically the purpose of the *indignatio* was to arouse anger against one's opponent, while the *conquestio* was intended to win sympathy for one's own cause. Otto's speech has elements of both: he laments that, contrary to both law and fairness, he has been humiliated in front of his friends *(ultra aequum et ius sese spretum memorans, ac coram amicis a sedili amotum)*, and he insists that the *insolentia* that William displayed toward him was sure to be manifested in the future toward Hugh and Arnulf. The effect of the speech, Richer tells us, was to arouse odium against Wil-

---

Alberada. Charles, Lothar, and Alberada shared a common mother, Queen Gerberga, but Alberada's father was Gislebert of Lotharingia—Gerberga's first husband—while the father of Charles and Lothar was King Louis IV. See Hoffmann, *Historiae*, 270, chap. 56, note 6. Arnulf was a bastard son of Lothar and thus Bruno's cousin.

91. *Historia* 4.56: *Indignatio Brunonis in Arnulfum.*

92. *Historia* 2.31.

93. *Historia* 2.31. The chapter title is *Otto iniuriam sub specie fidei habendae dissimulat, eiusque conquestio.*

94. Bamberg, Staatsbibliothek, MS Hist. 5, fol. 19^{V}, lines 27–28. The expunged text reads "de iniuria quae ei irrogata a Uuilelmo fuerat cum ab eo surgere a lecto coactus sit apud illos truculentus agitabat indignationem." Richer has replaced it with "de iniuria irrogata apud illos amplius conquerebatur. Ultra aequum et ius sese spretum memorans, ac coram amicis a sedili amotum."

liam. In that sense it is more *indignatio* than *conquestio,* but Richer seems to have realized that there was a fine line between the two. His tendency to conflate *conquestio* and *indignatio* may reflect the influence of Marius Victorinus, who states at the end of book 1 of his commentary that "there are many topics common to both the *indignatio* and the *conquestio,* and this is appropriate; for the judge cannot extend pity to us without becoming angry at our opponent, nor will he be able to grow angry with our opponent unless in the same matter he inclines to pity us."[95] For Victorinus, *conquestio* and *indignatio* were closely linked, and Richer seems to have adopted this view. His apparent lack of interest in the topics of the *conquestio* may also derive from a reliance on Victorinus, who mentions the applicability of the fifteen topics of the *indignatio* and the sixteen of the *conquestio,* but does not list them or discuss them in any detail.[96]

Why, then, did Richer (and Gerbert, on at least one occasion) use the terms *conquestio* and *indignatio* to designate entire speeches, when it is clear from the context of the *De inventione* that these were parts of the peroration, itself only one component of a larger speech? One possible answer is that the definitions of these terms in the *De inventione,* if plucked from their context, appear to designate self-contained speeches. Cicero's use of the word *oratio* to categorize each term might have led to confusion, since *oratio* commonly designated an entire speech, while in this case it describes only one part.[97] The most probable explanation, however,

95. *Explanationes in Ciceronis rhetoricam* 1.54, p. 178. Cf. Martianus Capella, *De nuptiis* 5.565: "conquestio, id est miseratio, isdem ex locis argumentorum sumitur quibus et indignatio."

96. John O. Ward, *Ciceronian Rhetoric in Treatise, Scholion, and Commentary,* Typologie des sources du Moyen Âge occidental 58 (Turnhout: Brepols, 1995), 96, notes that Victorinus's commentary tended to overshadow the text of the *De inventione* itself in the post-Carolingian period. Richer's citations of the *De inventione* prove that he knew both the text and the commentary—and Bamberg, Staatsbibliothek, MS Class. 25 contains both—but the instructional focus at Rheims may well have been on Victorinus.

97. *De inventione* 1.53.100: "Indignatio est oratio per quam conficitur ut in

is simply that *conquestio* and *indignatio* were fluid terms, serving both as rhetorical *termini technici* and as general terms for complaint and indignation, whether constructed according to technical rhetorical precepts or not. A writer could easily borrow from Cicero's discussion of the *conquestio* without adhering strictly to his divisions of the parts of a speech. This is exactly what Richer appears to have done.

In one important case Gerbert deploys the *conquestio* as an element of the conclusion of a (written) argument in accordance with the *De inventione.* In his letter to Wilderod of Strasbourg he divides his argument into the six parts of a speech *(exordium, narratio, partitio, confirmatio, reprehensio,* and *epilogus)* and gives the final section the title *epilogus per enumerationem et conquestionem*—that is, an epilogue that contains both an enumeration of arguments and a complaint, two of the three components of the peroration in the *De inventione.*[98] As with Richer's speeches of complaint, however, Gerbert does not turn to the topics of the *conquestio* to furnish himself with material. Instead, he first borrows an image from Virgil (*Aeneid* 1.3) to depict himself as a storm-tossed refugee, and then compares himself to the young Egyptian abandoned by his Amalekite master and rescued by King David (1 Sam. 30:11–16):

> I who have been driven to and fro on land and on sea while I have pursued the discoveries of philosophers and fled from unlearned peoples (and yet do not escape), I who was no small part of the captive and despoiled people of the great city of Rheims when it was betrayed, I flee to you as to a safe harbor. Therefore, extend your saving hand to me as I am tossed; give respite to one who is weary and will repay you if given the chance. For even the Amalekite who was restored was made one of David's commanders. I do not ask for gold; I do not seek land; it is only brotherly love that I require.[99]

---

aliquem hominem magnum odium aut in rem gravis offensio concitetur"; 1.55.106: "Conquestio est oratio auditorum misericordiam captans."

98. Letter 217 (Riché and Callu, 2.646).

99. Letter 217 (Riché and Callu, 2.646).

The writings of Gerbert and Richer indicate that the term *conquestio* could denote both a general complaint and the rhetorical *terminus technicus* discussed by Cicero in the *De inventione*.[100] The degree to which the rhetorical doctrines associated with the Ciceronian *conquestio* influenced the genre of the complaint in the literature of this period lies beyond the scope of this study, but in the speeches of Richer and Gerbert the influence seems to have gone in the other direction. That is, both writers tend to eschew the topics of the *conquestio* from the *De inventione* and draw their inspiration from other sources: literary or biblical themes, or perhaps even from an oral tradition of complaint literature, which seems to lie behind works like the *planctus* on the death of William Longsword.[101]

A characteristic example of Richer's use of a literary model as a source for the *conquestio* is the climactic moment of Ingo's speech when he reveals the scars that he has received in the service of King Odo. The baring of wounds as a sign of service to the state had already obtained the status of a rhetorical cliché by the first century A.D., when Petronius alluded to its overuse in the *Satyricon*.[102] It is nonetheless worth asking where Richer—who had not read Petronius—acquired his knowledge of this motif, since the answer could provide some insight into his reading habits and the sources of his rhetorical invention. Richer's familiarity with Sallust, Livy, and Hegesippus suggests that he might have derived the idea from their work, and in fact all three historians include a scene in which a speaker points to his scars before a crowd.

100. The fact that Richer treats *querimonia* and *conquestio* as synonyms seems to confirm that he conceived of the *conquestio* as a speech of complaint in general, and not merely in terms of Cicero's definition in the *De inventione*. Richer uses the word *querimonia* as the title for speeches of complaint at 2.16 and 2.52. Flodoard, *Annales*, s.a. 948, p. 111, introduces the speech of King Louis at the Synod of Ingelheim with the phrase *quaerimoniam propalavit*. At *Historia* 2.73 Richer rewrites Flodoard's version of the speech; he introduces it with the synonymous phrase *querelam effudit*, but designates the speech as a *conquestio* in the chapter title: *CONQUESTIO Ludovici apud Ottonem regem et sinodum regni*.

101. Lair, *Étude sur la vie et la mort de Guillaume Longue-Épée*, 61–70.

102. Kortüm, *Richer von Saint-Remi*, 100. See Patronius, *Satyricon* 1.1–2.

At chapter 85 of the *Bellum Iugurthinum* the consul Marius delivers a speech to an assembly of the people in which he admits to his lack of noble forebears and calls attention instead to his personal virtue. He admits that he cannot point to consulships, triumphs, or wax images of his ancestors as proof that he is qualified to serve as consul and command the Roman armies. Instead, Marius tells the crowd, he can point to prizes won for bravery and the scars on the front of his body *(cicatrices adverso corpore)* as evidence of his service to the people. The same topos appears in book 1 of the *Bellum Iudaicum,* where Antipater, the Idumaean adviser to the Judaean ethnarch Hyrcanus II, and father of the future king Herod, appears before Julius Caesar to defend himself against the slanders of his enemy Antigonus and make a show of his own loyalty to the dictator.[103] At the beginning of his speech Antipater tears off his cloak and points to his wounds as "pledges of his loyalty" *(fidei … pignora)* to Caesar.[104] Livy uses this topos no fewer than six times, once as the capstone of a speech of defense.[105] In book 6, M. Manlius Capitolinus is put on trial for sedition by the senate. After reminding his audience of his many services to the Roman people, Manlius "bared his breast, distinguished by the scars he had received in battle," and called upon the gods to come to his aid.[106] Given the frequency of this motif in his literary models, we can be virtually certain that Richer adapted Ingo's dramatic baring of his wounds from one or more of these passages.

A similar example of Richer's adaptation of material from a historiographical model occurs in a speech from book 2 in which Louis IV complains to his wife and his loyal followers about his persecution at the hands of Hugh the Great:[107]

103. Hegesippus, *Bellum Iudaicum* 1.13–1.25.

104. *Bellum Iudaicum* 1.25.2.

105. Livy 2.23.4, 2.27.2, 4.58.13, 6.14.6, 6.20.8, 45.39.16–17.

106. Livy 6.20.8.

107. *Historia* 2.52. The speech is labeled *querimonia* in the chapter title, but Richer uses the verb *conqueri* to describe Louis's speaking.

The king delivered a complaint to them in these words: "Alas, Hugh! Alas, Hugh! How many of my possessions you have deprived me of! What great evils you have inflicted upon me! In what miserable conditions I am now held captive! You have taken Rheims from me and snatched away Laon, the only two places where I could find refuge and security. My father was taken prisoner and thrown into a dungeon, but when he lost his life he also bid farewell to the miseries that now oppress me. I, on the other hand, who have been cast down into the same misfortunes, have nothing to show for my father's kingdom but a public spectacle. I do not care to live any more, but I am not permitted to die. Where then shall I betake myself?"[108]

This speech reveals just how formulaic the *conquestio*—or any speech—could become in Richer's hands. The beginning of Louis's complaint, with its apostrophe *("Eia tu, Hugo ... eia tu, Hugo")* and tricolon *(quantis ... quantis ... quanto),* closely echoes the address of Arnulf's men to Robert, the castellan of Montreuil-sur-Mer, earlier in book 2.[109] The parallel construction *His tantum duobus recipiebar, his duobus claudebar,* which features both anaphora and homoeoteleuton, is repeated almost verbatim a few chapters later when Louis complains of Hugh's persecution at the Synod of Ingelheim.[110] As Ingo did in his speech, Louis refers to death as the end of all misfortunes and uses the verb *precipitare* to describe his personal ruin, recalling the phrase *precipitare in miserias* used by Ingo in book 1 and by Bruno of Langres in his speech at the Synod of Saint-Basle.[111] In this case, however, Sallust's *Bellum Iugurthinum* is the source of both the commonplace about death and the verb *precipitare.* In fact, the two penultimate sentences are

108. *Historia* 2.52.

109. Cf. *Historia* 2.52: "'Eia tu,' inquiens, 'Hugo, eia tu Hugo. Quantis bonis a te privatus, quantis malis affectus, quanto etiam merore nunc detineor!,'" and *Historia* 2.11: "'Eia te,' inquiuunt, 'Rotberte, eia te Rotberte' (sic enim vocabatur). 'Quantis malis elapsus, quantis periculis exemptus es, et quanti insuper secundarum rerum tibi debentur successus.'"

110. *Historia* 2.73: "Hoc tantum claudebar, hoc solo cum uxore et natis recipiebar."

111. *Historia* 1.11: "Ob vestram salutem in has me miserias precipitavi"; 4.56: "Hunc unde hic sermo habetur, in has miserias precipitasse videor."

excerpted with minimal changes from Adherbal's address to the Roman senate in chapter 14 of the *Bellum Iugurthinum.* The rhetorical question that Richer uses to cap off the speech—*Quo me conferam?*—is found in Livy, Cicero, and Augustine, and is uncommon enough to suggest that Richer borrowed it from one of these sources.[112] In short, much of the language and many of the thematic elements of this speech are borrowed from other authors or else reused elsewhere in the *Historia.*

Ingo's plea before King Odo, Charles of Lotharingia's lament on the future sufferings of his children, and Louis's complaint to his men all employ themes or words borrowed from speeches written by classical historians. This feature is characteristic of Richer's approach to speech writing as a whole. It suggests that he consciously mined Sallust and Hegesippus (among others) for speeches as he read, and it may indicate that model speeches from classical historians were used to teach composition in the schools. The frequency of the *conquestio* form in particular, and the repetitive elements of these speeches in the *Historia,* suggests the possibility that the *conquestio* or perhaps a combined *conquestio/indignatio* was an exercise used by Gerbert to teach rhetoric. The fact that the *De inventione,* which was first studied at Rheims during Gerbert's tenure as *scholasticus,* defines the *conquestio* as a type of *oratio* (though not, according to Cicero, a separate speech), and the fact that Gerbert himself describes a speech in his *Acta* of the Synod of Saint-Basle as a *conquestio,* further suggests that Gerbert played a role in developing the complaint as a rhetorical genre at Rheims.

Deliberatio and the *Genus Demonstrativum*

The foregoing analysis of Richer's *conquestiones* suggests that for him speechwriting was as much about borrowing—language from Gerbert, Sallust, or Hegesippus; *sententiae* from the *Disticha Catonis;* motifs from classical historians—and imagining the

112. *De oratore* 3.214; Livy 40.10.4; Augustine, *Sermo* 106, chap. 1, *PL* 39.1952.

circumstances of historical actors, as it was about resorting to the rhetorical topics as sources of argument. There is no evidence that he felt compelled to hew closely to the precepts of the *De inventione.* Much the same holds true for the speeches that Richer designates with the term *deliberatio.*[113] In classical rhetoric the deliberative genre of oratory *(genus deliberativum)* encompassed speeches given before political assemblies or legislative bodies in which the speaker argued for or against the honor *(honestas)* or utility *(utilitas)* of an act.[114] In his contemporary treatise on the art of rhetoric, Notker Labeo (ca. 950–1022) included the "councils of princes" in deliberative bodies, and this is the context in which most of the deliberation in the *Historia* takes place.[115]

Cicero defines and enumerates the topics and rules *(praecepta)* for the deliberative genre of oratory in the second book of the *De inventione.*[116] He considers three categories of goods: the honorable *(honestum),* which is sought for its own sake; the useful *(utile),* which is sought because of the advantage it provides; and a third class that contains elements of both the honorable and the useful.[117] Under the heading of the purely honorable falls virtue, and Cicero goes on to define the four cardinal virtues of prudence *(prudentia),* justice *(iustitia),* bravery *(fortitudo),* and moderation *(temperantia),* as well as their subdivisions.[118] Included in this discussion are important definitions of natural and customary law.[119] There follows a list of things that are both good in and of themselves and good because of the advantages they bring: glory *(gloria),* rank *(dignitas),* influence *(amplitudo),* and friendship *(amicitia).*[120] Cicero then

113. For Kortüm's discussion of *deliberatio,* which focuses on the speech of King Radulf to the citizens of Rheims at 1.60, see *Richer von Saint-Remi,* 102–4.

114. *De inventione* 1.5.7; 2.51.156; Martianus Capella, *De nuptiis* 5.447.

115. *De arte rhetorica,* 180–81: "Sed invento occasione manifestam se praebet et in multitudine populi ubi sunt iudicia plebis et consilia principum curam regni administrantium ibi maxime gloriatur."

116. *De inventione* 2.52.157–76.

117. *De inventione* 2.52.157.

118. *De inventione* 2.53.159–2.54.165.

119. *De inventione* 2.53.161–2.54.162.

120. *De inventione* 2.55.166. I employ the translations of these terms used by Hubbell, 333.

turns to utility, which is divided into advantages of the body and those external to the body.[121] He closes with an examination of the related topics of necessity *(necessitudo)* and affection *(affectio)*.[122] As we shall see, Richer relies little on this detailed apparatus of deliberative topics in any of his accounts of deliberation or deliberative oratory.

At several places in the *Historia* Richer depicts kings or nobles deliberating on some matter of policy—weighing the advantages and disadvantages of one or more courses of action—in indirect discourse.[123] In some of these examples Richer characterizes the action of the characters with the words *deliberatio* or *deliberare*, but he is not thereby pointing to the delivery of a deliberative speech. Deliberation in this sense denotes a dispassionate analysis of the advantages and disadvantages of one or more courses of action, rather than a speech strongly advocating a certain point of view.

For example, when Hugh the Great and Arnulf of Flanders consider how best to respond to the threat posed by William Longsword, they conclude that killing him and letting him live both present problems. On the one hand, his death would leave King Louis without his most important ally and allow them to pursue their designs unopposed. On the other hand, their guilt would be obvious if they murdered him. Both choices are unappealing:

> They judged each one of these options dangerous, since if they killed [William], then the guilt for his murder would redound against them, and if they kept him alive then tyranny would manifest itself in the future.[124]

Hugh and Arnulf eventually agree to have William killed, but Richer glosses over the reasoning that leads to this decision with the phrase *de occisione tandem persuasi.* In this case, his interest lies

121. *De inventione* 2.56.168–69.
122. *De inventione* 2.57.170–172.58.176.
123. Cf. *Historia* 1.43, 2.32, 2.50, 3.78, 3.102, 4.49.
124. *Historia* 2.32.

not in showing why Hugh and Arnulf were eventually persuaded to carry out the murder, but in presenting the different courses of action that they considered.

In this and other instances of deliberation in the *Historia* Richer couches the arguments solely in terms of practical advantages and disadvantages. Honor and virtue do not enter into the calculus. When King Lothar debates whether to make peace with Otto II after the German emperor's campaign into West Francia in the fall of 978, he weighs the matter purely in terms of political expediency, specifically, how an alliance with Otto might strengthen his hand against Hugh Capet:

> If he continued to defy him, he thought that it was possible that the duke might be induced by bribes to go back to his alliance with Otto. If he himself were to be reconciled with Otto, however, then he would have to hurry so that the duke would not get wind of what he was doing and seek to be reconciled with Otto as well.[125]

This pattern of presenting two or more potential courses of action supported by arguments based on advantage—but not virtue—is a recurring feature of the *Historia*.[126] Richer always frames these deliberations in indirect discourse, and he dispenses with the persuasive speech delivered in support of one particular point of view. His goal is not to dramatize the process of persuasion, but to show the audience the options open to the actors.

Few speeches in the *Historia* clearly belong to the genre of deliberative oratory, that is, nonforensic speeches delivered before an assembly in which the speaker tries to persuade the audience to pursue a certain course of action. At the end of book 1, King Radulf, having captured the city of Rheims after a three-week siege, addresses the citizens in an attempt to persuade them to replace their archbishop, the five year-old Hugh, with a more suitable candidate.[127] Radulf's argument consists of two basic premises.

125. *Historia* 3.78.

126. *Historia* 2.32, 3.78, 3.102, 4.18, 4.49.

127. *Historia* 1.60. See also Kortüm, *Richer von Saint-Remi,*102–3.

First, the "little boy" *(infantulus)* Hugh is not a suitable occupant of the see of Rheims under the provisions of canon law. Second, although the citizens of Rheims are clearly reluctant to replace their elected archbishop with the king's candidate, they will not incur any dishonor by doing so, since they are being compelled to obey him by force:

> Nor will any dishonor redound against you, since necessity compels those who have been defeated and captured in war to change course.[128]

The necessity that Radulf invokes here is in fact a rhetorical *terminus technicus*. Necessity was a defensive plea that fell under the heading of the qualitative status *(constitutio generalis)*, the same category of rhetorical issue that encompassed Ingo's defense of *comparatio* at *Historia* 1.11 and Adalger's use of *remotio criminis* at the Synod of Saint-Basle.[129] *Necessitas* was employed when a defendant admitted to a deed but sought exculpation on the grounds that he had been compelled by force to act. The castellan Robert invoked necessity to assuage his shame at betraying Montreuil-sur-Mer to the forces of Arnulf of Flanders at 2.11, reasoning that his treachery could be excused by the fact that all the inhabitants of Montreuil would soon be exiled or put to death.[130]

The context of Radulf's speech—a persuasive address delivered before a citizen body urging them to choose a certain course of action—marks it out as an example of deliberative oratory. However, little in this speech directly reflects the precepts of the *genus*

128. *Historia* 1.60: "Nec dedecoris quicquam in vos redundabit, cum militari violentia victos et captos alia sequi necessitas adurgeat."

129. See *De inventione* 1.11.15 and 2.31.94–2.32.98. The assumptive branch of the equitable (iuridicialis) division of the qualitative status contained four subdivisions: *concessio, remotio criminis, relatio criminis*, and *comparatio*. *Concessio* ("confession") was divided into *purgatio* (where the intent of the agent was defended, but not the act) and *deprecatio* (where the defendant simply asked for pardon); *purgatio* was further subdivided into *imprudentia* ("ignorance"), *casus* ("accident"), and *necessitudo* ("necessity").

130. *Historia* 2.11: "Proponit sibi tandem proditionis dedecus ea posse necessitate purgari, quod omnes oppidanos in proximo aut exulaturos aut morituros sibi innotuit."

deliberativum as outlined in the *De inventione.* Radulf touches on the avoidance of dishonor and the advantages to be gained by the election of a new archbishop, but he does not mention *honestas* or *utilitas* specifically, nor does he delve into the deliberative topics enumerated by Cicero.

Another speech that we can assign to the *genus deliberativum* occurs at the beginning of book 2, when a council of West-Frankish magnates meets to discuss the royal succession after the death of Radulf in 936.[131] Hugh the Great delivers a speech in which he rejects his own candidacy for the throne and recommends that Louis, son of Charles the Simple, be brought back from England and crowned. Hugh makes two separate but related arguments. First, his father Robert erred in seizing the throne from Charles and continuing to reign while the true king was still alive. Second, the rule of the non-Carolingians Robert and Radulf fostered a lack of respect for the royal office and promoted discord in the kingdom. Absent from Hugh's speech is any consideration of the relative merits of the two leading candidates for the throne—himself and Louis. His argument is based purely on the question of which dynasty should occupy the throne, not who would make the better king. In general terms, this speech involves considerations of honor and advantage. Hugh admits that it was both wrong and ultimately bad for the kingdom for his father to have seized the throne. Once again, though, Richer avoids using programmatic words like *honestas* and *utilitas.* Nor does he mention the virtues and their subdivisions, or any of the different varieties of goods that are useful or both useful and honorable. In fact, in none of the deliberative speeches or accounts of deliberation in the *Historia* do we find any use of the specific argumentative topics of the deliberative genre as presented in the *De inventione.* As was the case with the *conquestio,* Richer is content to employ the general framework of a certain kind of speech without relying on Cicero's detailed inventory of rules.

131. *Historia* 2.2.

The longest, and arguably the most rhetorically sophisticated, speech in the *Historia* occurs at a moment of major historical importance: the assembly of Frankish nobles at Senlis in May 987 to determine the royal succession after the death of Louis V. Here Adalbero of Rheims delivers an oration in support of the candidacy of Hugh Capet and against the claims of Louis's uncle, Charles of Lotharingia.[132] The speech presents an interesting point of comparison with Hugh the Great's address in book 2. Hugh, in declining to put himself forward as a candidate for the throne and urging the magnates to crown Louis, argued for both the propriety and the utility of restoring the Carolingian line, claiming that Robert had acted unjustly in dethroning Charles the Simple and that a revived Carolingian dynasty might put an end to political disorder. He made no reference to his own or Louis's merits, instead framing the argument purely in impersonal terms. Adalbero is compelled to take the opposite approach. For the archbishop of Rheims, Hugh Capet's superior qualifications for the kingship count for more than the preservation of an unbroken Carolingian line of succession.[133] As a result, he presents his argument entirely in terms of the character of the respective candidates and ignores the possibility that dynastic change might lead to civil disorder—which is, in fact, exactly what happens. It is a mark of Richer's talent for *inventio* that in the case of these speeches concerning the royal succession he is able to devise two different and equally persuasive arguments whose basic premises are so contradictory.

The context of Adalbero's speech—a council of nobles who have assembled to consider the question of whom to support as the next king—appears to classify it as part of the *genus deliberativum*.

132. Carlrichard Brühl, *Deutschland-Frankreich: Die Geburt zweier Völker* (Cologne and Vienna: Böhlau, 1990), 589–93, emphasizes the fictional character of the speech and the danger of accepting it as a record of Adalbero's actual arguments. No evidence suggests that Richer was present or had any access to a record of what was said there.

133. Adalbero's real motives for supporting Hugh Capet were self-serving. See Brühl, *Deutschland-Frankreich,* 575–87, and Kienast, *Deutschland und Frankreich in der Kaiserzeit,* 1.99–120.

Adalbero does urge his audience to leave aside their personal loyalties and consider the "communal interest" *(utilitas communis)*—utility being one of the two chief considerations of deliberative oratory.[134] The content of the speech, however, which focuses largely on Charles's failings and Hugh's qualifications for the throne, suggests that it is an example of epideictic oratory, the branch of rhetoric that dealt with praise *(laus)* and censure *(vituperatio)*.[135] Indeed, immediately after his reference to *utilitas,* Adalbero employs terms that reflect the epideictic character of the speech, when he poses the rhetorical questions, "if you curse [*vituperetis*] the good, how will you praise [*laudabitis*] the bad? If you praise [*laudetis*] the bad, how will you scorn [*contempnetis*] the good?"

The topics of the *genus demonstrativum,* as outlined in the *De inventione,* involved the personal attributes of the subject: his name *(nomen),* nature *(natura),* way of life *(victus),* fortune *(fortuna),* disposition *(habitus),* feeling *(affectio),* interests *(studia),* purposes *(consilia),* deeds *(facta),* accidents *(casus),* and speeches *(orationes)*.[136] The themes to be considered in the epideictic oration were numerous, and they gave the speaker ample room to dilate on the good or bad qualities of his subject. Richer, however, makes very limited use of the topics *ex personis* in this speech. Adalbero first

134. The imperative to judge without *odium* or *amor* may reflect the opening of Julius Caesar's speech at Sallust, *Bellum Catilinae* 51: "Omnis homines, patres conscripti, qui de rebus dubiis consultant, ab odio, amicitia, ira atque misericordia vacuous esse decet."

135. *De inventione* 1.5.7: "demonstrativum est quod tribuitur in alicuius certae personae laudem aut vituperationem." Notker of Saint-Gall held that the epideictic genre involved "quis dignus sit imperio vel episcopatu." See *De arte rhetorica,* 114, lines 69–70, and 115, line 9. The first of these questions is precisely the topic being considered here.

136. *De inventione* 2.59.177: "Laudes autem et vituperationes ex eis locis sumentur qui loci personis sunt attributi." For an inventory of the topics, see *De inventione* 1.24.34. In the *De inventione* the topics *ex personis* were not limited to the epideictic genre, but could be applied to any speech during the *confirmatio,* the part of an oration following the *exordium, narratio,* and *partitio.* For an examination of the origin and later use of Cicero's topics *ex personis,* see Michael C. Leff, "The Topics of Argumentative Invention in Latin Rhetorical Theory from Cicero to Boethius," *Rhetorica* 1 (1983): 23–44.

describes the qualities that make a good king: nobility of body *(nobilitas corporis),* wisdom *(animi sapientia),* faith *(fides),* and greatness of spirit *(magnanimitas).* Charles is said to possess none of these and is characterized instead by faithlessness, lethargy, and dullness of mind. Hugh is "distinguished in deed, in nobility, and in wealth" *(actu, nobilitate, copiis clarissimum),* a "guardian of the state and of private possessions" *(tutor rei publicae ... et privatarum rerum),* a lord who provides protection *(patrocinium)* and aid *(auxilium).* Richer apparently saw no need to employ anything like the full range of topics *ex personis.* Only those external factors and qualities of mind and body relevant to exercising the kingship needed to be mentioned. Thus, while the speech is generally speaking an example of epideictic oratory, it reveals no detailed knowledge or application of the precepts of the *De inventione.*

Inductio

The speeches examined in this chapter demonstrate that by and large the divisions of classical rhetoric—the judicial, deliberative, and epideictic genres—as well as more specialized categories of speech such as the *conquestio* and *indignatio,* provided Richer with a basic framework within which to work. His application of Ciceronian rhetorical principles tended to remain on a fairly general level, however. Whether from limitations of space, lack of familiarity, or lack of inclination, he made little use of the topics specific to each of these various types of oratory when composing speeches for his characters.

A dialogue near the end of book 4, however, presents a unique case in which Richer engages with a more specialized kind of rhetorical argument. In chapter 3 we saw how Richer uses the same basic narrative template to describe the betrayal of several different strongholds. One instance was the attempt by a messenger sent by Count Odo I of Blois and Chartres to convince Walter, the castellan of Melun, to desert his lord, the royal vassal Burchard of Vendôme, and turn the castle over to Odo. In his marginal chapter title Richer designates the messenger's attempt to suborn the castellan as an *inductio.* This was a rhetorical term used to describe a particular type of argument by analogy.[137] In the *De inventione* Cicero describes two types of argument *(argumentatio)*: deductive reasoning *(ratiocinatio),* in which the speaker uses rhetorical syllogisms (epicheiremes or enthymemes) to demonstrate the probability of his assertion, and *inductio.*[138] This is not "induction" in the modern sense of the word (i.e., the generation of a general proposition from numerous particular cases); instead, as Cicero defines it:

> Induction is a form of argument which leads the person with whom one is arguing to give assent to certain undisputed facts; through this assent it wins his approval of a doubtful proposition because this resembles the facts to which he has assented.[139]

Cicero goes on to explain the use of *inductio* in detail, citing as an example a now-lost dialogue of the fourth-century B.C. philosopher Aeschines Socraticus in which Aspasia, the concubine of Pericles, poses a series of questions to Xenophon and his wife. The first two questions are designed to produce immediate answers: If the woman next door to Xenophon's wife possessed superior jewels, wouldn't she want these instead of her own? And if the neighbor possessed better clothes, surely Xenophon's wife would prefer them? Xenophon's wife answers both questions affirmatively. Two similar questions are posed to Xenophon himself. He is asked if he would prefer his neighbor's superior horse and farm to his own, and he also answers yes both times. Then Aspasia presents a third question, the doubtful proposition to which both are bound to give assent by virtue of their former answers. Would not Xenophon, by analogy, prefer his neighbor's wife if she were superior to his own wife? Likewise, wouldn't Xenophon's wife prefer the neighbor's husband, if he were a better husband than Xenophon? Husband

137. *Historia* 4.75: "Inductio ab legato Odonis in presidem Miliduni."

138. *De inventione* 1.31.51.

139. *De inventione* 1.31.51: "Inductio est oratio quae rebus non dubiis captat assensiones eius quicum instituta est; quibus assensionibus facit ut illi dubia quaedam res propter similitudinem earum rerum quibus assensit probetur"; trans. Hubbell, 93.

and wife alike remain silent when presented with this final question, seemingly caught in Aspasia's logical trap. By answering the first two questions in the affirmative, both have committed themselves to a line of reasoning that they cannot abandon when presented with the third question.

Now let us examine how Odo's messenger deceives Walter, the castellan of Melun. First, he feigns friendship with him and gains his trust. Then he begins to question him:

He addressed the castellan and asked him who the castle's previous owner had been. The castellan did not refuse to tell him whose it had been. The messenger then asked, "How then, did it come into the king's power?" The castellan also answered this question, whereupon the messenger asked, "Why is Odo being denied that which is rightfully his, when he has asked to have the castle returned to him on many occasions, and it is now held by someone inferior to him?" "Because," the castellan replied, "that was the king's decision." The messenger continued, "Don't you think that God is offended when, after the death of a father, an orphan is deprived of his patrimony without cause?" "Of course," the castellan replied. "And what is more, this is a source of despair for good men. For who among the magnates is more powerful than Odo? Who is more worthy of every honor?" In response the messenger said, "If you were willing to cross over to Odo's side, don't you think that you would be elevated to a position of greater authority? If you were Odo's man, you can be assured that you would enjoy his favor, his counsel, and his aid. Instead of one castle you would possess many, and the greater the height of the honor that you obtained, the further the glory of your reputation would reach." In response the castellan said, "How can you be sure that all this will happen without my being stained by sin and dishonor?" The messenger answered, "If you give yourself to Odo and turn the castle over to him, then whatever crime you think may result, let it be on my head and charged against me. I will pay the penalty for it and I will render an account of it to God on high. Now take thought for your own noble status and see to the increase of your fortune. The time to act is now. The circumstances recommend it, for the king's lack of authority has made him contemptible, while Odo is always attended by better fortune."[140]

140. *Historia* 4.75.

The rhetorical strategy pursued by Odo's messenger here bears a superficial resemblance to the *inductio* as defined by Cicero. He asks the castellan a series of questions (To whom did the castle of Melun belong formerly? How did Melun come to belong to the king? Why is it being unfairly denied to Odo?) before presenting an undeniable proposition to which the castellan must assent (surely it is wrong for an orphan to be deprived of his patrimony without cause?) But no relation of analogy holds between any of these four questions. Nor is there an analogical relationship between the fact that Odo and his family may have been unjustly deprived of Melun and the fact that the castellan would do much better for himself if he went over to Odo's side. The logical structure of the *inductio* as practiced by Odo's messenger is weak indeed. What marks this dialogue out as a form of *inductio*—if a somewhat tenuous one—is the fact that the castellan seems to be unaware of where the argument is leading when it begins. In this case, the first four questions soften him up and render him open to the suggestion that he go over to Odo's side, but they do not make it logically necessary that he do so. The *inductio* does not adhere to the tight logical structure outlined by Cicero, but it does use a series of propositions to win assent to a more doubtful proposition.

It is noteworthy that the speech of Odo's messenger looks more like an *inductio* if one ignores Cicero's example from Aeschines Socraticus and reads only the first part of the definition in the *De inventione:* "Induction is a form of argument which leads the person with whom one is arguing to give assent to certain undisputed facts."[141] Victorinus uses this statment as the lemma in his commentary, initially leaving out the second half of the definition where Cicero stresses that induction proceeds "through analogy" *(propter similitudinem).*[142] Victorinus goes on to discuss the use of analogous propositions, but it is possible that Richer remembered the definition better than the explanation that followed. Just as

141. *De inventione* 1.31.51, trans. Hubbell, 93.
142. *Explanationes in Ciceronis rhetoricam* 1.31, p. 150.

he neglected to delve very deep into the topics of the *conquestio,* the *indignatio,* the *deliberatio,* or the *genus demonstrativum* when using these forms of oratory in the *Historia,* Richer did not go to great lengths to see that his use of *inductio* developed according to the precise pattern laid out in the *De inventione.*

However inexact Richer's use of this technique, it is a clear instance of the application of rhetorical *ars* to the composition of a speech. Several other authors refer to *inductio* as a strategy of argument around the time when Richer was writing, which indicates an increasing familiarity with works like the *De inventione* and Cicero's *Topics* (which also describes *inductio*). Dudo of Saint-Quentin, Abbo of Fleury, and Fulbert of Chartres all use *inductio* to refer to a specific technique of argument, and in Abbo's case his knowledge of this term clearly derives from Cicero and/or Victorinus.[143]

Imitatio

While Ciceronian rhetoric provided Richer with a means of categorizing and labeling the various kinds of speeches in the *Historia,* only limited evidence suggests that he drew upon the *De inventione* as a source of content. Somewhat ironically, then, Cicero's treatise on rhetorical invention seems to have exercised comparatively little influence on Richer's own process of *inventio.* In devising material for individual speeches he relied to some extent on his own imagination, but he also borrowed ideas—and sometimes excerpted whole passages—from the works of classical and late an-

143. See *Gesta Normannorum* 4.93, p. 250, where Dudo refers to Hugh's technique of posing leading questions as *inductio propositionum.* In a letter to Gauzbert, abbot of Saint-Julien at Tours, Abbo alludes to the idea that *inductio* is successful whether the interlocutor speaks or keeps silent, which is almost certainly a reference to the *De inventione* and/or Victorinus. See letter 8, *PL* 139.431, and cf. *De inventione* 1.32.54, and Victorinus, *Explanationes in Ciceronis rhetoricam* 1.32, p. 152. Fulbert demonstrates knowledge of *inductio* as a type of argument from analogy *(per similitudinem).* See letter 22, in *The Letters and Poems of Fulbert of Chartres* (Oxford: Clarendon Press, 1976), ed. Frederick Behrends, 40.

tique historians. Richer's penchant for appropriating the words of Sallust in particular has been frequently commented on.[144] He also uses excerpts from the *Bellum Iudaicum* of Hegesippus and makes frequent allusions to Livy and Caesar's *Bellum Gallicum*. Since these were the model authors whom Richer knew best, it is important to consider the degree to which the content of these histories influenced Richer's speeches.

Apart from formal orations, the influence of Richer's classical and late antique models is evident to varying degrees in three different kinds of rhetorical *descriptio* in the *Historia*. We have already seen how Richer sought out words and phrases from Hegesippus and Livy to flesh out his accounts of battles and sieges.[145] Hegesippus also provides a model for the two other kinds of description in the *Historia:* the siege weapon and the progress of disease.

Richer gives a detailed account of the construction and deployment of three different siege weapons: a mobile war-cart used during Louis IV's siege of Laon in 938 (2.10), a forty-foot-high ox-driven siege tower employed at Lothar's siege of Verdun in 985 (3.105), and a battering ram built by Hugh Capet's army before the walls of Laon in 988 (4.22). In each case his language is precise and technical. He employs terminology drawn from Caesar, Livy, and Vegetius, but does not excerpt whole passages from their works, and it is clear that he had considerable independent knowledge of the art of siege craft. His decision to include such technical descriptions can be partly attributed to his penchant for ostentatious displays of learning, but he was also following his historiographical models.[146] The *Bellum Iudaicum* contains a detailed account of a battering ram used during Vespasian's siege of Jotapata in 67 A.D., and the *Bellum Gallicum* is filled with accounts of siegeworks, in-

144. Latouche, "Un imitateur de Salluste"; Smalley, "Sallust in the Middle Ages," 173–75.

145. See chap. 2 above.

146. Cf. Hoffmann, "Die *Historien* Richers von Saint-Remi," 485: "In der frühmittelalterlichen Geschichtschreibung war das ganz ungewöhnlich; die Anregung dazu kann nur von den antikern Historikern gekommen sein."

cluding a particularly detailed description of the fortifications constructed by Caesar's forces at the siege of Alesia in 52 B.C.[147]

Hegesippus also furnishes a precedent for descriptive passages about disease, a recurring motif in the *Historia.* Early in book 1, Aristobulus I, the Hasmonean king of Judaea (104–103 B.C.), stricken with guilt at having ordered the murder of his brother Antigonus, falls deathly ill. His insides are wracked with pain; he loses sleep; his breathing is troubled. Finally, he vomits up blood and dies.[148] Later Hegesippus describes the mortal illness of King Herod the Great (40–4 B.C.) with a graphic list of symptoms: fever, an intolerable itching, pains of the stomach and intestines, dropsy, the proliferation of worms in his body, spasms, and difficulty in breathing.[149] Just as the death of Aristobulus was brought on by an attack of conscience at his evil deeds, Hegesippus treats Herod's symptoms as punishment for his brutality and sacrilege. Richer uses some of the material in this passage to flesh out his account of the death of Winemar, the assassin sent by Baldwin of Flanders to kill Archbishop Fulk of Rheims, and, following Flodoard, he insinuates that Winemar's suffering and death were punishment for his sins.[150]

The descriptive passages of the *Historia* draw on both the general precedents and the specific language of Richer's classical and late antique models. The same is true of the speeches, in both form and content. The address of a commander to his troops before battle, for example, is a type of speech absent from consideration in medieval rhetorical handbooks, but one that occurs repeatedly in classical historiography and in the works of Richer's contemporaries.[151] Richer follows classical precedents as models for these

147. *Bellum Iudaicum* 3.11; *Bellum Gallicum* 7.69–74.

148. *Bellum Iudaicum* 1.7.2–1.8.1.

149. *Bellum Iudaicum* 1.45.9.

150. *Historia* 1.18. For a similar account of hideous disease as divine punishment, see Liudprand of Cremona's account of the death of King Arnulf of East Francia at *Antapodosis* 1.36.

151. See, e.g., Dudo, *Gesta Normannorum* 2.3; Aimoin, *Gesta Francorum* 1.20; Widukind, *Res gestae Saxonicae* 3.46. See Morse, *Truth and Convention in the Middle Ages,* 119–24, and David Bachrach, "Conforming with the Rhetorical Tradition of

speeches. Otto II's address to his troops during his campaign into West Francia in the fall of 978 is indebted to a speech that Catiline delivers to his followers at *Bellum Catilinae* 20.[152] Robert of Neustria's exhortation to his men before their battle with a Viking host draws on the speech Catiline gives to his troops (as well as the encouragement offered by the general Marcus Petreius) before the final encounter between his forces and the Roman legions.[153] Nothing suggests, however, that Richer intended these classical intertexts as a form of implicit commentary on the speakers. In an earlier chapter (1.21) he refers to Robert of Neustria as a "usurper" *(tyrannus)* for engineering a coup against Charles the Simple, but in this scene Robert is defending the kingdom from a ravaging Viking army, not leading a rebellion, and there is no link between him and Catiline. Similarly, Richer's treatment of Otto II is consistently positive, and the speech he delivers to his troops cannot be meant to associate him with the notorious Roman rebel.[154]

Richer's historiographical models also furnished him with examples of speeches of complaint, some of which he borrowed from directly. Thus, Charles of Lotharingia's complaint about the fate of his children (4.14) is modeled in part on Herod the Great's tearful lament to his friends and family about the misfortune of his grandsons, whom he himself had orphaned.[155] A particularly influential model was the speech of Adherbal, the Numidian king expelled from his lands by Jugurtha, to the Roman senate at chapter 14 of the *Bellum Iugurthinum*.[156] Adherbal's speech is much longer and

Plausibility: Clerical Representation of Battlefield Orations against Muslims, 1080–1170," *International History Review* 26 (2004): 1–19.

152. *Historia* 3.73.

153. *Historia* 1.28. Cf. *Bellum Catilinae* 58–59.

154. In two passages Richer draws on Sallust's descriptions of Catiline at *Bellum Catilinae* 5, 14, and 15 to describe Gislebert of Lotharingia (1.35) and Henry the Quarrelsome (3.97), but it is unlikely that he was trying to associate Gislebert and Henry with Catiline, any more than he wished to compare Gislebert to Julian the Apostate by borrowing a passage from the *Historia ecclesiastica tripartita* to describe him at 1.35.

155. *Bellum Iudaicum* 1.42.

156. *Bellum Iugurthinum* 14.

more rhetorically complex than any of Richer's *conquestiones,* but the goal of the speech—creating sympathy for the speaker by emphasizing the misfortunes he has suffered—is the same. We know that Richer used this speech as a model because there are allusions to it in six different places in the *Historia,* including lengthy excerpts in Louis's complaint to his men about his persecution at the hands of Hugh the Great at 2.52 and Charles of Lotharingia's complaint to Adalbero of Rheims at 4.9.[157]

The pattern of textual allusions in the *Historia* gives us some insight into how Richer used each of his four main historiographical models. The textual echoes of, and direct excerpts from, Sallust's two monographs cluster around speeches, personal descriptions, and scenes of battle. From the *Bellum Catilinae* Richer draws on descriptions of Catiline (5.1–5.8) and his accomplices (14); two speeches Catiline gives to his followers (20, 58); two passages immediately following speeches (22.2, 54.4); a letter from Volturcius to Catiline (44.5); and the preparations leading up to the moment when Catiline's army met the Roman legions in battle (58–60). The longest citations in the *Historia* come from the description of Catiline's men at 14.3 (3.97), Catiline's speech to his followers at 20.7 (3.73), the letter from Volturcius at 44.5 (2.51), and the lead-up to the final battle at 58–60 (1.28, 1.43, 1.46). Richer's favoring of Sallust's speeches as a source is more pronounced in the case of the *Bellum Iugurthinum.* Of the thirteen clear allusions to this text in the *Historia,* nine are from speeches in direct discourse, one is from a speech in indirect discourse, and one occurs directly after a speech.[158] Richer's most important sources were Micipsa's speech

157. Cf. *Bellum Iugurthinum* 14.1 and *Historia* 4.22; 14.2 and 1.17; 14.7 and 3.95; 14.8 and 4.9; 14.23 and 2.52; 14.25 and 4.14.

158. Micipsa's address at *Bellum Iugurthinum* 10 is echoed at *Historia* 1.4 and 2.51. Allusions to Adherbal's address to the senate at *Bellum Iugurthinum* 14 appear at 1.17, 2.52, 3.95, 4.2, 4.9, and 4.14. The speech of Gaius Memmius to the citizens at Rome at *Bellum Iugurthinum* 31 is echoed at *Historia* 1.24. At *Bellum Iugurthinum* 22.2 Jugurtha replies to the emissaries of Rome in indirect discourse. There is an allusion to this speech at *Historia* 2.3. Other textual allusions are to *Bellum Iugurthinum* 34.2 (the tribune Baebius tells Jugurtha to hold his peace) at *Historia* 4.33 and *Bellum Iugurthinum* 91.1 (Marius's preparations on the march) at *Historia* 3.69.

to Jugurtha, Adherbal, and Hiempsal in chapter ten and Adherbal's address to the senate in chapter fourteen. His close knowledge of these speeches suggests either that they were used as sample speeches in the rhetorical curriculum at Rheims, or that Richer paid particular attention to these parts of the *Bellum Catilinae* and the *Bellum Iugurthinum* as he read. The importance of Sallust as a stylistic model for the *Historia* prefigures the sudden and steep rise in the copying of manuscripts of the *Bellum Catilinae* and *Bellum Iugurthinum* north of the Alps in the first half of the eleventh century, so it appears that in this area, as in many others, Rheims was in the vanguard of the intellectual tradition in the Latin West.[159]

Hegesippus, as we have seen, served as a model for various kinds of descriptive passages, including battles, descriptions of siege weapons, and fatal diseases. The *Historia* contains well over two dozen textual echoes of the *Bellum Iudaicum*.[160] The longest excerpts are taken from Herod's disingenuous lament following his execution of his sons at 1.42 (in the lament of Charles of Lotharingia at *Historia* 4.14); Herod's death and burial at 1.45–46 (a model for the death and burial of King Lothar at 3.109 and 3.110); an account of the location of the town of Gamala at 4.1 (in Richer's description of Verdun at 3.101); the wounding of King Agrippa at the siege of Gamala at 4.1 (in the account of the wounding of Lothar at Verdun at 3.107); the slaughter of Jewish fugitives from Gadara and their allies by Roman forces at 4.15 (in the description of the attack on Lothar's army during his return journey through Lotharingia at 3.98); and a brief summary of the reign of Alexander (ruled 103–76 B.C.), the successor to Aristobulus as king of Judaea, and his enmity with Demetrius III of Syria at 2.13 (in Richer's description of the rule of Otto II and his quarrels with Lothar at 3.67). Once again, the pattern of these ci-

159. See Patricia J. Osmond and Robert Ulery, "Sallustius," *CTC* vol. 8 (Washington, D.C.: The Catholic University of America Press, 2003), 193; Birger Munk Olsen, *L'étude des auteurs classiques latins aux XIe et XIIe siècles*, 4 vols. (Paris: Editions du Centre national de la recherche scientifique, 1982–1989), 3.2.114–20; Reynolds, *Texts and Transmission*, 341–49, esp. 345–47; Cardelle de Hartmann, "Sallust in St. Emmeram," 6–7.

160. These allusions are collected in Hoffman, *Historiae*, 319–20.

tations, which cluster heavily around speeches and descriptions, is significant. It suggests that Hegesippus, like Sallust, was deliberately mined for material that could be used for formal orations and rhetorical set pieces.

As emphasized previously, there is no evidence that Richer intended any of these intertexts to serve as a means of implicit political commentary. When we consider, for example, the fact that Richer incorporates details from the death and burial of Herod the Great in his description of the death and burial of King Lothar, we might be tempted to look for parallels between the two. Such a comparison would be highly politically charged, since the New Testament presents Herod as a tyrant responsible for Massacre of the Innocents (Matt 2:16–18), while the *Bellum Iudaicum* focuses on his paranoia and execution of his own family members. One sign that we should not read the excerpt from the *Bellum Iudaicum* in the *Historia* as a comment on Lothar is the difference in the reaction of the crowds at the two funerals. At the end of Richer's account of Lothar's funeral procession from Laon to Rheims, he writes that "[the king's body] was borne the whole distance with great devotion and an equal degree of affection [*parique affectu*] on everyone's part."[161] In this case, all those accompanying the dead king to his place of burial mourn him with an equal amount of emotion. In Hegesippus's account of the burial of Herod, by contrast, the suite accompanying his funeral cortège shows the proper degree of outward devotion *(obsequium).* Yet, this show of grief is inspired not by true affection *(sed non omnium pari affectu),* but by fear.[162] Richer is using Hegesippus here only as a stylistic model; he does not try to draw a link between Lothar and Herod perceptible to those who are familiar with the *Bellum Iudaicum.*

The histories of Sallust and Hegesippus account for a substantial majority of the longer direct excerpts in the *Historia,* but

161. *Historia* 3.110.

162. *Bellum Iudaicum* 1.46.2: "magno obsequio per tantum spatii deductus universorum, sed non omnium pari affectu. Metus enim officium non votum extorserat, dolor intra se saltem liberam habebat sententiam. Hunc finem habuit Herodes."

Richer also echoes Livy frequently and Caesar's *Bellum Gallicum* somewhat less so. He appears to have read widely in the *Ab urbe condita* and he may have been familiar with up to twenty-five of Livy's books.[163] In a majority of cases he takes two- or three-word phrases from Livy when describing a scene of battle. In four other instances (1.11, 3.88, 4.14, 4.75) Livian language pops up in nonmartial situations: Ingo's speech (1.11), Hugh Capet's dramatic return journey from Rome to West Francia (3.88), Charles of Lotharingia's complaint to his friends (4.14) and possibly in the *inductio* of Walter of Melun (4.75).[164] The echoes of Livy in each of these instances are faint, and Richer does not seem to have drawn on him as a direct source for his speeches. Similarly, Caesar's *Bellum Gallicum* served Richer as a source of military terminology and geographical information rather than as a source of rhetorical themes.[165]

Conclusion

Richer's manner of speech writing derives from several different practices. Formal instruction in grammar and rhetoric at the monastery school of Saint-Rémi or the cathedral school at Rheims trained him in Latin prose composition and solidified certain stylistic habits that occur repeatedly in his speeches: parallelism, anaphora, "on the one hand … on the other hand" reasoning, rhetorical questions, and certain types of phrasing (e.g., the tricolon in which all three clauses are introduced by a form of the interrogative adjective *quantus*). Probably in concert with his school exercises, and cer-

163. Hoffmann gives thirty-six possible citations from Livy, from twenty-four books: 1–10, 22, 23–26, 30, 32, 33, 36–38, 41, 43, and 44. To this we may add the phrase *casus irrevocabilis* from 42.62.3, which Richer uses at *Historia* 4.14.

164. *Historia* 1.11 ("rerumque tranquillitas consequantur") draws on Livy 4.12.6; *Historia* 3.88 ("strictisque mucronibus postquam ei necem minati sunt si vocem emitteret") on Livy 1.58.2; *Historia* 4.75: ("quis omni honore dignior") possibly on Livy 4.49.14. In none of these dramatic scenes is the link between Livy and Richer anything more than verbal. Richer does not try to make a subtle connection between Tarquin's threat to Lucretia, for example, and the threats uttered by Hugh Capet's vassals against the man lodging them at 3.88.

165. See Hoffmann, "Die *Historien* Richers von Saint-Remi," 485–86.

tainly afterward as part of his own independent intellectual formation, Richer studied model speeches and descriptive passages from various sources. He read classical and late antique historians diligently, and he imitated these writers—principally Sallust and Hegesippus, but also Caesar, Livy, Orosius, the *Historia ecclesiastica tripartita* of Cassiodorus, and the *Historia ecclesiastica* of Rufinus—in the form of direct excerpts, indirect allusions, and the use of certain types of speech (e.g., the complaint, the address before battle) and descriptive passages such as the personal *descriptio,* the battle, the siege engine, and the progress of disease and death. We know, too, that Richer studied Gerbert's speeches carefully because he incorporates a revised version of Gerbert's *Acta* of the Synod of Saint-Basle in his history and recommends the *Acta* to his readers. Moreover, he uses elements of Gerbert's phrasing, vocabulary, and rhetorical terminology in his own speeches.

Once we take into account Richer's borrowing from and imitation of these rhetorical models, we find surprisingly little evidence for his use of the ideas and argumentative strategies found in the *De inventione* and the commentary of Victorinus. The exception to this rule is *status*-theory, which seems to have been a focus of rhetorical study at Rheims and elsewhere during this period.[166] The identification of the relevant issue in a case and the construction of a corresponding argument were most relevant to forensic oratory. Thus, it is not surprising that we find the clearest references to *status*-theory in the defense speech of Ingo and in the speeches at the Synod of Saint-Basle, where Arnulf attempted to defend himself from charges of treason. Richer's knowledge of *status* sometimes bleeds over into nonjudicial settings—for example, Robert of Montreuil's self-exculpation on the grounds of *necessitas* (2.11)—

166. For the importance of *status*-theory in rhetorical commentaries of the late tenth and early eleventh century, see Ward, *Ciceronian Rhetoric,* 100, and "From Antiquity to the Renaissance: Glosses and Commentaries on Cicero's *Rhetorica,*" in *Medieval Eloquence: Studies in the Theory and Practice of Medieval Rhetoric,* ed. James J. Murphy (Berkeley and Los Angeles: University of California Press, 1978), 48–49.

but in general *status*-theory was not very useful when it came to political oratory that took place outside of a legal context.

In general Richer uses Ciceronian rhetorical doctrine more as a means of labeling and categorizing speech than of generating it. Rather than using Cicero's topics of the *conquestio* as the basis for his own speeches, for example, he prefers to imitate the speeches of Sallust or Hegesippus or else to invent plausible lines of argument himself. He may well have taken note of sample speeches of complaint as he read, perhaps jotting terms like *conquestio* in the margins of the *Bellum Iugurthinum* or the *Bellum Iudaicum*, and then turning to these speeches as models later on. His engagement with the topics of the *De inventione* is limited, and, aside from the area of *status*-theory, his adaptation of the principles of Ciceronian rhetoric to his own speeches is comparatively superficial.

In this respect Richer was typical of his day. Widukind, Aimoin, and Dudo wrote speeches similar in length and content to Richer's, and none of these authors paid strict attention to the classical parts of a speech or the topics to be used in each section. Dudo, for example, gave his speeches the appearance of formal rhetoric by selectively employing devices like the *sententia* or the *captatio benivolentiae,* but made no further attempt to structure them according to classical rhetorical precepts.[167] Aimoin, like Richer, excerpted heavily from both Sallust and Hegesippus for the speeches in his *Gesta Francorum,* but made little use of rhetorical topics, even though he must have been familiar with the *De inventione.*[168] While Richer is particularly self-conscious in his deployment of rhetorical *termini technici,* his speeches are simply too short and too simple to incorporate anything like the full range and sophistication of Ciceronian oratory.

Richer's technique of categorizing his speeches in language that reflects the influence of *De inventione* while generally eschewing

167. Christiansen, *Dudo of St. Quentin,* xxxii.

168. See Karl Ferdinand Werner, "Die literarischen Vorbilder des Aimoin von Fleury," in *Medium Aevum Vivum: Festschrift für Walther Bulst,* ed. Hans Robert Jauss and Dieter Schaller (Heidelberg: Carl Winter, 1960), 69–103.

Cicero's topics as a source of material has parallels in other authors associated with Rheims in the late-tenth and early-eleventh centuries. Both Gerbert and Adalbero of Laon, the nephew of Adalbero of Rheims, wrote works in which they used the categories of Ciceronian rhetoric as a means of organization rather than invention. Gerbert divides his letter to Wilderod of Strasbourg into the parts of an oration, but grounds his argument in the Bible and patristic authorities rather than the Ciceronian topics.[169] Likewise, his speech before the Synod of Mouzon is organized according to the *partes orationis,* but makes little use of the techniques laid out in the *De inventione.*

Adalbero of Laon practiced a similar type of rhetorical labeling in the poem he wrote to King Robert II *(Carmen ad Rotbertum Regem)* between 1027 and 1031.[170] Adalbero had probably studied at the cathedral school of Rheims around the time of Gerbert's arrival and was presumably influenced by the rhetorical doctrines being taught at Rheims in the last three decades of the tenth century.[171] In the poem to Robert he supplies marginal glosses to divide the text into different sections based on the different parts of a speech *(exordium, narratio, partitio, confirmatio, reprehensio, conclusio),* the elements of a deductive argument *(propositio, approbatio, assumptio, conclusio),* and the components of the narration necessary to create trust *(fides)* in the audience,[172] taking his terminology directly from Marius Victorinus.[173] As with Gerbert's letter and Richer's speeches, there is a general correspondence be-

169. See Ward, "From Antiquity to the Renaissance: Glosses and Commentaries on Cicero's *Rhetorica,*" 45.

170. Claude Carozzi, ed. and trans., *Adalbéron de Laon: Poème au roi Robert* (Paris: Les Belles Lettres, 1979).

171. For Adalbero, see Robert T. Coolidge, "Adalbero, Bishop of Laon," *Studies in Medieval and Renaissance History* 2 (1965):1–114; for his education see 9–10, and Carozzi, *Adalbéron de Laon,* xi–xiii. Coolidge thinks that Adalbero probably left Rheims before Gerbert's arrival in 972. Carozzi thinks it equally likely that he remained until 974, when he became chancellor to King Lothar.

172. See Carozzi, *Adalbéron de Laon,* xxvi–xxxv.

173. See Carozzi, *Adalbéron de Laon,* xxiii–xxv and passim.

tween the text and the terms used to label it, but no deep engagement with the ideas of Cicero or Victorinus.

Each of these authors studied and wrote in the decades before the first new complete commentaries on the *De inventione* and the *Rhetorica ad Herennium* appeared in the Latin West. The lack of contemporary full-scale glosses on these texts is not an indication that they were not valued or studied, but that the tools needed to exploit them and make them fully accessible and useful for students were yet to be developed. For Richer, and for Gerbert, the classical art of rhetoric served as a means of defining, categorizing, and studying speech. Cicero's work even provided a philosophical ideal for those, like Gerbert, who believed in the correlation between eloquence and virtue. At the same time, works like the *De inventione* and the *Rhetorica ad Herennium* had limited usefulness as practical aids to composition. Nor, for all Richer's enthusiasm about the power of rhetoric, were his speeches suitable vehicles for the display of Ciceronian rhetoric in all of its sophistication. They are typically short and centered upon one idea, and they tend to rely on broad appeals to the emotions rather than subtle argumentation. The lack of sophistication that characterizes most of the speeches in the *Historia* does not imply that rhetorical study at Rheims was superficial or inadequate. Gerbert was assiduous in seeking out and copying new rhetorical manuscripts and he devised his own pedagogical aids for teaching rhetoric. But even self-professed students of rhetoric do not seem to have digested Ciceronian oratorical doctrines completely enough to make them useful for writers and speakers. For Richer, therefore, speech writing seems to have been more a matter of imagination and imitation than the deployment of the classical art of rhetoric.

[FIVE]

Authorial Intention and Authorial Ambition

WHEN SCHOLARS CONSIDER the questions of social function and authorial intention in medieval historiography, their analysis tends to revolve around two poles: the moral/exemplary and the political/propagandistic. These areas of focus follow naturally from the content of medieval histories and the stated goals of their authors. Medieval historians typically justified the writing of history on the grounds of its usefulness to posterity, and they located the utility of historiography in its ethical and/or didactic functions. History served both as a storehouse of human experience from which readers could draw moral lessons and as a written record of the unfolding of God's providence in the world. The political importance of medieval historiography derived from the ways in which a selective account of the past be could used to advance the interests of individuals, families, political entities, or institutions.[1]

The usefulness of history as a tool to teach moral lessons, to understand God's plan for mankind, and to promote political agendas of all sorts helps to explain the enduring popularity of the genre in the Middle Ages. Yet as important as these functions are, they should not be allowed to obscure the other factors that could motivate historical writing. To gain a fuller appreciation for the complex of impulses that might lead an author to write, and to choose what and how to write, we have to consider the social logic of the text (to borrow a phrase from Gabrielle Spiegel) in all

1. See in particular Goetz, "Die Gegenwart der Vergangenheit."

its dimensions.[2] The desire to entertain, for example, while not as frequently cited as the desire to instruct, was certainly important to many authors. Moreover, a host of less immediately obvious motives might lurk behind the historian's stated goal in writing. One facet of authorial motivation that should not be ignored is the potential of literary work to serve the writer's own self-interest. While medieval historians might profess to write for the utility of their audience, what they wrote could also be useful to themselves.

At a basic level, any author who wrote at the behest of a patron or an institution served the interests of his superiors and/or his community in such a way that he could expect to reap some sort of reward. Writing offered a means of winning status and esteem, and perhaps even more tangible remuneration. It could also be used to create and disseminate a particular image of the author to contemporaries, and a successful literary project could preserve the memory of the author for posterity, as his name was copied, read, and remembered along with his work. The text, then, could serve as a means of both self-representation and self-memorialization.

If the egoistic motivations of medieval historians have generally received less attention than their didactic or political goals, it is a consequence of their reluctance to speak openly about personal ambition. A strongly felt desire to avoid charges of presumption or ambition led authors to deploy familiar topoi as a preemptive defense. Thus, the topos of commission could shift the responsibility for writing to a patron, while the topi of hesitancy, humility, and ignorance were deployed to neutralize suspicions of the author's desire to write, literary ability, and knowledge, respectively.[3]

Moreover, medieval authors rarely wrote as independent agents with the freedom to determine when and what to write. History writing was time-consuming and required significant investments

2. See Spiegel, *The Past as Text,* 3–28.

3. For the topos of commission, see Simon, "Untersuchungen zur Topik der Widmungsbriefe," 1.59–64, 98–100, and Janson, *Latin Prose Prefaces,* 116–24; for hesitancy, see Simon, 1.65–67; for humility, see Simon, 1.108–19; for ignorance, see Simon, 1.111–12.

in training, labor, and material. To do it well—or even competently—required the kind of education that was generally limited (especially in the early Middle Ages) to a restricted class of trained monks and secular clerics. The authors of medieval histories were thus typically beholden to the interests of their monastery or cathedral church, or to the patrons who sought out their services. They were, in a sense, the mouthpieces for institutions and powerful individuals, and their histories were often designed to further monastic, episcopal, dynastic, or royal interests. If authors sought on occasion to direct their literary abilities toward personal advancement, their ambitions and the possible fruits of their labor remain largely invisible to modern readers.

Yet in spite of the power of patrons and institutions to influence subject matter and the social pressure to disguise literary ambitions, it is clear that some medieval historians wrote with an eye toward their reputation among their contemporaries and toward their remembrance by posterity. A case can be made that Richer was motivated in part by precisely this ambition, and that in his work he sought to fashion an image of himself as a literary stylist and scholar in the mold of his patron and mentor, Gerbert. Richer appears to have had several interrelated goals in writing, among them to narrate the wars of the West-Frankish kings in a classicizing style; to chronicle the faithlessness, treachery, and internecine squabbles of the magnates; and to praise and memorialize Gerbert. A less immediately obvious motive, but one that can nonetheless be perceived in his writing, was self-promotion. That is to say, in writing the *Historia* he set out to acquire intellectual esteem in the eyes of his audience—Gerbert, first and foremost, but also the clerical and monastic communities at Rheims and further afield—and to secure his own memory in written form through the composition of a literary work that would be copied alongside the annals of Hincmar and Flodoard, and read for years to come.

Text and Memory

The idea that a literary work might serve in part to preserve the memory of the author is found in a number of important texts that Richer had read. A *locus classicus* for this theme is the prologue to the *Bellum Catilinae,* where Sallust writes that men should not be content to live their lives in silence like mere animals, but should instead use their intellectual ability to leave a lasting memory of themselves:

> Therefore I find it becoming, in seeking renown, that we should employ the resources of the intellect rather than those of brute strength, to the end that, since the span of life which we enjoy is short, we may make the memory of our lives as long as possible.[4]

While a career of noble actions and glorious deeds was a sure path to lasting fame, the man who committed the deeds of others to writing could also expect to be honored:

> It is glorious to serve one's country by deeds; even to serve her by words is a thing not to be despised; one may become famous in peace as well as in war. Not only those who have acted, but those also who have recorded the acts of others oftentimes receive our approbation.[5]

It was not lost on the *litterati* of the Middle Ages that textual remains alone preserved the names of the poets, historians, and philosophers of classical antiquity down to their own time. Hrabanus Maurus composed verses on the ability of the written word to confer immortality.[6] In his commentary on book 5 of the *De nuptiis* of Martianus Capella, Remigius of Auxerre, contemplating the fame of Cicero and Demosthenes, the two most prominent members of the throng of famous orators who follow in Lady Rhetoric's train,

4. *Bellum Catilinae* 1.3–4, trans. John C. Rolfe, *Sallust,* rev. ed., Loeb Classical Library (Cambridge, Mass.: Harvard University Press, 1931), 3.

5. *Bellum Catilinae* 3.1, trans. Rolfe, 7.

6. *Carmen* 21, in *Hrabani Mauri carmina,* ed. Ernst Dümmler, MGH Poetae 2 (Berlin: Weidmann, 1884), 186, lines 9–10: "Grammata sola carent fato, mortemque repellunt/ Praeterita renovant grammata sola biblis."

noted that "Even after the passage of ages their glory remains immortal, because as long as their books are read, memory of them flourishes."[7]

Of course, Sallust and Cicero (as well as Martianus Capella and Boethius) wrote in an age when a general readership still existed to grant celebrity, and sometimes lasting fame, to successful authors. The context for literary production changed dramatically during the early Middle Ages, however. The collapse of Roman educational institutions in the fifth century, the severing of Latin from the Romance vernaculars as a consequence of Carolingian-era educational reforms, and the decline of literacy among the laity led to the disappearance of a true literary public in the Latin West.[8] It was replaced by a more restricted audience of literate monks and clerics (though works in Latin might be made accessible to a wider audience by being read aloud and/or simultaneously translated). Moreover, monastic authors, who became the most prominent writers of history in the post-Carolingian Latin West, were not necessarily free to indulge their authorial ambitions. The pursuit of fame in the present world was not deemed to be compatible with the goal of gaining salvation in the world to come. Hence the popularity of the topos of commission. To write at the request of a superior was to show love and obedience, while to write unbidden could suggest pride and literary ambition.

Yet the notion that a text could function in some part as a memorial to the author did not die out in the early Middle Ages. A writer might ask his audience to remember him in their prayers, as Bede did when he beseeched those who read or heard his history to

7. Cora E. Lutz, ed., *Remigii Autissiodorensis Commentum in Martianum Capellam,* 2 vols. (Leiden: Brill, 1962 and 1965), 2.68, lines 30–32: "Transeuntibus enim saeculis illorum gloria manet immortalis, quia quamdiu illorum libri leguntur, eorum semper memoria viget."

8. See Erich Auerbach, *Literary Language and Its Public in Late Latin Antiquity and in the Middle Ages,* trans. Ralph Manheim (Princeton, N.J.: Princeton University Press, 1993), 237–338, and Herbert Grundmann, "Litteratus-illiteratus: Der Wandel einer Bildungsnorm vom Altertum zum Mittelalter," *Archiv für Kulturgeschichte* 40 (1958): 1–65.

"remember to intercede often with the divine mercy for the sake of my infirmities of mind and body."[9] The text might also be presented to a patron as a token of remembrance of the author. In his commentary on Cicero's *Topics,* Boethius explains that Cicero composed and sent his book to Trebatius in part because he "wanted the book to be a token and memorial to rouse memory of himself."[10] This function of personal remembrance persisted in the Middle Ages. In the prologue to his commentary on Maccabees, Hrabanus Maurus states that he strives to serve Louis the Pious in any way that he can, "so that my memory might always be with you and the devotion of my mind to your service might be apparent."[11] This statement of purpose goes beyond the request for the dedicatee to remember the author in his prayers, a standard way in which Hrabanus ends dedicatory prefaces and epistles.[12] Here the text is to be seen as a sign of devotion, one that should provoke the reader to continuous remembrance of the author. Widukind of Corvey makes a similar request at the end of the prologue to book 1 of his *Saxon History,* when he asks his patroness, Mathilda, to read his work "in remembrance of me, with a piety equivalent to the devotion with which I wrote it."[13]

Occasionally medieval authors allude explicitly to the concrete rewards that literary activity could bring. In the prologue to his life of Charlemagne, Einhard (ca. 770–840) criticizes those who, "seduced by a desire for immortality, prefer to insert the outstanding deeds of others into whatever they write rather than remove the renown of their name from the memory of posterity by writing nothing."[14] The anonymous author of the older *Vita* of Queen

9. *Historia Ecclesiastica,* preface.

10. *In Ciceronis Topica, PL* 64.1044, trans. Eleonore Stump, *Boethius: In Ciceronis Topica* (Ithaca, N.Y.: Cornell University Press, 1988), 24.

11. *Commentaria in Libros Machabaeorum, PL* 109.1125.

12. See, e.g., the letter to Frederick of Utrecht that accompanies his commentary on Joshua (*PL* 108.999–1002); the epistle to Freculph of Lisieux at the beginning of his commentary on Genesis (*PL* 107.442); and the letter to Humbert that proceeds his commentary on Ruth and Judges (*PL* 108.1110).

13. *Res Gestae Saxonicae,* book 1, preface.

14. Einhard, *Vita Karoli Magni,* ed. Oswald Holder-Egger, MGH SRG 25 (Hanover: Hahn, 1911), 1.

Mathilda of Germany (ca. 895–968) invokes the words of Sulpicius Severus to deny that he (or she) is motivated by a desire for "eternal memory" or "the reward of human favor."[15] In a prefatory epistle to his *Chronica Boemorum*, Cosmas of Prague (ca. 1045–1125) tells his addressee, Archdeacon Gervase, that he is turning over his work to him for revisions so that others "might have [it] as material to make their own learning known to posterity and magnify their own names as an eternal memorial to themselves."[16] And in his memoirs, Guibert of Nogent (ca. 1060–ca.1125) declares that he pursued his studies so diligently out of a desire for temporal rewards, having been plied by his friends "with talk of fame and literary distinction and, through these things, the winning of high status and wealth."[17] Although such self-interested motives are inevitably brought up only to be condemned, renounced, or attributed to others, the fact that they are mentioned at all shows that they were not absent from the minds of medieval authors.

Autobiography and Self-Representation

Because writing was the province of a select few, and because it was laborious and difficult, the medieval author could expect his dedicatee to appreciate his effort and remember his service. Apart from the goal of winning the favor of a patron, some authors could expect to reach a wider audience that would continue to read and copy their works and perhaps preserve their names for posterity. The most successful could look forward to a degree of fame in their own time and continuing renown when they were gone. Thus, a literary work of great learning, stylistic genius, or pedagogical utility might secure for its author a place in the collective memory of learned men.

15. *Vita Mathildis reginae antiquior*, ed. Bernd Schütte, MGH SSRG 66 (Hanover: Hahn, 1994), 109. Cf. Sulpicius Severus, *Vita S. Martini* 1.1.

16. Cosmas of Prague, *Chronica Boemorum*, ed. Berthold Bretholz, MGH SRG 2 (Berlin: Weidmann, 1923), 2–3.

17. John F. Benton, ed., *Self and Society in Medieval France* (Toronto: University of Toronto Press, 1984), 78–79.

For a writer's name and work to be known by his contemporaries and remembered by future generations was an achievement in and of itself. Beyond this, an author might also choose to cultivate a certain image of himself by inserting autobiographical elements into his work.[18] Opportunities for literary self-representation were generally limited in the early Middle Ages, although this varied from genre to genre.[19] Autobiography as a literary form was virtually nonexistent between the time of Augustine's *Confessions* and the memoirs of Guibert of Nogent. For authors of biblical commentaries or pedagogical treatises the prologue was the only place where one could interpose oneself unobtrusively. A biographer might mention his relationship to his subject and seek to place himself in a favorable light through association, but this was impossible for those who wrote about figures from the distant past. Poetry offered more scope for the author to include autobiographical material, as is evident in Walter of Speyer's description of his studies in the first book of his life of Saint Christopher.[20]

Letters could impart much information about the author, and in many cases the surviving ones must have been composed or revised with an eye toward posterity.[21] Compiling and editing a letter collection offered even greater scope for self-representation, since the author could select which letters to include and the order in which to arrange them to create and propagate a particular im-

18. See Jay Rubenstein, "Biography and Autobiography in the Middle Ages," in *Writing Medieval History,* ed. Nancy Partner (London: Hodder Arnold, 2005), 22–41. For an exhaustive analysis of classical and medieval autobiography, see Georg Misch, *Geschichte der Autobiographie,* 4 vols. (Frankfurt: G. Schulte-Bulmke, 1949–1969). Particularly relevant for the tenth century is his discussion of Rather of Verona at 2.2.519–650.

19. See Rubenstein, "Biography and Autobiography," 26–27.

20. Peter Vossen, ed., *Der Libellus Scolasticus des Walther von Speyer: Ein Schulbericht aus dem Jahre 984* (Berlin: Walter de Gruyter, 1962).

21. For letters and letter collections in the Middle Ages, see Giles Constable, *Letters and Letter-Collections,* Typologie des sources du Moyen Âge occidental 17 (Turnhout: Brepols, 1976). For the potentially vast difference in literary style between purely utilitarian letters and those intended for future publication, see Constable, "An Unpublished Letter by Peter the Venerable to the Priors of Paray-le-Monial, Mesvres, and Luzy in 1147," *Studia Anselmiana* 85 (1982): 207–16.

age of himself. In the tenth and early eleventh centuries this genre bore fruit in the collections of Rather of Verona (ca. 890–974), Gerbert of Aurillac, Froumond of Tegernsee (ca. 960–ca. 1010), and Fulbert of Chartres (ca. 970–1028), and the trend of saving and editing one's correspondence flourished in the twelfth century with the letter collections of writers such as Peter the Venerable (ca. 1092–1156), Bernard of Clairvaux (1090–1153), and Peter of Blois (d. ca. 1212).

Historiography gave writers who took part in the events they described the opportunity to interpret the recent past in accordance with their personal political interests, as Nithard (d. 844/845) did in his account of the Frankish civil wars of the early 840s, or to justify and explain their actions, as Hincmar did in his entries in the *Annals of Saint-Bertin* for the years 861–882.[22] History and personal memoir could even be combined in a single work, as in the *Legatio* of Liudprand of Cremona, a highly self-referential account of the author's embassy to Constantinople on behalf of Otto I. While historiography might occasionally verge into autobiography in the works of important political actors like Hincmar, Nithard, and Liudprand, history writing offered a more limited scope to the autobiographical impulses of less prominent cathedral canons or monastic chroniclers. Nonetheless, the premium placed on eyewitness testimony and firsthand knowledge ensured that authors who had been present at important events or met the characters they described might insert themselves into their narratives when feasible. Moreover, the lack of a unifying theme beyond that of temporal progression in many medieval chronicles and narrative histories meant that these works tended to record a wide variety of different events, often in a diffuse and seemingly random way. This openness of structure afforded the writer considerable freedom to include autobiographical material. Finally, the highly personal tone of much medieval historical writing meant that authors frequently includ-

22. Wallace-Hadrill, "History in the Mind of Archbishop Hincmar," 53. For the purposes and audience(s) of Nithard's history, see Janet Nelson, "Public Histories and Private History in the Work of Nithard," *Speculum* 60 (1985): 251–95.

ed their own reflections and comments on their subject matter or their feelings about writing.[23]

Richer does not insert himself into the political narrative of his history, and we have no evidence that he was present at any of the events he describes. Although the autobiographical elements of the *Historia* are limited to two episodes involving his father and an account of his journey to Chartres in 991, these passages are important because they show that Richer conceived of his history at least in part as a means of self-representation, and they give us some insight into the image of himself and his family that he wanted to project.

Richer introduces his father, Rodulf, at the end of book 2, as King Louis IV awaits military aid from his brother-in-law King Otto to assist in his ongoing efforts to bring Hugh the Great to heel.[24] Deciding that Hugh's recent provocations (he had burned down a large part of the city of Soissons and ravaged the countryside around Rheims) had to be punished before Otto's reinforcements were due to arrive, Louis, Richer tells us, "sought the advice of my father, because he was his vassal [*miles*], a man useful in council and notable both for his eloquence and his daring, whence the king was on very familiar terms with him and sought his advice on many occasions."[25] Rodulf repays the king's trust by devising a plan to recapture Laon from Theobald le Tricheur, who was holding the city for Hugh, after Hugh had exacted it from the king three years earlier as the price of releasing him from captivity.[26] Laon was virtually impregnable because of its easily defensible lo-

23. Particularly interesting in this regard is the concluding poem of Dudo's *Gesta Normannorum* (Lair, 300–301; poem lxxxix in Christiansen, 174–75), in which the author describes the difficulty of his undertaking, enumerates his own faults, and asks for salvation. For an example of minor personal commentary in a historical work, see Aimoin, *Gesta Francorum* 3.13, where the author comments on his admiration for a poem of Venantius Fortunatus.

24. *Historia* 2.87.

25. *Historia* 2.87. For Hugh's attacks on Soissons and the county of Rheims, see *Historia* 2.85 and Flodoard, *Annales*, s.a. 948, p. 117.

26. Flodoard, *Annales*, s.a. 946, p. 101; *Historia* 2.51.

cation atop a steep hill, and Louis had failed to capture the city in a siege the previous year (2.84). After sending spies to observe the movements of the townsmen, however, Rodulf devised a plan to capture it through trickery.[27] He and a band of men disguised to look like the city's grooms went to Laon, waited in a concealed position by the hillside until the grooms had left to gather fodder, and then assumed their identity and made their way inside the city undetected. At this point they threw away the bundles of fodder behind which they were concealing their faces, sounded horns, and took control of the gate by which they had entered. Shortly thereafter the king's knights, who had been waiting in reserve, charged through the gate that Rodulf and his men were holding and inflicted a terrible slaughter on the men defending the city. The garrison was captured in short order, and Louis regained control of the city.[28]

Not surprisingly, the portrait of Richer's father that emerges from this story is that of an ideal retainer. Rodulf offers wise counsel, he is eloquent and daring, and he shows two of the virtues most desirable in a military leader: cleverness and personal bravery. Through his daring and ingenuity the crucially important royal seat of Laon is returned to Louis. Flodoard, interestingly, gives a rather different account of the capture of the city, one that does not include Rodulf. The *Annals* state that Louis's men scaled one of the walls at night and broke open the gates, after which the king was able to enter the city.[29] This version of events is hard to reconcile with what Richer tells us, and Rodulf's exploits may have been subject to considerable exaggeration or invention in the *Historia*.[30]

The second episode involving Richer's father concerns his capture of the citadel of Mons from Count Reginar of Hainaut, who had had seized property in Lotharingia belonging to Queen Gerberga.[31] In Richer's telling Rodulf is part of a close inner circle of

27. *Historia* 2.88.

28. *Historia* 2.90.

29. *Annales*, s.a. 949, p. 122.

30. See Lauer, *Le règne de Louis IV*, 199–200n3.

31. *Historia* 3.7–10. See Lot, *Les derniers Carolingiens*, 19–20. Gerberga's prop-

advisers who consider how best to respond to Reginar's provocations; not surprisingly he is deemed to be the one best suited to devising a plan.[32] He sends spies to the stronghold of Mons, where Reginar's wife and children are staying, to investigate the layout and identify the places where it is most vulnerable to a surprise attack. When the spies return, he leads a band of soldiers to the stronghold, takes control of it at night, and captures Reginar's wife and children, who later serve as bargaining chips in negotiations with Reginar.[33] The points of emphasis in this episode—Rodulf's close relationship with the ruler, and his cleverness, daring, and personal bravery—are the same as in his capture of Laon.

Richer's emphasis on Rodulf's advisory role to both Louis IV and Queen Gerberga is particularly interesting. At several points in the *Historia* Richer manifests a perceptible interest in social class, verging occasionally on snobbery against those of nonnoble status. Hagano, the man of "middling status" *(mediocritas)* who helps to bring down Charles the Simple, is the most obvious example.[34] Richer also expunged a statement in the first draft of the manuscript according to which King Odo's membership in the warrior class *(ordo militaris* or *ordo equestris)* made it difficult for him to enforce order among subjects unimpressed with his "middling status."[35] Elsewhere he appears particularly cognizant of class distinctions when reporting casualties. He states that during King Radulf's assault on a Viking warband in the county of Arras, "Count Hildegaud, who was of a very distinguished lineage, was killed, along with several others, although none of them were

erty in Lotharingia was part of the dower given to her in her first marriage, to Gislebert of Lotharingia.

32. *Historia* 3.6–7: "Inter quos cum pater meus huius rei dispositioni videretur idoneus, ab eo id summopere ordinandum petebatur."

33. *Historia* 3.8–10.

34. *Historia* 1.15–16.

35. *Historia* 1.5: "Creatusque rex, strenue atque utiliter omnia gessit, preter quod in militari tumultu raram componendi lites potestatem habuit, eo quod milites mediocri interdum subdi contempnerent." The underlined text is expunged at Bamberg, Staatsbibliothek, MS. Hist. 5, fol. 2ᵛ, lines 16–17.

of any repute,"[36] and that during Otto II's retreat across the River Aisne in 978 "quite a few men [were killed], but no one of any distinction."[37]

The mere status of *miles* was, in and of itself, not a particularly noble one,[38] but Rodulf's close personal relationship with Louis and Gerberga elevated him to a different station.[39] Proximity to the throne *(Königsnähe)* gave him an importance that he would not otherwise have possessed, an importance that must have rubbed off on Richer. For what exactly was the point of telling these stories about Rodulf? It cannot have been to introduce into the narrative material of guaranteed credibility and authenticity, for Richer never demonstrates the slightest interest in vouching for the truth of any of the orally derived material that he recounts. The reason for describing these episodes in so much detail was not to present the testimony of a reliable witness, but to celebrate and memorialize his father's accomplishments and proximity to the throne, and perhaps to share in the reputation and status that came with it.

The anecdotes about Rodulf are broadly speaking autobiographical, and they give us a sense of the way in which Richer sought to use the medium of history for his own ends. The only truly autobiographical passage in the *Historia,* however, is the description of his journey to Chartres in March 991. Considered in isolation, the passage is important because it gives us a rare glimpse at an episode in the life of a tenth-century monk. Viewed in a broader context,

36. *Historia* 1.51: "Hildegaudus vero clarissimi generis comes interemptus est, aliique nonnulli, nec tamen aliquo nomine clari."

37. *Historia* 3.77: "Qui reperti fuere, mox gladiis hostium fusi sunt, plures quidem, at nullo nomine clari."

38. See J. M. Van Winter, "Uxorem de militari ordinem sibi imparem," *Miscellanea Mediaevalia in memoriam Jan Frederik Niermeyer* (Groningen: J. B. Wolters, 1967), 113–24.

39. Lauer, *Les Annales de Flodoard,* 92n1, speculates that Rodulf may have been the treacherous castellan of Clastres who plundered the treasures of the fortress before abandoning it to Heribert of Vermandois in 944 (Flodoard, *Annales,* s.a. 944, pp. 91–92). The identification is impossible to verify, but if true it would suggest an even more specific motive for including these laudatory passages about Rodulf in the *Historia.*

it prompts the question of why Richer decided to include a travel narrative in a text otherwise devoted to the political and ecclesiastical history of West Francia. It is likely that Richer's account of his journey to Chartres was more than simply a narrative digression, and that he intended it to establish a certain image of himself, an image that was calculated to appeal to the values of the scholarly community at Rheims.

The account of Richer's journey occurs midway through book 4, between two major narrative blocks. It follows the civil war between Charles of Lotharingia and Hugh Capet, which began with Hugh's coronation in late May or early June of 987 and culminated in the capture of Charles and Arnulf of Rheims at the hands of Adalbero of Laon on the night of March 29–30 of 991.[40] It immediately precedes Richer's account of the Synod of Saint-Basle, which met on June 17–18 of that same year (4.51–73). Structurally, then, the journey functions as a *digressio,* an anecdote or descriptive passage designed to break up a long narrative and provide a respite for the reader.[41] Since Richer's journey actually took place two weeks before the capture of Charles and Arnulf, he deliberately violates the *ordo naturalis* of his history so that his digression will fall between these two major episodes without interrupting either one.

The story begins with a meeting between Richer and a knight sent from Chartres to deliver a message to him:[42]

One day, about fourteen days before they were captured, when I was thinking often and at length about the liberal arts out of a desire to learn the *logica* of Hippocrates of Cos, I encountered a knight from Chartres while I was in the city of Rheims. When I asked him who he

40. For the date of Hugh's coronation, see Hoffmann, *Historiae,* 239, chap. 12, note 4, and Brühl, *Deutschland-Frankreich,* 594–96.

41. See Quintilian, *Institutio oratoria* 4.3; Cicero, *De inventione* 1.19.27 and 1.51.97; Victorinus, *Explanationes in Ciceronis rhetoricam* 1.51, p. 175; Martianus Capella, *De nuptiis* 5.552. See also Lausberg § 340.

42. For discussions of this chapter, see also Arno Borst, *Lebensformen im Mittelalter* (Frankfurt: Verlag Ullstein, 1973), 146–50; Massimo Oldoni, "Il viaggio a Chartres de Richero: Un 'teatro' di medico nel Medioevo," *Ariel* 8, no. 1 (1993): 37–49; and Glenn, *Politics and History in the Tenth Century,* 252–66.

was and who had sent him, and why and whence he had come, he said that he was a messenger of Heribrand, a cleric of Chartres, and that he wished to speak with Richer, a monk of Saint-Rémi. Immediately recognizing the name of my friend and the reason for which he had been sent, I told him that I was the one he was looking for, and after bestowing a kiss upon him, we withdrew in private. He immediately produced a letter encouraging me to come and read the *Aphorisms* [of Hippocrates]. I was delighted at this, and taking a boy along with me, I arranged to make the journey to Chartres with the knight.

Interestingly, Richer does not mention asking for the abbot's approval for this journey. To the contrary, he begins making plans to leave as soon as he receives the letter from Heribrand. The fact that Richer was in contact with scholars in other locations, left the monastery to go to the city of Rheims by himself, and traveled when he wanted to, is instructive. It suggests that his movements were not restricted and he was not under the thumb of his abbot, which in turn implies he could have undertaken a literary project like the *Historia* on his own initiative, without waiting for a command, or approval, from above. That Richer's relationship with the abbot of Saint-Rémi was somewhat strained can be gleaned from his disappointment at the provisions he is given for the journey—particularly in light of the generous welcome that he receives elsewhere:

Upon my departure, however, I received from my abbot only a single horse to assist me. Lacking in money, a change of clothes, and other necessities, I arrived at Orbais, a place known for its great hospitality. There I was refreshed by the conversation of the lord abbot D[43] and sustained by his generosity, and on the next day I undertook to travel as far as Meaux. But when my two companions and I entered the winding paths of the woods, we were not spared the vicissitudes of bad fortune. For the choice of paths deceived us and we wandered six leagues out of our way. Then, after we had passed Château-Thierry, the horse, which up to now had seemed like Bucephalus, became slower than a reluctant little donkey.

43. The abbot's name is not known. See Hoffmann, *Historiae,* 264n11.

Richer's dissatisfaction with the single horse he received from his abbot is now justified, as the animal, worn out from its toil, collapses. In describing this and the other misfortunes that his little band must endure, Richer narrows the focus and adds a wealth of scenic detail:

> The sun had already passed mid-day and was edging into dusk, when the whole sky dissolved into a downpour, and that hardy Bucephalus, done in by his final exertions, collapsed and fell out from underneath the legs of the boy who was riding him, dropping dead at the sixth milestone from the city as if he had been struck by lightning. Those who have ever suffered similar misfortunes can judge from their own experiences how great my agitation and anxiety were at that moment. After the loss of his horse, the boy, who was not accustomed to the rigors of such a long journey, lay down, completely exhausted. The baggage sat there without anyone to carry it. Rain was coming down in a tremendous downpour. Clouds filled the sky. The sun was setting and casting threatening shadows. Amidst all of this, God's counsel was not lacking to one in doubt.

With night coming on, Richer and the knight opt to leave the exhausted boy behind and seek help up the road in Meaux. Before they can enter the town, however, they must cross a dangerous bridge:

> So I left the boy there with the baggage. After telling him what to say if he was questioned by passers-by, and urging him not to fall asleep, I arrived at Meaux, accompanied only by the knight of Chartres. I started out across the bridge, which I could scarcely make out in the dim light, and as I inspected it carefully I was tormented once more by new misfortunes. For it was riddled with so many and such large gaps that it was scarcely possible that those connected with the townsmen could have passed over it on that same day. The intrepid Chartrian, who showed considerable foresight during the journey, looked around everywhere for a boat, but finding none, returned to the perils of the bridge and secured the favor of heaven so that the horses could cross safely. Sometimes putting a shield down under the horses' feet in the gaping holes and sometimes joining together discarded planks, sometimes bending down and sometimes standing up straight, sometimes coming forward and sometimes running back, he successfully made it all the way across with the horses, while I accompanied him.

Thanks to the bravery—and agility—of the knight, Richer is able to cross the bridge and find lodging at the monastery of Saint-Faro.

Gloomy night had fallen and covered the world in foul darkness, when I arrived at the church of Saint-Faro, where the brothers were still preparing the fraternal libation. On that day they had celebrated a solemn feast, and the chapter of the rule concerning the cellarer[44] of the monastery had been read aloud, which was the reason that they were taking their drink so late. I was received by them as a brother and refreshed with pleasing conversation and ample food. I sent the knight of Chartres back with some horses to try the perils of the bridge (which we had escaped) once more and find the boy. He crossed the bridge in the manner previously described, and in the course of his wandering he came across the boy during the second watch of the night.[45] Despite calling out to him many times, he was scarcely able to find him. He took the boy along with him, and when he arrived at the city and considered the perils of the bridge (which he knew from experience to be exceedingly dangerous), he turned aside and took the boy and the horses to someone's cottage instead. Although they had eaten nothing the whole day, they stopped there that night only to rest and not to eat. Those who have ever been compelled to stay awake at night because they are worried about those dear to them can imagine how sleeplessly I passed that night and with what great torments I was afflicted. Shortly after the longed-for light of day had returned, they arrived, weak from their great hunger. Food was brought to them, and fodder and straw were set before the horses. After sending the boy away on foot to the abbot, I hastened to Chartres accompanied only by the knight. Then, after sending back the horses, I recalled the boy from Meaux.

Having overcome the various obstacles that threatened him on the way, Richer is now free to devote himself to the purpose of his visit: reading the *Aphorisms* of Hippocrates:

After he had returned and all of my worries had been put to rest, I applied myself diligently to the *Aphorisms* of Hippocrates with master Heribrand, a man of great generosity and learning. But since I only

44. *Regula Benedicti,* chap. 31. Neither the day on which Richer arrived at Meaux nor the feast that the monks were celebrating can be determined with certainty.

45. Around midnight.

learned about the prognosis of disease in this work, and a basic understanding of illnesses would not satisfy my desire, I also asked to read one of his books entitled *On the Concordance of Hippocrates, Galen, and Soranus.* This I obtained, since the powers of pharmacology, botany, and surgery were not hidden from one so skilled in the art of medicine.

The story is entertaining and well told, and it serves admirably as a digression. At the same time its length and autobiographical content suggest that it may have been intended as more than an amusing diversion. In narrating his journey to Chartres, Richer projects a certain image of himself to his audience, an image that, as we shall see, appears to have been calculated to appeal to their values. The journey is thus a kind of literary self-representation intended to create a sympathetic portrait of the author.

Formally, the story resembles a quest, since Richer is compelled to overcome several hardships to arrive at his final goal. The title he assigns to this chapter in the margin—*De difficultate sui itineris ab urbe Remorum ad Carnotum* ("On the Difficulty of His Journey from Rheims to Chartres")—implies that the theme of the chapter is surmounting obstacles. The goal of the "quest" is knowledge—specifically, secular knowledge—and part of what Richer seems to be doing in this episode is dramatizing his own perseverance in pursuit of learning.[46] It would be imprudent to push the quest comparison too far, however, since Richer does not assign to himself any traditional heroic qualities, and his success is due as much to the cleverness and courage of the knight of Chartres as to anything else. Aside from his interest in the liberal arts (medicine in particular), the most conspicuous aspect of Richer's character in this account is concern *(sollicitudo)*—for others and for himself. Awaiting the return of the knight and the boy at the monastery of Saint-Faro he tells the reader that "those who have ever been compelled to stay awake at night because they are worried about those dear to them can imagine how sleeplessly I passed that night and

46. Borst, *Lebensformen im Mittelalter,* 148, makes a similar observation.

with what great torment I was afflicted." Earlier, when the boy's horse dies, he makes a similar pronouncement, noting that "Those who have ever suffered similar misfortunes can judge how great my agitation and anxiety were at that time."

Equally telling are the qualities that the author does not ascribe to himself, most notably piety. Richer never prays during the travails of his journey. When the packhorse ridden by the boy collapses and his young companion can travel no further, he states that "God's counsel was not lacking to one in doubt," and in the next sentence he and the knight leave the boy behind to travel to Chartres together. Apparently it was God's counsel that they leave the boy alone in the forest! It is the knight who obtains the aid of heaven in devising a stratagem to get over the bridge. But these two mentions of God are almost perfunctory. Richer does not say that he or his companions prayed, that they begged God to help them, that they invoked the saints, or that they had no fear for their own safety because they put their trust in God. The absence of more explicit devotional overtones is even more striking when we consider that Richer undertook the journey during Lent, a time when monks were called upon to increase the measure of their devotion to God through prayer and abstinence from food and drink.[47] Yet there is no evidence of self-denial during the course of the journey. Instead, Richer laments that he has no spare horses, money, or extra clothing to take with him. At Orbais he dines with the abbot and is "refreshed by conversation" and "sustained by generosity" *(colloquio recreatus simulque et munificentia sustentatus)*. Likewise, at the monastery of Saint-Faro he is "refreshed with pleasing talk and sufficient food" *(dulcibus alloquiis cibisque sufficientibus recreatus)*.

Rather than showcasing his asceticism or spirituality, the journey narrative demonstrates Richer's allegiance to two types of virtues cultivated in the cathedral schools of the late tenth century and in the scholarly community at Saint-Rémi. The first is a set

47. *Regula Benedicti*, chap. 49.

of social graces, the polished *mores* that were thought to express inner virtue.[48] In this case Richer exhibits the virtues of friendship, congeniality, concern for others, and good humor. His relationship with Heribrand is an example of scholarly *amicitia*, the exalted form of intellectual friendship cultivated by learned clerics and monks. Gerbert's letter collection provides the best witness to the cult of *amicitia* at Rheims; his correspondence reveals a network of friends—both monks and secular clerics—among whom books were exchanged, manuscripts copied, and ideas discussed, all with frequent references to the obligations of one friend to another.[49] Two poems linked with Saint-Rémi from this period reveal a similar idealization of intellectual friendship. In a panegyric written to Constantine of Fleury by an anonymous monk of Saint-Rémi in the 980s, the poet uses the language of intimate friendship to praise his dedicatee, referring to him as his "long-beloved companion" *(Comis, amate diu)*.[50] Constantine is praised for his character and learning in abstruse Latin hexameters filled with Greek words and allusions to classical mythology. Adso of Montier-en-Der, who, like Constantine, was an important intellectual figure and a correspondant of Gerbert's, wrote a short, riddling, poem addressed to a Richer who is probably our historian.[51] Drawing upon Isidore of Seville's discussion of rough and smooth

48. For the importance of *mores* in the cathedral schools of this period, see Jaeger, *The Envy of Angels*, 53–117.

49. For Gerbert and the cult of *amicitia*, see Riché, *Gerbert d'Aurillac*, 251–54. For an eloquent expression of this ideal, see the opening of Gerbert's letter to Constantine of Fleury explaining the rules of the abacus (Riché and Callu, vol. 2, annexe 5, letter 1, 662): "vis amictiae impossibilia redigit ad possibilia." For letters as a means of cultivating *amicitia*, see Constable, *Letters and Letter-Collections*, 16–17 and 32.

50. Incipit "Constantine, meis opus est non promere verbis," in *Carmina medii aevi maximam partem inedita ex bibliothecis Helveticis collecta*, ed. H. Hagen (Bern, 1877; reprint, Hildesheim: Georg Olms, 1975), 130–34, line 52. For the cult of friendship in this poem, see Jaeger, *The Envy of Angels*, 58–59. See also Manitius, 2.506-8, and Szövérffy, 1.125–26.

51. *Versus domni Adsonis philosophi de dasian et silen*, discovered by André Vernet in Paris, Bibliothèque national, lat. 13068, fol. 81, and also found in Paris, Bibliothèque national, lat. 12699. See Vernet, *Annuaire de l'École Pratique des Hautes*

breathing-marks (*Etymologiae* 1.19.9–11), which are symbolized by the left- and right-hand side of the letter "H" respectively, he asks Richer to solve the riddle of these "discordant twin sisters," addressing him in the exalted language of *amicitia:*

If, Richer, you can untie my knots with your pen,
You shall be judged worthy [to take your place] between the altars of Apollo.[52]

Both poems show that praise for the intellectual accomplishments of one's friends was a hallmark of scholarly *amicitia.*

Richer and Heribrand cultivated just this sort of *amicitia,* a friendship that bore fruit in Richer's visit to Chartres to study medical texts unavailable to him at Rheims. Richer makes a point of complimenting his friend for his *mores* and his intellect, calling him "a man of great generosity and learning" *(magnae liberalitatis atque scientiae virum),* who was skilled in all aspects of medicine, including pharmacy, botany, and surgery. Significantly, these are the same three branches of medicine unfamiliar to the doctor of Salerno who competes with Derold, the bishop of Amiens, in a contest of medical knowledge before Charles the Simple.[53] In Richer's story the Salernitan is ashamed and says nothing when he cannot answer the king's questions on these subjects. In contrast, Heribrand possessed a thoroughgoing knowledge of the art of medicine.

Apart from showing his adherence to the norms of scholarly *amicitia,* Richer depicts himself as sympathetic, and prone to easily forgivable (perhaps even endearing) human weaknesses. He is disappointed by his abbot's frugality and glad to be entertained with food, drink, and conversation at Orbais and Meaux. He fears for his own safety amid bad weather, darkness, confusing roads,

---

Études, section 4.345–47; Monique Goullet, *Adsonis Dervensis Opera Hagiographica,* CCCM 198 (Turnhout: Brepols, 2003), xxviii–xxx; Glenn, *Politics and History,* 274–75.

52. Lines 10–11: "Si, Richere, meas kalamo dissolveris ansas, / inter Apollineas merito censeberis aras."

53. *Historia* 2.59.

and a structurally unsound bridge, but he is also tormented by worries for his companions. He can find humor even in a bad situation when he observes that a horse "that up to now had seemed like Bucephalus became slower than a reluctant little donkey."

The second type of virtue that Richer associates with himself in this narrative is the desire to learn *(aviditas discendi).* The wish to learn implies a recognition of one's own deficiencies, and as a result this chapter contains no intellectual boasting. Aside from his use of the comparatively obscure term *mesembrinum* for the more common *meridies* to mean "midday," and his reference to Alexander the Great's horse, Bucephalus, Richer does not go out of his way to show off his learning. Instead, he demonstrates his eagerness to learn and his perseverance in the pursuit of knowledge. He thinks "often and at length" *(saepe et multum,* an allusion to the first line of the *De inventione)* about the opportunity to read Hippocrates before Heribrand's messenger even arrives in Rheims. He endures a difficult journey to reach Chartres, and nothing indicates that he ever considers turning back. When he finally arrives, he is not content merely to study the *Aphorisms* "vigilantly" *(vigilanter)*; he also devotes himself to a more comprehensive medical compendium. The desire to learn and diligence in the acquisition of knowledge are key themes of this chapter.

It is precisely these qualities that distinguish the young Gerbert in Richer's account of his dedicatee's early scholarly career. When Gerbert is brought to Rome by his Spanish patrons, Count Borrell II of Barcelona and Bishop Hatto of Vich, he attracts the attention of Pope John XIII by virtue of his *industria* and his *discendi voluntas.*[54] We have no way of knowing whether Richer intended to create an explicit connection between himself and Gerbert through the parallel *aviditas discendi/discendi voluntas.* What is clear is that Richer and his audience agreed that scholarly ambition and intellectual curiosity were admirable qualities in a monk and future bishop. No less an authority than the pope himself approved

54. *Historia* 3.44.

of Gerbert's studies and helped to further his career. Thus, when Richer uses the narrative of his journey to Chartres to dramatize his own *aviditas discendi,* he signals his allegiance to a virtue exemplified by his patron and dedicatee and esteemed in the intellectual community at Rheims. If Richer did intend to draw an implicit comparison between himself and Gerbert in this account, the journey narrative was an ideal device. Gerbert's peregrinations in search of knowledge had led him from Aurillac in the Auvergne to Spain, and from there to Rome, Rheims, the abbey of Bobbio, and back to Rheims. Richer's comparatively short trip to Chartres can perhaps be understood as a kind of *imitatio Gerberti,* an attempt to show his intellectual mentor that he, too, would endure the hazards of travel in pursuit of knowledge.

Ostentatious Displays of Learning and Tenth-Century Intellectual Culture

To demonstrate a thirst for knowledge was to signal allegiance to a cherished scholarly ideal, but only by openly demonstrating a mastery of that knowledge could it be turned to practical use as a means of winning esteem or patronage. The ostentatious display of learning is a notable feature of tenth-century intellectual culture. Claudio Leonardi has argued that this period witnessed the "forerunner of the modern intellectual," when "knowledge came to be understood both as being a form of personal achievement and as having a social role."[55] Public displays of knowledge became part of the identity of self-styled scholars, a means of demonstrating their identity as intellectuals and showcasing their scholarly credentials.

Ostentatious displays of learning feature heavily in the writing of many of Richer's contemporaries. The rhetorical affectation, pedantic tone, and recherché *prosimetrum* form that Dudo of Saint-

55. Leonardi, "Intellectual Life," in *The New Cambridge Medieval History,* 3.189–90.

Quentin employs in his *Gesta Normannorum,* for example, all seem deliberately calculated to highlight the author's cleverness—notwithstanding his frequent invocations of the humility topos. Walter of Speyer's *Libellus scolasticus* is similar in the difficulties of interpretation it poses for the reader and the way in which it makes a show of its author's learning. Walter advertises his education to the reader both by describing the curriculum at the cathedral school of Speyer in detail and by composing hexameters dense with symbolism, allegory, obscure vocabulary, and difficult syntax.[56]

Gunzo of Novara's letter to the monks of Reichenau constitutes a particularly good example of the way in which intellectual pride could lead an author to showcase his learning in a heavy-handed fashion.[57] During his stay at the monastery of Saint-Gall in January 965 as a member of the retinue of Otto I, Gunzo, in a momentary lapse in concentration, employed an accusative case ending where an ablative would have been correct. This provoked a young monk to compose some impromptu poetic verses mocking Gunzo and satirizing his error.[58] Gunzo temporarily tolerated the insult, but upon his arrival in Germany he sent a letter to the monks of the nearby monastery of Reichenau (who were not necessarily on good terms with their brothers at Saint-Gall) in which he inveighed in the strongest possible terms against the young man's teacher.

Gunzo's letter is calculated quite clearly to put his opponents in their place by browbeating them with the evidence his own erudition. He lists, for example, all the books that he carried with him, including obscure and difficult works like Plato's *Timaeus.* He in-

56. See Vossen, *Der Libellus Scolasticus,* 32–34. Walter also verges on boasting when he speaks of the fame that his poem will obtain in an address to Saint Christopher at the end of book 1: "Here are the pages; if you deign to approach them, this poem will be celebrated in every land" (lines 261–62: "Praesto sunt cartae: quas si dignaris adire, omnibus in terris celebrabitur ista poesis").

57. *Epistola ad Augienses,* ed. Karl Manitius, MGH Quellen zur Geistesgeschichte des Mittelalters, vol. 2 (Weimar: Herman Böhlaus, 1958), 3–57.

58. *Epistola ad Augienses,* chap. 3, p. 22.

cludes a passage on the substitution of cases *(antiptosis)* in classical texts and in the Bible.[59] He quotes classical poets and even cites Homer in Greek (by way of Servius).[60] Much of the letter consists of a pedantic exposition of each one of the liberal arts. Although not particularly rich in autobiographical detail, the letter makes one aspect of Gunzo's personality abundantly clear: his extraordinary pride in his learning.[61] Occasionally, this pride flares into outright arrogance, as when he asks, "Who would suppose that one to whom God has granted so much would be criticized for changing one case?"[62]

For our purposes, the letter is valuable because it shows that learning could translate into esteem in monastic communities, and that an attack on the reputation of a self-styled scholar could be taken very seriously. The fact that Gunzo sent his invective to Reichenau, where it could be read and even copied by a sympathetic audience, rather than Saint-Gall, the home of the offending monk, is significant. It suggests that his primary goal was not to respond directly to his adversaries, but to demonstrate his erudition to his contemporaries (particularly those who shared his animosity for Saint-Gall), and perhaps also to preserve it in writing for posterity.

Certain aspects of the *Historia* suggest that Richer was interested in using his work to communicate a particular image of himself to his audience. His unusually assertive claim about his stylistic originality is one sign that he viewed his work in part as a platform for self-promotion. It was not unusual for hagiographers or historians in the ninth and tenth centuries to claim to be improving upon the faulty Latin style of their Merovingian-era sources. Aimoin of Fleury does just this in the prologue to his *Gesta Fran-*

59. *Epistola ad Augienses,* chap. 4, pp. 25–28.

60. *Episotla ad Augienses,* chap. 4, p. 25.

61. *Epistola ad Augienses,* chap. 1, p. 21: "Sciunt me vera fari qui munia literarum non mihi penitus abesse didicerunt."

62. *Epistola ad Augienses,* chap. 9, p. 37: "Quis putaret se reprehendendum in unius casus mutatione, cui deus plura concesserit."

corum, explaining that his abbot, Abbo, asked him "to reduce to the body of one small work and recall to a more correct standard of Latinity the deeds of the people and kings of the Franks that lay scattered throughout various books and were recounted in uncultivated language."[63] But unlike Aimoin, and unlike tenth-century hagiographers who typically spoke in terms of "correcting" and "polishing" earlier saints' lives, Richer claims to be recasting Flodoard's *Annals* in an entirely different literary form, and he was evidently keen that his audience be cognizant of that fact.[64] Literary ambition, the motive disclaimed by so many of Richer's contemporaries, lies close to the surface of the *Historia.*

Authorial self-promotion may also help to explain Richer's penchant for detailed descriptions of diseases and siege engines. Such passages can be explained on literary and aesthetic grounds as forms of *descriptio,* and both types of passage are found in the classical historians that Richer used as models. Yet it is also possible that Richer deliberately sought to showcase his knowledge of these two technically demanding and practically useful arts. Medical knowledge in particular was a valuable commodity that could bring tangible rewards to those skilled in its practice.[65] One gets a hint of this in the anecdote about Derold, who appears to have leveraged his position as court physician to Charles the Simple to become bishop of Amiens.[66] That monks and canons could and did use their knowledge of medicine for temporal gain can be seen in the conciliar prohibitions against the practice of medicine for profit beginning in the twelfth century.[67] In his letters Gerbert presents

63. *Gesta Francorum,* prologue. See also Werner, "Die literarischen Vorbilder des Aimoin von Fleury."

64. For stylistic claims in tenth-century hagiography, see Ludwig Zoepf, *Das Heiligenleben im 10 Jahrhundert* (Leipzig and Berlin: Teubner, 1908), 6–12.

65. See John J. Contreni, "Masters and Medicine in Northern France during the Reign of Charles the Bald," in *Charles the Bald: Court and Kingdom,* ed. Margaret T. Gibson and Janet T. Nelson (Hampshire: Variorum, 1990), 267–82. See also Rodulf Glaber's story about the monk Wulferius at *Historiae* 2.19–20.

66. *Historia* 2.59. Cf. Flodoard, *Annales,* s.a. 929, p. 44: "Deroldus medicus episcopatum Ambianensem adipiscitur."

67. Darrel W. Amundsen, "Medieval Canon Law on Medical and Surgical Prac-

himself as interested in, and knowledgeable about, medicine, but denies practicing it. Richer may thus have seen some benefit in advertising his medical knowledge to his dedicatee.[68]

The same possibility also applies to his knowledge of siege engineering, which is put on display in three passages in which he describes the construction of a mobile warcart (2.10), a siege tower (3.105), and a battering ram (4.22). The archbishops of Rheims wielded supreme power in the county,[69] and Gerbert's predecessors built fortresses, repaired walls, and undertook military operations to safeguard their possessions.[70] Bishops were also required to levy the *militia ecclesiae* for the king and possibly lead them in battle, an unwanted responsibility that had fallen upon Gerbert during his time as abbot of Bobbio.[71] Although the prospect of a monk giving advice on the conduct of war may seem far-fetched, Jean of Marmoutiers' life of Geoffrey Plantagenet describes how Walter of Compiègne, a monk of Marmoutiers, assisted Geoffrey in using the *De re militari* of Vegetius during the siege of Montreuil-Bellay in 1130.[72] It is not outside the realm of possibility, therefore, that

tice by the Clergy," *Bulletin of the History of Medicine* 52 (1978): 22–44. See also John of Salisbury's complaints about monks becoming medical students at *Metalogicon* 1.4.

68. Gerbert, letter 151 (Riché and Callu, 2.370–73).

69. Flodoard, *Annales*, s.a. 940, p. 75. But see Bur, "Reims, ville des sacres," 42–43, who thinks that the text of Flodoard has been interpolated here and denies that the archbishop ever had control over the *comitatus*.

70. Prinz, *Klerus und Krieg im früheren Mittelalter*, 150–64. Archbishop Hervey brought 1,500 troops to help Charles deal with Magyar raids in Lotharingia in 919; see *HRE* 4.14, p. 407. Seulf fought the Viking leader Ragenold with Heribert's army in 923; see Flodoard, *Annales*, s.a. 923, p. 26. Artald is mentioned several times campaigning with Louis IV and Lothar. See Flodoard, *Annales*, s.a. 945, p. 96; s.a. 947, p. 105; s.a. 952, p. 134; s.a. 958, p. 145. Arnulf fought alongside Charles of Lotharingia (*Historia* 4.34).

71. Gerbert was required to levy troops for Otto II, although he did not personally appear in battle. See letter 5 (Riché and Callu, 1.10–13); Riché, *Gerbert d'Aurillac*, 69.

72. Jean of Marmoutiers, *Historia Gaufredi Ducis Normannorum et Comitis Andegavorum*, ed. Louis Halphen and Rene Poupardin, *Chroniques des comtes d'Anjou et des seigneurs d'Amboise* (Paris: A. Picard, 1913), 218. For this incident and the use to which Vegetius was put in the early Middle Ages, see Bernard Bachrach, "The Practical Use of Vegetius' *De Re Militari* during the Early Middle Ages," *The Historian* 47 (1985): 239–55.

Richer had a specific interest in demonstrating his expertise in siege engines to Gerbert.

Intellectual Culture at Rheims

If Richer was subtler than some of his contemporaries in establishing his intellectual credentials, he nonetheless shared with them a reverence for secular learning and an appreciation of the status that it could confer. His literary self-fashioning as a classicizing historian and a student of the liberal arts, and his choice to dramatize his *aviditas discendi* rather than his humility, piety, or faith correspond to broader movements in intellectual culture during the second half of the tenth century. In the newly resurgent cathedral schools of this period the liberal arts were no longer cultivated predominantly as an aid to understanding the Bible. Instead, students pursued secular learning for practical reasons—as part of the training necessary to function as courtiers or ecclesiastical administrators—or even for its own sake.[73] At the same time, self-promotion, conspicuous pride in intellectual achievement, and even a certain combativeness in defending one's reputation became part of the scholastic culture of the Latin West.

Rheims was an important center for the study of the liberal arts at least from the time of Adalbero's arrival in 968. Richer makes a point of Adalbero's educational reforms, noting that "in order to satisfy in all things his own nobility of character, he sought to have the sons of his church instructed to their advantage in the liberal arts."[74] Abbo of Fleury visited Rheims in the late 960s to study astronomy, and Gerbert was drawn there in 972 to study *logica* (dialectic, and probably also rhetoric) with the celebrated Gerannus.[75] Gerbert's own tenure as *scholasticus* brought even more promi-

73. Notably, Richer's account of Gerbert's curriculum at Rheims makes no mention of the spiritual uses of secular learning.

74. *Historia* 3.42.

75. *Historia* 3.45. For Abbo's studies at Rheims, see Aimoin of Fleury, *Vita Abbonis,* chap. 3, *PL* 139.390.

nence to the cathedral school. The curriculum that he taught was distinctly secular, and in the scholarly community of Rheims literary genres such as poetry and historiography seem to have taken precedence over biblical exegesis. The author of the anonymous panegyric to Constantine of Fleury intermingles praise of his subject's piety and learning, but he lays the greatest stress on Constantine's scholarship in the *trivium*.[76] The poem's elevated tone, classicizing allusions, and smattering of Greek vocabulary point to the sophistication of literary culture at Rheims, and the praise bestowed on Constantine for his learning confirms the esteem that secular knowledge could confer.

Richer's biographical sketch of Gerbert's early career (3.43–65) is a particularly valuable source for contemporary attitudes about the relationship between spiritual duties and secular pursuits among the clergy at Rheims. In these chapters Richer describes Gerbert's studies in Spain and Italy, his arrival at Rheims and teaching at the cathedral school, and his disputation with Otric of Magdeburg at Ravenna. Although Richer clearly intended to praise and flatter his dedicatee in this section, he says nothing about Gerbert's spiritual life or his personal sanctity. He does not include a single anecdote that shows Gerbert's monastic devotion or his pursuit of Christian ideals such as charity or humility. Instead, Gerbert's learning is the dominant theme—indeed, it is the only theme.

When compared with the earlier examples of ecclesiastical biography at Rheims—Hincmar's *Life of Remigius* and Flodoard's *Historia Remensis Ecclesiae*—Richer's portrait of Gerbert bears witness to a notable shift in the values of the community.[77] The archetypal figures in the ecclesiastical history of Rheims prior to the arrival of Adalbero and Gerbert were Remigius (ca. 438–533), a figure of apostolic holiness who converted Clovis and the heathen Franks to Christianity, and Hincmar (806–882, b. 845–882),

76. E.g., the poet addresses Constantine as "beloved teacher of speech, light of rhetorical elegance" (lines 52–53: "doctor dulcissime fandi, rhetorici cultus lumen").

77. For Hincmar's life of Remigius, see Bruno Krusch, ed., *Vita Remigii*, MGH SSRM 3 (Hanover: Hahn, 1896), 239–341.

the model of the Christian bishop as administrator of his province and overseer of his flock. For these two men, as for the other archbishops of Rheims whose deeds Flodoard recounts in the *HRE*, learning is merely one facet of holiness and personal sanctity. In contrast, Gerbert is praised in terms that are almost exclusively secular.

Richer begins his account of Gerbert's career by stating that he was sent to Adalbero by God himself *(ab ipsa divinitate)*, and that as a consequence of his arrival "all of Gaul afterwards shone, glittering, as if with a blazing lamp."[78] Gerbert is thus divinely appointed, but he comes to Rheims to teach the liberal arts rather than Christian doctrine, and learning, not piety, is his most distinguishing characteristic. Richer employs the image of Gerbert as the bringer of divine light a second time when he declares that God inspired Gerbert's Spanish patrons to take him with them to Rome because he "wanted Gaul, which lay mired in darkness, to shine forth again with a great light."[79] Flodoard uses similar language to describe the coming of Saint Remigius to the Franks, declaring that he "arose as a brightly shining light to instruct the gentiles in the faith, one whom the divine piety … chose not only before he was born, but even before he was conceived."[80] The light metaphor and the idea of divine appointment echo Richer's description of Gerbert's arrival in Gaul, but whereas Saint Remigius came to spread the faith, the illumination that Gerbert brought was knowledge of the liberal arts.

Richer's account of Gerbert's life is essentially the story of his scholarly career. Gerbert is raised at the monastery of Saint-Gerald at Aurillac, where he is instructed in grammar, and is then taken to Spain by Count Borrell II of Barcelona (d. 992/3) to receive

78. *Historia* 3.43: "quo postmodum tota Gallia acsi lucerna ardente vibrabunda refulsit."

79. *Historia* 3.43: "Sed cum divinitas Galliam iam caligantem magno lumine relucere voluit, predictis duci et episcopo mentem dedit, ut Romam oraturi peterent."

80. *HRE* 1.10, p. 80: "Prefato Benagio beatissimus succedens Remigius imbuendis ad fidem prefulgidum surrexit lumen gentibus. Quem divina pietas … non solum priusquam nasceretur, sed et antequam conciperetur, elegit."

instruction in the liberal arts.[81] There he is entrusted to Bishop Hatto of Vich (d. 971/2), with whom he studies the *quadrivium.*[82] When Borrell and Hatto bring Gerbert to Rome, Pope John XIII (965–972) immediately recognizes his talents.[83] The pope recommends Gerbert to the German emperor Otto I on the basis of his knowledge of the *quadrivium,* but the emperor advises him to keep Gerbert in Rome.[84] Eventually Gerbert leaves for Rheims to study *logica* with the celebrated Gerannus.[85] Upon his arrival, the "loftiness of his studies" *(studiorum nobilitas)* recommends him to Archbishop Adalbero.[86] Soon thereafter he is appointed *scholasticus* at the cathedral school, where he attracts throngs of students to himself.[87] His fame spreads through Gaul, Germany, and Italy.[88] When a spy sent to Rheims by Otric of Magdeburg misinterprets Gerbert's taxonomy of the branches of knowledge *(divisio philosophiae),* and jealous rivals impugn his teaching, Otto II summons Gerbert to Ravenna, where Gerbert defeats Otric in a day-long disputation before the emperor and his court.[89]

Although Richer ascribes Gerbert's arrival in Gaul to divine providence, his abridged *vita* lacks any of the elements of sacred biography. There is no prefiguration of Gerbert's birth nor any miraculous stories about his youth; he is merely the most intellectually gifted of the young students at Saint-Gerald of Aurillac. Instead of recounting feats of asceticism or spiritual devotion, Richer describes Gerbert's curriculum at Rheims (3.46–54), where he teaches his students secular, rather than spiritual, lessons. Gerbert does not triumph over sin, heresy, or the temptations of the devil, but instead

81. *Historia* 3.43.

82. *Historia* 3.43.

83. *Historia* 3.44: "Nec latuit papam adolescentis industria, simulque et discendi voluntas."

84. *Historia* 3.44.

85. *Historia* 3.45.

86. *Historia* 3.45.

87. *Historia* 3.45.

88. *Historia* 3.55: "nomen etiam tanti doctoris ferebatur non solum per Gallias, sed etiam per Germaniae populos dilatabatur. Transiitque per Alpes ac diffunditur in Italiam, usque Thirrenum et Adriaticum."

89. *Historia* 3.55–65.

defeats a scholarly rival in the disputation at Ravenna. He toils over his work, but he is an intellectual athlete, not a spiritual one.[90]

Richer's portrait of the young Gerbert, singled out at a young age for his intellectual gifts and put on a path to scholarly fame, contrasts noticeably with Hincmar's account of the early life of Remigius. Like Gerbert, Remigius excels academically, but he chooses to pursue a solitary life of spiritual devotion rather than a public career of scholarship:

> [He] was entrusted to the school by his parents to be instructed in letters and quickly surpassed both his contemporaries and his elders in learning. He strove as well to conquer his tender years through the maturity of his character and to season his good will with the honey of charity, to avoid crowds of people that gathered together, and (as he learned the herald of his arrival had done) to serve the Lord through a solitary life in seclusion.[91]

Hincmar later enumerates the qualities that distinguish Remigius as bishop of Rheims (ca. 459/460–ca. 533):[92]

> He was thus generous in almsgiving, diligent in his vigils, devoted in prayer, perfect in charity, liberal in generosity, outstanding in learning, ready in speech, most holy in his way of life. He demonstrated the sincerity of his mind through the serenity of his countenance and showed the piety of his merciful heart in the gentleness of his speech. Whatever pertained to eternal salvation this most blessed man fulfilled in deed no less than he taught in his preaching.[93]

In Hincmar's portrait of Remigius learning is one among many qualities desired in a bishop, and by no means the most important. His role as a teacher is not to hand down knowledge of the

90. *Historia* 3.49: "in mathesi vero quantus sudor expensus sit, non incongruum dicere videtur."

91. *Vita Remigii,* chap. 2, p. 263. The "herald of his arrival" is the monk Montanus, to whom the birth of Remigius is announced in advance. See *Vita Remigii,* chap. 1, pp. 259–60, and *HRE* 1.10, p. 80.

92. Hincmar borrows this list of virtues from an earlier life of Remigius formerly attributed to Venantius Fortunatus. See Bruno Krusch, ed., *Vita Sancti Remedii,* MGH AA 4.2 (Berlin: Weidmann, 1885), 64–67.

93. *Vita Remigii,* chap. 4, p. 264.

liberal arts but to fire his students with the desire to live a holy life through his own example. In the *Historia Remensis Ecclesiae* Flodoard describes the way in which the young Saint Thierry learned from Remigius:

Of this angelic worship he had nearby a doctor to heal him, a patron to aid him, and a teacher to instruct him, namely Remigius, the blessed father of his religion. Enlightened by the example of this most pious teacher, burning with desire for the virtues, he strove to grow into a perfect man.[94]

Like Hincmar, whose *Vita Remigii* served as the principle source for the portrait of Remigius in the *Historia Remensis Ecclesiae,* Flodoard depicts the learning of Remigius as inseparable from his personal sanctity. Both were made manifest in good works:

His works bear witness to the radiance of learning, sanctity, and wisdom with which this most blessed father shone, since wisdom is known to be true and free from doubt when it is proven by a show of its works, as a tree is by its fruits.[95]

The life of Remigius as described by Hincmar and Flodoard shares little in common with the portrait of Gerbert in Richer's *Historia.* Remigius perfects his spiritual development by practicing a holy way of life *(sancta conversatio)* in isolation, while Gerbert is very much part of the world from the moment he leaves the Auvergne. The signal virtues of Remigius—charity, piety, and wisdom—stem from his devotion to the spiritual ideals of Christianity. He outstrips his peers in intelligence, but he directs it to a spiritual end. Like Remigius, Gerbert is distinguished by his industry and his intellectual gifts, but he is also possessed by the desire to learn, and he seeks knowledge for its own sake. For Remigius, knowledge is subordinate to holiness, and the role of the teacher

94. *HRE* 1.24, p. 122. See also *HRE* 1.24, p. 124: "At pius praesul [i.e., Remigius] molestia quadam corporis, ut fertur, detentus, beato Theoderico, quem pie casteque nutrierat, et spiritalibus doctrinis instruxerat ... negotium quod petebatur, ut pater filio, commendat." For Saint Thierry, see Sot, *Un historien et son église,* 408.

95. *HRE* 1.12, p. 85.

is to serve as an exemplar of Christian virtue. For Gerbert, knowledge does not constitute a means to an end, but an end in itself. God sends him to the Gauls specifically to enlighten them in the liberal arts.

It might be objected that Richer could hardly have modeled his account of Gerbert's early career on Remigius, an exemplar of legendary saintliness from the distant past, the apostle to the Franks, and the baptizer of Clovis. Yet if the life of Remigius did not necessarily offer a perfect template for future biography, the virtues that he exemplified were certainly important ecclesiastical ideals. Flodoard repeatedly emphasizes the virtues of charity and spiritual devotion in his accounts of other archbishops of Rheims from the ninth and tenth centuries. Hincmar's biography, for example, takes up all of book 3 of the *Historia Remensis Ecclesiae* and offers a point of comparison closer in time to Gerbert. Hincmar was famed as a canon lawyer, an administrator of the ecclesiastical province of Rheims, and a skilled politician who became the most powerful prelate in the West Frankish kingdom and the most important adviser to Charles the Bald. As we would expect, Flodoard devotes most of his life of Hincmar to his subject's pastoral and administrative duties (often by reproducing his letters), but he also describes his personal sanctity and spiritual devotion. Hincmar is brought up at the abbey of Saint-Denis, where, Flodoard writes, "he was nourished in the monastic way of life and imbued with the studies of letters."[96] Knowledge of the liberal arts here is connected explicitly to monastic discipline in a way that it is not in Richer's account of Gerbert's upbringing.[97] Moreover, Hincmar reforms the monastery of Saint-Denis through his own ascetic discipline, and the terms that Flodoard uses to describe his exemplary life there mirror the account of Remigius in Hincmar's *Vita:*

96. *HRE* 3.1, p. 190.

97. Cf. *Historia* 3.43: "Qui Aquitanus genere, in coenobio sancti confessoris Geroldi a puero altus, et grammatica edoctus est." It is significant that Richer mentions grammar, but not *monasterialis religio.* Hincmar also possesses *nobilitas,* a characteristic not ascribed to Gerbert, whose birth is never mentioned, and who came from a less august monastery than Saint-Denis.

And so that he could accomplish in deed what he urged in words, he too subjected himself to the religious way of life with the others, punishing his body and submitting to spiritual servitude.[98]

Like Saint Remigius before him, at the monastery of Saint-Denis Hincmar is a soldier for Christ.[99] Later, King Lothar I intervenes on his behalf and secures the archiepiscopal *pallium* for Hincmar out of respect for both his wisdom and his holiness.[100] Even though Hincmar was a prelate very much entangled in secular affairs, Flodoard continued to ascribe to him the virtues of monastic devotion and personal sanctity.

We find the same emphasis on spiritual virtues and service to the Church in Flodoard's descriptions of the other archbishops of Rheims, where he emphasizes prudent administration of the archiepiscopal province, upkeep of the church (in the form of building projects), concern for the poor, instruction of the clergy, and exemplification of the Christian virtues of piety, compassion, and generosity. Here, for example, is Flodoard's description of archbishop Hervey (900–922):

At once he strove to show that he was fit for this rank, inspiring affection in all good men and serving as a model even for his elders. He was a kind benefactor to the poor, a generous means of support for the monks, and a compassionate provider to the wretched in their need. He was especially well trained in liturgical chant, outstanding in singing the psalms and polished in performance, happy in mind and countenance, pleasant and mild, distinguished by every good quality, a father to the clergy and a devoted advocate of all of the people; he was slow to anger and quick to be merciful, a lover of the churches of God, and, with God's power, a steadfast defender of the sheepfold entrusted to him.[101]

98. *HRE* 3.1, pp. 190–91. Cf. *Vita Remigii,* chap. 4, p. 264: "Quicquid ad salutem pertinere posset aeternam, non minus implebat beatissimus opere, quam sermonis predicatione docebat."

99. *HRE* 3.1, p. 191. Cf. *Vita Remigii,* chap. 3, p. 263; *HRE* 1.10, p. 81.

100. *HRE* 3.10, p. 206.

101. *HRE* 4.11, p. 404.

Richer reproduces none of this material about Hervey in the *Historia.* He introduces him as a distinguished courtier (1.19: *vir spectabilis et palatinus*), and describes his bravery in rescuing Charles the Simple from his captors (1.22), and his eloquence and diplomatic skill at the court of Henry the Fowler (1.23). But he says next to nothing about Hervey's piety or his pastoral care of the province of Rheims, directing his readers instead to Flodoard's history.[102]

In his portrayal of Adalbero, Gerbert's predecessor as archbishop, Richer likewise says little about his subject's personal sanctity. He praises Adalbero for renovating the cathedral of Rheims, for organizing the canons of the cathedral under a rule, and for reforming monasteries, but with the exception of one reference to his "celibate life," he does not mention Adalbero's piety.[103] Adalbero is introduced as "a man of royal nobility" and later characterized as "noble and energetic."[104] During a council held at Compiègne in May 987, immediately after the death of King Louis V, Hugh Capet calls Adalbero "noble and famed for his great wisdom," and gives him the honor of addressing the assembled Frankish magnates because, Richer says, "he excelled in the knowledge of divine and human affairs and was so effective in his eloquence."[105] Knowledge of divine and human affairs *(divinarum et humanarum rerum scientia)* joined to the pursuit of living well *(studium bene vivendi)* was the definition of philosophy given by Isidore of Seville.[106] Adalbero, then, is praised for being an eloquent speaker and for being, in effect, a philosopher. These are the very same qualities to which Gerbert lays claim in his letter to Evrard of Tours, in which he

102. *Historia* 1.19.

103. At *Historia* 3.22–23 Richer describes Adalbero's renovations to the cathedral, at 3.24 his reform of the canonical life, and at 3.25 his zeal for monastic reform. At 3.25–29 Adalbero seeks a privilege for Saint-Rémi from Pope John XIII and at 3.30–42 he presides over a reform synod of abbots. At 3.25 Richer refers to Adalbero as "vir nobilis et strenuus, et fama celibis vitae omnibus clarus." He also calls him "religionis peritissimus" (3.42), but this appears to mean he was very knowledgeable about the rule, not that he was particularly diligent in observing it.

104. *Historia* 3.22: "regalis nobilitatis vir"; *Historia* 3.25: "vir nobilis et strenuus."

105. *Historia* 4.7.

106. *Etymologiae* 2.24.1; 8.6.1.

writes that "since the practice of moral behavior and that of speaking are not separate from philosophy, I have always joined my pursuit of speaking well with a desire to live properly."[107] Hugh's speech in praise of Adalbero at Compiègne, as invented by Richer, thus directly reflects the premium put on the virtues of eloquence and learning at Rheims.

Conclusion

Apart from one reference to Adalbero's "celibate life," Richer avoids any mention of interior spirituality or outward displays of Christian charity in his laudatory portraits of Gerbert and Adalbero. He depicts Gerbert as a teacher and scholar, a skilled dialectician and orator, and Adalbero as a noble, learned, and eloquent prelate who brings Gerbert to Rheims, renovates the cathedral, reforms monasteries, and institutes a rule among the canons. Richer's lack of attention to the personal holiness of his subjects is part of a general trend in the *Historia*. In contrast to Hincmar and Flodoard, Richer praises bishops and monks for their learning, eloquence, noble birth, and even wealth, but hardly ever for their piety.[108] While both Flodoard and Richer clearly felt that learning was a requirement of fundamental importance for bishops, they describe knowledge and erudition in different ways. In the *HRE* Flodoard invariably highlights knowledge of Scripture and the spiritual ends of education in the archbishops of Rheims, whereas Richer is generally silent about *religio, sacrae litterae,* or *doctrina ecclesiastica.*[109]

The terms of praise employed by Richer reflect the values of the

107. Letter 44 (Riché and Callu, 1.106).

108. A rare exception is Theotilo of Tours, who is described as "holy" *(sanctus)* at 2.46. See Giese, *"Genus" und "Virtus,"* 108–11.

109. See, e.g., *HRE* 1.16 (Remigius): "virum divinis eloquiis eruditissimum et doctrinis ecclesiasticis exercitatissimum"; 2.19 (Ebo): "vir industrius et liberalibus disciplinis eruditus ... qui multis ecclesiam curavit instruere commode"; 4.18 (Seulf): "vir tam ecclesiasticis quam secularibus disciplinis sufficienter instructus." Cf. this to *Historia* 2.41, where Richer describes Seulf as "vir strenuus, multaque rerum scientia inclitus."

community in which he lived and wrote: eloquence, erudition, and refined *mores*. The premium placed upon learning—and, in particular, on secular forms of knowledge—by the scholarly community at Rheims in turn affected both the content and the form of Richer's *Historia*. He chose as his principal theme the wars of the West Frankish kings, and, as we would expect, most of the *Historia* is devoted to political machinations and warfare. But an important secondary theme runs throughout the work, namely, respect for learning and recognition of the social prestige that it brings. This motif appears early on in the tale of the physician Derold of Amiens (2.59), a story that emphasizes the superiority of Derold's systematic knowledge of medicine over the practical experience of his rival.[110] The journey to Chartres can likewise be read as an expression of esteem for learning, since Richer endures an uncomfortable, even dangerous, trip, for the opportunity to read Hippocrates. The most obvious locus for this theme is Richer's account of Gerbert's scholarly career. Richer glorifies Gerbert by casting him as a heaven-sent emissary of learning; he includes a detailed account of his curriculum at the cathedral school of Rheims, and dwells in particular on his innovative use of devices such as the monochord, armillary sphere, and abacus. Richer's narrative of the *disputatio* at Ravenna serves a similar purpose, portraying Gerbert as a master of dialectic who vanquishes his opponent before an audience of assorted *sapientes* presided over by the emperor Otto II. Gerbert's display of wisdom at Ravenna also demonstrates very clearly the practical benefits of a reputation for learning, since Otto appointed him abbot of Bobbio soon after the disputation.

Just as the intellectual culture of Rheims influenced the content of the *Historia*, it also shaped Richer's manner of writing: his preference for classical authors as models, his composition of formal orations and rhetorical set-pieces like the *descriptio*, and his use of the technical terminology of medicine, siege craft, and rhetoric. On the one hand, these characteristics of the *Historia* reflect the

110. *Historia* 2.59. See Kortüm, *Richer von Saint-Remi*, 79–83.

high cultural level of Saint-Rémi and the sophistication of the education available there in the late tenth century. At the same time, Richer's self-conscious displays of erudition can also be read as a deliberate means of authorial self-representation, a way in which he could demonstrate his own learning to the rest of his community. Richer's claim of rewriting Flodoard in a new, and superior, prose style delivers the clearest evidence that he viewed his work as a means of showcasing his abilities, but he also laid claim to the mantle of learning in other, subtler ways. By dedicating his work to Gerbert and narrating his early career, Richer gives the impression of being an intimate of this most celebrated of tenth-century scholars. By describing in close detail the *disputatio* at Ravenna and Gerbert's curriculum at the cathedral school, and by recommending Gerbert's *acta* of synods for their rhetorical virtues, he implies his own familiarity with these specialized subjects. Finally, he uses the tale of his journey to Chartres to dramatize his desire for learning and his diligence in the pursuit of knowledge, the same virtues that he ascribes to the young Gerbert in his visit to Rome.

It is admittedly risky to hazard a guess at the unstated intentions of an author who lived a millennium ago in a culture governed by a set of mentalities and social practices very different from our own. An ever-present danger is that by importing present-day cultural assumptions into a world where they do not belong, evidence may be distorted or misinterpreted. Thus, it may seem anachronistic to read the motives of self-representation or even self-advertisement into Richer's history, precisely because these goals play such a large role in modern literary endeavors. Yet in spite of the shift in cultural assumptions surrounding writing and the idea of authorship between the Middle Ages and today, we should not overlook the ways in which medieval authors—even those who had been ordered to write and assigned specific subject matter—might use their texts for personal ends. The omnipresence of literary topoi intended to ward off charges of presumption or ambition confirms that these were seen to be very real motivations. Even authors who had no grand literary ambitions were presumably interested in imparting a favorable image of themselves to their audiences; the topoi of modesty were intended to do just this. Writing could be a way of winning esteem and securing patronage. Above all, it was a means by which an author could preserve the memory of his own name.

Thus, whatever Richer's ultimate goal was in writing history, and regardless of whether he was commissioned to write or not, he was able to use his work as a means of self-representation, of fashioning an image of himself that would be disseminated in his community and propagated as long as his text was read and copied. Although his history survives only by the slimmest of textual traditions, he was ultimately successful in this goal. All that we know of Richer is the faint portrait that emerges from the *Historia:* a studious monk who was the son of a warlike father, a devotee of medicine, siege engineering, and classical historiography, an admirer of Gerbert, and above all a follower of his patron in his desire to seek out and obtain knowledge, no unimpressive virtue in the world of the late tenth century.

Conclusion

"ALL HISTORY," wrote R. G. Collingwood, "is the re-enactment of past thought in the historian's own mind."[1] For Collingwood this was the expression of an ideal, not a statement of fact. Medieval historiography did not rate highly in his estimation, beholden as it was to a providential view of history that deemed human action to be important only insofar as it reflected God's will. Yet his dictum isolates one of the most salient features of Richer's methodology: his attempts to reimagine the circumstances of historical actors and explain their motivations to the reader.

Nowhere is his nuanced approach to elucidating motives clearer than in book 4, which deals with the polarizing events of the years 987 to 995. Here are recounted the coronation of Hugh Capet (987), the rebellion of Charles of Lotharingia (988–991), Arnulf's betrayal of the city of Rheims to Charles (989), and Adalbero of Laon's betrayal and capture of Charles and Arnulf (991). The perspective in these chapters is not that of a partisan or a polemicist; with few exceptions Richer avoids assigning praise or blame directly.[2] The virtues that qualify Hugh Capet to be king and the vices that disqualify Charles, for example, are put into the mouth of Adalbero of Rheims (4.11), not stated directly. Charles is twice referred to as *tyrannus,* but in both cases the perspective seems to be Hugh's

1. R. G. Collingwood, *The Idea of History,* rev. ed. (Oxford: Oxford University Press, 1994), 215.

2. The exceptions are his favorable assessment of Robert the Pious at 4.13, his praise of Gerbert at 4.73, and his repeated references to the treachery of Adalbero of Laon. Robert the Pious had been a student of Gerbert, and Adalbero had plotted to take possession of the see of Rheims from him.

rather than the author's.[3] As is typical of his approach, Richer works to clarify *rationes negotiorum* in such a way that his own loyalties remain murky. Charles's disappointment at the prospect of being passed over for the throne (4.9) and his grief at Hugh's coronation (4.14) are dramatized in two rhetorically effective speeches. Although Hugh receives handsome praise from Adalbero at the council at Senlis, his conscience accuses him of having despoiled Charles of an inheritance to which he was entitled (4.39). Even Arnulf's decision to break his oath to Hugh and Robert and throw his support behind Charles is couched in sympathetic terms:

> Although [Arnulf] had now advanced to a position of prominence by virtue of the prestigious office that he occupied, he nonetheless regarded it as a stroke of misfortune that he had no one left to him out of his father's family except for Charles. He thought it deplorable that Charles should be deprived of honor, when he remained the only hope for the restoration of his father's line. Arnulf pitied his uncle; he thought about him; he treated him with affection; and he cherished him as his dearest relative in place of his own parents. And after entering into deliberations with Charles, he sought to find a way to advance him to the height of power without seeming to be a traitor to the king.[4]

Later Richer goes to great lengths to show how Adalbero of Laon, a truly villainous figure who schemes to depose Hugh Capet and occupy Gerbert's see, wormed his way into Arnulf's confidence in order to betray him and Charles. This is not to suggest that Richer wrote from the perspective of a neutral observer. However understandable Arnulf's motivations, there is no suggestion in the *Historia* that he is anything but an oath breaker who is unworthy to occupy the see of Rheims. But the lack of a more obvious partisan slant in these chapters raises a question that is crucial to our understanding of Richer's whole historical enterprise: What view of the past was Richer trying to communicate, and for whom?

As we have seen, there is little to suggest that he wrote in an

3. *Historia* 4.18, 4.37; See Hoffmann, "Die *Historien* Richers von Saint-Remi," 478–79.

4. *Historia* 4.32.

effort to legitimate Carolingian or Capetian claims to the throne, for his perspective is not that of a dynastic loyalist. He begins by alluding twice to the inferiority of Odo's bloodlines, repeatedly tars Hugh the Great with the epithet *tyrannus,* depicts Hugh Capet (who is otherwise favorably portrayed) as being conscious of having robbed Charles of Lotharingia of his paternal inheritance, and criticizes Robert the Pious's treachery in reinstating Arnulf in one of the last of the annalistic notices on folio 57^{v}. Charles the Simple is portrayed as frivolous, unwarlike, and lacking in discipline. Louis IV is given favorable treatment, but, like his father, he is unable to bring the rebellious magnates to heel and must be rescued by his brother-in-law Otto. Lothar is an ambiguous figure linked to an act of treachery *(dolus)* against Hugh Capet. Louis V is dissolute and accuses Adalbero of Rheims of treason on baseless grounds, while Charles of Lotharingia (at least according to Adalbero) surrounds himself with unsavory associates and displays none of the qualities requisite in a king.

The ambiguity of Richer's political perspective suggests that he was not writing for an audience united by a common dynastic allegiance. That this audience was composed of the monastic and clerical communities at Rheims can be deduced from several factors: assumed familiarity with, and access to, the works of Hincmar and Flodoard, a focus on the archbishops of Rheims, the detailed and laudatory portraits of Adalbero and Gerbert, and the attention given to Adalbero's trip to Rome to secure a papal guarantee of immunity for Saint-Rémi (3.26–28). Although the evidence is limited, what we know about the monastic and clerical communities at Rheims in the late tenth century suggests a high level of intellectual sophistication. C. Stephen Jaeger has described Saint-Rémi during this period as, "a community of men who define[d] themselves as scholars, poets and statesmen/administrators," and this definition could equally well apply to the secular clergy under Adalbero and Gerbert.[5]

If we consider the *Historia* as a document written to appeal to

5. Jaeger, *The Envy of Angels,* 59.

this particular audience, then certain features of the text become easier to explain. Learning was clearly a valuable commodity both for the monks of Saint-Rémi and the secular clergy of Rheims. For those, like Gerbert, without local connections or kinship networks to further their progress, it could be the only way of rising in the world. Richer's minibiography of Gerbert proves just this point, for at every stage of his career Gerbert owed his advancement to the impression that his knowledge of the liberal arts made on powerful patrons. In the supposedly egalitarian world of the monastery knowledge could also be a means of differentiating oneself from the rest of the community, marking out those who possessed it for special responsibilities and promotion. If learning was a means of winning repute, then writing was the most tangible way of demonstrating that learning, and the *Historia* is filled with subtle and not-so-subtle indications of the author's knowledge. Viewed in that light, Richer's technical descriptions of diseases and siege engines, the attention he lavishes on Gerbert's curriculum and his disputation with Otric (in a manner that implies his own familiarity with the more intricate aspects of these subjects), his stylistic boasting and dramatization of his own *aviditas discendi* seem less like idiosyncrasies and more like a calculated strategy of intellectual self-representation.

The political views of this audience also clearly shaped the way in which Richer wrote about the history of tenth-century West Francia. The dangerous consequences of civil disorder, both for the church and for the kingdom as a whole, were a preoccupation for Gerbert, and were brought home to the clergy and monks of Rheims in brutal fashion after the sack of the city by Charles of Lotharingia's army in October 988. In a letter to Archbishop Willigis of Mainz written on behalf of Adalbero in March 984, Gerbert poses the rhetorical question: "[W]hat else is the disturbance of kingdoms but the desolation of churches?"[6] In April of the fol-

6. Letter 27 (Riché and Callu, 1.54): "Regnorum perturbatio, quid aliud est quam ecclesiarum desolatio?" See also letter 39 (1.94–97) written in Adalbero's name to Notker of Liège in late 984/early 985.

lowing year, writing to Theophanu, wife of Otto II, he declares that "discord among the nobility [*principum dissensio*] is the death of kingdoms."[7] In two letters, one to Remi of Trier, and the other to his former teacher, Raymond of Aurillac, he comments bitterly on the pillaging of Charles's troops.[8]

It is not surprising, therefore, that in the moral world evoked by the *Historia* the supreme political good is *concordia,* which is guaranteed by a strong and legitimate king. The greatest threat to a kingdom is *discordia,* which results from the acquisitive nature of the great men *(principes, primates, optimates);* from *invidia,* envy of what one's social rivals possess; and from *indignatio,* resentment at perceived slights to one's status. Discord among the leading men *(dissidentia principum)* is a recurring motif. In the very first chapter of the *narratio* proper Viking raiders invade Francia because, in the absence of a clear ruler, the magnates are each trying to get the better of one another, and the realm has collapsed into "complete disunity" *(summam discordiam).*[9] In book 2, Hugh the Great justifies his proposal to bring Louis IV back from England and crown him king on the grounds that "contempt for the king, and, as a result, discord among the leading men [*principum dissensus*]" flourished during Radulf's rule.[10] A year after Louis succeeds to the throne, Magyar raiders plunder towns, estates, and fields and burn churches, but they are allowed to retire unpunished "because of discord among the princes."[11] Richer learned of the Magyar raid from the 937 entry in Flodoard's *Annals,* but, significantly, he added the explanatory clause *ob principum dissidentiam* himself. Gislebert of Lotharingia, who fought against Charles the Simple in Lotharingia, and Heribert of Vermandois, who proved to be a continual thorn in the side of Charles, Radulf, and Louis IV, are

7. Letter 52 (Riché and Callu, 1.126–28): "Sed quia principum dissensio interitus regnorum est, principum vestrorum concordia remedium tantorum malorum nobis fore videtur."

8. Letters 162 and 163 (Riché and Callu, 2.402–3, 404–7).

9. *Historia* 1.4.

10. *Historia* 2.2.

11. *Historia* 2.7.

portrayed not merely as tyrants, but as fomenters of discord.[12] In book 3, when the ambassadors of King Lothar arrive at the court of Otto II to discuss peace terms between the two kings, both sides deliver speeches in which they condemn *dissidentia* as the cause of ruin for a state and praise the benefits of *concordia* and *amicitia.*[13] Shortly after his own coronation, Hugh Capet seeks to have his son Robert anointed king because he knows that after his death *discordia primatum* could lead to "the tyranny of the wicked against good men and, as a result, the captivity of all the people."[14] The references to *dissensus, dissidentia,* and *dissensio* in the *Historia* and in Gerbert's letters point to a fundamental anxiety about the fragmentation of royal power, and Richer's focus on the "conflicts" *(congressus)* and "disturbances" *(tumultus)* of the Gauls may reflect the unease among the clergy and monks of Rheims over the state of West-Frankish politics and the level of violence, particularly against church lands. In other words, this was an audience that would have been inclined to put a higher premium on peace, security, and the interests of their own institutions than dynastic loyalty.

The *Historia* can thus be read in part as the response of a monastic chronicler to violence unchecked by royal authority in the late tenth century. The degree to which the proliferation of castles, the devolution of power from counts to castellans, and the predatory nature of lordship in this period warrant the title of "Feudal Transformation" or "Feudal Revolution" is an open question.[15] Clearly, how-

12. See *Historia* 1.35, 1.47, 2.22, 2.37.

13. *Historia* 3.79.

14. *Historia* 4.12.

15. The bibliography on this topic is vast. For an analysis of this question from a pro-"mutationist" point of view, see Jean-Pierre Poly and Eric Bournazel, *The Feudal Transformation, 900–1200,* trans. Caroline Higgitt (New York: Holmes & Meier, 1991). For the main contours of the argument on each side, see the debate between Thomas Bisson and Dominique Barthélemy and Stephen D. White in *Past and Present:* Bisson, "The Feudal Revolution," *Past and Present* 142 (February 1994): 6–42; Barthélemy and White, "The 'Feudal' Revolution," *Past and Present* 152 (1996): 196–223. For clerical and popular responses, see Thomas Head and Richard Landes, eds., *The Peace of God: Social Violence and Religious Response in France around the Year 1000* (Ithaca, N.Y.: Cornell University Press, 1992).

ever, when Richer was writing, public order and royal justice in West Francia were in decline. As the power of the West-Frankish monarchy waned and counts began to lose control of the countryside to their former vassals, alienation and plundering of church lands was one of the consequences. Monks and clerics responded to this violence with frequent and vehement denunciations, and the *Historia* reflects this perspective.[16]

Criticism of the West-Frankish kings for their failure to stem this mayhem is at most implicit, however. Rather than complaining openly about the ineffectiveness of royal authority, Richer expends most of his effort portraying the quarreling and treachery of the nobility. In an important article analyzing the changing conceptions of lordship in this period, Thomas Bisson speaks of a "crisis of fidelity" and suggests that Richer's interest in scenes of treachery and betrayal resulted from his awareness of the increasing breakdown in obligations of fidelity.[17] Bisson calls attention to the fact that two spectacular examples of betrayal—those perpetrated by Walo of Melun against Burchard of Vendôme and by Adalbero of Laon against Charles of Lotharingia and Arnulf of Rheims—both occurred in the year 991, the year that Gerbert became archbishop of Rheims and the *terminus post quem* for the *Historia*.[18]

Bisson's hypothesis—that Richer looked at all of tenth-century West-Frankish history through a lens colored by the betrayals and domestic discord that he lived through—is persuasive. But is any

16. See Elisabeth Magnou-Nortier, "The Enemies of the Peace: Reflections on a Vocabulary, 500–1100," in Head and Landes, eds., *The Peace of God*, 58–79. In arguing for the distinctive nature of violence in the late tenth century, Bisson ("The Feudal Revolution," 40) cites the anonymous chronicler of Mouzon about conditions in the diocese of Rheims in the 970s: "While justice sleeps in the hearts of kings and princes, strong men agitated against [the archbishop] . . . [and] they began, each as he could, to make himself greater." See Michel Bur, ed., *Chronique, ou, Livre de fondation du Monastère de Mouzon* (Paris: Éditions du Centre national de la recherche scientifique, 1989), 152.

17. "The Feudal Revolution," *Past and Present* 142 (1994): 6–42.

18. "The Feudal Revolution," 25.

consistent message to be gleaned from these many acts of faithlessness? Does the traitor get his just desserts in the *Historia?* In many cases the answer is yes. The first major act of political betrayal is Robert of Neustria's rebellion against Charles the Simple, which ultimately results in Robert's death at the Battle of Soissons (1.46). Robert's son Hugh later admits that his father had acted unjustly in overthrowing Charles (2.3). Arnulf of Rheims and Charles of Lotharingia are both imprisoned by Hugh, and Charles dies in captivity (4.49). Between these major rebellions Richer describes numerous acts of treachery, and often remarks upon the consequences for the betrayer. Winemar, the murderer of Fulk of Rheims, is afflicted with a horrible disease as punishment for his crime and, deprived of last rites, he is "driven from this life a sinner and a perpetrator of sacrilege" (1.18). Count Adelelm of Arras and the anonymous cleric who scheme together to take over the town of Noyon are cut down inside a church by the enraged citizens (1.63). Walo, the castellan of Château-Thierry who betrays the fortress to Heribert of Vermandois, is put in chains by Heribert (2.7). The fate of Robert, the guard who betrays Montreuil to Arnulf of Flanders, is not specified, but when Erluin retakes Montreuil with the help of William Longsword, he puts many of Arnulf's men to the sword, and the luckless Robert may have been among them (2.14). Walter, the castellan who hands over Melun to Odo of Blois, is hanged alongside his wife outside the gates of the castle (4.78). Adalbero of Laon's most notable act of treachery, his betrayal of Arnulf and Charles to Hugh Capet in March 991, does not, in Richer's telling, have any immediate adverse consequences for him. Later, however, Richer describes how Adalbero hatches a plot with Count Odo of Blois and Otto III of Germany to take Hugh Capet and his son Robert captive and install Otto on the throne instead.[19] Hugh and

19. Odo was to become "Duke of the Franks," and Adalbero was to receive the archbishopric of Rheims. For Adalbero's involvement in this plot, see Coolidge, "Adalbero, Bishop of Laon," 54–61, and *Historia* 4.96–98. At 4.96 Richer writes that Adalbero of Laon and Odo of Blois intended to put on the throne a certain "O," whom Coolidge takes to be Charles of Lotharingia's youngest son, Otto, the duke

Robert are informed of the plot in advance, however, and Richer describes a scene in which the kings' guards confront Adalbero and accuse him of treachery (4.96–97). When one of Adalbero's vassals volunteers to fight a judicial duel on his behalf, he is warned by Count Landry of Nevers to ask his master whether he is really innocent or not (4.98). Questioned by his loyal vassal, Adalbero is forced to confess his wrongdoing, whereupon he is imprisoned by Hugh and Robert and deprived of his vassals.[20]

Given the frequency of these scenes of betrayal, and the detail in which Richer narrates them, he may have intended to make an ethical point about faithlessness and its consequences. But it would be a stretch to suppose that he shared the view articulated by Bede, and echoed by Hincmar in the preface to his *Vita Remigii,* that it was "a true law of history that what is gathered from public rumor should be committed to writing for the instruction of posterity."[21] Richer never alludes to instruction as a goal of his work, nor does he refer to the moral-exemplary utility of history as a storehouse of examples to imitate and avoid. The didactic utility of the *Historia* is also limited by the scarcity of explicit authorial commentary. Richer does not directly inveigh against disloyalty, dissension, and treachery, and his dramatization of scenes of betrayal can even be read as a somewhat cynical use of immoral behavior to entertain his audience.[22]

---

of Lower Lotharingia. Hoffmann, Historiae, 297n5, following Kienast, suspects that the reference is to Otto III of Germany.

20. Richer's portrait of Adalbero of Laon as a treacherous schemer may derive partially from the mutual hostility between Adalbero and Gerbert, which was only exacerbated by Adalbero's plot with Odo (an enemy of Gerbert) to acquire the see of Rheims for himself. See Coolidge, "Adalbero, Bishop of Laon," 54–56, and *Historia* 4.104 (Gerbert's speech at the synod of Mouzon): "Silent equidem leges inter arma quibus ille feralis bestia O[do] ita abusus est."

21. *Vita Remigii,* preface, 253: "vera est lex hystoriae simpliciter ea que fama vulgante colligitur ad instructionem posteritatis litteris commendare." Hincmar is quoting from the preface to Bede's *Historia Ecclesiastica.* For an analysis of what Bede means by *vera lex historiae,* see Roger Ray, "Bede's *Vera Lex Historiae,*" *Speculum* 55 (1980): 1–21.

22. Hoffmann, "Die *Historien* Richers von Saint-Remi," 504: "Wie immer bei Richer ist man der chronique scandaleuse näher als der Tragödie."

Richer's view of history was neither providential, nor apocalyptic, nor openly didactic. Nor did he write in the service of any contemporary political faction. To the extent that he can be said to have created a useful past, the beneficiary was Gerbert. Yet we might well wonder how useful the *Historia* would have been to Gerbert in practical terms. It may be the case that Richer, or Gerbert, or both, envisioned the text circulating among neutral parties inside and outside of Rheims and influencing opinions there. But if the principal goal of the work was the promotion of Gerbert's claims to the see of Rheims, then it is hard to explain why the pro-Gerbertian material is subsumed within a much larger narrative about the wars of the West-Frankish kings. Rather than designating these sections of the text as propaganda, a problematically anachronistic term when dealing with the early Middle Ages, it is probably more accurate to view them as encomium.[23] Whereas the goal of the propagandist is the widespread diffusion of the writer's tendentious point of view to outside parties, the primary goal of the encomiast is to earn the gratitude and patronage of his subject. The *Historia* looks very much like insider-literature, written primarily for a coterie that was already favorably inclined toward Adalbero and Gerbert.

Whether or not Richer wrote at Gerbert's request is an open question. The ubiquity of the topos of commission, and its usefulness to authors even when no commission actually existed, caution us not to accept Richer's claim in the prologue at face value. What is clear is that the *Historia*—a work that distinguishes itself from all prior Rheims historiography by virtue of its reliance on the techniques of rhetorical invention—was a product of Gerbert's intellectual influence.[24] Richer's boast of a *longe diversum orationis scema,* his composition of formal orations, his focus on explicating motives rather than overt moralizing, and his adherence to

23. For the problems associated with using the term "propaganda" to describe history in the tenth century, see Felice Lifshitz, "Dudo's Historical Narrative and the Norman Succession of 996," *Journal of Medieval History* 20 (1994): 101–20.

24. See Lake, "Truth, Plausibility, and the Virtues of Narrative."

the standard of *narratio probabilis* are all features of a new type of history dependent on classical models and Ciceronian doctrine. At the same time that Richer was writing, similar literary projects were being carried out at Fleury, where Aimoin was reworking his Merovingian-era sources in the *Gesta Francorum*, a work studded with formal orations and allusions to Hegesippus, and in the Vermandois, where Dudo of Saint-Quentin was laboring over the rhetorically ostentatious *Gesta Normannorum*. That these works were all written by authors educated in the schools of northern Francia in the late tenth century is not a coincidence; this period witnessed a revival of interest in Ciceronian rhetoric that would give rise in the early eleventh century to the first new commentaries on the *De inventione* and the *Rhetorica ad Herennium* since late antiquity.[25]

Stylistic innovation, therefore, was part of the raison d'etre of the *Historia*. In the absence of any overarching plot or consistent political agenda we need not seek to impose a spurious unity on the text. Richer's goal was to create a narrative history where none existed before. Rather than using the past as a form of political commentary on the present, the *Historia* was an attempt to explain and dramatize the history of the previous century through the techniques of rhetorical invention in a manner that would accord with the beliefs of its intended audience.

25. See Ward, *Ciceronian Rhetoric*, 90. For the proliferation of manuscripts of the *De inventione* and *Rhetoria* ad *Herennium* beginning in the tenth century, see Munk Olsen, *L'étude des auteurs classiques latins aux XIe et XIIe siècles*, 1.127–29. For the eleventh-century commentary tradition, see Ward, "Cicero's *De inventione* and the *Rhetorica ad Herennium*," 23–50 and 70–75, and Ward, "From Antiquity to the Renaissance," 37–38.

Bibliography

Manuscript Sources

Bamberg, Staatsbibliothek, MS Hist. 5

Bamberg, Staatsbibliothek, MS Class. 25

Bamberg, Staatsbibliothek, MS Class. 39

London, British Library, MS Royal 15A.XXXIII

Editions of Richer

Hoffmann, Hartmut. *Richer von Saint-Remi: Historiae.* MGH SS 38. Hanover: Hahn, 2000.

Latouche, Robert. *Richer, Histoire de France (885–995).* Les classiques de l'histoire de France au moyen âge. 2 vols. Paris: H. Champion, 1930 and 1937.

Pertz, G. H. *Richeri historiarum libri IIII.* MGH SS 3, 561–657. Hanover: Hahn 1839.

Waitz, Georg. *Richeri historiarum libri IIII.* MGH SRG 51. Hanover: Hahn, 1877.

Original Sources: Texts and Translations

Abbo of Fleury. *Vita S. Eadmundi.* Edited and translated by Michael Winterbottom. In *ThreeLives of English Saints.* Toronto: Pontifical Institute for Medieval Studies, 1972.

Acta concilii Mosomensis. Ernst-Dieter Hehl. MGH Concilia 6.1.495–507. Hanover: Hahn, 2007.

Acta concilii Remensis ad sanctum Basolum. Edited by Ernst-Dieter Hehl. MGH Concilia 6.2.380–469. Hanover: Hahn, 2007.

Adalbero of Laon. *Carmen ad Rotbertum regem.* Edited and translated by Claude Carozzi. In *Adalbéron de Laon: Poème au roi Robert.* Paris: Les Belles Lettres, 1979.

Ademar of Chabannes. *Chronicon.* Edited by P. Bourgain. CCCM 129. Turnhout, Belgium: Brepols, 1999.

Adso of Montier-en-Der. *Opera Hagiographica.* Edited by Monique Goullet. CCCM 198. Turnhout: Brepols, 2003.

Aimoin of Fleury. *Gesta Francorum.* Edited by André Duchesne. *Historiae*

Francorum Scriptores coaetanei 3.120. Paris: S. Cramoisy, 1641. Reprinted in *PL* 139.627–798.

Annales Bertiniani. Edited by Felix Grat, Jeanne Vielliard, and Suzanne Clémencet. La société de l'histoire de France. Paris: Librairie C. Klincksieck, 1964.

The Annals of St-Bertin. Translated with an introduction and notes by Janet Nelson. Manchester: Manchester University Press, 1991.

Annales regni Francorum. Edited by F. Kurze. MGH SRG 6. Hanover: Hahn, 1895.

Annales Vedastini. Edited by B. de Simson. MGH SRG 12. Hanover: Hahn, 1909.

Annales Vindocinenses. Edited by Louis Halphen. Recueil d'annales angevines et vendômoises, 50–79. Paris: Picard, 1903.

Augustine. *De doctrina christiana*. Edited by K.-D. Daur and J. Martin. CCSL 32. Turnhout, Belgium: Brepols, 1962.

———. *Enarrationes in Psalmos*. Edited by E. Dekkers and J. Fraipont. CCSL 38–40. Turnhout, Belgium: Brepols, 1956.

Bede. *Expositio Actuum apostolorum*. Edited by M. L. W. Laistner and D. Hurst. CCSL 121. Turnhout, Belgium: Brepols, 1983.

———. *Historia ecclesiastica gentis Anglorum*. Edited by Bertram Colgrave and R. A. B. Mynors. Oxford: Clarendon Press, 1969.

———. *In Tobiam, In Proverbia, In Cantica canticorum, In Habacuc*. Edited by D. Hurst and J. E. Hudson. CCSL 119B. Turnhout, Belgium: Brepols, 1983.

Boethius. *De topicis differentiis*. *PL* 64.1173–1216.

———. *In Ciceronis topica*. *PL* 64.1039–1174.

———. *In Isagogen Porphyrii commenta*. Edited by Samuel Brandt. CSEL 48. Vienna: F. Tempsky, 1906.

Cassiodorus. *Historia ecclesiastica tripartita*. Edited by W. Jacob and R. Hanslik. CSEL 71. Vienna: Hoelder-Pichler-Tempsky, 1952.

———. *Institutiones*. Edited by R. A. B. Mynors. Oxford: Clarendon Press, 1961.

Chronicon Virdunense. Edited by G. H. Pertz. MGH SS 8.280–503. Hanover: Hahn, 1848.

Chronique de Mouzon. Edited by Michel Bur. Paris: Éditions du Centre national de la recherche scientifique, 1989.

Cicero. *De inventione*. Edited by E. Stroebel. Stuttgart: Teubner, 1965.

———. *De inventione; De optimo genere oratorum; Topica*. Translated by H. M. Hubbell. Loeb Classical Library. Cambridge, Mass.: Harvard University Press, 1949.

———. *De oratore*. Edited by A. S. Wilkins. Oxford: Clarendon Press, 1902.

———. *Partitiones oratoriae*. Edited by A. S. Wilkins. Oxford: Clarendon Press, 1903.

———. *Topica*. Edited by A. S. Wilkins. Oxford: Clarendon Press, 1903.

Cicero [pseud.]. *Rhetorica ad Herennium*. Edited by F. Marx. Leipzig: Teubner, 1964.

[Incipit] "Constantine, meis opus est non promere verbis." Edited by H. Hagen. In *Carmina medii aevi maximam partem inedita ex bibliothecis Helveticis collecta*, 130–34. Bern, 1877. Reprint, Hildesheim, Germany: Georg Olms, 1975.

[Incipit] "Convenio signis quem convenisse loquelis." Edited by H. Hagen. In *Carmina medii aevi maximam partem inedita ex bibliothecis Helveticis collecta*, 134–36. Bern, 1877. Reprint, Hildesheim, Germany: Georg Olms, 1975.

Cosmas of Prague. *Chronica Boemorum*. Edited by Berthold Bretholz. MGH SRG n.s. 2. Berlin: Weidmann, 1923.

Disticha Catonis. Edited by Marcus Boas and H. J. Botschuyver. Amsterdam: North-Holland Publishing Co., 1952.

Dudo of Saint-Quentin. *Gesta Normannorum*. Edited by Jules Lair. *De moribus et actis primorum Normanniae ducum*. Paris: Derache, 1861.

———. *Dudo of St. Quentin: History of the Normans*. Translated with an introduction and notes by Eric Christiansen. Woodbridge, U.K.: Boydell Press, 1998.

Einhard. *Vita Karoli Magni*. Edited by Oswald Holder-Egger. MGH SRG 25. Hanover: Hahn, 1911.

Ekkehard IV. *Casus Sancti Galli*. Edited by Hans F. Haefele. Darmstadt: Wissenschaftliche Buchgesellschaft, 2002.

Flodoard. *Annales*. Edited by Philippe Lauer. *Les Annales de Flodoard*. Collection de textes pour servir à l'étude et à l'enseignement de l'histoire. Paris: Alphonse Picard, 1905.

———. *The "Annals" of Flodoard of Reims (919–966)*. Translated by Bernard Bachrach and Steven Fanning. Peterborough, Ont.: Broadview Press, 2004.

———. *De Triumphis Christi*. *PL* 135.491–886.

———. *Historia Remensis Ecclesiae*. Edited by Martina Stratmann. MGH SS 36. Hanover: Hahn, 1998.

Folcuin of Lobbes. *Gesta abbatum Lobiensium*. Edited by G. H. Pertz. MGH SS 4.52–74. Hanover: Hahn 1841.

———. *Gesta abbatum S. Bertini Sithiensium*. Edited by O. Holder-Egger. MGH SS 13.607–35. Hanover: Hahn, 1881.

Fulbert of Chartres. Letters. Edited and translated by Frederick Behrends. *The Letters and Poems of Fulbert of Chartres*. Oxford: Clarendon Press, 1976.

Gerbert of Aurillac. *De rationali et ratione uti*. *PL* 139.159–68.

———. Letters. Edited by Pierre Riché and J.-P. Callu. *Gerbert d'Aurillac: Correspondance*. Les classiques de l'histoire de France au moyen âge. 2 vols. Paris: Les Belles Lettres, 1993.

———. *The Letters of Gerbert with His Papal Privileges as Sylvester II.* Translated with an introduction and notes by Harriet Pratt Lattin. New York: Columbia University Press, 1961.

———. Mathematical Works. Edited by N. Bubnov. *Gerberti Opera Mathematica.* Berlin: R. Friedländer, 1899.

Gregory the Great. *Moralia in Job.* Edited by Marcus Adriaen. CCSL 143, 143A, 143B. Turnhout, Belgium: Brepols, 1979–1985.

Grillius. *Commentum in Ciceronis Rhetorica.* Edited by Rainer Jakobi. Leipzig: Teubner, 2002.

Guibert of Nogent. *Memoirs.* Translated by John F. Benton. *Self and Society in Medieval France.* Toronto: University of Toronto Press, 1984.

Hegesippus [pseud.] *Bellum Iudaicum.* Edited by Vincenzo Ussani. CSEL 66. Vienna: Hoelder- Pichler-Tempsky, 1932.

Helgaud of Fleury. *Epitoma vitae regis Rotberti Pii.* Edited and translated by Robert-Henri Bautier and Gillette Labory. Paris: Éditions du Centre national de la recherche scientifique, 1965.

Henry of Huntington. *Historia Anglorum.* Edited and translated by Diana Greenway. Oxford: Oxford University Press, 1996.

Hincmar of Rheims. *Vita Remigii.* Edited by Bruno Krusch. MGH SSRM 3.239–341. Hanover: Hahn, 1896.

———. *De divortio Lotharii regis et Tetbergae reginae. PL*125.619–772.

Historia Francorum Senonensis. Edited by G. Waitz. MGH SS 9.364–69. Hanover: Hahn, 1851.

Hrabanus Maurus. *Carmina.* Edited by Ernst Dümmler. MGH Poetae 2.154–258. Berlin: Weidmann, 1884.

———. *Commentaria in Libros Machabaeorum. PL* 109.1125–1256.

———. *Commentariorum in Genesim libri quatuor. PL* 107.439–670.

———. *De institutione clericorum libri tres.* Edited by Detlev Zimpel. Freiburger Beiträge zur mittelalterlichen Geschichte: Studien und Texte herausgegeben von Hubert Mordek 7. Frankfurt: Peter Lang, 1996.

———. *Epistola dedicatoria ad Fridurichum Episcopum Trajectensem. PL* 108.999–1002.

———. *Praefatio ad Hunbertum Episcopum dictata. PL* 108.1109–10.

Hrotsvita of Gandersheim. *Opera omnia.* Edited by Walter Berschin. Leipzig: Teubner, 2001.

Hugh of Flavigny. *Chronicon.* Edited by G. H. Pertz. MGH SS 8.80–503. Hanover: Hahn, 1848.

Isidore of Seville. *Etymologiarum sive originum libri XX.* Edited by W. M. Lindsay. 2 vols. Oxford: Clarendon Press, 1957 and 1962.

Jean de Marmoutier. *Historia Gaufredi Ducis Normannorum et Comitis Andegavorum.* Edited by Louis Halphen and Rene Poupardin. In *Chroniques des comtes d'Anjou et des seigneurs d'Amboise,* 172–231. Paris: A. Picard, 1913.

John of Salisbury. *Metalogicon*. Translated by Daniel D. McGarry. *The Metalogicon of John of Salisbury: A Twelfth-Century Defense of the Verbal and Logical Arts of the Trivium*. Gloucester, Mass.: Peter Smith, 1971.

Leonis abbatis et legati ad Hugonem et Rotbertum reges epistola. Edited by G. H. Pertz. MGH SS 3.686–90. Hanover: Hahn, 1839.

Liudprand of Cremona. *Opera*. Edited by P. Chiesa. CCCM 156. Turnhout: Brepols, 1998.

Martianus Capella. *De nuptiis Philologiae et Mercurii*. Edited by James Willis. Leipzig: Teubner, 1983.

Necrologium Ecclesiae Remensis. Edited by P. Varin. Archives législatives de la ville de Reims 2.1.62–105. Paris: Crapelet, 1844.

Notker Labeo. *De arte rhetorica*. Edited by James C. King and Petrus W. Tax. *Notker der Deutsche: Die kleineren Schriften* 7. Tübingen: Max Niemeyer Verlag, 1996.

Odo of Saint-Maur. *Vita domni Burcardi*. Edited by Charles Bourel de la Roncière. *Vie de Bouchard le Vénérable, comte de Vendôme, de Corbeil, de Melun et de Paris (Xe et XIe siècles) par Eudes de Saint-Maur*. Paris: Alphonse Picard, 1892.

Paul the Deacon. *Historia Romana*. Edited by H. Droysen. MGH SRG 49. Munich: Weidmann, 1879.

Peter the Venerable. Letters. Edited by Giles Constable. *The Letters of Peter the Venerable*. 2 vols. Cambridge, Mass.: Harvard University Press, 1967.

Quintilian. *Institutio Oratoria*. Edited and translated by Donald A. Russell. 5 vols. Loeb Classical Library. Cambridge, Mass.: Harvard University Press, 2001.

Regino of Prüm. *Chronicon*. Edited by F. Kurze. *Reginonis abbatis Prumiensis Chronicon cum continuatione Treverensi*. MGH SRG 50. Hanover: Hahn, 1890.

———. *History and Politics in Late Carolingian and Ottonian Europe: The Chronicle of Regino of Prüm and Adalbert of Magdeburg*. Translated with an introduction and notes by Simon MacLean. Manchester: Manchester University Press, 2009.

Regula Benedicti. Edited by Timothy Fry et al. *RB 1980: The Rule of St. Benedict in Latin and English with Notes*. Collegeville, Minn.: Liturgical Press, 1981.

Remigius of Auxerre. *Commentum in Martianum Capellam*. Edited by Cora E. Lutz. 2 vols. Leiden: Brill, 1962 and 1965.

Rodulf Glaber. *Historiarum libri quinque*. Edited and translated by John France. In *Rodulfus Glaber: Opera*. Oxford: Clarendon Press, 1989.

———. *Vita domni Willelmi abbatis*. Edited by Neithard Bulst. Translated by John France and Paul Reynolds. In *Rodulfus Glaber: Opera*. Oxford: Clarendon Press, 1989.

Sallust, *Bellum Catilinae and Bellum Iugurthinum*. Edited by L. D. Reynolds. Oxford: Clarendon Press, 1991.

———. *Sallust*. Edited and translated by John C. Rolfe. Revised edition. Loeb Classical Library. Cambridge, Mass.: Harvard University Press, 1931.

Terence. *Comoediae*. Edited by R. Kauer and W. M. Lindsay. Oxford: Clarendon Press, 1958.

Thegan. *Gesta Hludowici imperatoris*. Edited by Ernst Tremp. MGH SRG 64. Hanover: Hahn, 1995.

Thietmar of Merseberg. *Chronicon*. Edited by Robert Holtzmann. MGH SRG, n.s. 9. Berlin: Weidmann, 1935.

Trithemius, Johannes. *Annales Hirsaugienses*. Saint-Gallen, Switzerland, 1690.

Victorinus, Marius. *Explanationes in Ciceronis rhetoricam*. Edited by A. Ippolito. CCSL 132. Turnhout, Belgium: Brepols, 2006.

Vita Mathildis reginae antiquior. Edited by Bernd Schütte. *Die Lebensbeschreibungen der Königin Mathilde*. MGH SRG 66.109–42. Hanover: Hahn, 1994.

Walter of Speyer. *Libellus scolasticus*. Edited by Peter Vossen. *Der Libellus Scolasticus des Walther von Speyer: Ein Schulbericht aus dem Jahre 984*. Berlin: Walter de Gruyter, 1962.

Widukind of Corvey. *Rerum Gestarum Saxonicarum libri tres*. Edited by Paul Hirsch and Hans Eberhard Lohmann. MGH SRG 60. Hanover: Hahn, 1935.

Wipo. *Gesta Chuonradi imperatoris*. Edited by H. Bresslau. MGH SRG 61. Hanover: Hahn, 1915.

Secondary Sources

Althoff, Gerd. *Otto III*. Translated by Phyllis G. Jestice. University Park: Penn State University Press, 2003.

Amundsen, Darrel W. "Medieval Canon Law on Medical and Surgical Practice by the Clergy." *Bulletin of the History of Medicine* 52 (1978): 22–44.

Auerbach, Erich. *Mimesis: The Representation of Reality in Western Literature*. Translated by Willard R. Trask. Princeton, N.J.: Princeton University Press, 1953.

———. *Literary Language and Its Public in Late Latin Antiquity and in the Middle Ages*. Translated by Ralph Manheim. With a new foreword by Jan M. Ziolkowski. Princeton, N.J.: Princeton University Press, 1993.

Bachrach, Bernard. "The Practical Use of Vegetius' *De Re Militari* during the Early Middle Ages." *The Historian* 47 (1985): 239–55.

Bachrach, David. "Conforming with the Rhetorical Tradition of Plausibility: Clerical Representation of Battlefield Orations against Muslims, 1080–1170." *International History Review* 26 (2004): 1–19.

Bardot, Georges, "Remarques sur un passage de Richer." In *Mélanges carolingiens,* ed. G. Bardot, P. Pouzet, and A. Breyton. Bibl. de la Faculté des Lettres de Lyon 7 (Paris: Ernest Leroux, 1890), 1–39.

Barth, Rüdiger E. *Der Herzog in Lotharingien im 10. Jahrhundert.* Sigmaringen: Jan Thorbecke, 1990.

Barthélemy, Dominique, and Stephen D. White. "The 'Feudal' Revolution." *Past and Present* 152 (1996): 196–223.

Becker, Gustav. *Catalogi bibliothecarum antiqui.* Hildesheim, Germany: Georg Olms, 1973.

Becker, Phillipp August. "Der planctus auf den Normannenherzog Wilhelm Langschwert (942)." *Zeitschrift für französische Sprache und Literatur* 63 (1939): 190–97.

Beer, Jeanette. *Narrative Conventions of Truth in the Middle Ages.* Geneva: Librairie Droz, 1981.

Beumann, Helmut. "Der Schriftsteller und seine Kritiker im frühen Mittelalter." *Studium Generale* 12 (1959): 497–511.

———. "Topos und Gedankengefüge bei Einhard." *Archiv für Kulturgeschichte* 33 (1951): 337–50.

Bezzola, Gian Andria. *Das Ottonische Kaisertum in der französischen Geschichtsschreibung des 10. und beginnenden 11. Jahrhunderts.* Graz and Cologne: Hermann Böhlau, 1956.

Bisson, Thomas N. "The Feudal Revolution." *Past and Present* 142 (1994): 6–42.

Böhmer, J. F., and Harald Zimmerman, eds. *Regesta Imperii,* vol. 2, no. 5: *Papstregesten, 911-1024.* 2nd ed. Vienna: Böhlau, 1998.

Borst, Arno. *Lebensformen im Mittelalter.* Frankfurt: Verlag Ullstein, 1973.

Brinkman, Hennig. "Der Prolog im Mittelalter als literarische Erscheinung: Bau und Aussage." *Wirkendes Wort* 14 (1964): 1–21.

Bromet, A. "Étude sur la langue de Gerbert." *Revue de la Haute-Auvergne* 32 (1949): 217–230; 33 (1952): 91–109.

Brühl, Carlrichard. *Deutschland-Frankreich: Die Geburt zweier Völker.* Cologne and Vienna: Böhlau, 1990.

Buhrer-Thierry, Geneviève. "Le conseiller du roi: Les écrivains carolingiens et la tradition biblique." *Médiévales* 12 (1987): 111–23.

Bur, Michel, ed. *Saint-Thierry, une abbaye du VIe au XXe siècle. Actes du Colloque international d'Histoire monastique Reims-Saint-Thierry, 11 au 14 octobre 1976.* Saint-Thierry: Association des Amis de l'Abbaye de Saint-Thierry, 1979.

———. "A propos de la *Chronique de Mouzon* II: Architecture et liturgie à Reims au temps d'Adalbéron (vers 976)." *Cahiers de civilisation médiévale* 27 (1984): 297–302.

———. "Reims, ville des sacres." In *Le sacre des rois: Actes du colloque in-*

ternational d'histoire sur les sacres et couronnements royaux, Reims 1975 (Paris: Belles Lettres, 1985), 39–48.

———. "Adalbéron, archevêque de Reims, reconsidéré." In *Le roi de France et son royaume autour de l'an Mil: Actes du Colloque Hugues Capet 987–1987, La France de l'an Mil, Paris-Senlis, 22–25 juin 1987*, eds. Michel Parisse and Xavier Barral i Altet (Paris: Picard, 1992), 55–63.

Cardelle de Hartmann, Carmen. "Sallust in St. Emmeram: Handschriften und Kommentare in der Bibliothek des Klosters St. Emmeram (Regensburg)." *Journal of Medieval Latin* 18 (2008): 1–23.

Carey, F. M. "The Scriptorium of Reims during the Archbishopric of Hincmar (845–882 A.D.)." In *Classical and Mediaeval Studies in Honor of E. K. Rand*, ed. L. W. Jones (New York: Published by editor, 1938), 41–60.

Carozzi, Claude. "Gerbert et le concile de Saint-Basle." In *Gerberto, scienza, storia e mito. Atti del Gerberti Symposium 25–27 Iuglio 1983*, ed. M. Tozi (Piacenza: Archivum Bobiense, 1985), 661–76.

Collingwood, R. G. *The Idea of History*. Rev. ed. Oxford: Oxford University Press, 1994.

Constable, Giles. *Letters and Letter-Collections*. Typologie des sources du Moyen Âge occidental 17. Turnhout, Belgium: Brepols, 1976.

———. "An Unpublished Letter by Peter the Venerable to the Priors of Paray-le-Monial, Mesvres, and Luzy in 1147." *Studia Anselmiana* 85 (1982): 207–16.

Contreni, John J. *The Cathedral School of Laon from 850 to 930: Its Manuscripts and Masters*. Munich: Arbeo-Gesellschaft, 1978.

———. "Masters and Medicine in Northern France during the Reign of Charles the Bald." In *Charles the Bald: Court and Kingdom*, ed. Margaret T. Gibson and Janet T. Nelson (Hampshire, U.K.: Variorum, 1990), 267–82.

———. "The Tenth Century: The Perspective from the Schools." In *Haut Moyen-Age: Culture, éducation, et société, études offertes à Pierre Riché*, ed. Claude Lepelley, Michel Sot, and Pierre Riché (Nanterre: Éditions Publidix; La Garenne-Colombes, 1990), 379–87.

Coolidge, Robert T. "Adalbero, Bishop of Laon." *Studies in Medieval and Renaissance History* 2 (1965): 1–114.

Cox, Virginia, and John O. Wards, eds. *The Rhetoric of Cicero in Its Medieval and Early Renaissance Commentary Tradition*. Leiden: Brill, 2006.

Curtius, Ernst Robert. "Dichtung und Rhetorik im Mittelalter." *Deustsche Vierteljahrsschrift für Literaturwissenschaft und Geistesgeschichte* 16 (1938): 435–75.

———. "Zur Literarästhetik des Mittelalters II." *Zeitschrift für Romanische Philologie* 58, nos. 2–3 (1938): 129–232.

———. "Der Archipoeta und der Stil mittellateinischer Dichtung." *Romanische Forschungen* 54 (1940): 105–64.

———. "Mittelalterstudien." *Zeitschrift für Romanische Philologie* 63 (1943): 225–74.

———. *European Literature and the Latin Middle Ages.* Translated by Willard R. Trask. Princeton, N.J.: Princeton University Press, 1990.

Damon, Cynthia. "Rhetoric and Historiography." In *A Companion to Roman Rhetoric,* ed. William Dominik and Jon Hall (Malden, Mass.: Blackwell, 2007), 439–50.

Darlington, Oscar. "Gerbert, the Teacher." *American Historical Review* 52 (1946–1947):456–76.

Davies, Gwyn. *Roman Siege Works.* Stroud, U.K.: Tempus Publishing, 2006.

Deliyannis, Deborah Mauskopf, ed. *Historiography in the Middle Ages.* Leiden: Brill, 2003.

Depreux, Philippe. "Saint Remi et la royauté carolingienne." *Revue historique* 285 (1991): 235–60.

Devisse, Jean. *Hincmar, archevêque de Reims.* 3 vols. Travaux d'histoire ethico-politique 29. Geneva: Librairie Droz, 1976.

Dieter, Otto Alvin Loeb. "The Rhetoric of Notker Labeo." In *Papers in Rhetoric,* ed. Donald C. Bryant (St. Louis: Washington University Press, 1940), 27–43.

Dolbeau, François. "Un catalogue fragmentaire des manuscrits de Saint-Rémi de Reims au xiiie siècle." *Recherches augustiniennes* 23 (1988): 223–43.

Donnat, Lin. "Les coutumes monastiques autour de l'an Mil." In *Religion et culture autour de l'an mil: Royaume capétien et Lotharingie: Actes du colloque Hugues Capet 987–1987, la France de l'an mil, Auxerre, 26 et 27 juin 1987, Metz, 11 et 12 septembre 1987,* ed. Dominique Iogna-Prat and Jean-Charles Picard (Paris: Picard, 1990), 17–24.

Dumas, Auguste. "L'église de Reims au temps des luttes entre Carolingiens et Robertiens (888 –1027)." *Revue d'histoire de l'église de France* 30 (1944): 5–38.

Dümmler, Ernst. *Geschichte des Ostfränkischen Reiches.* 3 vols. Leipzig: Duncker & Humblot, 1887–1888.

Dunbabin, Jean. *France in the Making, 843–1180.* Oxford: Oxford University Press, 1985.

———."West Francia: The Kingdom." In *The New Cambridge Medieval History,* vol. 3, ed. Timothy Reuter (Cambridge: Cambridge University Press, 1999), 372–97.

Eckel, Auguste. *Charles le Simple.* Paris: Émile Bouillon, 1899.

Ehlers, Joachim. "Dom und Klosterschulen in Deutschland und Frankreich im 10. und 11. Jahrhundert." In *Schule und Schüler im Mittelalter. Beiträge zur europäischen Bildungsgeschichte des 9. bis 15. Jahrhunderts,* ed. M. Kintzinger, Sönke Lorenz, and Michael Walter (Cologne: Böhlau Verlag, 1996), 29–52.

Fauvarque, Bertrand. "Le pape Gerbert et l'empereur Otto III." In *Gerbert, moine, évêque et pape: D'un millénaire à l'autre: Actes des journées d'étude, Aurillac, 9–10 avril 1999* (Aurillac: Association cantalienne pour la commémoration du pape Gerbert, 2000), 271–84.

Favre, Édouard. *Eudes, comte de Paris et roi de France (882–898).* Paris: Émile Bouillon, 1893.

Fentress, James, and Christopher Wickham. *Social Memory.* Oxford: Blackwell, 1992.

Fichtenau, Heinrich. *Living in the Tenth Century: Mentalities and Social Orders.* Translated by Patrick J. Geary. Chicago: University of Chicago Press, 1991.

Fleischman, Suzanne. "On the Representation of History and Fiction in the Middle Ages." *History and Theory* 23 (1983): 278–310.

France, John. "La guerre dans la France féodale à la fin du IXe et au Xe siècle." *Revue belge d'histoire militaire* 23 (1979): 177–98.

Ganshof, F. L. *Feudalism.* Translated by Philip Grierson. 1964; reprint, Toronto: University of Toronto Press, 1996.

Gasc, Hélène. "Gerbert et la pédagogie des arts libéraux à la fin du dixième siècle." *Journal of Medieval History* 12 (1986): 111–21.

Geary, Patrick. *Phantoms of Remembrance: Memory and Oblivion at the End of the First Millennium.* Princeton, N.J.: Princeton University Press, 1994.

Gibson, Margaret. "The Continuity of Learning circa 850–circa 1050." *Viator* 6 (1975): 1–13.

———. "Boethius in the Tenth Century." *Mittellateinisches Jahrbuch* 24–25 (1989–1990): 117–24.

Giese, Wolfgang. *"Genus" und "Virtus": Studien zum Geschichtswerk des Richer von St. Remi.* Diss. Munich, 1967. Augsburg: W. Blasaditsch, 1969.

Glauche, Günter. *Schullektüre im Mittelalter.* Münchener Beiträge zur Mediävistik und Renaissance-Forschung 5. Munich: Arbeo-Gesellschaft, 1970.

Glenn, Jason. "The Composition of Richer's Autograph Manuscript." *Revue d'histoire des textes* 27 (1997): 151–89.

———. "The Lost Works of Richer: The *Gesta Adalberonis* and the *Vita Gerberti.*" *Filologia Mediolatina* 4 (1997): 153–90.

———. *Politics and History in the Tenth Century: The Work and World of Richer of Reims.* Cambridge: Cambridge University Press, 2004.

———. "Master and Community in Tenth-Century Reims." In *Teaching and Learning in Northern Europe, 1000–1200,* ed. Sally N. Vaughn and Jay Rubenstein (Turnhout, Belgium: Brepols, 2006), 51–68.

Goetz, Hans-Werner. “Die Gegenwart der Vergangenheit im früh- und hochmittelalterlichen Geschichtsbewußtsein.” *Historische Zeitschrift* 255, no. 1 (1992): 612–97.

———. “Vergangenheitswahrnehmung, Vergangenheitsgebrauch und Geschichtssymbolismus in der Geschichtsschreibung der Karolingerzeit.” *Settimane di Studio* 46 (1999): 177–225.

Goffart, Walter. *The Narrators of Barbarian History (A.D. 550–800): Jordanes, Gregory of Tours, Bede, and Paul the Deacon.* Princeton, N.J.: Princeton University Press, 1988.

Gottlieb, Theodor. *Mittelalterliche Bibliotheken.* Leipzig: Otto Harrassowitz, 1890.

Grundmann, Herbert. “Litteratus-illiteratus: Der Wandel einer Bildungsnorm vom Altertum zum Mittelalter.” *Archiv für Kulturgeschichte* 40 (1958): 1–65.

———. *Geschichtsschreibung im Mittelalter: Gattungen, Epochen, Eigenart.* Göttingen, Germany: Vandenhoeck & Ruprecht, 1965.

Guenée, Bernard. “Histoire, mémoire, écriture. Contribution à une étude des lieux communs.” *Comptes Rendus des Séances de l'Académie des Inscriptions et Belles Lettres* 127 (1983): 441–56.

Guillot, Olivier. “Les étapes de l'accession d'Eudes au pouvoir royal.” In *Media in Francia: Recueil de mélanges offert à Karl Ferdinand Werner,* 199–223. Maulévrier, France: Hérault, 1989.

Guyotjeannin, Olivier. *Episcopus et comes: Affirmation et déclin de la seigneurie épiscopale au nord du royaume de France (Beauvais-Noyon, Xe–début XIIIe siècle).* Geneva: Librairie Droz, 1987.

Hadot, Pierre. *Marius Victorinus. Recherches sur sa vie et ses oeuvres.* Paris: Études augustiniennes, 1971.

Head, Thomas, and Richard Landes, eds. *The Peace of God: Social Violence and Religious Response in France around the Year 1000.* Ithaca, N.Y.: Cornell University Press, 1992.

Healy, Patrick. *The Chronicle of Hugh of Flavigny: Reform and the Investiture Contest in the Late Eleventh Century.* Aldhershot, U.K.: Ashgate, 2006.

Hehl, Ernst-Dieter. “Erzbischof Ruotbert von Trier und der Reimser Streit.” In *Deus qui mutat tempora: Menschen und Institutionen im Wandel des Mittelalters: Festschrift für Alfons Becker zu seinem fünfundsechzigsten Geburtstag,* ed. Ernst-Dieter Hehl, Hubertus Seibert, and Franz Staab (Sigmaringen: Jan Thorbecke, 1987), 55–68.

Hen, Yitzhak, and Matthew Innes. *The Uses of the Past in the Early Middle Ages.* Cambridge: Cambridge University Press, 2000.

Hoffmann, Harmut. *Bamberger Handschriften des 10. und des 11. Jahrhunderts.* MGH Schriften 39. Hanover: Hahn, 1995.

———. "Die *Historien* Richers von Saint-Remi." *Deutsches Archiv für Erforschung des Mittelalters* 54 (1998): 445–532.

———. "Autographa des früheren Mittelalters." *Deutsches Archiv für Erforschung des Mittelalters* 57 (2001): 1–62.

Innes, Matthew. "Memory, Orality, and Literacy in an Early Medieval Society." *Past and Present* 158 (1998): 3–36.

Iogna-Prat, Dominique, and Jean-Charles Picard, eds. *Religion et culture autour de l'an mil: Royaume capétien et Lotharingie : Actes du colloque Hugues Capet 987–1987, la France de l'an mil, Auxerre, 26 et 27 juin 1987, Metz, 11 et 12 septembre 1987.* Paris: Picard, 1990.

Jacobsen, Peter Christian. *Flodoard von Reims: Sein Leben und seine Dichtung "De triumphis Christi."* Mittellateinische Studien und Texte 10. Leiden: Brill, 1978.

Jaeger, C. Stephen. *The Envy of Angels: Cathedral Schools and Social Ideals in Medieval Europe, 950–1200.* Philadelphia: University of Pennsylvania Press, 1994.

Jakobi, Rainer. *Grillius: Überlieferung und Kommentar.* Untersuchungen zur antiken Literatur und Geschichte 77. Berlin: Walter de Gruyter, 2005.

Janson, Tore. *Latin Prose Prefaces: Studies in Literary Conventions.* Studia Latina Stockholmiensia 13. Stockholm: Almquist & Wiksell, 1964.

Kalckstein, Carl von. *Geschichte des französischen Königthums unter den ersten Capetingern.* Vol. 1. Leipzig: T. O. Weigel, 1877.

Kardong, Terence G. *Benedict's Rule: A Translation and Commentary.* Collegeville, Minn.: Liturgical Press, 1996.

Kienast, Walther. *Deutschland und Frankreich in der Kaiserzeit (900–1270).* 3 vols. Stuttgart: Anton Hiersemann, 1974–1975.

Kortüm, Hans-Henning. *Richer von Saint-Remi: Studien zu einem Geschichtsschreiber des 10. Jahrhunderts.* Stuttgart: Franz Steiner Verlag, 1985.

Koziol, Geoffrey. *Begging Pardon and Favor: Ritual and Political Order in Early Medieval France.* Ithaca, N.Y.: Cornell University Press, 1992.

———. "Charles the Simple, Robert of Neustria, and the *Vexilla* of Saint-Denis." *Early Medieval Europe* 14, no. 4 (2006): 355–90.

———. "Is Robert I in Hell? The Diploma for Saint-Denis and the Mind of a Rebel King (Jan. 25, 923)." *Early Medieval Europe* 14, no. 3 (2006): 233–67.

Laffitte, Marie-Pierre. "Esquisse d'une Bibliothèque Médievale: Le Fonds de Manuscrits de l'Abbaye de Saint-Thierry." In *Saint-Thierry, une abbaye du VIe au XXe siècle. Actes du Colloque international d'Histoire monastique Reims-Saint-Thierry, 11 au 14 octobre 1976*, ed. Michel Bur (Saint-Thierry: Association des Amis de l'Abbaye de Saint-Thierry, 1979), 73–100.

Lair, Jules. *Étude sur la vie et la mort de Guillaume Longue-Épée, duc de Normandie.* Paris: A. Picard, 1893.

Lake, Justin. "Truth, Plausibility, and the Virtues of Narrative at the Millennium." *Journal of Medieval History* 35 (2009): 221–38.

Lattin, Harriet Pratt. "The Eleventh Century MS Munich 14436: Its Contribution to the History of Coordinates, of Logic, of German Studies in France." *Isis* 38 (1948): 205–25.

Latouche, Robert. "Un imitateur de Salluste au Xe siècle: L'historien Richer." *Annales de l'Université de Grenoble*, section lettres droit, n. s., 6 (1929): 289–306.

Lauer, Philippe. *Le règne de Louis IV d'Outre-Mer.* Paris: É. Bouillon, 1900.

———. *Robert Ier et Raoul de Bourgogne, rois de France (923–936).* Paris: H. Champion, 1910; reprint, Geneva: Slatkine, 1976.

Lauranson-Rosaz, Christian. *L'Auvergne et ses marges (Velay, Gévaudan) du VIIIe au XIe siècle: La fin du monde antique?* Le Puy-en-Velay, France: Les Cahiers de la Haute-Loire, 1987.

Leff, Michael C. "The Topics of Argumentative Invention in Latin Rhetorical Theory from Cicero to Boethius." *Rhetorica* 1 (1983): 23–44.

Leitschuh, Friedrich, and Hans Fischer. *Katalog der Handschriften der Königlichen Bibliothek zu Bamberg.* Bamberg, 1887–1912; reprint, Wiesbaden: Harrassowitz, 1966.

Leonardi, Claudio. "I codici di Marziano Capella." *Aevum* 33 (1959): 434–89; 34 (1960): 1–99, 411–524.

———. "Intellectual Life." In *The New Cambridge Medieval History*, vol. 3, ed. Timothy Reuter (Cambridge: Cambridge University Press, 1999), 186–211.

Lesne, Emile. *Histoire de la propriété ecclésiastique en France.* 6 vols. Lille: R. Giard; Paris: H. Champion, 1910–1943.

Lifshitz, Felice. "Dudo's Historical Narrative and the Norman Succession of 996." *Journal of Medieval History* 20 (1994): 101–20.

Lindgren, Uta. *Gerbert von Aurillac und das Quadrivium: Untersuchungen zur Bildung im Zeitalter der Ottonen.* Sudhoffs Archiv 18. Wiesbaden: Franz Steiner Verlag, 1976.

Lot, Ferdinand. *Les derniers Carolingiens: Lothaire, Louis V, Charles de Lorraine (954–991).* Paris: É. Bouillon, 1891.

———."La date de naissance du roi Robert II et le siège de Melun." In *Mélanges Julien Havet: Recueil de travaux d'érudition dédiés à la mémoire de Julien Havet (1853–1893)* (Paris: Ernest Leroux, 1895), 149–56.

———. *Études sur le règne de Hugues Capet et la fin du Xe siècle.* Paris: É. Bouillon: 1903.

———. "L'origine de Thibaud le Tricheur." *Le Moyen Age* 20 (1907): 169–89

———. *Études sur les légendes épiques françaises.* Paris: H. Champion, 1958.

Löwe, Heinz. "Dialogus de statu sanctae ecclesiae: Das Werk eines Iren im Laon des 10. Jahrhunderts." *Deutsches Archiv für Erforschung des Mittelalters* 17 (1961): 12–90.

Lutz, Cora E. "The Commentary of Remigius of Auxerre on Martianus Capella." *Medieval Studies* 19 (1957): 137–56.

MacKinney, L. C. "Tenth-Century Medicine as Seen in the *Historia* of Richer of Rheims." *Bulletin of the Institute of the History of Medicine* 2 (1934): 347–75.

MacLean, Simon. *Kingship and Politics in the Late Ninth Century: Charles the Fat and the End of the Carolingian Empire.* Cambridge: Cambridge University Press, 2003.

Manitius, Max. *Geschichte der lateinischen Literatur des Mittelalters.* 3 vols. Munich: Beck, 1911–1931.

Marenbon, John. *Boethius.* Oxford: Oxford University Press, 2003.

Martínez Pizarro, Joaquín. *A Rhetoric of the Scene: Dramatic Narrative in the Early Middle Ages.* Toronto: University of Toronto Press, 1989.

McCormick, Michael. *Les Annales du Haut Moyen Âge.* Typologie des sources du Moyen Âge occidental 14. Turnhout: Brepols, 1975.

McKitterick, Rosamond. "The Carolingian Kings and the See of Rheims (883–987)." In *Ideal and Reality in Frankish and Anglo-Saxon Society: Studies Presented to J. M. Wallace-Hadrill,* ed. P. Wormald, D. Bullough, and R. Collins (Oxford: Blackwell, 1983), 228–49.

———. *The Frankish Kingdoms under the Carolingians (751–987).* London: Longman, 1983.

Melville, Gert. "Wozu Geschichte schreiben? Stellung und Funktion der Historie im Mittelalter." In *Formen der Geschichtsschreibung,* Beiträge zur Historik 4, ed. R. Koselleck, H. Lutz, and J. Rüsen (Munich: Deutsche Taschenbuch Verlag, 1982), 86–146.

Meyer-Gebel, Marlene. "Zur annalistischen Arbeitsweise Hinkmars von Reims." *Francia* 15 (1987): 75–108.

Misch, Georg. *Geschichte der Autobiographie.* 4 vols. Frankfurt: G. Schulte Bulmke, 1949– 1969.

Moehs, Teta E. "Gerbert of Aurillac as Link between Classicism and Medieval Scholarship." In *Gerberto, scienza, storia e mito. Arri del Gerberti Symposium 25–27 Iuglio 1983,* ed. Michele Tosi (Piacenza: Archivum Bobiense, 1985), 331–50.

Momigliano, Arnaldo. "Tradition and the Classical Historian." *History and Theory* 11 (1972): 279–93.

Monod, Gabriel. "Études sur l'histoire de Hugues Capet." *Revue historique* 28 (1885): 241–82.

Morin, Dom Germain. "Le catalogue des manuscrits de l'abbaye de Gorze au XIe siècle." *Revue Bénédictine* 22 (1905): 1–14.

Morse, Ruth. *Truth and Convention in the Middle Ages: Rhetoric, Representation and Reality.* Cambridge: Cambridge University Press, 1991.

Munk Olsen, Birger. *L'étude des auteurs classiques latins aux XIe et XIIe siècles*. 4 vols. Paris: Editions du Centre national de la recherche scientifique, 1982–1989.

———. *I classici nel canone scolastico altomedievale*. Spoleto: Centro italiano di studi sull'alto Medioevo, 1991.

Murphy, James J. *Rhetoric in the Middle Ages: A History of Rhetorical Theory from Saint Augustine to the Renaissance*. Berkeley and Los Angeles: University of California Press, 1974.

Mütherich, F. "The Library of Otto III." In *The Role of the Book in Medieval Culture*, vol. 2, ed. Peter Ganz (Turnout, Belgium: Brepols, 1986), 11–26.

Nelson, Janet. "Public Histories and Private History in the Work of Nithard." *Speculum* 60 (1985): 251–95.

———. "The *Annals of St Bertin*." In *Charles the Bald: Court and Kingdom*, ed. Margaret T. Gibson and Janet T. Nelson, 2nd rev. ed. (Hampshire, U.K.: Variorum, 1990), 23–40.

Oldoni, Massimo. "Il viaggio a Chartres de Richero: Un 'teatro' di medico nel Medioevo." *Ariel* 8, no. 1 (1993): 37–49.

Parisse, Michel. "Les évêques de France et le pape, à la lumière des actes du concile de Saint Basle (991). In *Gerbert, moine, évêque et pape: D'un millénaire à l'autre, Actes des journées d'étude, Aurillac, 9–10 avril* 1999 (Aurillac: Association cantalienne pour la commémoration du pape Gerbert, 2000), 171–93.

Parisse, Michel, and Xavier Barral i Altet, eds. *Le roi de France et son royaume autour de l'an Mil: Actes du Colloque Hugues Capet 987–1987, La France de l'an Mil, Paris-Senlis, 22–25 juin 1987*. Paris: Picard, 1992.

Poly, Jean-Pierre, and Eric Bournazel. *The Feudal Transformation, 900–1200*. Translated by Caroline Higgitt. New York: Holmes & Meier, 1991.

Prinz, Friedrich. *Klerus und Krieg im früheren Mittelalter: Untersuchungen zur Rolle der Kirche beim Aufbau der Königsherrschaft*. Stuttgart: Anton Hiersemann, 1971.

Ray, Roger. "Orderic Vitalis and His Readers." *Studia Monastica* 14 (1972): 17–33.

———. "Bede's *Vera Lex Historiae*." *Speculum* 55 (1980): 1–21.

———. "The Triumph of Greco-Roman Rhetorical Assumptions in Pre-Carolingian Historiography." In *The Inheritance of Historiography, 350–900*, ed. Christopher Holdsworth and T. P. Wiseman (Exeter: University of Exeter Press, 1986), 67–81.

Reinhardt, Hans. *La Cathédrale de Reims. Son histoire, son architecture, sa sculpture, ses vitraux*. Paris: Presses universitaires de France, 1963.

Renouard, Yves. *Études d'histoire médiévale*. 2 vols. Paris: S.E.V.P.E.N., 1968.

Reynolds, L. D., ed. *Texts and Transmission: A Survey of the Latin Classics*. Oxford: Clarendon Press, 1983.

Riché, Pierre. *Les écoles et l'enseignement dans l'Occident chrétien de la fin du Ve siècle au milieu du XIe siècle.* Paris: Aubier Montaigne, 1979.

———. "L'enseignement de Gerbert à Reims dans le contexte européen." In *Gerberto, scienza, storia e mito. Atti del Gerberti Symposium (25–27 Iuglio 1983),* ed. Michele Tosi (Piacenza: Archivum Bobiense, 1985), 51–69.

———. *Gerbert d'Aurillac, le pape de l'an mil.* Paris: Fayard, 1987.

———. "La bibliothèque de Gerbert d'Aurillac." Mélanges de la Bibliothèque de la Sorbonne 8 (1988): 94–103.

———. *Abbon de Fleury: Un moine savant et combatif.* Turnhout, Belgium: Brepols, 2004.

Rubenstein, Jay. "Biography and Autobiography in the Middle Ages." In *Writing Medieval History,* ed. Nancy Partner (London: Hodder Arnold, 2005), 22–41.

Ruf, Paul. *Mittelalterliche Bibliothekskataloge Deutschlands und der Schweiz* 3.3. Munich: C. H. Beck, 1939.

Sassier, Yves. *Hugues Capet: Naissance d'une dynastie.* Paris: Fayard, 1987.

Scharer, Anton, and Georg Scheibelreiter, eds. *Historiographie im frühen Mittelalter.* Vienna: R. Oldenbourg, 1994.

Schmale, Franz-Josef. *Funktionen und Formen mittelalterlicher Geschichtsschreibung.* Darmstadt, Germany: Wissenschaftliche Buchgesellschaft, 1985.

Schneidmüller, Bernd. "Widukind von Corvey, Richer von Reims und der Wandel politischen Bewußtseins im 10. Jahrhundert." *In Beiträge zur mittelalterlichen Reichs- und Nationsbildung in Deutschland und Frankreich,* ed. Bernd Schneidmüller and Carlrichard Brühl (Munich: R. Oldenbourg, 1997), 83–102.

Schulz, Marie. *Die Lehre von der historischen Methode bei den Geschichtsschreibern des Mittelalters.* Berlin: Walther Rothschild, 1909.

Schwager, Helmut. *Graf Heribert II. von Soissons, Omois, Meaux, Madrie sowie Vermandois (900/06–943) und die Francia (Nord-Frankreich) in der ersten Hälfte des 10. Jahrhunderts.* Münchener historische Studien, Abteilung Mittelalterliche Geschichte 6. Kallmünz/Opf, Germany: Lassleben, 1994.

Schwartz, Gerhard. *Die Besetzung der Bistümer Reichsitaliens unter den sächsischen und salischen Kaisern mit den Listen der Bischöfe 951–1122.* Leipzig: Teubner, 1913.

Simon, Gertrud. "Untersuchungen zur Topik der Widmungsbriefe mittelalterlicher Geschichtsschreibung bis zum Ende des 12. Jahrhunderts." *Archiv für Diplomatik* 4 (1958): 52–119; 5–6 (1959–1960): 73–153.

Smalley, Beryl. "Sallust in the Middle Ages." In *Classical Influences on European Culture, A.D. 500 to 1500,* ed. R. R. Bolgar (Cambridge: Cambridge University Press, 1971), 165–76.

Sot, Michel. *Un historien et son église au Xe siècle: Flodoard de Reims.* Paris: Fayard, 1993.

———. "Richer de Reims a-t-il écrit une Histoire de France?" In *Histoires de France, historiens de la France: Actes du colloque international, Reims, 14 et 15 mai 1993*, ed. Yves-Marie Bercé and Philippe Contamine (Paris: H. Champion, 1994), 47–58.

Stratmann, Martina. "Die *Historia Remensis Ecclesiae:* Flodoard's Umgang mit seinen Quellen." *Filologia Mediolatina* 1 (1994): 111–27.

Stump, Eleonore, trans. *Boethius: De Topicis Differentiis.* Ithaca, N.Y.: Cornell University Press, 1978.

———, trans. *Boethius: In Ciceronis Topica.* Ithaca, N.Y.: Cornell University Press, 1988.

Szövérffy, Joseph. *Secular Latin Lyrics and Minor Poetic Forms of the Middle Ages: A Historical Survey and Literary Repertory from the Tenth to the Late Fifteenth Century.* 3 vols. Concord, N.H.: Classical Folia Editions, 1992–1995.

Teeuwen, Mariken. "The Study of Martianus Capella's *De nuptiis* in the Ninth Century." In *Learned Antiquity: Scholarship and Society in the Near-East, the Greco-Roman World, and the Early Medieval West,* ed. A. A. MacDonald, M. W. Twomey, and G. J. Reinink (Leuven: Peeters, 2003), 185–94.

Tellenbach, Gerd. "Über Herzogskronen und Herzogshüte im Mittelalter." *Deutsches Archiv für Erforschung des Mittelalters* 5 (1942): 55–71.

Tosi, Michele. "Il governo abbaziale di Gerberto a Bobbio." In *Gerberto, scienza, storia e mito. Atti del Gerberti Symposium 25–27 Iuglio 1983*, ed. M. Tosi (Piacenza: Archivum Bobiense, 1985), 71–234.

Van Winter, J. M. "Uxorem de militari ordinem sibi imparem." In *Miscellanea Mediaevalia in memoriam Jan Frederik Niermeyer,* 113–24. Groningen: J. B. Wolters, 1967.

Vansina, Jan. *Oral Tradition: A Study in Historical Methodology.* Translated by H. M. Wright. Chicago: Aldine, 1965.

Verhelst, Daniel. "Adson de Montier-en-Der." In *Religion et culture autour de l'an mil: Royaume capétien et Lotharingie : Actes du colloque Hugues Capet 987–1987, la France de l'an mil, Auxerre, 26 et 27 juin 1987, Metz, 11 et 12 septembre 1987*, ed. Dominique Iogna-Prat and Jean-Charles Picard (Paris: Picard, 1990), 25–30.

Vogel, Walther. *Die Normannen und das Fränkische Reich bis zur Gründung der Normandie (799–911).* Heidelberg: Karl Winter, 1906.

Vogüé, Adalbert de. *La communauté et l'abbé dans la règle de Saint Benoît.* Paris: Desclée de Brouwer, 1961.

Waitz, Georg. *Jahrbücher des deutschen Reichs unter König Heinrich I.* Leipzig: Duncker & Humblot, 1885.

Wallace-Hadrill, J. M. "History in the Mind of Archbishop Hincmar." In *The Writing of History in the Middle Ages*, ed. R. H. C. Davis and J. M. Wallace-Hadrill (Oxford: Clarendon Press, 1981), 43–70.

Ward, John O. "From Antiquity to the Renaissance: Glosses and Commentaries on Cicero's *Rhetorica*." In *Medieval Eloquence: Studies in the Theory and Practice of Medieval Rhetoric*, ed. James J. Murphy (Berkeley and Los Angeles: University of California Press, 1978), 25–67.

———. *Ciceronian Rhetoric in Treatise, Scholion, and Commentary*. Typologie des sources du Moyen Âge occidental 58. Turnhout, Belgium: Brepols, 1995.

———. "Cicero's *De inventione* and the *Rhetorica ad Herennium*: Commentaries and Contexts." In *The Rhetoric of Cicero in Its Medieval and Early Renaissance Commentary Tradition*, ed. Virginia Cox and John O. Ward (Leiden: Brill, 2006), 3–75.

Wattenbach, Wilhelm. *Deutschlands Geschichtsquellen im Mittelalter bis zur Mitte des dreizehnten Jahrhunderts*. Vol. 1. Berlin: Wilhelm Hertz, 1893.

Werner, Karl Ferdinand. "Die literarischen Vorbilder des Aimoin von Fleury." In *Medium Aevum Vivum: Festschrift für Walther Bulst*, ed. Hans Robert Jauss and Dieter Schaller (Heidelberg: Carl Winter: 1960), 69–103.

Williams, John R. "The Cathedral School of Rheims in the Eleventh Century." *Speculum* 29 (1954): 661–77.

Winterbottom, Michael. "Grillius on Cicero's *De inventione*." *Classical Quarterly* 54 (2004): 592–605.

Wittich, Karl. "Richer über die Herzoge Giselbert von Lothringen und Heinrich von Sachsen." *Forschungen zur Deutschen Geschichte* 3.107–41. Göttingen: Verlag der Dieterichschen Buchhandlung, 1863.

Woodman, A. J. *Rhetoric in Classical Historiography: Four Studies*. London: Routledge, 1988.

Ziolkowski, Jan. "Theories of Obscurity in the Latin Tradition." *Mediaevalia* 19 (1996, for 1993): 101–70.

Zoepf, Ludwig. *Das Heiligenleben im 10 Jahrhundert*. Leipzig and Berlin: Teubner, 1908.

Index

Richer of Saint-Rémi: The Methods and Mentality of a Tenth-Century Historian was designed in Minion by Kachergis Book Design of Pittsboro, North Carolina. It was printed on 60-pound Natures Natural and bound by Thomson-Shore of Dexter, Michigan.